Accountancy in Transition

Edited by Richard P. Brief, NEW YORK UNIVERSITY

A GARLAND SERIES

The Development of Accounting Theory:
Significant Contributors to Accounting Thought in the 20th Century

edited by
Michael J. R. Gaffikin
Michael J. Aitken

Garland Publishing, Inc.
New York & London   1982

Library of Congress Cataloging in Publication Data
Main entry under title:

The Development of accounting theory.

   (Accountancy in transition)
   Bibliography: p.
   1. Accounting—Addresses, essays, lectures.
I. Gaffikin, M.J.R.   II. Aitken, Michael J.   III. Se-
ries.
HF5625.D44   1982   657'.01   82-82489
ISBN 0-8240-5336-2

The volumes in this series are printed on acid-free,
250-year-life paper.

Printed in the United States of America

Contents

ACKNOWLEDGMENTS

"The Economics of Accountancy" by Irving Fisher has been reprinted by permission of the editor of the *American Economic Review* as has the book review of R J Chambers, *Accounting Evaluation & Economic Behavior* by George J Benston.

"Edwards & Bell on Business Income," by R J Chambers has been reprinted by permission of the editor of the *Accounting Review* and the author.

The book review by Charles Reitell of Stephen Gilman, *Accounting Concepts of Profit* has been reprinted by permission of the editor of the *Annals* of the American Academy of Political & Social Sciences.

R H Montgomery's book review of Henry Rand Hatfield, *Accounting—Its Principles & Problems* has been reprinted by permission of the editor of the *Accounting Review.*

The review article "The Foundations of Accounting Measurement," by Norton M Bedford has been reprinted by permission of the editor of the *Journal of Accounting Research* and the author.

"The Contributions of A C Littleton to Accounting Thought and Practice," has been reprinted by permission of the editor of the *Accounting Review* and by Norton M Bedford.

The University of Chicago Press has granted permission to reprint W A Paton's book review of *Truth in Accounting* by Kenneth MacNeal. (*Journal of Political Economy*, 1940)

"Accounting & Analytical Methods: A Review Article," by R J Chambers has been reprinted by permission of the editor of the *Journal of Accounting Research* and the author.

Permission to reprint Ralph J Baker's review of *Financial Accounting* by George O May has been granted by the Harvard Law Review Association © 1945.

The editor of the *Journal of Accountancy* has granted permission to reprint "Comment on 'The Basic Postulates of Accounting'" (Copyright 1963 by the American Institute of Certified Public Accountants) and H R Hatfield's review of Charles E Sprague, *The Philosophy of Accounts.*

The editor of the *Accounting Review* and the author have permitted the reprinting of the book review of W A Paton, *Accounting Theory* by R J Chambers.

"Accounting Related to Social Institutions—The Theoretical Formulations of D,R.Scott" (sic) by L J Benninger has been reprinted by permission of the editor of *Accounting and Business Research.*

"The Market Value according to Sterling: A Review Article," by Richard Mattessich has been reprinted by permission of the editor of *Abacus* and the author.

"A Closer Look at Sweeney's Stabilised Accounting Proposals" by F L Clarke has been reprinted by permission of the editor of *Accounting and Business Research* and the author.

The extract from *A Critical Examination of the Orientation Postulate in Accounting* (1961 reprinted 1978, Arno Press) has been reprinted by permission of the author, Stephen A Zeff.

The book review by E C Moyer of *The Fund Theory and its Implications for Financial Accounting*, by W J Vatter, has been reprinted by permission of the editor of the *Accounting Review.*

INTRODUCTION

A statement such as "historical cost accounting no longer produces
results that are useful for decision making", is to exploit the insight
that a tradition's history is relevant to an appraisal of its cognitive
status. However, if such appraisal is to be reliable then it is
necessary to have more than a superficial appreciation of the temporal
dimension of any research tradition. It was on this premise that this
book was conceived.

Some years ago a book entitled The Development of Accounting Thought
by Harvey Deinzer was published. It served for us as a textbook, first
as students and later as teachers. It was not an entirely satisfactory
book especially in that it included in its title, "development", yet
seemed more directed to (the then) contemporary accounting thought. We
felt another text was needed. One which would utilize a Deinzer-type
structure yet be more directed to the actual temporal features process
of accounting thought. This aspect, we believe, is important, even
crucial, to an understanding of accounting theory (see last Chapter). It
was an important element in our accounting theory courses.

Later we discovered, at the University of Sydney, Professor R J Chambers,
had, with his typical intellectual thoroughness, developed a comprehensive
course in the development of accounting thought. It is compulsory for
all postgraduate accounting students. Rather than rely on the usually
superficial "appreciation" of past writers' works given in so-called
accounting theory texts, it was considered better to study the actual
works. Many other institutions have developed similar courses. The
difficulty with teaching such a course is that the support material was
not available or so spread as to make recourse to it extremely difficult;
especially where several students are after the same material.

This book seeks to serve as a resource book for such study. It is
designed to facilitate the study of the original works - not replace
them. However, two problems immediately spring to mind. First, teachers
will possibly not agree as to what constitutes suitable source material,
and, secondly, which books are worthy of study, given usual time
constraints. Perhaps the second problem presupposes the first. Our

1

choice of authors is obviously subjective. However, in keeping with the
spirit (if not the method) of modern research methodology we did examine
the literature in an attempt to make our choice more objective. We
were concerned with accounting theory so looked at those works which
were designed to contribute to the theoretical basis of accounting rather
than serve as textbooks of method (eg Dicksee's, Auditing). We were
concerned with the works of individual theorists which meant the exclusion
of the, sometimes valuable (eg ASOBAT), committee presentations. We
were concerned with major works, hence excluded those who, while making
significant contributions through the journal literature, had not
authored a major work on accounting theory.

We compared our "list" with those in widely used accounting theory
expositions. All those belonging to Most's (1977) "American School",
except Thomas, are included in this study. Although a little more
difficult to determine, all writers of major works referenced by
Hendriksen (1977) also appear in our list. Possible exceptions are Ladd,
Prince and Pattillo (see Hendriksen, Chapters 1-3). All those discussed
in SATTA (1977), except Alexander are included in our study and of those
discussed by McDonald (1972) we have only excluded Grady (not a theoretical
presentation). All those discussed in Henderson & Peirson (1977) except
Grady, are included in our study. We have included some not generally
included in some of the above textbooks. Sprague we feel is representative
of an early theoretical exposition. We agree with (and go beyond)
Hendriksen, that Gambling is a suitable case for study. While he is not
widely known in the American literature his work is specifically designed
to present a theory of accounting (acceptable or not). He seems to be
one of the very few British authors to have done this. Baxter and
Sewell Bray may have been included but are difficult to "pin down" to a
single theoretical exposition: they have written widely and more generally.

How does one study a book? It is the ideas contained within that book
which are important. Our course of study proposes that the book first
be read and this followed by some general background to the author -
including life and other works. A review is representative of a reaction
to the book. Where possible some guided discussion would enable a more
complete understanding. Consequently, some questions have been included
in this book. It does not seem reasonable to expect the same questions

to be directed to all the works studied. However, as indicated in the concluding essay, for a work to be considered a contribution to the theoretical literature, some criteria must be met. Chambers, in the course he designed at the University of Sydney, directs discussion to nine basic considerations: function, subject, orientation, context, quantification, auxilliary notions, categories, system and method. These, he argues, provide a framework for general evaluation of the works considered - not all aspects will be covered in every book.

To present one review of a book is possibly unfair to the author. Some reviews of MacNeal's Truth in Accounting can only be described as devastatingly critical. It is presenting one side of the story. Some of the authors have reacted to the reviews (especially the review articles). These reactions are included in the listed bibliographies and should also be read to "judge the judgement" - provide a balance. Nevertheless, any author wishes to communicate ideas: it is the readers who can best describe the communication they have received.

We encountered one or two difficulties in our attempt to produce as complete a work as possible. Our major source for bibliographic material was the Accountants Index. However, it was, especially in respect of earlier years, inadequate. Not all relevant journals are indexed. There have been changes in journals indexed. Some journals had rather short lives and it was often impossible for us to have access to these (and some others). Not being resident in the US we may not have uncovered some sources of biography. However, as far as we know we had access to all the generally available biographical indexes. We chose to present only brief biographical details and selected bibliographies. We accept there may be some material we have not been able to observe. Surprisingly we discovered several inconsistencies in our biographical sources. It was surprising in that many of these are historiographically speaking, very recent.

Our bibliographical searches uncovered some interesting details. It is not appropriate that they be discussed here. However, what should be stressed is that the bibliographies prescribed here are "selected" - we attempted to include all relevant references. Some writers, such as Chambers, Littleton, May & Paton, have written so extensively that they warrant separate volumes devoted to each of them (as indeed there has been). Some writers (eg Canning, Edwards & Bell) have made contributions in areas other than accounting. Some of these have been included to give an idea of their interests; but not all.

Overall, although we faced many typical research difficulties which may have affected the quality of this book, we feel it meets a need. It fills a gap in the textbook literature. Hopefully it will provide a useful resource to stimulate the study of the works of our important accounting theory forbears. Consequently we wish to acknowledge our appreciation of Murray Wells who promoted our cause, Dick Brief for supporting our cause and our colleagues who helped us formulate our cause. We also thank Swee-Eng Chia and Sheilah Markham for typing the chronologies, bibliographies and other material. We cannot provide the usual author's disclaimer because the ideas are those of the original theorists.

Michael Gaffikin
University of Sydney

Michael Aitken
University of Sydney

REFERENCES

American Accounting Association, Committee on Concepts and Standards
    for External Financial Reports, Statement of Accounting Theory and
    Theory Acceptance (SATTA), AAA, 1977.

Henderson, S & Peirson, G, An Introduction to Financial Accounting Theory,
    Longman Cheshire Pty, 1977.

Hendriksen, E S, Accounting Theory, 3 ed, Richard D Irwin, 1977.

McDonald, D L, Comparative Accounting Theory, Addison-Wesley, 1972.

Most, K, Accounting Theory, Grid, 1977.

2

The Philosophy of Accounts

Biographical Chronology

1842	Born (9 October), Nassau, New York
1860	Bachelor's degree from Union College, with Phi Beta Kappa honours
1862	Master's degree
1860-62	Taught at Greenwich Union Academy
1862	Enlisted in the New York National Guard
1866	Married Ray Ellison (from which union later emerged four children)
1868	As a result of bravery in service made Colonel in New York Volunteers
1870	Joined staff (as clerk) of Union Dime Savings Bank, New York and rose to become its president in 1892, a position he held until his death.
1881-84	Associate Editor, The Bookkeeper
1893	Honorary Ph.D from Union College
1896	Certified CPA (New York); served as member of Board of Directors of New York Society of CPA's.
1900	From this time on the Faculty of New York University, having been instrumental in organizing and developing its School of Commerce, Accounts & Finance.
1904-05	President, Savings Bank Section, American Bankers Association
1910	Awarded honorary Doctor of Letters from Olivet College.
1912 (12 March) Died	

Sprague was one of the first people to hold the position of Professor of Accounting. It is worth noting that he spoke sixteen languages and was a champion of the cause of Volpük, a proposed international language. Previts (1972) refers to him as the "Patriarch of the Preclassical system of accounting", who, "more than any other of his ilk...significantly advanced the theoretical framework of early American accountancy".

Selected Bibliography

1880   "The Algebra of Accounts," The Bookkeeper, 20 July, pp 2-4;
        3 Aug, pp 19-22; 17 Aug, pp 34-5; 31 Aug, pp 51-3.

        "The Cheque Bank," The Bookkeeper, 28 Sept, pp 81-2.

        "The Detecting of Errors in Balance Sheets," The Bookkeeper,
        12 Oct, pp 97-101.

        "Addition by Means of Subtraction." The Bookkeeper, 26 Oct,
        p 119.

1889   "Outlay and Income," The Office, Nov, pp 207-8.

        "Algebra of Accounts," The Office, May, pp 91-2; July,
        pp 122-3; Aug, pp 144-5.

1890   "Tabular Bookkeeping." The Office, Sept, pp 240-41

1896   "Line by Line Accounts," Business, Jan, pp 29-31

1897   "Detecting Errors in Accounts," Business, June, pp 176-9.

1900   "Proposed Tax on Mortgages," Banking Law Journal, pp 70-2.

        "Proposed Mortgage Tax in New York State." Gunton's
        Magazine, pp 218-25.

1902   Handbook of Volapük, Grammer, Exercises and Vocabulary,
        Steiger, (New York).

1904   "The Basis for Valuation for Securities," The Book Keeper,
        January, 1904, pp 76-80.

        "Premium on Bonds," Business Man's Magazine and the Book
        Keeper, July, pp 883-4.

        The Accountancy of Investment, Business Publishing Company;
        3rd Edn, 1906; Rev. Edn, 1914 (Ronald Press).

1905   "Computing Present Values," Business Man's Magazine and the
        Book Keeper, July, pp 755-6.

        Extended Bond Tables, Business Publishing Company, (New York).

1906   Problems and Studies in the Accountancy of Investment, The
        Author, 1906. (Reproduced in monthly instalments in
        Business World, Oct 1905 to May 1906).

        "Premiums and Discounts," Journal of Accountancy, v.2, August,
        pp 294-6.

1907   The Philosophy of Accounts, The Author (New York) (Reproduced
        in monthly instalments in Journal of Accountancy, vv. Jan
        1907 through Jan 1908). 4 Edn, 1918; 5 Edn, 1922 (Ronald
        Press). Reprinted, Scholars Book Co., 1971.

        Tables of Compound Interest, The Author (New York)

        "Fallacy in Bond Values," Journal of Accountancy, Nov, v.5,
        pp 1-4.

1908   "Stock Value of a Bond," <u>Journal of Accountancy</u>, July,v.6. pp 174-6 (<u>Accountant</u>, 12 September, pp 314-5).

"<u>Amortization</u>, The Author, (New York).

1909   <u>Text-book of the Accountancy of Investment</u>, The Author, (New York).

"Embezzlement and Accountability," <u>Journal of Accountancy</u>, v.8. June, pp 85-96.

1910   "Continuity of Interest," <u>Journal of Accountancy</u>, v.9, pp 340-3 (Accountant, 7 May, pp 655-7).

<u>Logarithms to 12 Places and Their Use in Interest Calculations</u>, The Author, (New York).

1915   <u>Extended Bond Tables</u>, Ronald Press (New York).

1917   "Conscription of Income a Sound Basis of War Finance," <u>Accountant</u>, May, pp 486-91.

REFERENCES

Book Reviews: <u>Journal of Accountancy</u>, v 6, 1908, p.67-9(H R Hatfield). <u>Accounting Review</u>, v.49, 1974, pp.216-7 (G J Previts).

Mann, Helen S, <u>Charles Ezra Sprague</u>, New York University, 1931.

New York State Society of CPAs Committee on History, "Charles Ezra Sprague, Public Accountant", <u>NYCPA</u>, v.22, July 1952, pp.430-2.

Previts, G J, <u>A Critical Evaluation of Comparative Financial Accounting Thought in America 1900-1920</u>, 1972 (Reprint), Arno Press, 1980.

Book Department.

THE PHILOSOPHY OF ACCOUNTS. By Charles E. Sprague. New York. The author. 1908. xx, 8°. ix + 161pp. Price, $3.00.

To outline in these pages the contents of Colonel Sprague's Philosophy of Accounts is needless, for the readers of the JOURNAL OF ACCOUNTANCY are already familiar with the work; to criticise it is indeed a difficult task, for the author has so combined scholarly erudition, philosophic insight and practical experience as to disarm any reviewer. There remains therefore only the pleasant, though somewhat superfluous task of paying tribute to the masterly little treatise, with which no other American work can properly even be compared, with which even the wide literature of Germany can furnish but few rivals.

Despite its forbidding and somewhat misleading title Colonel Sprague's work is of great practical value, not only in the sense that any sane exposition of theory has practical value but because it contains much more than a theory of accounts, at least half the book being made up of suggestions based on the author's own experience in accounting practice.

American works on accounting and bookkeeping have almost without exception been mere practical manuals, not scientific or theoretical treatises. Yet even in these practical handbooks occasionally gleams a theory of double entry bookkeeping. But most of these follow the same model, and the theory that has been steadfastly presented has not only been fragmentary but misleading and valueless. The present author has broken with the line of theory traditional with American writers, and agrees in general, although not in detail, with that current in Germany and known as the theory of Hügli and Schär.

The conventional explanation of the theory of accounting is to treat each account as though it represented an actual relationship of debtor and creditor, carrying out the principle by a forced and unnatural personification. Connected with this has been the formulation of a rule of thumb for debiting and crediting, which in its most extreme form appears in the common formula "Debit all that comes in and credit all that goes out." In this treatise the author rejects the principle that there is in all cases a debtor—either assumed or real—and shows that the various accounts, instead of uniformly presenting the single relationship of debtor and creditor, are essentially different in their nature and are to be divided into contrasting groups. With this understanding of the nature of the accounts the uniform formula for debiting and crediting of course fails, and the author clearly shows that "debit" has an altogether different meaning in one set of accounts from what it has in another.

The system of classifying accounts differs too from the traditional one. For some strange reason most American texts have clung to the antique and illogical classification of accounts as "real, personal and fictitious." This is abandoned in favor of two groups: Specific Accounts (that is those indicating assets and liabilities), and Proprietorship Accounts. But unfortunately the author's terminology is not entirely clear, for he introduces occasionally the phrase "basic accounts" as including cash and merchandise, without clearly defining the term, nor showing how these accounts fit into his general scheme of classification. There is also a little vagueness, although no real contradiction in the use of the term "economic accounts," it being at times uncertain whether these are or are not proprietorship accounts. The author also classifies accounts as exterior and interior but this is merely a variation in nomenclature and corresponds in lines of cleavage with the original division into specific and proprietorship accounts.

Even so lucid an exposition of theory as that given by Colonel Sprague must contain points which seem less clearly and felicitously put. But these are points of minor detail, generally mere matters of questionable expression which in no way affect the argument, or the soundness of the author's theses. Such infelicities occur where the author speaks of outlay as in every case implying service received, which may be true where there is an outlay for expense but it is not where a pure loss is concerned. Again the distinction between the two sides of the balance sheet that "the credit side gives the distribution not of actual assets but of the value" is unsatisfactory, for in any case every account, on either side, deals only with its value. The statement that "the right hand side of the balance sheet is entirely composed of claims against or rights over the left hand side" while capable of correct interpretation is apparently too close an approach to the personalistic theory rejected by the author. And, finally, the author's discussion of the so-called materialistic and personalistic schools hardly does justice to the point at issue. The schools are divided not so much on the question as to whether assets are things or rights against persons as they are on the treatment of the proprietorship and economic accounts. The real dispute is as to whether these too are to be treated as representing an assumed debt relationship, or whether the specific and proprietorship accounts are two distinct groups of accounts (Kontenriehen) each with a distinct significance and distinguished by having the positive and negative sides reversed.

Turning to the more practical portion of the book it would be invidious to select particular section as being especially meritorious, for each chapter, whether dealing with the history and use of the journal, the description of posting mediums, the prevention and detection of errors, or other topics of practical importance, is lucidly written and both scholarly and suggestive. The monographs on the cash account and the merchandise account are also so valuable that one can not but regret that the author altered his original plan of treating in detail all the principal forms of accounts.

A most valuable feature of the book is the emphasis placed on the relativity of accounting forms. In many texts on accounting the student is told that some transaction must be recorded in a certain way, that particular books are to be used, that certain forms are to be observed. If for nothing else the present work has done a service in showing that accounting forms are not fixed and absolute; that "they may be deviated from when anything is to be gained." A most refreshing contrast to the rigid prescriptions which so frequently mar accounting treatises is the author's statement that the propriety of using a particular account "depends on personal and administrative considerations, theoretically either procedure is correct," or again: "It is not necessary that a trial balance or a balance sheet should always be two-sided."

H. R. H.

QUESTIONS

(1) "As a branch of mathematical and classificatory science the prin-
     ciples of accountancy may be determined by a priori reasoning, and
     do not depend on the customs and traditions which surround the
     art" (ix).
     - Does Sprague define the term 'principles of accounting'?
     - To what extent is Sprague's work devoted to explicating
       the principles of accounting?
     - What is 'a priori' reasoning?
     - Is Sprague correct in his assertion that 'a priori' reason-
       ing is sufficient for the determination of accounting
       principles?
     - To what extent do customs and traditions figure in a dis-
       cipline's development?

(2) Sprague describes the function of accounting as "... to analyse
     (the) success or failure (in increasing wealth) so as to ascer-
     tain its causes, as a guide to future conduct? (paragraph 165).
     He also (mathematically) defines "present worth" as historic
     cost adjusted for depreciation (para.136).
     - To what extent can Sprague's definition of present worth
       (in the valuation of assets) be useful as a guide to future
       conduct?

(3) "To seek the truth and follow the facts is safer than to compress
     everything into the mold of a 'theory'"(para.108).
     - Does Sprague expand on the term "mold of a theory"?

(4) "Assets + Insolvency = Liabilities" (Para.145)
     - In view of the above equation does the way in which Sprague
       describes the valuation of assets imply any new understand-
       ing of the term 'insolvency'?

(5) Sprague speaks of "The all importance of the proprietary accounts
     (as) to measure the success or failure in increasing wealth"
     (para. 165).
     - Does Sprague define wealth?
     - What implications would the lack of such a definition have
       in the context of asset valuation?

3

Accounting: Its Principles and Some of its Problems

Biographical Chronology

1866	Born (27 November) in Chicago, Illinois.
1886-90	Affiliated with the municipal bond business
1898	Married Ethel A Glover
1892	Bachelor's degree, Northwestern University
1894-8	On Faculty of Washington University, St Louis, as instructor in political economy
1897	Doctorate, University of Chicago
1898-1902	Instructor then assistant professor, University of Chicago
1902-04	Dean of the College of Commerce & Administration, University of Chicago.
1904-09	Associate professor, University of California, Berkeley.
1909-37	Professor
1909	Published Modern Accounting
1914-18	President, Berkeley, California Commission of Charities
1909-20	Dean of the College of Commerce (Berkeley)
1917	Vice-President, American Accounting Association (AAA; then called American Assoc of University Instructors in Accounting)
1917-18	Dean of Faculties (Berkeley)
1918	Vice-President, AAA; Vice-President, American Economic Association; Director, Division of Planning and Statistics, War Industries Board.
1919	President, AAA.
1920-23	Dean of Faculties
1923-28	Senator of Phi Beta Kappa
1927	Revised version of Modern Accounting published under the title of Accounting: Its Principles and Some of its Problems
1928	Award of merit - outstanding contribution to accounting literature (Beta Alpha Psi).
1929	US representative to Amsterdam International Congress on Commercial Education.
1933	AAA representative to London, Fourth International Congress of Accountants
1937	Retired, University of California
1938	A Statement of Accounting Principles (with Sanders & Moore)
1941-2	Dickinson Lecturer, Harvard University
1942	Member, Berkeley War Appeals Board
1945	Died, 25 December
[1951	Elected Ohio Accounting Hall of Fame]

Selected Bibliography

1909   "Zwei Pfadfinder" (Two Pathfinders), Zeitschrift für
            Buchhaltung (Linz), no.4, pp 80-6.

            Modern Accounting: Its Principles and Some of Its
            Problems, D. Appleton & Co (New York).

1911   "Some Variations in Accounting Practice," Journal of
            Accounting Research, Autumn, 1966, pp 169-82, (Paper
            presented in 1911 to American Association of Public
            Accountants)

1915   "Some Neglected Phases of Accounting," Electric Railway
            Journal, 16 October, pp 799-802.

1923   "Historical Defense of Bookkeeping," Papers and Proceedings,
            American Association of University Instructors in
            Accounting, pp 65-75; Journal of Accountancy,
            (April, 1924), pp 241-53. NB. This is reproduced in
            several anthologies.

1926   "Earliest Use in English of the Term Capital," Quarterly
            Journal of Economics, May, pp 547-8.

1927   "What is the Matter with Accounting?," Journal in
            Accountancy, October, v 44, pp 267-9 (also in,
            Canadian Chartered Accountant, January, 1928, pp 213-
            25; Licentiate in Accountancy, January, 1928, pp 237-
            48).

            Accounting: Its Principles and Problems, D. Appleton and
            Co. (New York). Reproduced, Scholars Book Co., 1971.

1928   "Accounting Paradox," Accounting Review, v.3, pp 342-4.

1930   "Comments on 'A Symposium on Appreciation'," Accounting
            Review, v.5, pp 12-14, 26-7, 33-4, 53-4.

1932   "Check-list of Early Bookkeeping Texts," Accounting Review,
            v.7, pp 194-206, with A.C. Littleton.

1934   "Accounting Principles and the Statutes," Journal of
            Accountancy, Aug, v.58, pp 90-7.

            "Operating Deficit and Paid-In," Accounting Review,
            September, v.9, pp 237-41.

1936   "What they say about Depreciation," Accounting Review,
            v.11, pp 18-26.

1938   A Statement of Accounting Principles, American Accounting
            Association, 1938. With T.H. Sanders and U. Moore.

1939   "Survey of Developments in Accounting," AIA Papers on
            Auditing Procedure and Other Subjects, pp 5-11.

1940   "Accountants Adventures in Wonderland," Journal of
Accountancy, Dec, v.70, pp 527-32.

"Financial Aspects of Depreciation" (Correspondence),
Journal of Accountancy, Jan. v.69, pp 48-9.

"Accounting Trivia" (Accounting Exchange), Accounting
Review, v.15, pp 417-9.

Accounting, Principles and Practices, Ginn and Company,
(Boston), with T.H. Sanders and N.L. Burton.

1943   Surplus and Dividends (Dickinson Lectures), Harvard
University Press, (Massachusetts).

1944   "Replacement and Book Value," Accounting Review, v.19,
pp 66-7.

REFERENCES

Book Reviews of Accounting:
        ALA Booklist, v.24, Nov 1927, p.81
        Boston Transcript, 2 July 1927, p.4 (430w)
        Manufacturing Index, v.14, July 1927, p.63 (400w)
        Accounting Review, v.2, 1927, pp.189-93 (Montgomery, R H)
        Accounting Review, v.52, 1973, p.224-5 (Stone, W E)

Book Reviews of Modern Accounting:
        ALA Booklist, v.5, June 1909, p.168
        Journal of Political Economy, v.17, 1909, p.647
        (Cole, W: 850w)
        Economic Bulletin, v.2, Sept 1909, p.235 (Clevland, A:
        780w)
        Political Science Quarterly, v.26, 1911, p.345
        Accounting Review, v.57, 1977, p.770 (Moonitz, M)

Hatfield, John, "Recollections About Father", Accounting Historians
Journal, v.4, 1977, pp.14-17.

Homburger, R & G J Previts, "The Significance of 'Zwei Pfadfinder'",
Accounting Historians Journal, v.4, 1977, pp.9-13.

Mumford, M J, "An Historical Defence of Henry Rand Hatfield", Abacus,
v.16, 1980, pp.151-8.

Previts, G J, A Critical Evaluation of Comparative Financial Accounting
Thought in America 1900-1920, 1972 ,(Reprint),Arno Press, 1980.

REVIEWS

Accounting—Its Principles and Problems, by HENRY RAND HATFIELD. D.
Appleton and Company, New York, 1927. xviii, 548 pp.

I have just finished reading Professor Hatfield's new book. It is not often
that a writer who has the same delicacy of touch, humor, and keen knowledge
of accounts as Professor Hatfield possesses permits so long a period as
eighteen years to elapse between a first and second edition. A rather careful reading of the book has created in me a passion to be honest, and I
must confess that if I had not been asked to review the book I probably
would not have read it for a long time, if at all. If I had neglected to read
it I would have missed a real treat. In addition to the pleasure of reading
live comments on dry subjects, I have learned something new and my views
regarding some old-fashioned theories are strengthened.

Professor Hatfield, in referring to the field of accounting, states in his
preface that during the last eighteen years "more serious study has been
given to its scientific aspects than in any other period of similar length, perhaps more than in preceding centuries since Pacioli." I am afraid that
some of us who are very busy and who used to read with avidity all of the
new books on accounting read fewer books now than we did some years ago,
because we are quite unable to keep up with the number of creditable works
which are being issued. Professor Hatfield also says, "the enactment of the
Federal income tax law has, more than any other single event, emphasized
the necessity of keeping accounts that will exhibit with approximate accuracy
the annual income." But no mention is made of the very serious departures
from good accounting practice which appear in the Federal law and the
regulations. All accountants have more or less to do with Federal income
tax problems and it is most confusing to try to harmonize good accounting
practice with technical income tax procedure. I am not criticizing in principle the departures in the law and the regulations since it must be recognized
that it will never be feasible to impose a tax on book net income. I merely
mention the confusion because it has certainly made the writing of a book
on accounting far more difficult than was the case in 1909 when Professor
Hatfield's first edition was published.

Perhaps the outstanding feature of the new edition is the attention given
to other writers on accounting subjects, and to court and other authoritative
decisions. In addition to extended comments a satisfactory bibliography appears at the end of almost every chapter.

Professor Hatfield's method of presentation is easy to follow and grasp.
His comments and criticisms on the writings of others are good tempered
and in most cases convincing. I am glad to find that Chapter I deals with
the balance sheet as a whole, as my own experience in teaching and in practice has convinced me that the discussion of the balance sheet comes first

either in the instruction of a novice or in technical discussions with practitioners. I shall not have time to review the various chapters individually, but I would like to list the chapter headings in order that the full scope of the work may be seen:

In addition to the foregoing there is an appendix of sixty-five pages containing questions and problems, arranged in groups to correspond with the relative chapters of the text. The questions are well framed. As to the answers, Professor Hatfield says: "Answers to the questions imply an application of the principles set forth in the text, rather than a repetition of the words of the text."

Many of the criticisms in the book are directed at the misleading and inaccurate terminology in wide use at the present time. There is little uniformity about published statements and while I personally deprecate any general standardization of form, I heartily agree with Professor Hatfield that there should be more standardization than now applies. His suggestion that what is usually called "reserve for depreciation" should be changed to "allowance for depreciation" is a very good one. I hope it will be generally adopted. I also hope that there will be more rapid improvement in the designation of assets and liabilities in many published balance sheets. It seems rather ridiculous that the only agreement among accountants is that the two sides of a balance sheet should balance, whereas there are listed among assets items which by no stretch of the imagination could be called assets and there are items listed among liabilities which under no possible construction of the word could be called liabilities.

Professor Hatfield also calls attention to the inaccurate use of the word "reserves" in connection with liabilities, the exact amount of which is known or in regard to which an estimate is made.

Professor Hatfield has a keen grasp of the present inconsistency in balance sheets in which some accounts are meticulously adjusted to odd dollars and cents as to cost, other items are included at value, and still others at some figure in between cost and value, the net result of the whole being unsatisfactory.

I hope that Professor Hatfield's criticisms of the American Institute's report on terminology will result in an early revision. The Committee never intended that in its first attempts anything very satisfactory could be achieved, and is itself keen about frequent correction and revision. If the work had been frequently revised it is not likely that Professor Hatfield would have been able to refer to the Institute's definition of "working assets" as "crudely materialistic and meaningless."

Having finished the book I am somewhat in doubt regarding Professor Hatfield's idea of an ideal balance sheet. He very properly refers to past costs as merely historic and often wholly out of line with present-day values. On the other hand apparently he is not prepared to accept the idea that a balance sheet should show present values since in his comment he says that such a balance sheet "strangely halts and stumbles toward its goal." This criticism is quite justified when specifically applied to concrete cases. I think that in this case, as well as in some others, Professor Hatfield does not make sufficient allowance for the practical difficulties of public accountants who must deal with lawyers, bankers, and business executives who have opinions of their own regarding the interpretation of accounts and who, to the astonishment of accountants, sometimes are right.

The rules for distinguishing between capital and income are discussed in relation to court decisions and other authoritative data and will repay reading.

Professor Hatfield discusses at some length the necessity for basing values on the "going concern" theory. Perhaps we are not ready for any departure from this basis, but I think someone should be courageous enough to distinguish between the values of a concern which is going down and the values of a concern which is going up. When one considers that about ninety-nine per cent of the value of a balance sheet lies in its future working out it is altogether wrong to ignore the trend. This is well illustrated in the rule for valuing inventories at "cost or market whichever is lower." In all cases of fluctuating markets the true financial position of a concern is quite different on the day the balance sheet is published than it was on the closing day and thus the fiction of the basis becomes apparent since the "true" financial position as set forth in the balance sheet is a most unreliable guide.

It is obvious that Professor Hatfield does not like to show average costs. He says that a second purchase at a lower price than the first does not reduce the cost of the first, and that the only excuse for this is ease of administration. I am not sure that this is a sound comment. When one buys at different prices different quantities of precisely the same thing it would seem to be more accurate to divide the total quantity purchased by the total cost price and use this as the new cost of the unit than to assume later on that some had been bought at a high price and some at a low price and thus leave to chance or manipulation the showing of a profit or loss which might be wholly misleading. I am afraid that some of the unsound and illogical Treasury interpretations have been given too much weight by Professor Hatfield in this and other places.

I am sorry that space will not permit of detailed comment on Professor Hatfield's differentiation between "use" and "value" as these terms relate to depreciation. It is obvious that the straight line method of depreciation is highly inaccurate but no one has yet worked out any more satisfactory method. I do not refer at this point to recognized methods of dealing with depreciation which can be accurately measured, such as the unit method, but I refer to depreciation of such large items as buildings and equipment and machinery of indefinite life. Even though Professor Hatfield has not invented a new rule his keen analysis of the deficiencies of the present rule will be very helpful to those who have an open mind on the subject of accounting for depreciation.

Professor Hatfield, discussing unissued capital stock, says that many accountants prefer to bring the amount of the unissued stock into the books and accounts. I do not recall ever seeing such entries in books of account and if I ever did see any it made no impression on me. The difference between unissued stock and non-authorized stock in reality is almost no difference at all. Professor Hatfield says that it may be of some importance if new funds are needed, etc., but he does not mention that most corporations which need new funds do not have authorized stock issues and yet they find no difficulty whatever in securing statutory approval. This reduces the difference between unissued and non-authorized stock to a legal gesture which is hardly important enough to justify book entries. In other words, the mere right to sell stock which is authorized is not an asset of importance since the "right" is so easily procured that it lacks everything of the elements of an actual asset. The *ability* to sell new stock is a real asset which belongs to a vast number of corporations with no unissued stock, whereas there are a great many corporations with unissued stock which could not possibly sell the stock if they tried.

In dealing with treasury stock Professor Hatfield quotes Sir Arthur Lowes Dickinson, who says that showing treasury stock as an asset "is erroneous and misleading." This may be true, but in examining a great many balance sheets certified to by leading firms of accountants I have frequently noticed the item set up as an asset and I doubt very much whether anyone has been misled.

Professor Hatfield fails to see the inherent vice in the return to stockholders as cash dividends of premiums paid on capital stock. There may be court decisions which operate to keep the offending directors out of jail, but that does not lessen their moral turpitude. The lawyers are too versatile in their interpretation of accounts and they have been bringing pressure in the recent past in other directions such as the distinction between "surplus," "earned surplus," and "paid in surplus." The lawyers say that accountants should not be allowed to decide whether surplus is or is not available for dividends. We will have some weird accounting if the lawyers are permitted to take charge of our terminology. I am afraid that Professor Hatfield is influenced by the lawyers when he discusses the difference between "contributed capital" and "capital contributed to surplus." The whole point of issue is one of morals rather than law, since dishonest or unscrupulous directors are the only ones who pay dividends out of premiums received on capital stock. I am afraid that if accountants do not take a firm stand regarding the whole subject of surplus, particularly as related to no-par stock, the dishonest corporations will take advantage of the situation and stockholders will receive dividends, believing they are out of profits, whereas the dividends are out of either contributed capital or capital contributed to surplus, in either of which cases the stockholders will surely be deceived.

The only chapter in the book with which I can find fault is that dealing with the consolidated balance sheet. All of us have a great deal to learn on this subject but I was confused rather than enlightened by some of the discussions. Departing from his usual rule of citing authority in detail, Professor Hatfield, on page 452, sets up a consolidated balance sheet which he says is advocated "by accountants of high repute." To my mind the balance sheet is obviously wrong, and I doubt whether there is much authority for the form. I have had much of actual practice with consolidated balance sheets and I still favor the existing rules, some of which Professor Hatfield criticizes. For instance, I think that the surplus of a subsidiary company at its acquisition should be deducted from the goodwill of a holding company. I also think accountants are justified in setting up on the asset side the par value of stocks issued for property, and I do not believe that Professor Hatfield can sustain his position that "the fact of over-valuation can be adequately represented by crediting an allowance for over-valuation."

I read with some interest Professor Hatfield's comments on the interpretation of the balance sheet. I am inclined to think that too much value is being placed on interpretation of past results. Many of our outstanding successful manufacturers and traders know little about accounts. Is it not because they are vastly more concerned with the future than with the past? What real advantage would derive from an intensive study of the results of past periods when to their certain knowledge conditions are changing and they do have before them the costs and expenses of the present month and trustworthy estimates of the costs and expenses of future months? I do not wish to underestimate the value of past records, since no business can get along without them, but I think their value may be overemphasized. Present values may be misleading but past values are more misleading.

On the whole, Professor Hatfield has produced a fine book and I feel deeply grateful that I was given the opportunity of reading and reviewing it. I commend the book withoutout hesitation to everyone interested in accounting.

R. H. MONTGOMERY

Columbia University

(1) Hatfield states that various values including cost and present
     value are relevant depending on the purpose of the balance sheet.
     (Pg.25) In view of his statement that "the Balance Sheet shows
     the financial status of a concern, giving information on solvency,
     and in a less degree its exhibits accumulated profits" (Pg.21).
     - Does the latter quote point to a particular valuation
       method?
       (Bear in mind the commonsense and legal definitions of solvency).

(2) Liabilities are described by Hatfield as "negative assets" (Pg.221).
     However, apart from giving examples of what are and are not
     assets (Pg.13-16) he does not actually define an asset.
     - To what extent is the above assertion true?
     - What implications do the lack of definitions of assets,
       liabilities, etc. have in terms of the development and
       acceptance of ideas in accounting?

(3) "Accounting is an attempt to present two aspects of business
     affairs concerning which every businessman needs to be informed
     ... a showing of what one owns and owes ... and how the propr-
     ietor's worth increases or decreases from time to time" (Pg.1).
     - Does Hatfield explain why every businessman wants to know
       this information?
     - What importance is there in knowing why something is needed?
     - What are the consequences of not knowing the above?

(4) "... the general principle must be adopted that the basis of
     inventory values is the present value of the assets to the
     holder as a "going concern" (Pg.75).
     - What relationship does Hatfield establish between the
       notion of going concern and value?
     - Is Hatfield correct in positing a necessary difference,
       between items valued in the normal course of business and
       items valued in the course of a forced liquidation.

(5) Hatfield on pages 22 and 23 speaks of terminological problems
     of accounting. He laments that "there is at present no
     accepted authority to whom appeal can be made" (Pg.23).

     - To what extent does terminology continue to be a problem
       in Accounting?
     - Is Hatfield's attitude to the resolution of the problem a
       useful one?

19

4

WILLIAM ANDREW PATON

Accounting Theory - With Special Reference to the
Corporate Enterprise

Biographical Chronology

1889	19 June born, Michigan (near Calumet), the son of Andrew and Mary (Nowlin) Paton (both teachers)
1905	Passed 8th grade examination after having completed not more than three years of formal schooling
1906	Attended Imlay City High School
1907	Attended Michigan State Normal School (now Eastern Michigan University) until 1912 with the exception of a two year period (1908-1910)
1912	Entered the University of Michigan
1914	Appointed to a part-time teaching position with the University of Michigan
1915	Awarded a bachelor's degree from the University of Michigan nearly a year after fulfilling necessary curriculum requirements. Advanced to full time instructorship.
1916	Awarded a master's degree from the University of Michigan
1917	Awarded doctorate from the above university Appointed assistant professor at University of Michigan
1918-19	Relocated in Washington DC where he was appointed, first to the War Trade Board and, later, to the Income Tax Unit of the Bureau of Internal Revenue
1919	Advanced to associate professor on his return to the University of Michigan
1921	Advanced to full professor at University of Michigan
1922	Became the sixth president of the American Association of University Instructors in Accounting. Accounting Theory published.
1926	Served until 1929 as the inaugural editor of The Accounting Review
1927	Became a CPA (Michigan) after taking CPA examination
1936	Became the first Research Director of the American Accounting Association
1939	Became a charter member of the Committee on Accounting Procedure of the AICPA serving for eleven years
1940	Dickinson Lecturer in Accounting, Harvard University, the first academic to be selected for the honour
1944	Awarded an honorary doctor of letters from Lehigh University
1947	Appointed to a special chair as Edwin Francis Gray University Professor of Accounting
1950	One of the first three (and the first academic) to be elected to Ohio State University's Accounting Hall of Fame
1953	Awarded the Alpha Kappa Psi Foundation's Accounting Award
1955	An Accounting Scholarship and Fellowship fund set up in his name by former friends and students. The object of the fund was to provide financial assistanct to graduate students in accounting.

1959	Retired from the University of Michigan
1961	Honoured by the Michigan Association of Certified Public Accountants who set up bronze medal award, the "William Paton Award", bestowed upon candidates having the highest score in the semi-annual CPA examinations
1965	Awarded a Doctor of Laws from Eastern Michigan University
	Awarded a Doctor of Economic Science from Olivet College
1971	Awarded a Doctor of Laws from Northwood Institute
1976	Opening of the William A Paton Centre for Accounting Education and Research building, financed by contributions from former friends and students

SELECTED BIBLIOGRAPHY

1917   "Theory of the Double-Entry System," Journal of Accountancy, v.23 (Jan), pp 7-26.

1918   Principles of Accounting, The Macmillan Co. (with R.A. Stevenson).

1919   "Some Phases of Capital Stock," Journal of Accountancy. v.27 (May), pp 321-35.

1920   "Proprietors' Salaries," Journal of Political Economy, v.28 (March), pp 240-56.

       "Some Current Valuation Accounts," Journal of Accountancy, v.29 (May), pp 335-50.

       "Depreciation, Appreciation and Productive Capacity," Journal of Accountancy, v.30 (July), pp 1-11.

1921   "Methods of Measuring Business Income," Administration, v.1 (April), pp 509-26.

       "Assumptions of the Accountant," Administration, v.1 (June), pp 786-802.

1922   "Valuation of Inventories," Journal of Accountancy, v.34 (Dec), pp 432-50.

       Accounting Theory, With Special Reference to the Corporate Enterprise, The Ronald Press Co. Reprinted, Chicago: A.S.P. Accounting Studies Press Ltd., 1962, Lawrence, Kan.: Scholars Book Co., 1973.

1924   Accounting, The Macmillan Co.

1927   "Distribution Costs and Inventory Values," Accounting Review, v.2, pp 246-53.

1928   "Special Applications of Discounting," Journal of Accountancy, v.46 (Oct), pp 270-82.

1931   "Economic Theory in Relation to Accounting Valuation," Accounting Review, v.6, pp 89-96.

       "Working Capital in Public Utility Regulation," Journal of Accountancy, v.54, pp 287-99.

1932 "Accounting Problems of the Depression," <u>Accounting Review</u>, v.7, pp 258-67.

1934 "Shortcomings of Present-Day Financial Statements," <u>Journal of Accountancy</u>, v.57 (Feb), pp 108-32.

"Aspects of Asset Valuations," <u>Accounting Review</u>, v.9, pp 122-29.

"Costs and Profits in Present-Day Accounting," <u>National Association of Cost Accountants Bulletin</u>, v.16 (October 1), pp 123-39.

1938 "Comments on <u>A Statement of Accounting Principles</u>," <u>Journal of Accountancy</u>, v.65 (March), pp 196-207.

<u>Essentials of Accounting</u>, The Macmillan Co., 2d ed. revised, 1949.

1940 "Analysis of Financial Statements," <u>Cost and Management</u>, v.22 (Sept) pp. 303-19.

<u>An Introduction to Corporate Accounting Standards</u>, American Accounting Association, (with A.C. Littleton).

1941 <u>Advanced Accounting</u>, The Macmillan Co.

1945 "Transactions between Affiliates," <u>Accounting Review</u>, v.20, pp 255-66.

1948 "Accounting Procedures and Private Enterprise," <u>Journal of Accountancy</u>, v.85, (April), 278-91.

1950 "Measuring Profits under Inflation Conditions: A Serious Problem for Accountants," <u>Journal of Accountancy</u>, v.89 (Jan), pp 16-27.

1952 <u>Asset Accounting</u>, The Macmillan Co., (with W.A. Paton, Jnr).

<u>Shirtsleeve Economics: A Commonsense Survey</u>, Appleton-Century-Crofts, Inc.

1955 <u>Corporation Accounts and Statements: An Advanced Course</u>, The Macmillan Co., (with W.A. Paton, Jnr).

1958 <u>Essentials of Accounting</u>, The Macmillan Co., (with R.L. Dixon).

1963 "Accounting and Utilization of Resources," <u>Journal of Accounting Research</u>, v.1, pp 44-72.

1965 <u>Corporate Profits: Measurement, Reporting, Distributing, Taxation; A Survey for Laymen and Accountants</u>, Irwin.

1968 "Observations on Inflation from an Accounting Stance," <u>Journal of Accounting Research</u>, v.6, pp 72-85.

1971 <u>Assets-Accounting and Administration</u>, Warren, Mich., Roberts & Roehl, Inc., (with W.A. Paton, Jnr).

1973 "Financial Misrepresentation and Measurement," <u>Financial Executive</u>, v.41 (April), pp 14-21.

1976   "Notes on Handicapping," The Accounting Historian, v.3, p 4.

1980   "Statement by William A. Paton," Accounting Review, v.55, pp 629-30 (a response to Ijiri's review article on An Introduction to Corporate Accounting Standards, 1940, same issue)

1981   "Recalling George Oliver May and Me," Accounting Historians Journal, v.8 (Fall), pp 91-5.

NOTE: A full bibliography (to 1976) is contained in Essays in Honor of William A. Paton. Pioneer Accounting Theorist, ed, Zeff, S.A., J. Demski and N. Dopuch, University of Michigan, 1979.

REFERENCES

Book Reviews: Journal of Accountancy, v.35, April 1923.
Journal of Accountancy, v.15, Jan 1963, p.94 (R I D).
Accounting Review, v.38, 1963, pp.448-9 (R J Chambers).

Book Review of Paton & Littleton:
Accounting Review, v.38, 1963, pp.470-77 (W J Vatter).

Edwards, J D & R F Salmonson, "Contributions of Four Accounting Pioneers" (Digests), Michigan State University, 1961.

Fox, J G, "A Comparative Study of Selected Areas of the Accounting Thought of William Andrew Paton & Prevailing Accounting Thought, 1915-1970", PhD Thesis, George Washington University, 1974.

Ijiri, Y, "An Introduction to Corporate Accounting Standards: A Review", Accounting Review, v.55, 1980, pp.620-28 (reply by Paton, pp.629-30).

Lawrence, H J, "William Paton: Pioneer Accounting Theorist", PhD Thesis, University of Mississippi, 1972.

Stabler, H F & N X Dressel, "May & Paton: Two Giants Revisited", Accounting Historians Journal, v.8, 1981, pp.79-90.

Taggart, H F (ed) Paton on Paton, University of Michigan, 1964.

Zeff, S A, J Demski & N Dopuch, Essays in Honor of William A Paton, Pioneer Accounting Theorist, University of Michigan, 1979.

WILLIAM ANDREW PATON, *Accounting Theory—With Special Reference to the Corporate Enterprise*, new printing with foreword by Herbert F. Taggart (Chicago: A.S.P. Accounting Studies Press, Ltd., 100 N. LaSalle St., 1962, pp. 8, xii, 508, $5.00). Originally printed in 1922 by The Ronald Press Company, New York.

[Ed. Note: Ordinarily, reprintings are not accorded full-fledged reviews. However, the original printing of this volume appeared four years before the launching of THE ACCOUNTING REVIEW, and hence has never been reviewed in this journal.]

The publication of *Accounting Theory* in 1922 was potentially epoch making. Paton's treatment of accounting cut through the technical "bookkeeping" treatment of many of the earlier texts. Although he acknowledged obligations to Sprague and Hatfield, and although the orientation is foreshadowed in the earlier *Principles of Accounting* of which he was co-author with Stevenson, there was not previously in the English language anything like so comprehensive an examination of some of the crucial problems of accounting as this work presented. The long title of the book is *Accounting Theory—With Special Reference to the Corporate Enterprise;* and it is perhaps the selection of corporate business as the field of interest which gave it one of its distinctive features. Corporate business had arrived, to stay; and Paton was among the first to link accounting with the problems of choice confronting business managers, as distinct from investors and creditors. "Accounting . . . is perhaps the principal instrument by which the directors of business are enabled to conduct their affairs rationally" (p. 7). So thoroughly is the managerial viewpoint adopted that the role of accounting information in directing the flow of investible funds to the more efficient corporations—a matter recurrently dealt with in later Patoniana—receives scant attention.

Here then is the progenitor of all the books and articles which have since attached to their titles such terms as decision-making, business decisions, and the like. But it deals with the matter in a much more consistent manner than much latter day writing. In the first quarter of this century writers often took quite a nonchalant view of the basic character of the financial statements. On one occasion, for example, Hatfield observed that some say the basis of accounting should be cost, others say it should be value; but he himself took no particular line on the controversy. As is now known, the thirties saw a hardening, to the point of ossification, of the view that cost should be the basis, and much of the "accounting for decision-making" literature merely grafts a new set of words on to the regular treatment of historical-cost-based accounting. But Paton's insight and point of view told him quite clearly that managers wanted information expressive of values: "It is the function of accounting to record values, classify values, and to organize and present value data in such a fashion that the owners and their representatives may utilize wisely the capital at their disposal" (p. 7). And with reference to then recent inflationary experiences—"It is coming to be recognized that accounting systems must become more sensitive and accurate gauges of values if the purposes of the various interests involved are to be adequately served" (p. 12). "Valuation is the crux of accountancy . . . . any adequate system of accounts must be so constructed as to facilitate a presentation of all possible fluctuations and transpositions with respect to asset values" (pp. 92, 93). True, there is also the statement: "cost gives true value for purpose of initial statement"

—which has become so much a part of the literature that the last five words in it have tended to lose their significance. Not so in Paton's book. His chapter on Revaluation and Capital Maintenance weighs the arguments in a masterly, even-tempered fashion, but leaves the reader in no doubt that the insistence on the importance of values is carried through consistently, and that there are many more cogent reasons for accepting revaluation than the "general grounds" on which "many accountants would object" to it (p. 442). Systematic discussion of the problems of revaluation—other than in this closely argued chapter—is foregone, with the remark: "Any such study would require one or more volumes in itself." From hindsight one might say this was the prophetical understatement of 1922!

The only other outstanding feature of the book which can be discussed here is the final chapter entitled The Postulates of Accounting. Here for the first time is an "attempt" (Paton's own word) to present "a systematic statement of all the important postulates of accounting," its "basic assumptions" (p. 472). The distinct business entity, the continuity of the entity, the equality of assets and equities, the representation of financial condition by statements of assets and equities, the invariance of the unit of account, the initial propriety of cost as a measure of value, the transfer of values in the transformation of goods and services, the propriety of accrual accounting and timing conventions—are all discussed. Here was the beginning of opportunities for serious students of the subject to come to grips with its basic character. A start was made; but what happened? Its reviewer in the *Journal of Accountancy* of April, 1923, found little that was unusual and devoted one-third of the space to some argument about explanations of the difference between balance sheet presentations in Britain and the United States! Not many years later the cost doctrine was enthroned in a mood of hasty revolt against the misdemeanors of some and the misfortunes of others during the late 20's and early 30's. Ad hoc rules and rulings began to proliferate unsystematically. Whereas Paton averred that "in a study of the theory of accounts, the income statement is of little importance . . . . the balance sheet is of the utmost consequence" (p. 20), the opposite view gained wide and prevailing support. And it is only in recent years that these upstart views have begun to be reconsidered.

It was said at the outset that Paton's book was potentially epoch-making. But, as is the case with many ideas born of wide and penetrating insight, it appears to have been about 40 years ahead of its time. To judge from the "theoretical" literature it would seem as though the greater part of a whole generation of accountants has either not known of it or has chosen to disregard it as a foundation from which to progress. In so many respects it expresses contemporary moods that its republication is perhaps more timely than its original publication. So much for progress.

The academic world—at least—owes a considerable debt of gratitude to the small group of teachers, all former students of Professor Paton, whose enterprise has made this classic again readily available. Professor Taggart, a life long colleague of Paton, has contributed a lively foreword which provides both the setting of the book and a tribute to its author. *Accounting Theory* should, in the reviewer's opinion, be required reading, as an antidote to much that is doctrinaire in more recent literature, by all serious students of the subject whether in college or in practice.

R. J. CHAMBERS
Professor of Accounting
University of Sydney

24

(1)   "The balance sheet, as a true statement of financial condition, should not be taken too seriously (because) it depends on the future for its validation" (Pg.486).

"... the balance sheet and the income sheet, presents the results of the entire accounting process" (Pg.20).

"The balance sheet ... is of the utmost consequence" (Pg.20).

"Accounting ... is the principal instrument by which the directors of business are enabled to conduct their affairs rationally" (Pg.7).
- What can be inferred about Paton's work from the information contained in the above quotations from his work?

(2)   "In a study of the theory of accounts, the income statements is of little importance ..." (Pg.20).
- To what does the term "theory of accounts" refer?
- Is Paton justified in his remark?

(3)   Paton provides support for both original cost and replacement cost in his exposition.
- What justifications does he use?
- How do these justifications link up with his proposed function of accounting detailed on pages 6,7,16 and 20?
- Does Paton opt for any particular valuation base and what is his primary criteria of final choice?

(4)   "In this book, no attempt has been made to discuss the problems of valuation except in so far as the explanation of the structure of accounts has a bearing upon these matters". (Pg.xvii)
"Valuation is the crux of accountancy" (Pg.92).
- Would one be justified in connecting these two statements?
- If so, what implications do they have for Paton's work?
- In what sense is valuation the crux of accountancy?

(5)   "The accountant should develop his classifications ... from the point of view of the owners ... in terms of the needs and purposes of those furnishing the bulk of the capital of the business" (Pg.354)

- Does Paton explain and/or expressly demonstrate what the needs of owners are?
- What evidence does Paton cite to support his implication that small capital suppliers may have different needs to bulk suppliers?

(6)   What is the basis of Paton's suggestion that supplementary financial statements should be used in accounting?

5

JOHN BENNETT CANNING

The Economics of Accountancy

Biographical Chronology

1884	Born, Huron, Michigan
1913	Bachelor of Philosophy in political economy, University of Chicago.
1915-17	Instructor, political economy, University of Chicago.
1917-19	Military service
1919-41	Assistant (later full) Professor of Economics, Stanford University.
1921-29	Member Board of Examiners of California State Board of Accountancy.
1929	PhD in Economics, University of Chicago.
1941-45	War Food Administration, US Department of Agriculture
1946	Retired Stanford University; US representative on the Quadripartite Council, Berlin.
1948	Retired US Government
1962	Died

Selected Bibliography

1929   Economics of Accountancy, A Critical Analysis of Accounting Theory, Ronald Press Company, (New York).

"Hatfield's Paradox", Accounting Review, v.4, pp 111-115.

"Some Divergencies of Accounting Theory from Economic Theory," Accounting Review, v.4, pp 1-8.

"Depreciation Elements in Burden Estimates," National Association of Cost Accountants, N.A.C.A. Bulletin, v.11, No.11, Section 1, pp 1-14.

1931   "Cost of Production and Market Price," Accounting Review, v.6, pp 161-64.

1934   "Relation of Budget Balance to Economic Stabilization: a Suggested Federal Treasury Policy," American Economic Review, March, pp 312-16; with Edward G Nelson.

REFERENCES

Book Reviews: Annals of American Academy of Political & Social Science,
                 v.149, 1930, p.213 (Alden, W H).
                 American Economic Review, March 1930, p.112 (Beatty, W C).
                 Accounting Review, v.3, 1931, pp.242-3 (Meriam, R S).

Chambers, R J, "Canning's The Economics of Accountancy - After 50 Years",
       Accounting Review, v.54, 1979, pp.764-76.

Fisher, I, "Review of Canning's, The Economics of Accountancy", American
       Economic Review, v.20, Dec 1930, pp.603-18.

Smith, W R, "Profile: John Bennett Canning", The Accounting Historian,
       v.1, No.3, July 1974, p.6.

The

American Economic Review

VOL. XX   DECEMBER, 1930   No. 4

THE ECONOMICS OF ACCOUNTANCY[1]

This book is neither a manual for the bookkeeper, nor a purely theoretical work on accountancy. It is best described as an exposition of accountancy theory in harmony with sound economic theory. The theme centers on *income*, which the author regards as the all-important concept in both economics and accountancy. The problem of the accountant is to value the inflows and outflows of payments incident to business enterprises.

Accountants take cognizance of the costs of durable instruments chiefly or solely as a means of evaluating the future services which these instruments may render. When the capacity of a capital good to render further services melts away, its value melts away no matter what its original cost. Accounting should be made, not solely for the benefit of the management, but for the benefit of individual shareholders and of the public who are potential investors in the corporation and purchasers of the services it renders.

The book points the way to a sounder science of economics and a better theory and practice of accountancy.

It would not seem an exaggeration to say that *The Economics of Accountancy: A Critical Analysis of Accounting Theory*, by John B. Canning marks an epoch in the two branches of knowledge to which it relates—economics and accountancy—and none the less because it is a border-line study rather than strictly within the domain of either branch. It has come to be recognized as a good sign when any two sciences begin to encroach on each other so that the twilight zone becomes a new field for study. We all know that a new impulse was given to physics and chemistry when the traditional fence separating them was thrown down, and the new science of physico-chemistry established.

There is a fundamental reason why such studies as Canning's must be of value to economics. Any quantitative economic concept, to be of any use, should be capable of actual measurement. Accounts represent primarily those measures of business which are practical. They apply to business the acid test of practical workability—a test which might have saved much useless labor and disputation in economic literature. The "wage fund" theory, for instance, could scarcely have been proposed in an atmosphere of actual accounts. No one ever has or ever could set up an account of a wage fund. And if he could set it up in a capital account, he would see the inherent impossibility of transmuting it into

[1] Published by Ronald Press, 1929. Reviewed in AMERICAN ECONOMIC REVIEW, March, 1930, p. 112.

wages in the income account. So also we might have been spared the wearisome discussions of the supposed important distinction between productive and unproductive labor. The illusory "wage fund" concept and the illusory "unproductive labor" concept each died a natural death, slowly and unobtrusively. Professor Canning's book will hasten the inevitable and unobtrusive death of many illusory concepts of capital and income such as the once popular formula, "capital is wealth used to produce more wealth," which is fully as futile as the notion of "productive labor" (as distinct from "unproductive labor") to which it is analogous.

Professor Canning keeps his feet on the ground. His work shows a painstaking effort to deal with many baffling problems of practice and theory. The book is not a manual for the bookkeeper nor is it primarily a purely theoretical study. It may perhaps best be described as an exposition of accounting procedure in harmony with sound economic theory. The author avoids, for the most part, inferences as to the intentions of accountants in their various procedures; for what accountants' intentions may have been must always be a matter of conjecture. Instead, he studies the statistical effects of these procedures and points out their economic significance. He complains that too little attention has been given to accounting in the colleges. Only in the last two decades have the university curricula given courses in accounting from the economic point of view, despite the fact that the practice of bookkeeping is centuries old.

The central theme of the work is the concept of *income*, which conforms to that which I have found essential in my own studies, namely, a series of services rendered. The author repeatedly calls attention to the importance of this income-concept, and criticises me for not emphasizing it enough. He says:

In a late article Fisher says: "I believe that the concept of income is, without exception, the most vital central concept in economic science and that on fully grasping its nature and interrelations with other concepts largely depends the full fruition both of economic theory and of its applications to taxation and statistics." If he had written instead that *income is, without exception, the simplest and most fundamental concept of economic science, that only by means of this concept can other economic concepts ever be fully developed and understood, and that upon beginning with this concept depends the full fruition of economic theory in economic statistics,* it would have been an equally true and a more significant statement (p. 175). (The italics are Canning's.)

Income may not consist entirely of money income, and even money income is not literally money.

Note that it is the *fruition* in money—not the money-fruit—that is gross income. When a grocer makes a cash sale, the money he receives is an asset—not income. It is the *bringing in* that is income, it is this *last con-version* in a long chain of events, *i.e.,* of establishing a place of business, of equipping the sales-rooms, of acquiring stock in trade, of preparing the wares for exhibit and delivery, and so on, that constitutes gross income. Many objects and persons within the establishment will have rendered non-monetary though valuable services to the grocer that are necessary antecedents to this final service of the object sold. It is this final service only, this service of bringing in money, that counts as income. To the extent that these antecedent services are applicable to future sales, future bringings-in of money, the grocer has assets—not income. In a "cash" business the income cycle and the operation cycle are co-terminous. The cycle begins with money passing from the proprietor; it ends with the receipt of money that cannot be recovered by the person paying it (pp. 101-102). (Compare my *Nature of Capital and Income,* Part II.)

In an ordinary modern enterprise, the author points out, the whole problem of services is that of bringing in or paying out money and, since this money flows irregularly, the valuation of these flows fairly allocated to short periods can never be given any exact meaning. The accounting for all gains and losses can never be given completely and accurately until the business is wound up. For any interval between the date of founding, or first putting in of money, and the date of winding-up, or last taking out of money, only estimates or appraisals are possible. These intermediate year-by-year or month-by-month accounts can be only reports of progress. The income and outgo for a given week cannot consist merely of the money transactions which happen to occur within that particular week. There may be none; or there may be a whole quarter's disbursements. We must obviously include only the pro rata share for that week of any big items within it as well as the pro rata share of big items occurring before and after that week. It is this pro-rating, or spreading over time, of the irregular and unequally lumped receipts and expenditures which makes the chief trouble for accountants. These pro-ratings are necessarily estimates, not facts. The only actual facts of corporate income are the money receipts and expenditures in all their jagged irregularities; but unless there is some pro-rating the results of accounting are of little practical use.

It is possible, but not very useful, to prepare all income statistics of the past on the basis of realized income and cost valuations. This would be a cash receipts and disbursements accounting only. No accruals or earnings, positive or negative, would be included. That is to say, no depreciation and no appreciation could find a place, no costs of assets like manufactured inventories other than the cost of materials embodied in the goods and of direct labor services, could be shown. Such an accounting can show very little that is significant with respect either to a present financial and operating position or to performance during a period that is closed (pp. 320-321)

30

On the other hand, it is very difficult to define gross income under actual accounting. The concept includes two very unlike parts.

In a book of this kind the definition of gross income is of critical importance. But the writer has been unable to find anywhere in the literature either a simple definition, or a simple set of propositions amounting to a definition, that satisfactorily meets the tests just proposed. Nor has he ever been able to phrase a definition of his own that, tested upon good students, seemed to be a sufficiently apt one on the score of convenience (p. 100).

The gross income of a specified period is a mere summation. It is a measure only. *It is the summation of the amount of gross operating income plus the amount of gross financial income.* It is a summation only, both because the nature of the two classes of income have nothing in common that is peculiar to gross income, and because the *methods of measuring* (not the *unit of measure*) of the two kinds of income are different (p. 100).

When professional accountants speak of the gross operating income of a period they mean the *fruition in money (or the equivalent of money), effected within the period of all those elementary services which are the components of enterprise operations* (p. 101).

The gross financial income of a period consists of the hire earnings, effected within the period, arising from grants of moneyed funds made by one person (or persons) to another (or others) (p. 109). (Italics are the author's.)

Net income, however, is merely a difference; there are no separable series of services that can be ascribed to it. The separable series all belong to gross income.

No propositions that assign a qualitative nature to *net* income can be maintained (p. 126).

. . . . Since what is true for each particular proprietor must be true for any succession of them, there can also be a final net income to an enterprise for the whole period of its existence. Just as with gross income, too, no measure of net income earned in an enterprise in a period shorter than a proprietor's tenure can ever be anything more than an index of progress (p. 127).

There seems to be no brief expression less general than "net income is equal to gross income less deductions" that is wholly true; and this expression comes perilously near being meaningless. It is idle to attach any single term to the whole congeries of items that enter into the subtrahend summation unless some new term wholly free of alternative usages is invented (p. 127).

It would seem that the vagueness in the concept of gross income which troubles Mr. Canning is of no great consequence because to whatever degree gross income is subject to fluctuation, in that same degree will the "deductions" therefrom likewise be necessary. Just as in the complete accounting of the payment of 5 cents for a glass of soda water, it makes very little difference whether any attention is paid to "making change." If a customer first changes a dollar bill and then hands over a quarter, receiving back 20 cents in change, it might be difficult to decide whether a full accounting should state that a gross payment of 25 cents was made in exchange for 20 cents plus a glass of soda water, or that a gross payment of a dollar was made in exchange for 95 cents plus a glass of soda water, or even that $1.25 was paid for $1.20 and a glass of soda water. The only important fact is that the glass of soda water costs a net of 5 cents. So gross income and net deductions are important only as methods of computing net income. The only complication comes from the pro-rating process which must apply equally to gross income and its "deductions" if double counting is to be avoided.

No treatise on the subject of income could avoid some discussion of the pitfalls of double counting. The accountant, like the economist, must ever be on the lookout for these pitfalls.

The accountant, in scheduling these adverse events, is extremely careful to avoid double counting. The spoiling of a partly manufactured product is an adverse event; so, too, are the payment for the materials that have gone into it, the wages paid for work done upon it, and the overhead charges incurred in its partial manufacture; but the loss of the article and the cost of the article lost have one, not several, adverse effects. If the damage due to spoilage were to be listed as a deduction item, then the items shown for wages, purchases, and a myriad of overhead accounts would have to be diminished below the corresponding account balances. The outlay for a new factory building is an adverse event just as the acquisition of the building is favorable. But the benefit from acquisition cannot be experienced in a period less than the entire tenure of it. The accountant parcels out the adverse element, the outlay, over the series of years in which the beneficial services are to be received. Just as he avoids counting both the receipt of the building and the receipt of the services of the building but counts only one, he avoids counting both the outlay and the expiration of service value. Depreciation expense is not an expense in and of itself; it is the outlay for the depreciating object that is the primary expense. By the end of the tenure of the building it makes no statistical difference in the balance sheet whether the outlay was treated as a single deduction from gross income when the outlay occurred or as a series of annual deduction items the summation of which is equal to the outlay. Obviously, the latter treatment is the more convenient for those who wish periodic information about net income. In the avoidance of double counting the accountant's statistical procedure is above reproach. Definitions of income, common in economic literature, that include both goods and services do not have this great statistical merit (pp. 128-129).

Professor Canning closely links the income concept of a series of services with the concept of assets. He points out that the essential idea of an asset is that it stands for a separable series of *future* services.

What is essential is that there must be some anticipated, identifiable, separate (or separable) services (or income) to be had by a proprietor as a matter of legal or equitable right, from some person or object, though not necessarily from an ascertainable person(s) or object(s). One speaks of a motor truck owned by a corporation and operated in its enterprise as an asset of the company. But neither the legal title in the object nor the existence of the object, nor the two together, constitutes the asset. That which is fundamental is that certain anticipated services of the truck will inure to the benefit of the corporation. Note that it is not the whole of the possible services of the truck, nor even all those services that could be rendered by it with maximum economy to society, but only those services which the company can *advantageously* obtain from it in the course of *its operation in their enterprise* (p. 14).

Thus, the idea of a series of future services is the essence of an asset rather than any specific source or means of those services like a motor truck or a person.

To distinguish between the source and the services from that source would be, for some items (indeed, for most), to split hairs, both practically and logically. But the source of the service to the holder of a negotiable note receivable, for example, may be either the person primarily liable, intermediate parties secondarily liable, or unascertained transferees, whether by full negotiation or by assignment "without recourse" and/or "without warranty," or it may be some person who "pays for honor." Obviously some source must be anticipated; but no particular or ascertained source, nor even an unconditional source is requisite. It is not the *source* that is the note holder's asset; nor is it the thing (or person) that will *prove to be* the source that is valued. It is the anticipated service, the payment of money at some future time, that is valued and that is fundamental to the existence of the asset (p. 15).

The idea is that as long as a group of future services can be wrapped up in a separate package, so to speak, bought or sold, or at any rate valued, under whatever label, the question of the physical or other means by which this package of services is secured is of no consequence.

The whole subject of accountancy, if not the whole essence of economics, lies in the study of series of services. Capital accounts, that is, accounts of assets and liabilities, merely represent the discounted valuation at a particular date of the series of services and disservices or "outlays" which are expected to be rendered subsequent to that date.

It is worth noting that the author exonerates the accountants from the error of holding that past costs determine values. This will come as a surprise to many economists who have long complained that accountants deal solely, or principally, with past costs.

Economists and others have often made the gross mistake of attributing to accountants a confusion of cost and value, or of identifying cost and valuation. No such crude association can be shown from the facts of modern accounting procedure. Others, particularly the writers on accounts, have said that accountants adopt cost less depreciation as the measure of valuation. This is much nearer the mark. But even if depreciation be

:efined in the most refined and accurate sense, with respect to that which
s found in practice, the statement is still wide of the mark. Modern
accounting procedure abounds in instances that do not conform to this
oversimplified description. To make this assertion about accountants' valuations would make the modern balance sheet assert things that the underlying
procedures do not assert at all and would make it omit saying many things
that it does assert. Cost is only one class of evidence considered; depreciation, however defined and measured, is only one class of evidence among
many. In a multitude of cases, initial valuations greater than cost are
recognized; in a like multitude, increases in value are exhibited (p. 186).

Accountants are properly sceptical of valuation bases other than original
cost. But when the weight of evidence tends to show that some higher or
lower basis is *really* more probable they are not unwilling to revise valuations (p. 254).

Past costs are utilized by accountants chiefly, if not solely, as a
means of valuing future or anticipated services. No competent accountant would value any asset or liability except by valuing the anticipated future services and outlays. Just as soon as these anticipated
future services melt away, the present value melts away too; and the
valuation must be written off or reduced, however great the past cost
may have been. One of the chief tasks of the accountants is, through
"valuation accounts," or "reserves," to do this work of writing off or
revising original valuations, whether these original valuations were
taken from cost figures or not.

This attitude of the author, which is that of professional accountants, toward cost or expense as a valuation, though imperfect, of future services is shown in the discussion of "organization expenses:"

The real meaning of the item, "organization expenses," is, therefore,
"this amount was paid to procure the adopted form of organization in the
expectation that the services or assets to be utilized under it would be
worth more to the proprietary interest (by at least the amount of the
outlay) than they would otherwise be worth" (p. 32).

Professor Canning points out that where an asset and a liability are
evenly matched by the substantial equivalence and simultaneity of a
future series of services, on the one hand, and a corresponding future
series of outlays or payments therefor, on the other, both are usually
omitted in the accounts. For instance, if a man acquires a lease of
a house and contracts to pay rent, the lease is not usually put down as
an asset nor the obligation to pay rent as a liability, for the reason
that the series of services, namely, the shelter of the house, and the
series of outlays, namely the payments of rent, are supposed to match
each other. But, if the two series are not substantially equivalent or
not substantially simultaneous, the accountant may express the pre-
ponderance as an asset or as a liability or even set forth the present

value of both. In the latter case it is better not to separate such pairs
by placing one on one side of the balance sheet and the other on the
other, but to set up the bigger one as an asset or liability, as the case
may be, and the other as a deduction therefrom.

Some such procedure is called for not only in cases where, because
of an increase, say, of shelter value over and above the rent contracted
for, the lease has a salable value, but also in cases where the rent is
prepaid, in other words where the simultaneity has been materially in-
terfered with. In such cases there is apt to be confusion in the economic interpretation if the interpreter does not realize what is really
represented.

Thus one often sees in balance sheets items of "prepaid wages," "prepaid
rent," etc. A *wage* cannot be an asset to the employer, nor a rent to a
tenant. But the labor services and the services of the rented object still
to be rendered are clearly assets within the meaning of the definition
given in the preceding chapter; and supposedly, the services will be worth
at least as much as they have cost (p. 24).

The author emphasizes the importance of taking more specific account of commitments. It occasionally happens that accounts con-
forming to the best criterion of accountants mislead purchasers of a
business because of the omission of certain commitments, such as a long-
time guarantee to replace a machine or else to refund its purchase
price. Good accounting practice is moving toward a better procedure
regarding commitments. Professor Canning intimates that it may
shortly become the general practice to include all vital commitments in
the balance sheet by giving more inclusive meanings to assets and liabilities.

That is to say, some accountants are beginning to list, as assets and as
liabilities, the services to be had and the services to be performed under
wholly unperformed contracts (p. 57).

Among the most interesting and penetrating of the author's observations are those on so-called "good will." He points out that, just as
a pair of shoes is worth more than twice the value of a single shoe, since
a single shoe is scarcely usable by itself, and just as an automobile
is worth more than the sum of the values of its separate parts, so a
business as 'a going concern may be worth more than the sum of the
valuations of its separate parts (by "sum" is meant, of course, the al-
gebraic sum, including liabilities as negative assets). This difference
between the value of the whole combination and the sum of the values
of its constituent parts taken piecemeal, is, the author tells us, what
accountants mean by "good will." From a dictionary point of view and
still more from an etymological point of view, this interpretation might
be accused of perverting the meaning of the term "good will," or of

extending it to include patents, trade marks, franchises, and all other "intangibles;" but that is a mere matter of words. It might be better, from a verbal point of view, to return to the original meaning of "good will" as merely one of many kinds of intangibles, namely the valuation of the probability of continued patronage of satisfied customers—customers feeling literally a good will toward the concern—in which case there would still remain an excess of the total valuation of an enterprise and the sum of the valuations of its separable parts.

In practice, however, it is seldom, if ever, possible to separate "good will" from other intangibles. Thus good will in the strict and original sense has very little useful meaning. It is the "going-concern excess," including other intangibles, which has the useful meaning—the excess of the total valuation over the sum of the valuations of the separable parts. If accountants call this entire sum "good will," there can be little objection either from the accountant or the economist. This excess, whether called good will or not, explains the excess of market value over book value. Of course the "excess" may be negative.

In this connection the author raises the question as to whether good will, in the sense of going-concern excess is properly to be regarded as an asset at all, or whether, as he inclines to think, the concept of "assets" should be restricted to designate only the piecemeal parts.

In discussing this problem, Professor Canning helps us to see the justification for the reluctance of accountants to make their book values correspond more nearly to actual or market values by refusing, in general, fully to evaluate "good will." The accountant's proper business under the terms for which he is usually engaged is primarily confined to making a correct valuation of *the separable parts* and does not include making a valuation of the going concern *as a whole*.

Sometimes, therefore, the accountant puts down the so-called good will as worth "one dollar"—not, of course, because he thinks that one dollar is its true worth, but merely as a memorandum that good will exists and that the accountant has not attempted to evaluate it. To evaluate it properly requires an entirely different sort of expert than an accountant, with a different sort of training.

Of course where the "good will" has actually been sold in good faith for a definite sum or, for any other reason, has a specific measurable valuation, the accountant is justified in placing such valuation upon it and he can then do so by the same methods he uses in his ordinary professional work.

This problem of the discrepancy between the valuation of a concern as a whole and the valuation of its parts is at bottom the same as the much discussed problem of economists as to whether the sum of the marginal productivities of the agents of production will account for the whole product, or whether, instead, there emerges a residual element.

Another problem with which Professor Canning deals is the "equation of proprietorship." It has long been an aphorism of economists that the value of the assets is equal to the value of the liabilities plus the value of the proprietorship.

Is this "equation of accounts" an identity or is it an equivalence between three independently measurable magnitudes? If it is an identity, which two of the three magnitudes are really the independent ones? The author answers these questions by concluding that the two independent items are assets and liabilities and that the derivative item is the net proprietorship. In a still more simplified way we may regard liabilities as a form of assets merely having a negative sign. The assets represent the series of services running to the proprietor and the liabilities represent the series running from the proprietor.

Arithmetically there are but two quantities exhibited: (1) the money valuation (importance to the proprietor) of the ultimate benefits to be received from the services proceeding from the several items to the proprietor; and (2) the money valuation of the services which the proprietor has bound himself to render to other persons. Statistically the equation of accounts is epitomized in the difference between the volume of benefits expected to flow in (with reference to the proprietor) and the volume of adverse elements to flow out.

In the matter of valuation, liabilities do not differ from assets except in characteristic direction of flow. Those writers who urge consideration of liabilities as negative assets express a view more fruitfully suggestive than do those who habitually associate liabilities and *net* proprietorship in their discussion. But the problems of revenue-getting are so vastly different from those of procuring funds for it and from those of dividing the fruits of enterprise that no degree of similarity of quantitative aspects of the single items can ever make the groups of assets and the groups of liabilities homogeneous with respect to the accountant's principal inquiries.

The association in speech and writing of liabilities and of net proprietorship as though these two quantities were coördinate and had an independent existence, cannot but be misleading to those not fully informed. That they usually appear in the same member of the balance sheet as though they were coördinate is a mere statistical convention (pp. 50-51).

He concludes:

Proprietorship consists of the entire beneficial interest of a holder of a set of assets in those assets. A liability is a service, valuable in money, which a proprietor is under an existing legal (or equitable) duty to render to a second person (or set of persons) and which is not unconditionally an agreed set-off to its full amount against specific services of equal or greater money value due from this second person to the proprietor.

Net proprietorship cannot be qualitatively defined except as a mere difference. It is the *difference found by subtracting the summation of the liabilities from the amount of the proprietorship* (pp. 55-56). (Italics are the author's.)

I think this statement, which the author offers not as his personal
solution but as his interpretation of the best usage of accountants,
does not fully clear up the difficulties and ambiguities involved in the
concept of a "proprietor." In the old days, when accounting began, the
proprietor was a very definite individual with specific liabilities; but
today with a multitude of investment forms and with contracts in
which creditors share in profits and take explicit risks instead of en-
joying returns which are theoretically guaranteed, the whole concept
of a proprietor becomes more and more difficult, if indeed it does not
vanish into thin air, while the concept of the corporation as a fictitious
or artificial person which, for bookkeeping purposes, receives and dis-
penses all elements of the accounts becomes increasingly useful.

Today the essential differences, economically speaking, between investments such as common stocks of various types, preferred stocks of
various types, and bonds of various types, are chiefly differences of
risks. The problem cannot, it seems to me, be worked out from a
merely legalistic point of view, though legal rights are of great importance and the author pays much attention to their bearing on the
subject (*e.g.*, pp. 60-63). He is not at all convincing when he concludes that a debenture bond is not a bond at all and so is "clearly
not a liability." And in this he clearly departs from his rule of interpreting accounting procedure.

"That is to say, so long as there is any contract between the company and
another person not wholly and completely performed on the company's
part, and so long as any tort or criminal liability exists undischarged, no claim
can be enforced (p.62).

But a good debenture bond is ordinarily regarded by its owner as
almost identical with a mortgage bond. It is merely a matter of the
relative chances involved. In fact, a debenture bond of one company
may be far safer than a mortgage bond of another. When there is no
chance of insolvency, the distinction becomes a distinction without a difference. With our modern mixtures of bonds and stocks and with so
many persons in many rôles of stockholder and bondholder, with customer stock ownership and employee stock ownership, with profit-shar-
ing and coöperation, the idea of "the" residual ownership becomes too
complicated to be covered by the share of any one "responsible proprietor" or group of proprietors. The author himself seems to regard
the owner of a debenture or of an "income bond" as almost as purely
a proprietor as the owner of preferred stock. Many bonds today are
convertible into stock or have stock warrants attached so that the
"residual" claims include a part of the interests of "creditors."

In short, the old idea of a proprietor as one insider with specific
and simple obligations to outsiders called creditors will no longer serve;

for certain types of "creditors" instead of being really outsiders are partly inside the business and partake of the nature of proprietors.

For this reason I venture to think that there is more value than the author seems to assign to it of the concept of a "fictitious person," such as a corporation considered as a bookkeeping entity. This "person" is the sole proprietor and its liabilities include stocks as well as bonds. Thus, with respect to a corporation, the residual element in the balance sheet is a true liability, a liability to stockholders.

We could even imagine a company in which each of the parties at interest has precisely the same rights and obligations as every other, owning the same quota of bonds, preferred stock and common stock, etc. Who then is "the proprietor?"

The valuation of some kinds of assets is far more *direct* than that of others. This leads Professor Canning to make a broad distinction between direct and indirect valuation although there are many imperceptible gradations between the two, according to how definitely one can estimate the contribution of the asset to the money making which is the supreme object of the enterprise. Among the assets capable of what he calls "direct" valuation are cash and accounts receivable.

Cash involves no estimate. Accounts receivable involves an estimate of collectibility only. Merchandise involves likewise merely an estimate of funds to be collected as a result of sales, though, of course, a highly reliable estimate is not always possible. In the case of cash the enterprise services have all been rendered. In the case of the accounts receivable and the merchandise, only one service, the bringing in of money, is involved (p 183).

As to "indirect valuations," he says:

But not all assets are of this kind. In a manufacturing establishment many kinds of machines are employed each of which renders a kind of service peculiar to itself. None of these services consists in the direct and immediate bringing in of money. And while no one will question the proposition that the value of a machine is derived from the value of its services and from the outlays incident to procuring its services, no one can make a direct money valuation of those services unless they are to be sold separately (pp. 183-184).

Professor Canning thinks that one of the improvements to which we may look forward in accounting procedure is the substitution of direct valuations in certain cases such as inventories, where indirect valuations are now employed because they are easier.

If any substantial increase in reliability can be had at reasonable expense by resorting to direct valuation, clearly it is worth getting, and, in any event, the direct valuation gives *additional* information. The inventory is almost always the biggest single current item in merchandising concerns. In mercantile establishments, too, it is often the largest item in the balance sheet. The present writer's belief is that, in proportion to the effort needed to

...complish it, improvement of inventory valuation offers a prospect for a ...eater gain in usefulness of accounting reports than does any other element ... technique in accountancy (p. 227).

Sometimes—all too often in the writer's opinion—accountants employ ...direct valuations when legitimate and reasonably reliable direct capital ...lues can be found. This is the case with finished goods inventory (p. ...6).

Professor Canning considers carefully the various formulas which ...ave been proposed for correcting valuations of assets, especially in ...preciation accounts. He discusses various types including the or-...inary straight line formula by which an asset is supposed to depreciate ...venly through a certain specific period until it vanishes, and also the "sinking fund" formula in which interest is taken into account.

The writer has made a test of every formula proposed in the literature and ...as invented some hundreds of modifications upon these. But every one of ...hese can be demonstrated to be inferior in the conditions that prevail in ...se to the modifications of the service unit rule proposed here (p. 284).

He concludes that a modification of the service unit formula is the best, since it possesses none of the demerits of the other formulas dis-cussed and

possesses not only all of the merits of all of them but many more. If the postulates laid down for its support approximate the truth, the formula produces useful answers to the questions:

1. Of that which has been paid or must be paid for services of long-lived devices, how much expense was impliedly incurred on behalf of services already realized and how much for services that are still to be had?

2. Of those services paid for or to be paid for how much is applicable to the services used this year?

3. How much has been or will have to be paid out per unit of service realized (p. 294)?

The author believes in the judicious use of mathematics but does not wish to be too meticulous in this regard, as the cost of the mathematics may have to be taken into account as itself a material element in cost.

But any one who has the patience to find out for himself what accountants actually do and who will reflect upon what he finds, will discover that mod-ern accounting practice is, on the whole, sounder than that which has been written about it (pp. 45-46).

Professor Canning impresses upon the reader that accounts are not prepared primarily for economists but for employers who are anxious to get the most practical valuations possible and who are interested in economic theory only to the extent that it leads to an improvement in such practical valuations.

Many economists are grieved to find that the balance sheet valuations of accountants are of mongrel origin (from the economist's point of view). They find that cash has been counted (a present valuation); that accounts, bills, and notes receivable have been valued at the number of dollars expected to come in (a future valuation); that interim receivable interest accruals are valued separately from the principals to which they attach (an earning); that inventories are valued at cost or market (a purely arbitrary index); that items like organization expense, purchased good will, etc., having no attributes in common with the assets grouped with them are included (valuation account balances); that fixed assets are valued at an approximation to the cost of the future services expected to become available provided that cost does not exceed the cost of available substitute services (a division of costs into past and future charges). They find, moreover, that these diverse valuations of diverse things are added to find an asset total that, dollar for dollar, cannot possibly have a common significance.

In the other branch of the balance sheet they find a group of current liabilities valued at the amount to become payable (a future valuation); that fixed liabilities are valued to yield the effective rate implicit in their net issue price (a present valuation); and that a more or less arbitrary distribution of the difference between asset and liability totals is made among capital stock and elements of surplus or deficit (the total thus divided being merely the resultant of the diverse measures of assets and of liabilities). They find that this net proprietary interest figure bears no stable relation to the true capital value (if the latter could be found) of the enterprise as a whole.

No less are they distressed by the figures they find in the income statement for a specified period. They find a mixture of realized income positive and negative, of many negative earnings, of some positive earnings; and of a figure like that resulting from the difference between (1) the sum of purchase costs and beginning inventory valued at cost or market, and (2) the closing inventory valued at cost or market—a difference figure that is neither a realized (negative) income nor a (negative) earning.

The statistical state of affairs complained of does exist. No competent student of the joint field of economics and accounting can doubt that the measurements in accountants' reports are of diverse statistical orders. But that is a very different matter from charging professional accountants with responsibility for statistical absurdities. To such a charge the accountants could make the perfect rejoinder, "Show us a better way of doing this work that is both practicable and that clients would pay to have done" (pp. 319-320).

The author suggests that, in view of the importance of the information given in the balance sheet, it would be well to supersede the single "all purpose" balance sheet by various balance sheets constructed for various purposes. He hopes the day may come when public accountants will serve notice that a particular balance sheet was framed for a particular purpose and that he who uses it for any other purpose "does so at his own risk" (p. 88).

In short, while the author is critical of the economists' criticism of accountants, he points out the need for better accounting and the necessity of providing the money to pay for it. He stresses the importance of having an accounting made, not simply by and for the interested management, but by and for those whom the management serves. Thus, the shareholders in an enterprise might well have their own accountants report to them on the state of the financial condition of the company from their point of view.

There can be no doubt of the too great apathy of the financially interested public in the past in procuring disinterested expert reviews of corporate affairs. There can be no doubt, however, that bankers, in the interest of their depositors and shareholders, that investment houses, in the interest of their customers, and that governing boards of the stock exchanges, in the interest of their members and their members' clients, have in recent years done much to press the protective services of public accountants upon corporate business. The comment excited both in the popular press and in financial and trade journals by Professor Ripley's "Stop, Look, Listen" article,[2] in which among other measures, he urged an annual accounting by public accountants acting in the interests of shareholders other than directors and officers, could hardly have followed the publication of such an article fifteen years ago. Pressure for better service by those entitled to receive it can be counted on both to extend and to better the service (p. 327).

While the great bulk of the work done by public accountants still consists of "balance sheet audits" and of "detailed audits" covering the activities of a fiscal year, many more important and far-reaching investigations have been required of them in recent years. "Financial and industrial surveys" are often asked for. In these, something more than the history of the concern under examination is brought in. The prospect for the industry as a whole, the form and magnitude of the enterprise most likely to succeed in the industry, the appropriate capital "set-up," the most advantageous mode of market development, and so on, are considered. Such tasks give scope for the best service of broadly trained, experienced professional men, men whose competence and vision go far beyond that requisite for the conventional procedures of account keeping (pp. 327-328).

The author points out that the profession of accounting, with its rules, associations, and training, has become increasingly ethical and therefore increasingly important to all concerned. While the accountant is almost universally paid by the employer, he will not, if in a reputable firm, falsify accounts for his own or his employers' benefit. He is in a semi-judicial position and under obligation to report correct valuations for the benefit of the creditors or others interested besides the proprietor who pays for his work. As interest in and understanding of the importance of accounting grow, the economists, the statisticians and the general public will demand that accountants furnish the information needed by investors and the consumers as well as that required by the proprietor. If some day our census taking, which has already grown vast in scope and complexity, should include an accounting survey, or if some future Rockefeller Foundation should make such a survey, presumably the accountants making the survey would find

[2] *Atlantic Monthly,* September, 1926.

themselves seeking to reach such valuations as will serve the purposes of economists and statisticians rather than proprietors.

The most of the book is given up to accounts of money making enterprises. But to me, because of my own studies in this line, one of the most interesting portions of the book is that which gives an ideal accounting of a person's individual income (pp. 163-168).

The shortcomings of economists who have neglected accounting studies are pointed out with much plain speaking. The author shows (page 7) that the economist is prone to assume that those who are in the market possess and use certain information about cost which they have not and can never get. He also points out (page 7) that much in economic theory is only quasi-quantitative; that, for instance, the notions of increasing or decreasing returns are "too coarse for practical analysis."

He criticises the often cited case of the telephone business as subject to decreasing returns or increasing cost, pointing out that when the cost *per subscriber* increases with the increasing size of a telephone business the cost *per unit of service* may be decreasing. And in general, a service unit is suggested to replace the time unit which is a poor makeshift for a standard for measuring amounts and values of services.

It takes no great insight to see that one year's use of a truck may vastly differ from another year's uses in everything that is really significant. But if a ton-mile-under-useful-load has a stabler significance, and if the ratio of miles run to ton-miles-under-useful-load for periods as long as a year is relatively constant, then miles run is a better (that is, more convenient and, hence, more significant) measure than is a year of use (p. 281).

Any one who drives an automobile and watches his expenses knows that gasoline cost, tire costs, valve grinding, greasing, bearing adjustments, reboring of cylinders, etc., are much more closely related to miles run, under given road and use conditions, than they are to months or years in service (p. 282).

The author does not claim to have covered the whole ground of the economics of accountancy; nor does he claim to have solved satisfactorily all the problems with which he does deal. The vitally important subject of cost accounting he has deliberately refrained from treating. It is to be hoped that he will deal with this subject in a future book.

Professor Canning has written a sound and penetrating book which should be highly serviceable to accountants and economists alike. Although he defends the accountants against the unjustified criticisms of statisticians and economists, he does not attempt to make out that accountants can do no wrong. His book points the way to a sounder science of economics as well as better theory and practice of accountancy.

IRVING FISHER

Yale University

(1)   "The accountants have no complete philosophical system of thought about income; nor is there evidence that they have greatly felt the need for one" (Pg.160).

"The accountants can properly be said to adhere to one highly useful and intricately articulated theory (of income) (Pg.143).
- To what extent are the above quotes complementary/ contradictory?

(2)   Canning's treatment, although to be admired in many respects, clearly suffers from a confusion of "... the different but complementary roles of past information, present facts, and future prospects in the decision-making process" (Chambers, 1979, 774).
- What validity (if any) lies in this claim?
(Consider especially Canning's use of the phrase "financially difficult position" and his asset valuation rules).

(3)   Canning makes a point of refering to the terminological problems in accounting explaining that resolution of such problems is a necessary prerequisite to understanding the accounting equation.
- To what extent does Canning solve this problem?
(Pay particular attention to his treatment of income and proprietorship).

(4)   What criteria does Canning favour for choosing between his "direct valuations" and "cost" or "cost or market" valuations?

(5)   On page 199-200 Canning details six rules for aggregated measurements.
- In his treatment of inventory what (if any) contravention is suggested?
- How might such contravention (assuming it occurs) affect the end product of Canning's work?

6

DR SCOTT

The Cultural Significance of Accounts

Biographical Chronology

1887	Born, 24 October, near Montecello, Missouri; son of David Roland Scott
1907-10	Attended the University of Missouri where he was awarded AB and BS degrees (in journalism)
1910-11	Fellow in Economics, University of Missouri
1911	Instructor, University of Michigan
1912-13	Reporter, Detroit Times
1914	Re-employed as Instructor at the University of Missouri
1917	Advanced to Assistant Professor in Economics at University of Missouri
1918-19	Statistician with US army in France
1919	Promoted to Associate Professor at University of Missouri
1920	Appointed Professor of Economics at University of Missouri Married Carrie Lind Pancoast on 28 April
1925	Theory of Accounts published
1930	Chairman, Department of Accounting and Statistics (Scott now became Professor of Accounting and Statistics)
1931	The Cultural Significance of Accounts Published
1941	Vice-President, American Accounting Association
1952-54	First Vice-President, American Association of University Professors
1954	Died, 8 February

45

SELECTED BIBLIOGRAPHY

1925   Theory of Accounts, Henry Holt and Company, (New York) 284p.

1926   "Conservatism in Inventory Valuations," Accounting Review,
        (March) v.1, pp 18-30.

1928   "Valuation of Investment Securities," Accounting Review,
        (December) v.3, pp 375-382.

1929   "Depreciation and Repair Costs," Accounting Review, (June)
        v.4, pp 116-120.

        "Valuation of Depreciation and the Financing of Replacements,"
        Accounting Review, (Dec) v.4, pp 221-226.

1931   The Cultural Significance of Accounts, Henry Holt and Company,
        (New York), 316p.

        "Unity in Accounting Theory," Accounting Review, (June)
        v.6, pp 106-112.

1933   "Observed vs Theoretical Depreciation," American Accountant,
        (June) pp 170-71.

        "Communication," American Economic Review, v.23, pp 274-77.

1936   "Toward More Effective Participation," Journal of Higher
        Education, v.7 (Oct), pp 383-86.

1937   "Tentative Statement of Principles," Accounting Review,
        (Sept) v.12, pp 296-303.

        "Trends in the Technique and Tools of Management,"
        Accounting Review, (June) v.12, pp 138-145.

        "Freedom in An Age of Science and Machines," Journal of
        Social Philosophy, v.11, pp 317-26.

1938   "What the AAUP is and What it is Not," American Association
        of University Professors Bulletin, v.24 (March), pp 241-45.

        "Science and Social Guidance," Philosophical Review, v.47,
        pp 638-42.

1939   "Accounting Principles and Cost Accounting," Journal of
        Accountancy, (Feb) v.67, pp 70-76,

        "Responsibilities of Accountants in a Changing Economy,"
        Accounting Review, (Dec) v.14, pp 396-401.

        "Science and the Association," American Association University
        Professors Bulletin, v.25 (Dec), pp 567-73.

1940   "Selling Accounting Short," Accounting Review, (Dec) v.15,
        pp 507-09.

1941   "The Basis for Accounting Principles," Accounting Review,
        (Dec) v.16, pp 341-349.

1942   "Professors Administrant," American Association of University Professors Bulletin, v.28, (April), pp 247-56.

1943   "A Simplified Solution of Circuit Ratio Problems," Accounting Review, (April) v.18, pp 99-103.

1945   "Defining and Accounting for Depreciation," Accounting Review, (July) v.20, pp 308-315.

           "Due Process in Higher Education," American Association University Professors Bulletin, v.32 (Summer), pp 367-73.

1947   "Role of Accounting in Public Utility Regulation," Accounting Review, (July) v.22, pp 227-240.

1949   "Influence of Statistics Upon Accounting Technique and Theory, Accounting Review, (June) v.24, pp 81-87.

1950   "Rationale of Academic Freedom," American Association of University Professors Bulletin, v.36 (Winter), pp 629-43.

REFERENCES

Book Reviews of Cultural:
           Accounting Review, v.7, 1932, pp.147-8 (H C Miller).
           Accounting Review, v.40, 1965, pp.932-3 (L J Benninger).

Book Reviews of Theory:
           Journal of American Statistical Association, v.21, Mar 1926, pp.102-5 (W A Paton).
           Accounting Review, v.1 , 1926, pp.90-1 (E A Saliers).
           Accounting Historians Journal, v.5, 1978, pp.84-5 (J R Oliver).

Benninger, L J, "Accounting Related to Social Institutions the Theoretical Writings of D R Scott", Accounting Research, v.9, 1958, pp.17-30.

Elam, R, "The Cultural Significance of Accounts - the Philosophy of DR Scott", Accounting Historians Journal, v.8, 1981, pp.51-9.

Kvam, R L, The Collected Writings of DR Scott, University of Missouri, (Lucas Bros), 1964.

Morton, J R, "Profile: DR Scott", Accounting Historian, v.1, April 1974, p.5.

Shelley, R E, "DR Scott, Accounting Teacher Extra-Ordinary", DR Scott Memorial Lectures, 1968, pp.3-5.

ACCOUNTING RELATED TO
SOCIAL INSTITUTIONS—THE THEORETICAL
FORMULATIONS OF D. R. SCOTT*

By L. J. BENNINGER

Some accountants have become aware of Professor Scott's ideas through his work *The Cultural Significance of Accounts*.[1] Often I have encountered the puzzled query, "What is it all about?" Others know of him for his writings in professional journals. To still other accountants, Scott is virtually unknown. Any who are interested in a scholarly attempt to place accounting on a broader philosophical base, will, in any event, find Scott's theoretical formulations provocative.

It might be well at the outset to present briefly Scott's biography, most of which I have drawn from *Who's Who in America*. Professor D. R. Scott was born at Monticello, Missouri, on October 24, 1887. He received his A.B. and B.S. degrees in Journalism from the University of Missouri in 1910 and the Ph.D. in Economics from Harvard in 1930. From 1912 to 1914 he worked with the *Detroit Times*. In 1914 he began his teaching career as Instructor in Economics at the University of Missouri. Here he became acquainted with Thorstein Veblen, a leader of the institutional school of economics, who deeply affected Scott's thinking both on economic and accounting subjects. Scott's later *The Cultural Significance of Accounts* indicates throughout the tremendous influence of Veblen. As a personal reminiscence, I can remember the pride with which Scott pointed to his own desk as once having been used by Veblen. From 1918 to 1919 Scott served as a statistician in the United States Army. He then returned to the University of Missouri, where he served until his death in 1954. At that time Scott was Professor of Accounting and Statistics and held the post of vice-president of the American Association of University Professors.

Scott's major academic interests lay in two areas, separate in nature but closely interrelated within his general philosophy. These areas were: (1) a philosophical understanding of economic and social problems and (2) the development of accounting, particularly accounting principles. The basis of his theoretical formulations in both of these areas is presented in his major work *The Cultural Significance of Accounts*.

The Cultural Significance of Accounts

The economist will, in all probability, grasp much of Scott's *Cultural Significance* more readily than will the accountant, for Scott is indebted

---

* A paper presented on November 29, 1956, to the Accounting Seminar of the University of Florida, U.S.A.
[1] D. R. Scott, *The Cultural Significance of Accounts* (Henry Holt, New York, 1931).

heavily to Veblen and the institutional school of economics. Furthermore, it is probably true that, if Scott had been less interested in accounting and more in economics, he may well have achieved a niche in the institutional school as a disciple of Veblen.

As an institutionalist, Scott believed firmly in the evolution of human society. As a corollary, he believed that any set of ideas, concepts and institutions were tentative and relative in nature, referring to only a particular stage in the evolution of society and having validity only for the duration of that stage of evolution. To Scott, change was a normal phenomenon. Constantly, a new social pattern in process of evolution sounded the death knell to an established social order. However, in certain periods of social evolution, change took place at a slower pace than in others. Each of those periods represented an equilibrium or calm during which frictions between man and man and between man and his environment were minimised. During such periods, certain basic concepts and principles were widely accepted by all segments of society.

To Scott mediæval civilisation was such a time of relative equilibrium. During the eighth to the twelfth centuries the chaos left from the fall of Rome gave way to relative order and security, based in the main on the outstanding institution of the time, the Roman Church. The thirteenth to the fifteenth centuries saw the disintegration of mediæval society without any corresponding reintegration of social values; this period was to Scott the first stage of a transition between one social pattern and another. The sixteenth and seventeenth centuries saw the Protestant Reformation, the Renaissance, the rise of national States, the development of mercantilism, expanded handicraft technology, the breakdown of the guilds and the Commercial Revolution. The absorption of the law merchant into the common law and the opening of trade to all-comers represented not only revolt against the mediæval way of life, but also a second and last stage of a period of transition leading positively toward a new social order. The focus of interest in society was shifting away from an ideal of the rights and interests of individuals as conceived under a régime of status to an ideal of the rights and interests of individuals freed from fixed status, each to follow independently his own pursuits of life, liberty and happiness. In the eighteenth century there was a maturity of the new social pattern, described by Scott as individualism. The idea of divine rights was supplanted by natural rights. Political democracies arose in England, France and the United States. Simple handicraft technology was on the way to being supplanted by production by power machinery. The economics of *laissez-faire* became the vogue. Labour cost became a measure of value. In a very real sense, man's aspirations shifted from objectives pertaining to the next life towards the Greek emphasis on the present. A philosophy of individualism dominated religion, law, government, education and economics. In all society the common social philosophy held that authority emanated upwards from the individual.

Trading for a profit became the cornerstone of the economics of the new period. Trade was governed by a free system of markets, in which the forces of demand and supply were adjusted to each other. Behind market control there lay newly-developed systems of exchange, currency, law and a stable government. Not only would the market settle economic conflicts, but it would do so in such a way to further the best interests of society at large. At the heyday of the period of individualism, a management class such as we know today had not yet materialised. Accounting remained a simple recording device carried on by minor clerks devoid of professional status.

In Scott's view, diametrically-opposing forces are at work during a transitional period. On the one hand, there are those who would attempt to solve current problems by appeal to established concepts and institutions; on the other, there are those who would call for solutions in entirely new terms, emphasising the need for institutional change and the need for the development of new concepts. As an institutionalist and evolutionist, Scott tended to deprecate the old and glorify the new.

Since his interest lay primarily in the solution of economic problems, he levelled his sharpest criticism at the institution of the competitive market. Explained on the demand side by subjective concepts of marginal utility and on the supply side by similarly subjective concepts of the pain and irksomeness of labour, the competitive market, Scott thought, was a rationalisation of what people believed rather than a concrete fact. Although the idea of a competitive market was the controlling economic force during the period of individualism, any attempt to give the institution the same influence in a different period would make adjustment to changed conditions more difficult. It was in this connection that he presented the theory that classical economics, or for that matter any body of theory, achieved its full development only after the social pattern to which it referred had already begun to disintegrate.

Scott pointed out that today western society is essentially pluralistic in nature, lacking a comprehensive and unifying philosophy such as had existed in the mediæval and individualistic periods. For example, it was once thought that the greatest group good came from the free interplay of individuals in a competitive market, but today economic control is shared positively by government, labour organisations, voluntary associations, the management of large-scale enterprise, the market and accounting. These diverse forces are likely to come into conflict—and so on. When conflict ensues, the group may be seriously hurt.

Scott felt that he personally had a role to play in what he considered to be an evolving social order. Furthermore, he realised the risks incurred in attempting to give leadership:

> When we look back upon past social conflicts, it is comparatively easy to tell who was right and why, but when the conflict is in progress the choice is not so simple. It is not always easy to tell whether a would-be reformer is a hero and perhaps a martyr or merely a fool and a fanatic. For every proposal which represents an effective adjustment to society to new conditions, there are many suggestions which are grounded in the ignorance of their supporters. The man who would reform society must take the risk that his proposals may not prove to be constructive suggestions. In a period of crisis the realist who has

the understanding necessary to appraise the difficulties ahead and the ability to see what will work under the given situation provides social guidance and new social ideals. The true leader is not a visionary or an idealist except in the sense that his insight is greater than that of other men.[2]

He believed that a philosophy would unify and co-ordinate human conduct in the coming social order would have as its base a common belief in the efficacy of science. Evolution in this direction was already in progress. As partial proof, he pointed to the man-in-the-street, who increasingly relies on what he thinks is scientific fact for an answer to the truth of various situations. Modern advertising programmes rest, to a large extent, on a recognition of the common man's belief in science. To Scott, however, the science believed in by the uneducated was a thing of the past. Nineteenth-century science was primarily a science of absolute laws: modern science recognises its generalisations to be tentative and relative, and a philosophy based upon this interpretation, in Scott's view, would be the foundation of a new society. Science and its accompanying machine technology would call for a development of human personality different from that in force in the period of individualism. Just as the machine calls for a close co-ordination of men and materials in a factory, similarly in the larger social realm increasingly the group would base its values on teamwork and the interests of the group rather than upon unrestricted individual rights.

In the coming society, the controlling force over economic affairs would be a subtle but coercive one. Such a force, Scott felt, would be the institution of accounting itself, adjusted to an underlying philosophy based upon science. This point needs considerable and detailed elaboration. Details leading to its explanation may appear at first as evasive and elusive, but they are essential to an understanding of Scott's thesis.

Scott considered that the steady drift away from *laissez-faire* in government would continue. The long-term trend spelled an increase in control over economic life by government. Such control would be effected by the increasing use of commissions of experts. This type of control had already been foreshadowed by commission control over public utilities. Eventually, Scott seemed to imply, conflicts among different types of commission control would arise and would need to be resolved by some central economic commission charged with planning the major objectives of the social and economic system.

It should be emphasised that Scott was both anti-fascist and anti-communistic. To Scott, fascism was a temporary aberration of a group making a transition by resort to violence rather than processes of law. Both communism and socialism were backward-looking ideologies attempting to solve economic and social problems through "revolution by agreement—a social contract" without an accompanying change in underlying philosophy.

Commission control would have as its foundations that which was funda-

---

[2] D. R. Scott, "Science and Social Science", *The Philosophical Review*, xlvii, November, 1938, page 641.

mental to all other activities and aspects of the evolving society—a common belief in the efficacy of science. The scientific viewpoint would be applied to economic problems in large, partly through dependence upon an institution which had successfully adapted itself to change over the centuries—accounting. A new accounting would develop its principles in close conformity with the methodology and spirit of science. It would move increasingly in the direction of becoming a statistical methodology. Its data would become the recorded economic facts of the new society. Decisions made by commissions on all levels of government would be directly affected by the data and methodology of a science drawing its principles from a large social philosophy. Furthermore, with the increasing reliance upon accounting, increasingly the advice and opinions of professional accountants would be sought in the interpretation and solution of economic problems.

Although regulated by commissions utilising accounting data and methodology, the super-corporation would exercise great power in the new society. The management of such business would one day become professionalised. Of the various segments of management, Scott felt those in controllership would be the first to achieve professionalisation. The close relationship of the controller to the public accounting profession, the force of government and the demands of investors would call for controllers with professional status. The influence of such controllers would be felt in the exercise of economic power by the corporation of the future.

To Scott, the management of large-scale enterprise was fast becoming a forward-looking, policy-type management. The trend is epitomised by the development in larger businesses of policy executives separated, to a large extent, from the immediate operations of the business. This division of executive responsibility in business has a parallel in the development of the chancellor in university administrations. Policy-type management calls increasingly for data capable of projection and comparison. Such data would be provided by the controller drawing at first from two competing accounting methodologies, accounting and statistics. Eventually, accounting would partake largely of the methodology of statistics and would be largely relied upon by the new policy-type management. Data presented by accountants would be in accord with accepted principles of accountancy. Formulation of such principles would affect both policies and immediate operations of businesses in the evolving social order.

Scott believed that the market would continue to function in the new society, though on a highly restricted scale. He pointed to what he considered to be a present-day weakness, that although the market may be an effective device for regulating conflicts between corporations coming to it, it fails to reconcile the many divergent interests within a particular corporation:

> ...If a given manufacturing company has non-cumulative preferred stockholders as well as common stockholders, accounting is called upon to draw the line of division between their interests. The market does not automatically adjust this conflict. The market does not determine whether a profit was earned during a given period.

Similarly, accounting, rather than the market or the law, draws the line between the interests of present and those of future stockholders. Of course, the market fixes the price at which present stockholders sell to future stockholders, in so far as the stock is sold, but even in such sales the bids behind the resultant market price commonly rest upon accounting reports of profits earned and asset values. . . .

Perhaps the best illustration of how the adjustment of conflicting economic interests has come to be dependent upon accounts is in the regulation of public utilities. Issues involving rates charged and profits allowed require an accounting basis for their settlement. In its decisions aiming at justice as between investors and consumers, the regulating commission is as much dependent upon accounts as is the manager of any competitive enterprise; more so in fact, if that is possible. . . .[3]

Even today, therefore, the principles and practices of accounting play a major role in the adjudication of economic interests. In the developing social pattern, corporate interests as well as others will rely, in the settlement of economic problems, on the ideology of accounting rather than the ideology of classical economics.

Consequently, Scott felt that, as the principles and practices of accounting would be increasingly applied both by government and by private business to economic problems, accounting would in essence become the basic controlling force in economic activities and would play a role tantamount to that of the market in the individualistic period. The production and distribution of wealth would be guided by ideas inherent in the institution of accounting. All elements of society are ultimately and significantly affected by an accounting presentation of revenue and cost data. Accounting would become a dynamic, controlling force wholly in tune with men's larger concept of a philosophy of science. As the competitive market was a process of valuation in the individualistic period, accounting, in turn, was to become a process of valuation in the evolving social period.

As market machinery has become less and less effective in a changing economic situation, accounting technique has been developed to supplement and supplant it. So pervasive is this increasing dependence upon accounts that it suggests an organisation of economic institutions around accounts comparable to the earlier organisation around the market. . . .[4]

The Need for a Cultural Orientation

Scott consistently applied his general philosophical tenets to his classroom teaching. In an age of transition, pluralism and conflict, he felt it urgent that students be provided with an orientation to modern society. He deemed the old liberal arts tradition of a man with a universal grasp of the arts and sciences practically dead and incapable of revival. In its place must come orientation throughout all courses, as well as perhaps a single course devoted to the problem of orientation of a particular professional field.

---

[3] Ibid., pages 201-202.
[4] Ibid., page 285.

In Scott's view there were two possible approaches to an orientation course. One would represent a series of lectures to be presented by professors drawn from the various departments and colleges of the university. This approach, he thought, would be foredoomed to failure, for there would be little to relate diverse points of view to a common cultural background. Another approach would be to have the orientation course taught by one individual who had a grasp of the professional area and a philosophical background such as would permit him to direct readings and discussions designed to give a comprehensible and integrated picture of modern society and its direction. Such instruction, Scott felt, should come late in the student's course of study. The later it came, the more there would be to integrate.

An insight into Scott's interest in cultural orientation as applied to a more restricted sphere is given by the following quotation concerning Scott's presentation of a course in managerial accounts and statistics:

> ...The burden of this course runs to the effect that it is the fundamental function of accounts and statistics to so analyse and present the facts that the decisions of the management will be automatic. Instead of presenting accounts and statistics as tools through which management controls operations under its authority, this course presents them as a means by which the management is itself controlled by the facts. This ideal for management is precisely the same as that of the practitioner of medicine who seeks to rest his diagnosis and prescription upon conclusive objective evidence.
>
> If we accept the implications of the foregoing discussion, we cannot escape the conclusion that business administration is actually coming to rest upon a scientific foundation....[5]

Development of Accounting Principles

A major objective of the orientation course was to attune the student to broad social principles. Principles relevant to a specific science must inevitably dovetail with broader social principles, or they become out of touch with reality. In Scott's thinking, accounting principles need to be tested against general social principles, just as accounting rules of thumb needed to be tested against broader accounting rules and principles. As social principles evolve, it becomes essential that the entire hierarchy of accounting rules and principles also change. Scott felt that the present-day development of accounting had lagged to such an extent that on many points accounting data had lost touch with reality.

Examples of Scott's interpretation of accounting principles are listed below. The first is a major principle followed by amplifying principles of a lesser order.

"The procedures, rules and techniques of accounting must afford equitable treatment of all interests actually and potentially involved in the financial situations covered by accounts."

---

[5] D. R. Scott, "Unity in Accounting Theory", *The Accounting Review*, vi, June, 1931, page 207.

"The accounting record and summary reports drawn from it should present a true and accurate statement of the information which they purport to record and present. Accounts must not be made a means of misrepresentation."

"Accounting rules, procedures and techniques must be continuously revised to allow for changing economic conditions in order that they may continue to embody the principles of justice, fairness and truth."

"Accounting rules, procedures and techniques should be consistently applied. They should never be changed arbitrarily to serve the temporary purposes of management. When changes are necessary they should be controlled by the principles of justice, fairness and truth."[6]

Note that in an elucidation of accounting principles Scott refers to what he would consider broader but applicable social principles.

Cost Accounting

Scott believed cost accounting to be the most representative aspect of the phenomenon of institutional change within the broader area of accounting. Cost accounting, he pointed out, had its modern development as a conflicting methodology to general accounting. It developed outside the realm of generally accepted accounting principles, and although since integrated, the union was somewhat forced. Cost accounting is less concerned with recording and more with problems of management. It therefore often utilises concepts not fully in accord with generally accepted principles of accounting. In time, however, Scott felt that cost accounting practices would give rise to cost accounting principles which would not only be applicable to cost accounting conceived as a narrow sphere of specialised accounting interest but, with the spread of cost accounting theory and technique to all accounting processes, would be applicable to accounting as a whole. The accounting principles of tomorrow would be found in large part in principles now in process of development by cost accountants.

Distinction between Cost and Expense

Scott held that, historically, periodical revenues were matched by the cost of merchandise sold and the expenses of a period. With the advent of cost accounting, manufacturing expenses were divided between those to be apportioned to cost of goods sold and hence to periodical revenues and those remaining on hand in inventory. The word "cost" was applied, therefore, at first to cost of merchandise purchased and sold and later to goods manufactured and sold. The word "cost", consequently, in Scott's view, has an historical connotation of an accurate measurement of cost.

Today, Scott would say, sales revenue is matched by either purchased merchandise cost or manufacturing cost of goods sold plus, in either case, periodical expenses. Accounting is now in process of developing a plan of

---

[6] D. R. Scott, "The Basis of Accounting Principles", *The Accounting Review*, xvi, December, 1941, pages 342-3.

cost accounting for distribution costs which, when completed, would lead to a designation of distribution expenses to be matched against sales revenue as "distribution cost of goods sold". The word "expense" would continue to be applied to those items not capable of matching with sales revenue on a cost accounting basis.

Current Replacement Cost

Consistently throughout his lifetime Professor Scott believed in the valuation of assets in terms of current replacement cost and their issuance, depreciation or amortisation in the same terms. I quote from an article written by him in December, 1929, in the course of an argument with Professor Kester:

> ... Present market value and future market value are two quite distinct concepts and it is the present market value which expresses that competitive significance which makes an asset an asset. If there are such things as "real and actual costs of production", they surely are costs in the current competitive situation. The price which may have been paid for an asset at some more or less distant time in the past is of itself no more significant than the price which may be paid to replace it at some more or less distant time in the future."[7]

Except at one odd point, investments representing a controlling interest, Scott held consistently to the use of current costs in the accounts. Inventories were to be carried at latest invoice cost. Stocks held for speculation were to be carried at market value. Long-term investments in stocks were to be carried at cost plus adjustments for increases or decreases in book value due to undisturbed earnings or losses, plus adjustments for changes in the market price above and below this amount. Bonds owned were to be carried at cost plus applicable premium or less applicable discount, plus or minus any change in the market value of the bonds. Fixed assets were to be valued at cost plus or minus changes in replacement cost less depreciation on replacement cost.

Credits accompanying asset write-ups, except when related to speculative investments, were to be taken to special appraisal surplus accounts. Such accounts were to remain open to be credited in times of price rise and debited in times of price decline. Credit additions to these accounts meant simply that more dollars than formerly were required to measure the same equity.

Patents, copyrights, franchises and the like were to be carried in the books ordinarily at cost, if purchased; it would be still better if they were carried at an amount representing the discounted value of their future revenues. Amortisation of such assets was to take place in proportion to value loss, and if the asset was assumed to have value in perpetuity, its cost was to be permanently carried on the books.

Scott believed that many intangible values were left out in the conventional construction of a balance sheet. He argued, for example, that an established firm had a *bona fide* asset in the form of the value of a skilled labour force. The value of such an asset could be put approximately at 50 per cent. of the

---

[7] D. R. Scott, "Valuation for Depreciation and the Financing of Replacements", *The Accounting Review*, iv, December, 1929, page 27.

cost of training the present force, on the assumption that the number of new workers being added to the force was about equal to the number about to retire and that all others had reached the mid-point in their training.

Peculiarly enough, Scott changed his position on current costs when he dealt with investments representing a controlling interest in other companies. Either he felt statements prepared for the controlling legal entity had no significance by themselves or his interest in such investments centred entirely on the technique of consolidated statements:

> ... Keeping such stock at cost gives an indication of the controlling company's equity in the subsidiary at the time of purchase of the stock. At the same time it does not interfere with an accurate statement of assets and equities included in the consolidated unit. Hence such investments are best carried at cost.[8]

Depreciation Accounting

Scott abhorred much of current thinking on the subject of depreciation. He believed first of all that depreciation should be computed on the basis of current replacement cost and second that "depreciation is an accruing loss of value which begins with cost new and ends with scrap value at the end of an asset's useful life".

In criticising a definition of depreciation based upon a report of the Committee on Terminology of the American Institute of Accountants, dated October, 1942, Scott wrote:

> The definition which is criticised in the foregoing discussion was formulated to tie in with a preconceived theory of the nature of accounting, whereas definitions in accounting, as in other fields, should be arrived at in the spirit of an open-minded approach to the subject matter and the problems which are to be considered. This error arises from uncritical habits of thought which are moving in the direction of making accounting theory a closed and perfected system. The dictum that accounting is essentially a record of historical cost divorces the viewpoint of accounting from that of management. The present attempt to make depreciation a term of art peculiar to an accounting cult would, if successful, widen still further the breach between accounting theory and the everyday sphere of concrete affairs in which management must act.
>
> In a price system values are in proportion to utility or usefulness. Price and value are terms in which businessmen commonly make comparisons and decisions. ...
>
> When assets are new, businessmen and accountants both appraise them in terms of cost. This is not because that cost is significant *per se*. It is not. The importance attached to it arises from the fact that it is a present appraisal or evaluation of the total usefulness of the asset in question. ...[9]

---

[8] D. R. Scott, "Valuation of Securities", *The Accounting Review*, III, December, 1928, page 19.

[9] D. R. Scott, "Defining and Accounting for Depreciation", *The Accounting Review*, xx, July, 1945, page 314.

With respect to the method to be chosen to measure the "accruing loss of value" of a depreciable asset, Scott wrote:

The cost new of an asset is a valuation of its usefulness just as any market price is such an evaluation. The process of allowing for depreciation by one method or another writes down the book value of the asset from cost new to scrap value. The appropriateness of the method chosen and the equitableness of the result which it affords depends upon the degree to which the writing down of the book value corresponds with the actual change in the value of the asset from cost new to scrap value.[10]

Although Scott felt depreciation took place in an infinite variety of ways, he pointed to three general factors which should be considered in the selection of a depreciation method. These were: (1) "the distribution of income over the expected life of the asset"; (2) the influence of imputed interest; and (3) "the distribution of the repair costs necessary to keep the asset in working order".[11] If an asset was expected to render most of its service during its early life, some decreasing amount method of depreciation should be employed. If depreciable assets required heavy investment over long periods of time, the influence of interest should be recognised by the use of some interest method of depreciation which would give rise to increasing amounts of depreciation over the useful life. If repair costs were significant in amount and irregular in incidence, net income would be diminished when they take place, a consequence that should be taken into consideration in constructing the depreciation formula. Irregularity in use of an asset might directly affect income realisation and physical deterioration of the asset, and in such circumstances a units-of-output or service hours method of depreciation should be employed.

Proprietorship Accounts

Scott segregated three types of proprietorship account: (1) accounts indicating investment in a business not ordinarily reducible through cash dividend distributions, including elements of capital stock, capital surplus and retained earning brought into the capital category; (2) accounts indicating retained earnings potentially available for dividends; and (3) operating reserves in the nature of proprietorship.

Departures from current practice can be illustrated by assuming a business to have established a reserve for post-war expansion. According to Scott, once the expansion had taken place the reserve should be closed to a capital surplus account or be included in the invested capital category to become part of permanent equity.

To Scott an operating reserve was established by a charge to revenue— for example, a provision for repair guarantees or a provision for self-insurance. The former reserve he would classify as a curent liability, on the assumption that repairs to be made under a guarantee would give rise to a

---

[10] Ibid., page 311.
[11] Ibid., page 312.

rather speedy reduction in working capital. The latter reserve he would carry among surplus reserves. Although a reserve for self-insurance would be decreased with the advent of the contingency anticipated, the timing of the event was indeterminate, and until it occurred the reserve represented a portion of the general ownership in the business.

Some Closing Comments

The objective of this article has been to present rather than to evaluate the theoretical formulations of Professor Scott. A full-scale criticism of his works would entail still another article and preferably should be made by someone other than one of his former students. Nevertheless, a few comments and a brief evaluation may serve as a conclusion to bring into focus some of his major ideas.

Scott's formulations of a cultural background of accounts shares many of the limitations of institutionalists writing in the first third of this century. Scott saw mankind pushing its restless way towards vague, unknown but desirable goals which, when achieved, would in turn be replaced by still other uncertain but desirable goals. Implicitly, he assumed that change meant progress and that progress meant change. Although in his description of the evolution of western society he pointed to the Renaissance as a return in part to Greek and Roman ideas, he was impatient with those who would turn or return to traditional concepts and institutions for a settlement of modern problems. His motto with respect to social change might well have been: "always forward, never backward".

Scott's scorn for subjective thinking in economics was matched only by his own penchant for subjective thinking in accounting. To Scott the line between the two would be sharp and clear; to the observer, it appears vague and indistinct. Often he preached relatively but practised the absolute. As a consequence, his own concept of economics became divorced from reality.

Man's subjective thoughts are the stuff which engenders the production and distribution of wealth. To claim that marginal utilities were not capable of measurement and to treat them in consequence as lacking reality was to express a defeatism of a sort that Scott himself abhorred when it showed itself in the face of the problem of measuring such imponderables as the value of a working force, depreciation or the distribution costs applicable to a unit of a particular product. To hold that marginal utility was simply a rationalisation of a particular society was to ignore basic elements of human personality as expressed by human wants and desires. Finally, to argue against the influence of the competitive market but at the same time to rely upon it in a number of situations as a basis of value determination in accounting posed a paradox in logic.

On the level of business and accounting, Scott expressed a buoyant optimism on the possibility of basic changes in group personality, whereby problems will be solved not by selfishness or emotionalism but by a reliance upon science and matter-of-factness. All present-day pluralistic forces will some day resolve their differences on the basis of reason and the group interest. In the light of history to date, this is romantic idealism much on a par with that expressed by Voltaire's *Candide*.

Despite his vagueness, his occasional inconsistency and his undue optimism, Scott, held forth a useful concept of social change and a dynamic and unified concept of accountancy. That societies as well as organisms evolve and that adaptation to change is imperative to survival is a generalisation worthy of consideration, not only with respect to larger social problems but also to the constituent institutions, arts and sciences of a particular society. A pragmatic test of the efficacy of either economics or accounting rests in their ability to help solve present-day problems.

Within the specific area of accounting, Scott made his greatest contribution in his writings on and postulations of accounting principles. Although he would be the last to minimise the services of accounting to management, clearly and incisively he expressed the moral basis behind accounting and the accounting profession: that a successful society would attempt to secure justice for its individual components and that accounting, as one of the great social institutions, was charged specifically with the protection of a variety of economic interests. Whether or not one agrees with his general concepts of evolution and institutional change, it is in the area of principles that Scott precisely related the everyday environment to larger social concepts and principles.

Scott achieved a unity of his accounting theory by building his structure about a framework of morality and utilitarianism. Income represented an increase in net assets due to enterprise profit-making activities: price-level gains should be excluded from income reporting. His test of revenue realisation lay in that procedure or convention which best protected the various interests at stake. Cost of production at current cost nominally determined the book value of items manufactured; however, value so determined was to be tested by market values or amounts arrived at by a discounting of putative incomes. Cost of production ideally included not only so-called actual costs but also imputed costs.

Considering some of Scott's other tenets and theories, it is apparent that accounting has gained tremendously both in stature and prestige. Whether or not accounting will, as in his vision, become the economic cornerstone of a future society supplanting the market in importance is debatable. Nevertheless, it does appear that accounting will play an increasingly important role in economic affairs. The need for a revaluation and adaptation of accounting as a statistical and economic methodology is gradually becoming apparent to accountants. The use of replacement costs in connection with the valuation of fixed assets has come within the realm of generally accepted accounting principles. The measure of depreciation in the same terms appears to be on the way to a similar acceptance.

Today much of Scott's thinking has achieved, or is in process of achieving, respectability—in such degree that to one well versed in accounting theory, Scott appears to offer little not already included within the sum total of accounting knowledge. But the same may be said in various degrees of other great personalities, in accounting as in other subjects. Relative to the total achievement, little would appear to have been lost had any single one of them not lived or written. However, bearing in mind the period during which he did most of his work, Scott played an influential role in establishing a favourable intellectual climate for the further advancement of accounting. Moreover, the trend appears to bear out many of his predictions on the character of our evolving society, the nature of prospective changes in accountancy and the increased importance of accounting among the various institutions of society.

Gainesville, Florida, U.S.A.

(1) At the centre of Scott's theoretical development are ethical norms, epitomising the responsibility of accounting in society?
- What are these?

(2) What evidence is there to suggest the Scott saw accounting as a control device in economic life? What precisely is accounting meant to control?

(3) Scott makes mention of the disintegration of a market control period and the advent of an individualistic period.
- To what does he refer?
- What is the context and relevance of his discussion for accounting purposes?

(4) Scott explains the process of cultural evolution in a step-like manner, similar to that used by a modern day philosopher.
- What are these steps?

(5) How does what Scott refers to as 'the scientific point of view' figure in his explanation of the cultural underpinnings of accounting?

(6) What importance does Scott ascribe to the concept of "pluralism"?

(7) Inspite of the fact that Scott prefers no particular valuation procedure he refers to the choice between valuation procedures as resting "... upon social ends and values" (Pg.94).
- What ends and values (if any) does Scott divulge?
- Is general purchasing power a social end?
- Assuming a positive response to the former question - what valuation procedure does this imply?

(8) "On this account, it appears to the writer a mistake to use the term value except in a subjective sense" (Pg.96).
- What is the context in which this quote appears?
- Might one infer that Scott has not recognised the notion of "value in exchange"?

7

HENRY WHITCOMB SWEENEY

Stabilised Accounting

Biographical Chronology

1898	Born Springfield, Massachusetts, 12 September.
1915-17	Amherst College (Winner Billings Latin Prize, 1917)
1919	Bachelor of Arts, Columbia University
1920	Bachelor of Science, Columbia University; Beta Gamma Sigma; Instructor Commercial Subjects, Barnard School for Boys, New York; Montgomery Accounting Prize.
1921	Master of Science, Columbia.
1922	Instructor Business Administration, University of Wisconsin, then Assistant Professor.
1923/4	(3 months) with Lybrand, Ross Brothers and Montgomery.
1924	Assistant Professor of Accounting, University of Pittsburgh; Master of Arts; Bookkeeping and Introductory Accounting.
1925 (Dec to 1931 (June)	Price Waterhouse and Co., New York.
1927	Manuscript of Stabilized Accounting won the $500 prize in a National Economics Contest.
1928 (Sept) to 1929 (June)	Professor of Accounting and Head of Accounting Department, Long Island University, Brooklyn, New York.
1931-2	S.D. Leidesdorf and Co., New York
1932-4	R.G. Rankin & Co., New York
1934	Married, Mae Edith Fichter
1934-5	Asst. Comptroller, Commercial Investment Trust Corporation (Automobile and Industrial Finance), NY.
1935	Accounting Supervisor and Depreciation Expert, Federal Communications Commission, Washington DC; Senior Land Bank Examiner, Farm Credit Admin., Washington DC. Other Government positions until 1943.
1936	Stabilized Accounting; Asst. Editor The Accounting Review; Ph.D. Columbia.
1936-44	Professor of Accounting, Georgetown University.
1940	LL.B, Georgetown University.
1941-58	Professor of Law, Georgetown Law School.
1943	Partnership in New York law firm.
1944	Own accounting, CPA, practice, specializing in government contracts and income taxation.
1956-67	Adjunct Professor of Accounting, Graduate School of Business, Columbia University.
1960	LL.M, Columbia.
1967	Died

NB. Sweeney switched positions regularly in his earlier life. He often withdrew from these positions for short periods in order to concentrate on his writing. His teaching positions overlapped or were held concurrently with his business appointments. He was a member of several state CPAs.

Selected Bibliography

1924   Bookkeeping and Introductory Accounting, McGraw-Hill
        Book Co.

1927   "Effects of Inflation on German Accounting," Journal of
        Accountancy, March, v.43, pp 180-191

1928   "German Inflation Accounting," Journal of Accountancy,
        Feb, v.45, pp 104-116.

1930   "Maintenance of Capital," Accounting Review, v.5, pp 277-
        287.

1931   "Stabilized Depreciation," Accounting Review, v.6, pp.
        165-178.

1932   "Stabilized Appreciation," Accounting Review, v.7, pp 115-21

        "Making reports to stockholders tell the truth,"
        Forbes, April.

        "Balance-Sheet Treatment of Long-Term Liabilities
        Maturing Within One Year," American Accountant, Oct.

1933   "Capital", Accounting Review, v.8, pp 185-99

        "Income", Accounting Review, v.8, pp 323-35

1934   "How Inflation Affects Balance Sheets," Accounting Review,
        v.9, pp 275-99.

        "How New Dollar Will Affect Your Assets," Forbes, 15 Feb.

        "Approximation of Appraisal Values by Index Numbers,"
        Harvard Business Review, Oct.

1935   "The Technique of Stabilized Accounting," Accounting
        Review, v.10, pp 185-205

1936   Stabilized Accounting, Harper and Brothers (Reissued,
        with Foreward by W.A. Paton in 1964 by Holt, Rinehart
        and Winston Inc.).

1947   "Nonresident Estate Taxes under United States and United
        Kingdom Conventions," Taxes - the Tax Magazine, v.25,
        pp 903-10.

1948   "Avoidance of Double Income Taxation - The United States -
        United Kingdom Convention," Taxes - the Tax Magazine,
        v.26, pp 732-40.

1957   "Tax Effects of Operating as a Corporation or Partnership
        Prentice-Hall, with H. Shockey.

1962   "Accounting for Government Contracts," Prentice-Hall
        Accountant's Encyclopedia, v.3, pp 1261-1315.

1965   "Consolidation of Defense Contracts Audit," <u>Armed Forces Comptroller</u>, v.10, June, pp 6-8.

1967   "Examination of Defense Contracts by the General Accounting Office," <u>New York Certified Public Accountant</u>, v.37, Aug, pp 609-14.

<u>REFERENCES</u>

<u>Book Reviews</u>: <u>Accounting Historians Journal</u>, v.8, 1981, pp.126-7 (D Buckmaster).
     <u>Accounting Review</u>, v.11, 1936, pp.296-99 (A C Littleton).
     <u>Accounting Review</u>, v.40, 1965, pp.934-6 (D A Corbin).
     <u>Journal of Accountancy</u>, v.124, March 1967, pp.87-8 (B G King).

Causey, D Y, "Sweeney's Price Level Accounting Revisited", <u>South African Chartered Accountant</u>, Jan 1975, pp.25-6.

Clarke, F L, "A Closer Look at Sweeney's Stabilized Accounting Proposals", <u>Accounting & Business Research</u>, Autumn, 1976, pp.264-275.

Mosich, A N, "Profile: Henry Whitcomb Sweeney", <u>The Accounting Historian</u>, v.1, Jan 1974, p.4.

New York Times, <u>Obituary</u>, 3 Sept 1964.

Zeff, S A, "Introduction" to his (ed) <u>Asset Appreciation, Business Income & Price-Level Accounting</u>, Arno Press, 1976.

Sanders, T H, "Significant Recent Accounting Literature", <u>Harvard Business Review</u>, v.15, 1937, pp.376-77.

A Closer Look at Sweeney's Stabilised Accounting Proposals

F. L. Clarke

Reviewing the first edition of Henry Whitcomb Sweeney's[1] *Stabilized Accounting* (1936) in *The Accounting Review*, Littleton (pp. 296–99) declared that:

> ... the book suffers from the relegation of much of the discussions of theory to magazine articles scattered over the past ten years ... But that does not help most of us. ... we probably have not, nor will we, read the dozen or so more supplementary articles by the author himself.

Those comments were somewhat prophetic, for it seems that Sweeney is one of the persons most often mentioned in the context of the price level problem in accounting, and one of those whose work has been read the least.

In a sense that is understandable, for although the reputation of Sweeney's book as a leader survives, his contributions to the literature on the price level problem are not contemporary. After the first edition of *Stabilized Accounting* appeared in 1936, he did not publish on the issue in the general literature again for nearly thirty years.

In the Foreword to the 1964 reprint Sweeney explained under the caption 'Forty Years After: or Stabilized Accounting Revisited' that during the 1920s his interest in the general problem of accounting valuation had been stimulated by Paton's 1920

Journal of Accountancy article on 'Depreciation, Appreciation and Productive Capacity' which illustrated how depreciation charges might be revised to show the changing purchasing power of money, his own awareness of the efforts made in post World War I Germany to construct balance sheets which stabilised the measuring unit and his reading of Mahlberg's solution to the problem in *Bilanztechnik und Bewertung bei schwankender Wachrung (Balance Sheet Presentation and Valuation During Inflation)*, and his own general dissatisfaction with the valuation rules of traditional accounting (pp. xvii–xxi). For Sweeney, *Stabilized Accounting* was the final product of that interest; for others, it has been the object of misunderstanding.

In this article some aspects of Sweeney's explanation and illustration of stabilised accounting are subjected to a closer scrutiny than they appear to have been in the past, with the view to disposing of some misleading descriptions of his proposals.

Summary

The general conclusions drawn in this paper are:

(a) Most current reference to Sweeney's proposals is drawn from *Stabilized Accounting*, but much of the substance of Sweeney's proposals there has been missed, ignored or not understood.

(b) There is little evidence that descriptions and illustrations of stabilised accounting in the articles Littleton referred to have been read by those who mention Sweeney in their own work.

(c) Grouping Sweeney and stabilised accounting with the various proposals for 'measuring the effect of inflation on firms' is misleading; the primary purpose of stabilised accounting was to achieve 'homogeneous measurement'.

(d) Grouping Sweeney and stabilised accounting with proposals for price level adjusted accounting

[1]Sweeney, Henry Whitcomb (1898–1967) was assistant professor of accounting in the School of Business Administration at the University of Pittsburg (1924–1925), professor of accounting at Georgetown University (1936–1944) and also professor of law at Georgetown Law School (1941–1958), and adjunct professor of accounting at Columbia Graduate School of Business (1956–1967). Between 1935 and 1943 he was also employed by the United States Government; first as Depreciation Expert in the Federal Communications Commission for a year, then in the Farm Credit Administration to 1939, and as Chief Accountant of the Navy Board of Contract Appeals, to 1943. In 1944 he entered practice as a CPA to concentrate on the legal and accounting aspects of contracting with Government agencies.

of the CPP variety is misleading: Sweeney preferred stabilisation on the basis of replacement cost or 'reproductive' cost.

(e) The mode of stabilisation on the basis of replacement or reproductive cost preferred by Sweeney did not overcome any of his objections to the features of ordinary accounting.

Reference to Sweeney

Although *Stabilized Accounting* (1936 and 1964) is the most often referred to description of Sweeney's proposals, it has only a corroborative use in the piecing together of the ideas that underlie them. In that context it is of little more use than his 1964 review of Accounting Research Study No. 6 'Reporting the Financial Effects of Price-Level Changes' (ARS 6),[2] as both merely provide evidence of his continued support for some of the views he had

----

[2]"Reporting the Financial Effects of Price-Level Changes' (Accounting and Research Division of the American Institute of Certified Public Accountants, October, 1963).

expressed in journal articles between 1927 and 1935.

The 1936 edition of *Stabilized Accounting* was limited to 1,000 copies. It is likely, therefore, that most current reference to Sweeney's ideas has been through familiarity with the 1964 reprint. Sweeney, however, explained there in the Foreword that he had spun-off his main ideas in the earlier articles and that the manuscript of his thesis upon which they were based, ' . . . had been cut to less than half and the style changed so that *Stabilized Accounting* would be ' . . . a practical elementary treatise on economics and accounting' (p. xxii). It is surprising that so much reliance has been placed upon the book for a detailed description of stabilisation techniques and so little attention has been given to the articles. (The main articles and their cross referencing to *Stabilized Accounting* are set out in table (i). Later reference to those articles is designated by year of publication.) It seems reasonable to suggest that distorted descriptions of both stabilised accounting and what Sweeney was trying to achieve through it are products of misplaced emphasis on such a secondary source of reference.

	Reference to Articles in Stabilized Accounting (*Holt, Rinehart and Winston, 1964 reprint*)
TABLE (i) **Sweeney's works referred to**	
Article	
'Effects of Inflation on German Accounting' *Journal of Accountancy* (March, 1927, pp. 180–191)	p. 8
'German Inflation Accounting' *Journal of Accountancy* (February, 1928, pp. 104–116) and letter to Editor of *Journal of Accountancy* in reply to J. H. Allen (April, 1928, pp. 310–311)	pp. 38, 40, 182
'Maintenance of Capital' *Accounting Review* (December, 1930, pp. 277–287) [*]	p. 6
'Stabilized Depreciation' *Accounting Review* (September, 1931, pp. 165–178)	p. 47
'Stabilized Appreciation' *Accounting Review* (June, 1932, pp. 115–121)	pp. 23, 50
'Capital' *Accounting Review* (September, 1933, pp. 185–199)	pp. 48, 53
'Income' *Accounting Review* (December, 1933, pp. 323–335)	pp. 19, 21
'Approximation of Appraisal Values by Index Numbers' *Harvard Business Review* (October, 1934, pp. 108–115)	pp. 18, 49
'How Inflation Affects Balance Sheets' *Accounting Review* (December, 1934, pp. 275–299)	pp. 8, 18, 49, 182
'The Technique of Stabilized Accounting' *Accounting Review* (June, 1935 pp. 185–205)	pp. 18, 38, 75

[*]Reprinted in M. Moonitz and A. C. Littleton, *Significant Accounting Essays* (Prentice-Hall, 1965)

Generally, stabilised accounting is referred to in the accounting literature in the context of the various attempts to *account for the effects of inflation on particular firms*, and is described solely as an early exercise in adjusting financial data for changes in the general level of prices only. In this way it is implied that the prescriptions for such adjustments in *Statement of Standard Accounting Practice 7* in the United Kingdom[3] and as set out in exposure drafts in the United States,[4] Australia,[5] Canada[6] and New Zealand[7] are properly in line with Sweeney's proposals.

Littleton and Zimmerman (p. 188), for example, explain that *Stabilized Accounting* was a 'pioneer work' and ' . . . presented a comprehensive methodology for computing and disclosing the impact of inflation on accounting data'; Hendriksen (p. 59) referring to Sweeney's 'contribution to Theory' says that he recommended the adjustment of financial statements 'by the use of a *single* conversion purchasing power index' (emphasis added), and in his own price level study (p. 16) links Sweeney's work with that of Jones and Mason as if they necessarily represented the same ideas; Blough (p. 309) describes Sweeney's work in much the same terms as do Littleton and Zimmerman; Mathews and Grant (p. 23) mention Sweeney's proposals under the subhead 'Alternative Methods of Accounting for Inflation' and explain that his approach involved conversion into current values of every item appearing in the profit and loss account and balance sheet by means of a general index of purchasing power; Paton and Littleton (p. 139) refer to stabilised accounting (though not to Sweeney by name) as a method of 'common dollar' accounting and explain that such a system is 'quite different' from replacement price accounting; Baxter on a number of occasions has given credit to Sweeney for the term 'stabilisation' as a description of a method by which 'it is possible to restate every figure in both the income account

and balance sheet with the help of price-index numbers' (1975, p. 30; and for example 1949, p. 456; 1959, p. 251), but gives no indication that Sweeney intended stabilised accounting to do much more. Baxter's extension of simple stabilisation to incorporate replacement prices (1959, p. 252; 1975, p. 74) is made as a supplementary procedure rather than as an integral part of stabilisation, as Sweeney devised it; Kirkman (p. 112) only mentions Sweeney in the context for proposals for making adjustments for changes in the general level of prices; Gynther (p. 2) notes Sweeney's 'now famous book' but, as explained below, missed half of its message; Wilk (p. 28) argues that 'conversions should be made with an index portraying changes in the value of the monetary unit and not indices for any particular assets . . . This is the system which was adopted by H. W. Sweeney in his book *Stabilized Accounting*'; The Association of Certified and Corporate Accountants (p. 58–9) implies that stabilised accounting ignores differential increases in prices and that it therefore 'attempts to exclude the monetary factor'; Causey (p. 26) describes Sweeney as promoting a straight price level adjusted system' in which a general index was the ideal deflator'. He refers for support to ' . . . Sweeney's illustration for the A Corporation' in chapters I and II of *Stabilized Accounting* and ignores the comprehensive examples that follow in later chapters; Weston (p. 381), reviewing stabilisation procedures, notes Sweeney's contribution in *Stabilized Accounting* but identifies it only with adjustments through the use of a general index; and MacNeal (p. 116) in criticising stabilised accounting refers only to an example in which the general commodities index is used.

None of the above refers to any of Sweeney's work other than *Stabilized Accounting*.

Homogeneous unit

Contrary to the current linking of Sweeney with attempts to account for the effect of inflation, his primary aim with stabilised accounting was to correct conventional accounting so that profit and loss and balance sheet data would be stated in 'homogeneous terms'; that is, in terms of monetary units entailing equalised purchasing power.

The 1927 and 1928 articles introduced his concern over the mathematical impropriety of comparing, adding and subtracting heterogeneous money units. 'Such comparisons' he noted, 'violate the mathematical principle that dissimilar items cannot properly be compared with one another' (1927, p. 183; 1928, p. 104); and 'There is no advantage in finding the total of heterogeneous units. It would be meaningless' (1927, p. 189), and further that 'Costs and

[3]'Accounting for Changes in the Purchasing Power of Money' (The Institute of Chartered Accountants in England and Wales, *et al.*, May 1974).

[4]'Financial Reporting in Units of General Purchasing Power' (Financial Accounting Standards Board, 31 December, 1974).

[5]'A method of "Accounting for Changes in the Purchasing Power of Money"', (The Institute of Chartered Accountants in Australia and the Australian Society of Accountants, December 1974).

[6]'Accounting for Changes in the Purchasing Power of Money' (Accounting Research Committee, Canadian Institute of Chartered Accountants, July 1975).

[7]'Accounting for Changes in the Purchasing Power of Money' (Board of Research and Publications, The New Zealand Society of Accountants, March 1975).

expenses expressed in marks having particular purchasing power could not be deducted from income expressed in marks having a different purchasing power if true profit or loss was to be ascertained' (1928, p. 104).

Reference in the 1928 article to the impropriety of adding heterogeneous units was a subtle, though nevertheless definite, indication that the primary purpose of the stabilised accounting techniques was to achieve the homogeneity of units in accounts, even rather than contemporaneity. In an example there, numbers representing paper mark units were deflated to represent their purchasing power equivalent in pre-war gold marks, to stabilise amounts appearing in a 'factory building account'. If contemporaneity had been the major issue the 1914 gold marks should have been inflated to represent their equivalent purchasing power in terms of the contemporary 1923 paper marks.

Further reference to the primacy of achieving the homogeneity of units in accounts filtered through Sweeney's other articles appearing prior to *Stabilized Accounting*. For example:

> . . . stabilized accounting is primarily concerned with homogeneously representing the money units of former dates in the general price level . . . (1932, p. 115);

and referring to the consequences of inflation on accounting data he noted that, 'financial figures . . . become non-uniform, dissimilar, heterogeneous in nature' (1934, p. 277). Demonstrating stabilisation he further explained:

> . . . because valuation at cost of reproduction or replacement necessarily conduces toward a much more homogeneous measurement of all assets . . . it cannot help being viewed with approbation by stabilized accounting, which is primarily concerned with homogeneous measurement (1935, p. 197).

The emphasis was retained in *Stabilized Accounting*. It might be argued that that is to be expected since Sweeney admitted the book was based on the same source as the articles. But the cutting and trimming of his thesis in the preparation of *Stabilized Accounting* gave him the opportunity to tone down that emphasis if he chose to. Clearly he did not.

Though it is only one of three major complaints that Sweeney levelled at conventional accounting, the objection that it is 'mathematically unsound' (p. 7) because ' . . . the figures on the ordinary balance sheet and profit and loss account are all scrambled together' is reinforced at several places in the text and his primary aim of removing that defect is stated explicitly in a number of places; for example,

> . . . stabilized accounting is *primarily* concerned

with the use of homogeneous measurement (p. 42) (emphasis added);

> . . . stabilized accounting, although *primarily* interested in homogeneous measurement . . . (p. 51) (emphasis added);

Stabilized means *uniformly* expressed in the value of the dollar as of the date represented by the balance sheet rather than . . . a mixture of the dollar values of many different dates and periods (p. 159) (emphasis added).

Sweeney's declaration that stabilised accounting was primarily concerned with homogeneous measurement is understandable, for the homogeneity of the product of the profit or loss calculation and of the amounts set out in the balance sheet was a necessary condition for rectification of the other two defects he noted in *ordinary accounting*. It was also described as being (i) *irrelevant*, insofar as it did not show progress made by an entity in gaining greater command over goods and services in general, 'the customary main object of economic activity' (1930, p. 277, 287; 1933 'Capital', p. 193; 1935, p. 194; and *Stabilized Accounting*, p. 4, 17 and 189), and (ii) *incomplete* insofar as ordinary accounting did not show all the financial gains and losses of an entity in the period in which they arose (p. 15). Whilst homogeneity could be achieved independently (the deflation style of stabilisation in the 1927 article illustrated that), measuring changes in a firm's command over goods and services in general and the reporting of all its financial gains and losses necessitated that the profit or loss of each period and the data in the balance sheet be expressed in terms of contemporary (and therefore homogeneous) purchasing power. Removal of the objections that ordinary accounting was irrelevant and incomplete merely necessitated that stabilisation had to be in terms of current, rather than past, purchasing power.

Sweeney's criticism of ordinary accounting is just as valid in relation to deflationary conditions as it is in the context of inflation. The proper context of the criticism is 'price level fluctuations', of every kind. Homogeneous measurement is just as primary a matter and ordinary accounting could be equally as irrelevant and incomplete under deflationary, as under inflationary conditions. He in fact argues along those lines in *Stabilized Accounting* (p. 183) when defending his proposals in the context of the deflated US economy in the early 1930s. So, although directed at the problems of accounting under inflationary conditions, the stabilisation techniques were not intended to be linked uniquely to them.

We might expect that specific reference to 'inflationary gains and losses' would be a feature of the product of stabilisation if those techniques were intended to 'account for' or to 'measure' the effect of inflation on particular entities. But no such label is given to any item in the works referenced in Table (i), nor is there any clue in those articles that doing so was ever contemplated by Sweeney. This is in direct contrast with descriptions such as 'inflation gains or losses' and 'Statement of income and inflation gains (loss)' in ARS 6 (p. 128). Sweeney's stabilisation method was merely intended by him to make the data in the stabilised profit and loss account and balance sheet homogeneous, so far as purchasing power was concerned, and to show whether the particular entity's command over goods and services in general (its purchasing power) had increased or decreased during the accounting period. Unlike price level adjustment proposals such as those in ARS 6, Sweeney's stabilisation was not a method for measuring the effects of inflation on specific entities and clearly was not intended to be.

Preference for 'replacement cost version'

Sweeney's hypothesis that the main object of economic activity was to gain greater command over goods and services in general predicated his argument that income could not be calculated unless a charge was made for the maintenance of 'real (purchasing power) capital' based on movements in a *general index* (1930, p. 182). But in the 1930 article he was less rigid than the previous rejection by him of basing depreciation on the replacement costs of assets, because doing so 'was directed towards the maintenance of real (physical) capital' (1927, p. 187). The use of 'specific' index numbers (representing replacement costs or costs of reproduction) was permitted 'if the intention is to increase economic power over one good' (p. 185) and

> . . . under certain conditions measurement may, with more justification, be based on the price of a single commodity . . . Although stabilized accounting customarily employs, with apparent justification, the general index . . . it is not essentially related to any particular kind of measuring unit (p. 287).

The 1927 objection to depreciation based on replacement cost was reiterated in 1931 in 'Stabilized Depreciation'. However, like the 1930 article that preceded it, the line was softer than it had been. Replacement cost depreciation was acknowledged as a 'safer and more conservative plan of procedure to adopt during the inflation years than the old original cost based theory . . . ' (p. 173) and it possessed 'notable merit' (p. 174).

Three years after the 1929 Symposium on Apprecia-

tion[8] had reached the conclusion that asset appreciation ought to be accounted for (though there was no consensus regarding how it ought to be reported) Sweeney illustrated how appreciation might be stabilised. *Stabilised appreciation* was 'limited to an increase in the purchasing power that a particular asset commanded over growth in the value of all goods in general' (1932, p. 115–6). The development of stabilised appreciation was significant so far as the future development of stabilised accounting was concerned; it settled the depreciation on replacement cost issue that had been raised in the 1927 and 1930 articles, and clearly Sweeney was approving of it as part of the method (p. 119); it firmed up the distinction between realised and unrealised gains and losses which he had been developing since the letter by Allen to his 1928 article; and it provided the basis for the later distinction between *general and specific changes in the value of money* (1935, p. 197).

Further support for stabilisation on the basis of replacement or reproductive cost appears in both of the 1933 articles. There, Sweeney argued that 'capital valuation' should be based on present-cost-of-production ('Capital', p. 190), that depreciation based on replacement cost was 'conservative' and implied that it therefore was desirable (p. 191), and explained that stabilised income was composed of two parts, '1. Current income, and 2. Gains or losses in the value of property owned' ('Income', p. 323).

The mechanism of using specific index numbers to approximate appraisal values was demonstrated by Sweeney in 1934 and accompanied by the explanation that reproduction costs and appraisal values are entitled to a higher place in asset valuation (p. 108) and further reiteration that depreciation based on replacement cost was conservative (p. 191).

Preference for stabilisation on the basis of reproductive cost estimated by using numbers drawn from a specific index was made explicit in the discussion accompanying the illustrations in 'The Technique of Stabilized Accounting' (1935). Reproductive cost stabilisation was shown there *for completeness* (pp. 182 and 192), and:

> because valuation at cost of reproduction . . . conduces towards a much more homogeneous measurement of all assets than does valuation at original cost it cannot help being received with approbation by stabilized accounting (p. 197).

Evidence of Sweeney's preference for that mode of stabilisation is equally explicit in *Stabilized Accounting*. There, he argued that stabilisation

> . . . must be able to give effect to valuation at

---

[8]See *Accounting Review*, Vol. V, March 1930, pp. 1 59, for a review of the proceedings.

replacement cost, as well as to valuation at original cost. This it is easily able to do . . . In fact, stabilization based on cost of replacement will be found still more informative than stabilization based on original cost (p. 44),

and described it as showing the 'sound value' of assets (p. 49).

Further support for stabilising on the basis of replacement costs and its link with the homogeneity aim is stated explicitly in the comment referred to above, noting that,

. . . stabilized accounting, although primarily interested in homogeneous measurement, cannot refrain from giving more approval to replacement cost as a valuation base than to ordinary original cost (p. 51).

Stabilisation based on replacement costs was further meshed into the scheme of his proposals by linking it with the notion of 'capital valuation' developed in the September 1933 article, with the explanation that,

Valuation at cost of replacement seems capable of giving more useful information to all concerned than does valuation at original cost. Also it is thought to yield values that in the long run approximate more closely the values derived from the ideal method of determining value of capital . . . The *ideal method makes value depend upon future income* . . . For these reasons the replacement-cost version of stabilized accounting is the one to be preferred (p. 53).

In *Stabilized Accounting* the stabilisation of estimated replacement costs was illustrated in chapter II which was devoted entirely to 'that version' of the method. And the illustration in chapter VI relating to the factoring company (Mill Agents) was based on accounts in which the non-monetary assets were stated at current market prices (p. 129). Sweeney, however, mistakenly identified the stabilisation of Mill Agents' accounts as a further example based on replacement costs (p. 171). The description in chapter VI indicates that Mill Agents' inventories and securities were stated at their current selling prices, not their replacement costs.

Unawareness of Sweeney's preference for stabilisation based on replacement or reproductive costs is supported also by circumstantial evidence. Some authors who have referred to Sweeney in the context of price level accounting with general index based adjustments, have gone on to propose replacement price accounting in various forms themselves and the use of specific index numbers for approximating replacement prices, without any further reference to Sweeney. Mathews and Grant (pp. 20–1), Gynther (p. 56) and Weston (p. 385) from among those

mentioned above, for example, do so without any mention of Sweeney's affinity with such proposals. Gynther, for example, turns to Ladd and to Edwards and Bell for support when proposing the approximation of replacement prices with the aid of index numbers.

Sweeney's review of ARS 6 may have contributed to the belief that he supported adjusting accounts by using general index numbers only. There he stated: 'To review the Study's main concepts, therefore, places this reviewer in the anomalous position of practically reviewing his own work' (p. 1100), and 'The Study recapitulates well the entire field of stabilized accounting in the first 58 pages' (p. 1111). It invites the inference that a reading of ARS 6 is a substitute for reading *Stabilized Accounting*.

Chatfield, for example, drew attention to that statement by Sweeney and suggested that both ARS 6 and *Accounting Principles Board Opinion No. 3 (APB 3,* 'Financial Statements Restated for General Price-level Changes') followed ' . . . the basic method described in stabilized accounting'. In a sense they do, but only in respect of the *mechanics* of using index numbers to adjust accounting data. ARS 6, however, argued that 'Replacement Cost is a Separate Problem' (p. 29) and that 'It is not the function of this report to debate the merits of original cost or replacement cost as possible principles of valuation . . . price-level adjustments of accounting data are not the same thing as the adoption of replacement costs, either in theory or in the nature of the results'. Yet, Sweeney regarded them as integral parts of the same exercise. It is curious that Chatfield did not regard using replacement prices as part of Sweeney's basic method. When reviewing the 'changing concepts of asset valuation' he acknowledged Sweeney's recommendation that replacement prices be used in the stabilisation process. Furthermore he argued that 'MacNeal was only trying to do on the conceptual level what Sweeney had done with the practical problem of asset valuation'.[9]

We might also note that Sweeney's review is critical of most of the Study for its deviations from even the simple form of stabilised accounting. General price level adjusted accounting does not contain provision for the incorporation of replacement price or the use of specific index numbers, does not distinguish between realised and unrealised gains and losses and does not distinguish between 'general' and 'special' money value gains and losses. Stabilised accounting as it was described by Sweeney does each of these things.

---

[9] Chatfield, M. *A History of Accounting Thought* (Dryden Press, 1974), pp. 241–2.

Some of the reviewers of *Stabilized Accounting* have been no more precise or thorough when describing Sweeney's ideas than those persons who mention his work casually. Littleton in his 1936 review picked up Sweeney's use of general index numbers, but did not mention either his desire for homogeneous measurement or his preference for stabilisation based on replacement prices. Though Littleton interpreted Sweeney as having *substituted purchasing power for prices* as the 'keynote of orthodox accounting', he apparently missed Sweeney's attempt to establish a relationship between replacement prices and purchasing power. *Stabilized Accounting* was reviewed informally by MacNeal in his *Truth in Accounting*.[10] In many respects he did so more thoroughly than Littleton, for Sweeney's use of replacement prices was described as an integral part of the stabilising procedures. However, MacNeal did not draw attention to the homogeneity motive that underlay them. King and Corbin did little better in their reviews of the 1965 reprint.[11] King noted that Sweeney's major concern was homogeneity, but described his use of replacement prices in the illustration of stabilisation that appeared in chapter III as '. . . a digression . . . more appropriately placed in the chapter devoted to sundry topics'.[12] Whilst Corbin expressed his regret that 'The recommendation to use replacement costs in the stabilisation process has been missed by many "rediscoverers" of Sweeney', he, like Littleton and MacNeal twenty-nine years before him, did not comment on the emphasis Sweeney placed on achieving homogeneity in the units in accounts.[13]

Irrelevant, mathematically unsound, incomplete

Despite Sweeney's preference for stabilised accounting based on replacement cost, it does not overcome any of his three objections to ordinary accounting. The balance sheet and profit and loss data in the example given in 'The Technique of Stabilized Accounting' are reproduced in Tables (ii) and (iii) respectively, to illustrate why it fails to do so.

The first objection, that ordinary accounting fails to show progress in gaining greater command over goods and services, and the third, that it fails to show all purchasing power gains and losses as they occur, can be dealt with together.

The $14,996 stated for total assets in the stabilised reproductive cost balance sheet for X Corporation will only represent the purchasing power (the command over goods and services in general) embodied in the total assets, *if* the amounts set out beside the assets represent either actual money or money's worth. For purchasing power is entailed only by the possession of money or its equivalent. Neither the $8,000 set out against 'Merchandise inventory' nor the $3,996 amount of 'Total fixed assets' represent either actual money amounts or money's worth. Each is an approximation of reproductive or replacement cost and (at best) indicates only how much money the company would have to pay to acquire or produce those assets, rather than the purchasing power entailed by the possession of them. 'Total net worth' of $13,296, therefore, is not a representation of the money's worth of the net assets at that time, and therefore does not represent purchasing power at any time. Comparison with purchasing power positions at other times, therefore, is impossible. The first objection stands.

So does the third. The financial gains and losses to which the third objection relates are components of the measure of the change in the purchasing power commanded by the firm. If such a measure cannot be established to overcome the first objection, then the third objection must also remain.

Sweeney argued in *Stabilized Accounting* (p. 51) that indexed amounts representing current replacement prices are 'expressed in current dollars' and therefore 'are expressions of current general purchasing power'. He proposed that such amounts could properly be added to other expressions of current general purchasing power, such as cash balances and the like, to give a meaningful total. In a restricted sense the notion Sweeney referred to is correct, but the way he described it is not.

The product of multiplying a past amount of money by index numbers is not an amount of current dollars; rather, it is an expression of the number of current dollars needed to confer the equivalent purchasing power of that past amount. If the numbers are drawn from a *specific index*, then the expression is of *equivalent specific purchasing power*.

But the essence of Sweeney's objection to the mathematical impropriety of ordinary accounting was not the addition or subtraction of units representing past and current dollars during times of changing price levels, it was the impropriety of representing the product of those calculations as amounts of any specified kind of purchasing power. Since possession

---

[10]MacNeal, K. *Truth in Accounting*, (Scholars, reprinted 1970), pp. 115–26.

[11]King, B. C. review of *Stabilized Accounting* in *Journal of Accountancy*, March 1967, pp. 87–8 and Corbin, D. A. review of *Stabilized Accounting* in *Accounting Review*, Vol. XL, October, 1965, pp. 935–6.

[12]Ibid, p. 87.

[13]Ibid, p. 936.

of actual money or money's worth entails the power to purchase goods and services in general, it necessarily entails the power to purchase specific commodities such as those to which replacement price indices relate. It seems reasonable to accept a proposition that the part of the dimension of *actual* money representing power to purchase those specific goods, and the expression of equivalent specific purchasing power derived in the indexed calculation, *are* homogeneous. But the reverse, claimed by Sweeney, is not the case. For the choice of extracting the specific purchasing power dimension of actual money is possible only because it embodies the whole purchasing power dimension. The numbers derived using a specific index, however, embody only that part of the dimension related to the goods specified in each case.

Amounts set out in the X Corporation's 'stabilized reproductive cost' balance sheet for cash, $2,500, and for receivables, $500, may properly be added to the $8,000 estimated reproductive cost of inventory and yield a valid and interpretable total of $11,000. But note that it can only be related to the power to purchase inventory. The $14,996 product of adding to that total the $3,996 stated as the total worth of fixed assets, however, is uninterpretable. The $2,880 and $1,116, for equipment and land respectively, are not expressions of homogeneous purchasing power, of any kind. The different index number series used in their calculation related to the movements in the price of equipment and land respectively, but neither related to changes in the prices of *any* other goods. The numbers represent different purchasing power dimensions, are heterogeneous and the product of adding them is meaningless.

The consequences of the different purchasing power dimensions of the fixed asset amounts and of the inventory are carried into the calculations of the *Net deficit* of $1,704 through the 'changes in the special value of money' entries ($1,000 in respect to inventory and ($204) in respect to fixed assets) in the stabilised reproductive cost profit and loss account. It does not express current purchasing power of any identifiable dimension, and renders the $13,296 stated as 'Total net worth' uninterpretable in respect to its purchasing power significance.

None of Sweeney's objections to ordinary accounting were overcome in the replacement-reproductive cost version of stabilised accounting. Yet stabilisation on the basis of original cost (the mode least preferred by him) overcame in principle the heterogeneity objection and therefore satisfied his primary aim, since each amount restated by using the general index numbers represented general purchasing power. The other objections of course remain unsatisfied.

Curiously, despite the frequent references to stabilised accounting in the literature its general failure to overcome Sweeney's objections has either not been detected by commentators on the method, or has not been admitted by them. In particular the mathematical impropriety of the reproductive cost version has gone completely unnoticed, even by those who indicated their understanding of it. Neither Corbin nor Chatfield made any comment on the issue, whilst MacNeal clearly was unaware of it in stating that stabilised accounting was

an exhaustive and mathematically impregnable system for displaying changes in purchasing power. Whether or not one approves the concept employed . . . he must admit that it completely achieves its purpose (p. 123).

Conclusion

A summary of the main conclusions appears at the beginning of this paper. Collectively they amount to a general proposition that Sweeney and his stabilised accounting method have been misrepresented in much of the literature on the price level problem in accounting.

Inflation over the past twenty-five years has created the conditions in which the efficacy of making indexed price level adjustments to conventional accounts has been re-examined. Understandably Sweeney's pioneering work has been resurrected. But generally the reporting and analysis of its results have been less than accurate.

The effects of the loose descriptions and analyses of Sweeney's proposals are difficult to identify. It is reasonable to suppose, however, that the pursuit of excellence in any discipline is impeded by an imperfect record of the development over time of its underlying ideas. In the context of accounting thought it is almost certain to be, for the mere survival of a line of thought appears sometimes to be substituted for logic as a test of its rigour. Long-standing ideas in accounting seem to take on a mantle of respectability, to which they often are not entitled.

It is interesting to ponder whether inaccurate descriptions and analyses of stabilised accounting and the continued support by some for the indexation of conventionally prepared accounts, is coincidence or consequence.

References

Association of Certified and Corporate Accountants, *Accounting for Inflation* (1952).

Blough, C., 'Depreciation to Measure Income or to Provide Funds for Replacement?', *NAA Bulletin*, August, 1959, pp. 47-55.

Baxter, W. T., 'Accountants and the Inflation', *Accountant*, 4 June, 1949, pp. 456-461. 'Inflation and the Accounts of Steel Companies', *Accountancy*, May 1959, pp. 250-51. *Accounting Values and Inflation*, (McGraw Hill, 1975).

Causey, D. T., 'Sweeney's Price-Level Accounting - Revisited', *South African Chartered Accountant*, January, 1975, pp. 25-6.

Edwards, E. O. and Bell, P. W., *The Theory and Measurement of Business Income* (University of California Press, 1960).

Gynther, R. S., *Accounting for Price-Level Changes: Theory and Procedures* (Pergamon, 1966).

Hendriksen, E., *Accounting Theory* (Irwin, 1962). *Price-Level Adjustments of Financial Statements* (University of Washington, 1961).

Jones, R. C., *Price-Level Changes and Financial Statements* (American Accounting Association, 1955). *Effects of Price-Level Changes on Business Income, Capital, and Taxes* (American Accounting Association, 1956).

Ladd, D. R., *Contemporary Corporate Accounting and the Public* (Irwin, 1963).

Littleton, A. C., Review of Stabilized Accounting, *Accounting Review*, Vol. XI, September, 1936, pp. 296-99.

Littleton, A. C. and Zimmerman, V. K., *Accounting Theory: Continuity and Change* (Prentice - Hall, 1962).

MacNeal, K., *Truth in Accounting* (Scholars reprint, 1970).

Mason, P., *Price-Level Changes and Financial Statements* (American Accounting Association, 1956).

Mathews, R., and Grant, J. McB., *Inflation and Company Finance* (Law Book Company, 1962).

Paton, W., 'Depreciation, Appreciation and Productive Capacity', *Journal of Accountancy*, July, 1920, pp. 1-11.

Weston, J. F., 'Consistency and Changing Price-Levels' *Accounting Review*, October, 1949, pp. 379-86.

Wilk, L., *Accounting for Inflation* (Sweet and Maxwell, 1960).

TABLE (ii)
Extract from 'The Technique of Stabilized Accounting', *Accounting Review*, June, 1935, (p. 195)
The X Corporation Stabilized and Unstabilized Balance Sheets as at the Close of the Firs: Fiscal Period

Assets	Original cost				Reproductive cost			
	Unstabilized		Stabilized		Unstabilized		Stabilized	
Current Assets								
Cash	$2,500		$2,500		$2,500		$2,500	
Accounts receivable	500		500		500		500	
Merchandise inventory	5,750		7,000		8,000		8,000	
Total current assets		$8,750		$10,000		$11,000		$11,000
Fixed Assets:								
Equipment	$2,400		$3,000		$3,200		$3,200	
Less-Reserve for depreciation	240		300		320		320	
Net	$2,160		$2,700		$2,880		$2,880	
Land	1,550		1,500		1,116		1,116	
Total fixed assets		3,710		4,200		3,996		3,996
Total assets		$12,460		$14,200		$14,996		$14,996
Liabilities								
Current Liabilities:								
Accounts payable		$1,700		$1,700		$1,700		$1,700
Net Worth								
Capital Stock		$10,000		$15,000		$10,000		$15,000
Surplus or *Deficit*:								
Realized:								
Net income for the period	$2,160		*$1,456*		$2,160		*$1,496*	
Less-Dividend paid	1,400		1,500		1,400		1,500	
Balance	$760		$2,996		$760		$2,996	
Unrealized:								
Net income for the period			496		2,536		1,292	
Net surplus or *deficit*		760		2,500		3,296		1,704
Total net worth		$10,750		$12,500		$13,296		$13,296

Realized Income	Original cost				Reproductive cost			
	Unstabilized		Stabilized		Unstabilized		Stabilized	
Changes in the Special Value of Money:								
Merchandise:								
Net sales		$14,200		$15 000		$14 200		$15,000
Less—Cost of goods sold:								
Net Purchases	$13,500		$16,500		$13,500		$16,500	
Deduct—Final merchandise inventory	5,750	7,750	7,000	9,500	5,750	7,750	7,000	9,500
Gross profit on sales		$6,450		$5,500		$6,450		$5,500
Less—Selling, administrative, and financial expenses:								
Salaries	$2,700		$3,000		$2,700		$3,000	
General expenses	2,800		3,000		2,800		3,000	
Depreciation	240	5,740	300	6,300	240	5,740	300	6,300
Net profit on operations		$710		$800		$710		$800
Fixed assets:								
Profit on sale of land		1,450		1,313		1,450		1,313
Net income from realized changes in the special value of money		$2,160		$513		$2,160		$513
Changes in the General Value of Money:								
Loss on cash			$3,469				$3,469	
Less—Profit on:								
Accounts receivable			$500				$500	
Accounts payable			960				960	
Total			$1 460				$1,460	
Net loss on realized changes in the general value of money				$2,009				$2,009
Realized net income for the period		$2,160		$1,496		$2,160		$1,496
Unrealized Income								
Changes in the Special Value of Money:								
Merchandise						$2,250		$1,000
Fixed assets:								
Equipment (net)					$720		$180	
Less—Land					434	286	384	204
Net income from unrealized changes in the special value of money						$2,536		$796
Changes in the General Value of Money:								
Profit on:								
Cash			$156				$156	
Accounts payable			340				340	
Net income from unrealized changes in the general value of money				$496				496
Unrealized net income for the period				$496		$2,536		$1,292
Final net income for the period		$2,160		$1,000		$4,696		$204

75

(1) To what extent is Sweeney concerned with specific/general price changes?

(2) "....the ultimate goal of accounting is to produce relevant, accurate, and complete information ..., for sucessful and intelligent business management must rely upon being given such information" (Pg.101)

- Does Sweeney explain or demonstrate why successful and intelligent business management needs this information and/or how it uses it?

(3) Sweeney refers to three necessary steps to achieve the goal explicated in question 2. Stabilization is one of the three.

- What are the other two?
- Why is stabilization considered necessary?
- What is the basis of the stabilization procedures?

(4) Sweeney claims that stabilization is more appropriate than accepted accounting procedures for indicating whether an enterprise has approached nearer the goal of economic activity, viz., an increase in the general purchasing power of the owner's investment in the enterprise.

- What do you understand by the term "general purchasing power" in the context of money?
- In view of the procedures of stabilization and your understanding of general purchasing power, can this claim be sustained?

(5) How might the arguments developed in reponse to question four be used to dispute Sweeney's claim that stabilized accounting is better than traditional accounting because it includes all kinds of realised and unrealised profit and loss for changes in the value of money.

(6) What does Sweeney have to say about the definition of assets, liabilities; valuation rules? To what extent does your answer to the former questions affect the scope and significance of Sweeney's work?

(7) Sweeney maintains the stabilized accounting accounts for a deficiency in traditional accounting which combines figures not expressed in the same kind of measuring unit, thus violating the basis mathematical axiom that "Like added to like gives like".

- To what extent does stabilized accounting rectify the situation?

(8) What problem of accounting is Sweeney most concerned to rectify via his book?

8

STEPHEN GILMAN

Accounting Concepts of Profit

Biographical Chronology

1887	Born, Illinois.
	Attended University of Wisconsin - studied engineering.
	Became interested in accounting when assisting his father in the preparation of a book on cost accounting.
1913-16	Worked for Tennessee Coal & Iron Company.
1916-17	Moved to Chicago, studied accounting through La Salle Extension Institute, became a CPA.
1918	With John Tanner acquired the International Accountants Society (Chicago) - developed it into a leading correspondence accounting school.
1920-23	Editor of Accountants Forum.
1925	Analyzing Financial Statements published: his first book.
1939	Accounting Concepts of Profits published.
1944-6	Editor, The Accounting Review (one of a panel of three).
1959	Died.

Selected Bibliography

1907   "Accounting Education," Journal of Accountancy, Dec, v.5, pp 125-126 (authorship uncertain)

1917   Principles of Accounting, La Salle Extension University, Chicago

1921   "Relation of Business Statistics to Management Control," Paper, 11 May, pp 14-5, 42.

"When Profits Fall Off," Administration, Sept, pp 376-80.

1922   "Fundamentals of the Business Budget," Accountants' Forum, Nov, pp 3-5.

1924   "Method of Balance Sheet Analysis," Management Administration, August, pp 147-150.

1925   Analysing Financial Statments, Ronald Press (New York) Revised Edition in 1934.

1926   Observations on Balance Sheet Analysis," Canadian Chartered Accountant, March, p.313 (and CPA, Feb, pp 37-40).

1928   "High-hatting the Boss with Figures," Manufacturers News, May, pp 31, 62.

"Get the Range and Study the Target, you Technical Marksmen!", Certified Public Accountant, Aug, pp 233-4, 240.

"Two Methods of Analyzing Statement," Certified Public Accountant, July, pp 203-4, 216-7.

1930	"How to Use Trend Percentages in Analyzing Progress of a Business of a Business, American Accountant, May, pp 215-7.

1930   "How to Use Trend Percentages in Analyzing Progress of a
            Business of a Business, American Accountant, May, pp 215-7.

1937   "Is College the Only Way," Accounting Review, v.12, pp 105-
            111.

1939   Accounting Concepts of Profit, Ronald Press (New York).

1940   "Audit Record of the Internal Control Survey," Journal of
            Accountancy, Dec, v. 70 pp 489-95.

1941   "The Accounting Meaning of Income," AIA, Accounting Auditing
            and Taxes, pp 118-21.

            "Bankers Look at the Cost on Market Rule," Journal of
            Accountancy, May, v.71 pp 418-21.

            "Trends in Financial Statement Analysis," Accounting
            Forum, June, pp 5-8, 60.

1943   "Reporting of War Accounting Practices," Journal of
            Accountancy, Sept, v.72   pp 200-10.

1944   "Accounting Principles and the Current Classification,"
            Accounting Review, v.19, pp 109-116.

            What the Figures Mean, Ronald Press Co (New York).

1946   "Correspondence Courses in the Accounting Education
            Programme," Accounting Review, v.21, pp 396-404.

1949   "Graphic and Arithmetic Financial Analysis Techniques
            Need a Pre-examination," Journal of Accountancy, July,
            v.88, pp 30-39.

1956   "How to Use Charting in Business," in Lasser, J.K., ed.
            Standard Handbook for Accountants, Part 5, pp 99-127.

REFERENCES

Book Reviews of Concepts:
                    Management Review, v.28, July 1939, p.251 (7Ow).
                    Annals of American Academy of Political Science,
                    v.206, Nov 1939, p.198 (C Reitell).
                    Journal of Business, v.13, 1940, pp.206-8 (R L Dixon).
                    Journal of Accountancy, v.69, 1940, p.505
                    (C G Blough).
                    Accountant, 13 April 1940, p.426 (R F Fowler).

Walker, R G, "Explorations in Accounting", Harvard Business Review, v.18,
       1939, pp.384-96.

GILMAN, STEPHEN. *Accounting Concepts of Profit.* Pp. xv, 635. New York: Ronald Press Co., 1939. $5.00.

The author states with much accuracy that the justification for his book "is to be found in the history of the past half-dozen years which have witnessed a shift in accounting emphasis from the balance sheet to the profit and loss viewpoint," attributable to the "awakened interest in the investor's viewpoint" as a most important force.

This book was written primarily for the "accountant in search of accounting 'principles' articulating with present-day practice" and for those "with a collateral interest in accounting problems, particularly lawyers, engineers, economists, statisticians, credit men, investors, and business managers."

Accounting practices are being challenged by both informed and uninformed critics—the motives of some being laudatory. This in itself would be a sufficient justification for this timely treatise.

The sequential pattern of the book is as follows: Accounting Conventions; Doctrines, Rules and Principles; Classification; Expenditures and Income; Inventories; Fixed Assets; Profit and Loss Statement; and Summary.

The impact of law, especially income-tax law, business and economic influences or accounting is succinctly stated. The frequent and sometimes pernicious effect of tax laws on profit determination and profit distortion is made vivid.

The author is a bit dubious about the existence of many accounting "principles," so-called, but one has the decided feeling as he reads that in this respect the author is not a hypercritic but a realist. He does state and comment on various "principles of accounting" that have been enunciated.

At the heart of the presentation are three accounting conventions: the entity (not proprietorship) convention, the valuation convention, and the accounting period convention.

To a certain extent the book is more descriptive than definitive, although there are notable exceptions, especially in the salty and penetrating castigation of the "cost-or-market,-whichever-is-lower" rule of inventory valuation.

The entire book is no "scissors-and-paste" performance, despite the fact that it is replete with judicious selections from other writers—all germane—to whom the author generously accords credit. The book is excellently annotated.

Standard costs receive treatment. Here is a sample: "Recognition of the possibility of profit distortion inherent in standard costs is the best insurance against deceptive annual reports. The undeniable value of standard cost accounting seems to justify the modification of academic rules, traditional viewpoints, and strict accounting theory" (p. 391).

Why leave the word "seems" in the foregoing? Standard costs made their appearance mainly because of the limitations of historical costs in their usefulness to management. Their rapid growth as a vehicle for managerial control is a glowing testimonial to their effectiveness, and also to the impotence of costs as mere historicity.

Elsewhere the author states: "As Canning has so truly remarked: the term 'standard cost' is a grievous misnomer. Whatever may be the true character of the things called by that name, they are certainly not 'costs.'"

While some use the term "cost standards" as preferable to "standard costs," since when has the word "cost" been a uniform and rigid concept even in "actual" cost accounting? Is depreciation always an actual cost? Experience of those with cost codes under the N.R.A. conclusively demonstrated that even actual costs were far from meaning the same thing in different enterprises. Historical costs are far from perfect, as Gilman has so cogently brought out in his volume.

One wishes that the author had paid some attention to the contention of some cost men and management engineers that standard costs are the only "true" costs; otherwise the author's treatment of inventory charges, credits and valuation is rather inclusive.

The author has little respect for the last-in, first-out, and normal or base stock methods, despite their high sanction. This reviewer assumes that he is familiar with the Endicott-Johnson method of showing all inventories in the main body of the balance sheet with a footnote reference to normal inventories carried at base stock prices; and a reserve on liability side to bring only the portion of the inventory known as normal down to the base or fixed prices shown as footnote on the asset side of the balance sheet. Does this not give full disclosure of material facts with the exception that the cost valuation of inventory is not shown where the market valuation is lower?

The author does not formulate a rigid definition of accounting profit. Instead, he seeks by description more than definition to deposit in the reader's mind the fact that the concepts of profits are diverse. He has succeeded admirably. His book, in the reviewer's opinion, will hold a high standing as one of the most scholarly and valuable books in our time; but only an accomplished student of accounting can extract the most out of it. It is not a book for novices.

This reviewer does not believe that accounting is a mere recording of historical costs, income, and valuations, important as these are. Critics of accounting should bear in mind that accounting has many purposes and uses.

Some of the limitations of accounting are "inherent in its functional design." Accounting as a technique and as a tool for management is no better than the men who record, interpret, and use accounting data.

CHARLES REITELL

New York, N. Y.

79

QUESTIONS

(1)   In chapter 13 Gilman seeks to clear up some terminology disputes
       by seeking mutually exclusive definitions of the terms, principle,
       doctrine, rule and convention etc.
          - To what extent is this sort of discussion necessary in the
            intellectual development of a discipline?
          - Were the distinctions drawn of significance in attaining
            the above objective?

(2)   "Since double-entry accounting became the accepted method of
       recording the financial history of business, the balance sheet
       viewpoint has dominated. Within the last few years accounting
       emphasis has shifted somewhat to the profit and loss viewpoint.
       (Pg.25) Consider this quote in the context of a further state-
       ment that "Since periodic revaluations of fixed assets have be-
       come unnecessary, few informed people attach much importance to
       the figures representing unexpired fixed assets" (Pg.96).
          - What evidence does Gilman provide to support his view?
          - To what does "accounting emphasis" refer?
          - Given that an estimation of one's present worth is a necess-
            ary factor of choice, did this reported change mark a
            corresponding change in the theoretical explication of
            accounting; if so,how has this become apparent?
          - In the second quote does the phrase "become unnecessary"
            refer to unnecessary by law or unnecessary for decision
            purposes?

(3)   While according praise to H.W. Sweeney, Gilman details some
       objections to Sweeney's stablised accounting.
          - What are these objections?
          - Are they of consequence?

(4)   In the context of asset valuation Gilman posits an argument very
       similar to May's.
          - What is this argument?
          - What, if any, are the differences?
          - What evidence does Gilman cite to support his view?
          - What, if any, excuses does May offer in addition to the
            feasibility argument.

(5)   "... the recognition of unrealised losses due to decreasing mar-
       ket prices deliberately contradicts the general policy of match-
       ing" (Pg.131).
          - To what does the term "unrealised losses" refer?
          - What is the "general policy of matching"?
          - In what sense are decreased market prices unrealised losses?

9

K F MACNEAL

Truth in Accounting

Biographical Chronology

1895	Born, 20 December, in Berwyn, Illinois
1912	Entered University of Chicago after attending J Sterling Morton High School
1916	Dismissed from University of Chicago
1916-17	Joined the staff of Price Waterhouse and Co
1917-19	Service with US Army in France
1920	Passed the Illinois CPA examinations earning a gold medal in the process
1921	Married Marguerite Giroud, 19 March
1920-43	Occupied a number of financial and accounting positions in Philadelphia business enterprises including manufacturing, building construction, hoteliery and real estate.
1929-30	As treasurer for an investment trust he supervised an ongoing (five year) analysis of the published financial statements of all companies listed on the New York Stock Exchange.
1939	Truth in Accounting, published
1943	Founded a small firm of CPA's in Philadelphia, MacNeal, Keetz and Allen
1972	Died, 16 March.

Selected Bibliography

1939   "Shortcomings of Some Accepted Accounting Principles
            Under Modern Conditions," Annalist, 13 July, pp 38-39.

            Truth in Accounting, University of Pennsylvannia Press
            (Philadelphia), 334 p.

            "What's Wrong With Accounting?", Nation, 7 Oct, pp 370-72;
            14 Oct, pp 409-412.

1941   "Is Our System of Financial Reporting Sound?", Accounting
            Forum, April, pp 7-11 (and Irish Accountant and Secretary
            May, pp 261-4).

            "Caveat Investor, Nation, 8 Feb, pp 151-53.

REFERENCES

Book Reviews of Truth:
            Journal of Accountancy, v.67, June 1939, pp.345-6
              (Lenhart, N J).
            Commonweal, v.30, 21 July 1939, p.322 (Binsse, H L: 550w)
            Management Review, v.28, Sept 1939, p.331 (600w).
            New Republic, v.100, 6 Sept 1939, p.138 (Norton, J D: 550
            Yale Law Journal, Nov 1939, pp.167-70 (Hunt, P).
            Journal of the American Statistical Association, Dec 1939
              pp.757-58 (Canning, J B).
            American Economic Review, Dec 1939, pp.853-55, (Jackson,
              J H).
            Review Supplement, Accounting Research Association,
              No.10, Jan 1940, pp.14-16 (Hatfield, H R).
            Journal of Political Economy, April 1940, pp.296-98
              (Paton, W A).
            Accounting Review, v.46, 1971, pp.634-36 (Philips, G E).

Zeff, S A, "Truth in Accounting: The Ordeal of Kenneth MacNeal",
            Accounting Review (forthcoming).

Walker, R G, "Explorations in Accounting", Harvard Business Review, v.18,
            1939, pp.384-96.

Truth in Accounting. By KENNETH MACNEAL. Philadelphia: University of Pennsylvania Press, 1939. Pp. xvii+334. $3.50.

With a number of the observations made in this attack on present-day accounting, particularly as reflected in the efforts of public accountants, I find myself in sympathy. There is some merit in the claim that the "most important party at interest in modern business is the small uninformed security holder" rather than the commercial banker or trade creditor, and there is force in the contention that the needs of the detached investor have not received adequate consideration in the preparation of financial reports. The author is justified, too, in emphasizing the importance of "economic values" in business affairs and the limitations of conventional statements as representations of such values and their interactions. Recorded dollar cost, as Mr. MacNeal points out again and again, does not continuously measure currently-significant value, and cost is no lodestar to which a fluctuating value has a tendency to return. The use of "cost or market, whichever is lower" as an expedient in inventory pricing does not appeal to the author, and it is to be doubted if a sound defense for this widely recognized convention of accounting can be found. Unrealized profit represented by appreciation of marketable securities held, Mr. MacNeal correctly states, is just as real and "safe" as a realized profit reinvested in such securities. That earning rates of different companies as computed on the respective investments as recorded are often lacking in comparability as a result of basing the respective accounts on costs, likewise cannot be gainsaid. Of particular interest is the author's expressed belief that "the year-to-year profits or losses of a normal business, as well as its ultimate showing, are more dependent upon the so-called outside forces than they are upon the skill or lack of skill shown in the operation of the business itself." There are numerous cases, without much question, in which this holds true.

On the other hand, the book is literally loaded with exaggerations, inconsistencies, and unsound propositions. What is this "truth" which Mr. MacNeal is continually stressing? Of course we all believe in truth just as we do in "justice" and the other cardinal virtues. But is there any agreement as to what constitutes truth in the periodic measurement of the economic data of the business enterprise—a living, continuing stream of activity, a complex of interrelated and progressing relationships? Is truth in this situation a single, clear-cut set of "values" lying right before the eyes of the accountant now that Mr. MacNeal has furnished the "open sesame"? Unfortunately the situation is not as simple as the author tries to make it appear. Currently-significant values are easily determined for wheat and marketable securities (the author's favorite examples) but for many of the assets of most of our half-million business corporations no reliable evidences of day-to-day values are available. There is no justification, moreover, for the assumption that recorded costs are generally false or misleading data as compared to estimated current market values. Costs are facts, and for some purposes, at least, costs are truths. I wonder if Mr. MacNeal has ever examined any of the many thousands of prospectuses covering bond issues of predepression days. In all or nearly all the statements included in such prospectuses estimated market values were given, with no indication of what the property to be mortgaged had cost. Many people now feel that had the emphasis in these documents been laid on actual cash costs rather than on estimated values the small investor would have been better informed. From the standpoint of disclosing legally-recognizable income, too, there is at present no possibility of substituting estimated values all along the line for costs—a condition which the author consistently ignores. The legal point of view, it is true, does not always harmonize with the economic, but the fact remains that the accountant must operate within a structure of general and corporate law. In preparing a statement of taxable income, or a showing of realized income assignable to various classes of security holders, the essence of the accountant's task is a matching of revenues and costs. This does not deny the possibility or desirability of supplementary computations.

The author takes many hard-and-fast positions where actually he hasn't a leg to stand on. He denies legitimate organization costs a position in assets or invested capital. To him bond discount is an outright loss and bond premium an immediate gain. What nonsense! Apparently he sees no propriety at all in the accumulation of construction costs, transportation charges, or any form of cost reckoning, at least as far as the balance sheet is concerned. In the discussion of depreciation there is little indication of familiarity with the subject. "Many a business has shown dismal operating losses over a period of years and has finally liquidated at a figure sufficient to make its owners rich, all because of appreciation in fixed assets which the accountant would scorn to put upon the books." I doubt if Mr. MacNeal has any substantial evidence to support such a sweeping assertion.

After laying great emphasis on the importance of using nothing but market values in reporting assets the author accepts conventional practice with respect to the treatment of accounts and notes receivable as "they commonly have no market price and their replacement cost would normally be the exact equivalent of their face value." Actually there is good evidence of the immediate market value of standard commercial paper in the discounted values set by banks and other financial institutions. In discussing prepaid insurance Mr. MacNeal advises valuation at either unexpired cost or "replacement cost," and makes no mention of the possible use of surrender value.

The author criticizes "Stabilized Accounting" as proposed by H. W. Sweeney on the ground that the concept employed is beyond the "comprehension of the ordinary man or woman who would have to depend for financial information upon the figures presented." He seems convinced, however, that the array of estimated values and unrealized gains and losses that he proposes to have presented would be as clear as crystal to the man on the street and would almost automatically result in rational judgments all along the line.

Mr. MacNeal scores the accounting profession without mercy, and by his very unreasonableness overshoots his mark. "The typical public accountant of today is, in actual fact, little more than a graduate bookkeeper. . . . . Of what use is the accountant except as a sort of accessory in a confidence game. . . . . Public respect for the accounting profession is now less high than it was a decade ago." Such wild statements, with which the book abounds, show complete disregard for or lack of knowledge of the facts. Granting that accounting is subject to improvement, it remains perfectly clear that a truly remarkable advance has been made in American accounting in the last twenty-five years, an advance which is especially noticeable in the very area in question—corporate reporting to stockholders.

W. A. Paton

University of Michigan

Truth in Accounting
by Kenneth MacNeal, C.P.A.

(Pennsylvania : University of Pennsylvania Press : Oxford University Press. xvii + 334 pp. 20s. net.)

The opening chapter of this book portrays, by means of three clever fables, the ways in which investors and others may be grievously misled by mistakenly attributing to balance sheets a meaning which they should not convey.

This is the thesis of the entire book. From its title one might expect it would discuss fraudulent and purposefully misleading statements, such as too frequently come before the Courts. On the contrary, it is merely a vigorous argument in favour of showing in the accounts present values, rather than costs, and of so doing whether that value is above or below cost.

To this much-debated question the author contributes some good arguments. But he is somewhat ungenerous to those who hold the other view in that he repeatedly speaks of their statements as being untrue. It is just as truthful (whether as serviceable or not) to present a statement which professedly shows unamortized costs as it is to state estimated present value. One may prefer present value to original, or cost, value, but one is as much a fact as the other. And, as in all accounting discussion, much depends on the debater's use of terms. If " profits " is limited by definition to that which, in common parlance, is said to have been " realized," it is rather severe to criticize one for not including, in the showing of profits, the appreciation of fixed assets. Mr. MacNeal makes a strong presentation of his side of the argument. He is supported by some prominent accountants on both sides of the Atlantic. But it must be remembered that there are others among whom, to mention only two, are George O. May and Professor Eugen Schmalenbach, who hold that accounting is essentially a process of allocating historical costs, and not one of valuation. This is not the proper place to enter into the discussion as to which view is preferable. Those interested in hearing one side ably presented will enjoy reading this book.

Some of the author's statements may be questioned. Among these are the statements : that when assets are secured by the issue of shares they are to be valued at the par of such shares ; that goodwill is not a proper asset ; that discount on shares is a loss ; that discount on a note payable differs essentially from that on a long-term debenture ; that premium received on debentures is a gain : that amortizing discount on debentures payable falsifies the accounts ; that, in this case, the effective rate of interest is " theoretical " interest, and the nominal rate is " actual " interest. The author is also to be questioned as to his use of the economic term " subjective value."

It is probably incorrect to say, as does the author, that the rulings in *Excelsior Water and Mining Co. v. Pierce* and in the *Verner* case hold that the reduction in the value of capital assets does not enter into the calculation of profits. The decisions seem merely to hold that in certain peculiar situations such reduction does not affect the amount which may legally be paid as dividends.

To be highly commended are : the clear refutation of the dictum, often used as an argument against showing appreciation, that " what goes up may come down " ; his explanation of goodwill ; his attitude regarding dividends received on shares of a subsidiary, and his criticism of lumping together different kinds of reserves.

It is to be regretted that the author included a section dealing with the history of bookkeeping. That is an *excursus*, not really pertinent to the subject of the book. Unfortunately it contains a number of inaccuracies as to names of authors, titles and dates of books, and even as to the nature of their contents. These errors are evidently due to the author having accepted without further inquiry the statements contained in a crudely inaccurate book published in the United States a few years previously. The moral is that it is wise for an author dealing with bibliography either to make independent research or to be careful in selecting his authority. For the selection in this case one should sympathise with the author, rather than criticise him.

Henry Rand Hatfield.

(1)   MacNeal speaks of the financial statements of accounting as being
        an "... incomprehensible mixture of present facts, historical
        data and accounting conventions" (Pg.184).
            - How true is this assertion today?
            - What is MacNeal's ideal solution to the problem?
            - Are his ideal solution and his practical suggestions for
              change complementary?
            - By what criteria are his practical suggestions introduced
              and justified?

(2)   "In the writers opinion goodwill should have no place in a balance
        sheet" (Pg.237).
            - What justification does McNeal provide for the above view?
            - To what extent is MacNeal's view a common one?

(3)   How does MacNeal define assets and liabilities?
            - To what extent are such definitions necessary in the
              explication of his ideas?

(4)   MacNeal maintains that for an asset to have economic value it
        must possess the following properties (1) Scarcity (2) Exchange-
        ability and (3) Utility. In view of the second property this
        would imply that non-marketable assets have no economic value.
            - Is this latter statement justifiable?
            - What does MacNeal mean by economic value?
            - Given that this is MacNeal's ideal solution is his practical
              suggestion for valuing non-marketable assets any different?

(5)   In favouring the cost price of assets to zero values, MacNeal
        maintained that "such (refering to zero values) would be farther
        from the truth than the use of original cost as value" (Pg.188).
            - To what extent does this and other aspects of MacNeal's
              book reveal his inability to break away from the value in
              use notion (as opposed to his ideal value in exchange).
            - What other author(s) suggested zero values for non-marketable
              assets?

(6)   "In this work it has been my aim to present a comprehensive
        analysis of modern accounting theory and practice ..." (Pg.vii).
            - What do you understand by the term 'accounting theory'?
            - How is this term changed by the addition of the adjective
              'modern'?
            - In view of your answers to question 1 and other specific
              aspects of MacNeals' book, does he succeed in his aim?

(7)   "... the Economic value of anything is its 'value in exchange'
        which, measured in money, is its market price" (Pg.87).
            - How did MacNeal propose finding out a market price?

10

GEORGE OLIVER MAY

Financial Accounting: A Distillation of Experience

Biographical Chronology

1875	Born in Teignmouth, Devon, England (22 May), the son of George England and Bessie (Gooland) May
1889	Awarded a scholarship and entered Blundell's school in September
1892	15 February, entered Thomas Andrew's chartered accountants office as an "articled pupil" where he continued his education until 1897
1897	Admitted on 3 February, as an associate to the Institute of Chartered Accountants in England and Wales. Entered the employ of Price Waterhouse and Co. 28 July moved to the United States of America and began work in Jones, Caeser & Co, associated to Price Waterhouse.
1904	1 January, married, Edith Mary Slocombe; became a partner of Price Waterhouse, USA
1909	Granted US citizenship
1911	1 July succeeded Sir Arthur Lowes Dickinson as a senior partner of Price Waterhouse & Co, USA
1916	Appointed to an American Institute of Accountants committee to confer with the Secretary of Commerce and Federal Reserve Board on the preparation of financial statements and the audit thereof for credit purposes
1926	President and Chairman of the Board (1928-29) of the National Bureau of Economic Research
1927	On 1 January relinquished administrative duties as senior partner of Price Waterhouse and Co. Elected to Board of the Council of Foreign Relations. Began a five year period in which he was a consultant to the Treasury Department
1930	Appointed chairman of a joint committee of the New York Stock Exchange and American Institute of Accountants investigating the need for greater uniformity in accounting principles Vice-president of the American Economic Association
1936	First Dickinson Lecturer at Harvard University
1937-40	Director of American Statistical Association
1950	Elected to Ohio State University's Accounting Hall of Fame
1961	Died on 25 May.

Selected Bibliography

1906   "Proper Treatment of Premiums and Discounts on Bonds, "
            Journal of Accountancy, v.2 (July), pp 174-86.

1915   "Problems of Depreciation," Journal of Accountancy, v.19
            (Jan), pp 1-13.

            "Qualifications in Certificates, "Journal of Accountancy,
            v.20 (Oct), pp 248-59.

1922   "Taxation of Capital Gains, "Harvard Business Review,
            v.1 (Oct), pp 11-18; also in Journal of Accountancy,
            v.34 (Nov), pp 321-33.

1925   "Taxable Income and Accounting Bases for Determining It, "
            Journal of Accountancy, v.40 (Oct), pp 248-66; also
            Canadian Chartered Accountant, July 1926, pp 2-21.

1926   "Corporate Publicity and the Auditor, "Journal of Accountancy,
            v.42 (Nov), pp 321-26.

1929   "Carrier Property Consumed in Operation and Regulation of
            Profits, "Quarterly Journal of Economics, v.43, pp 193-220.

1931   "Further Thoughts on Depreciation and a Rate Base, "The
            Quarterly Journal of Economics, v.44, pp 687-97.

1932   "Influence of the Depression on the Practice of Accountancy, "
            Journal of Accountancy, v.54 (Nov), pp 336-50.

1934   "Position of Accountants Under the Securities Act, "Journal
            of Accountancy, v.57 (Jan), pp 9-23.

1936   "Influence of Accounting on the Development of an Economy, "
            Journal of Accountancy, v.61 (Jan), pp 11-22.

1937   "Eating Peas with your Knife, "Journal of Accountancy, v.63
            (Jan), pp 15-22.

            "Principles of Accounting, "Journal of Accountancy, v.64
            (Dec), pp 423-5.

1938   "Uniformity in Accounting, "Harvard Business Review,
            v.17 (Autumn), pp 17-22.

1940   "Valuation of Historical Cost: Some Recent Developments, "
            Journal of Accountancy, v.69 (Jan) pp 14-21.

            "Recent Trends in Accounting "(address-accounting division
            of the Association of American Railroads, White Sulphur
            Springs, West Virginia, June 18, 1940, 28 p.),
            Canadian Chartered Accountant, Sept. pp 151-68.

1941   "(An) Accountant's Adventures in Wonderland, "Journal of
            Accountancy, v.71 (Jan) pp 72-3.

1942 "War and Accounting Procedures," <u>Journal of Accountancy</u>,
     v.73 (May), pp 393-400.

1943 "<u>Financial Accounting: a Distillation of Experience</u>,"
     The Macmillan Co (NY), 274 p.

     "The Nature of the Financial Accounting Process,"
     <u>Accounting Review</u>, v.18, pp 189-93.

     "Accounting and Regulation," <u>Journal of Accountancy</u>,
     v.76 (Oct), pp 295-301.

     "Improvement in Financial Accounts," <u>Dickinson Lectures
     in Accounting</u>, Harvard University Press, pp 1-48.

1944 "Accounting as a Social Force," The Author (New York),
     55 p; also <u>Canadian Chartered Accountant</u>, v.44 (May),
     pp 274-80.

1945 "Long Term Liabilities and Capital Stock," in
     <u>Contemporary Accounting</u>. A.I.A., Chapter 9.

1947 "The Future of the Balance Sheet," <u>Journal of Accountancy</u>,
     v.84 (Aug) pp 98-101.

1948 "Postulates of Income Accounting," <u>Journal of Accountancy</u>,
     v.86 (Aug) pp 107-11.

     "Accounting Research," <u>Accounting Research</u>, v.1 (Nov),
     pp 13-19.

1950 "The Case Against Change in Present Methods of Accounting
     For Exhaustion of Business Property," in A.I.A. Study
     Group on Business Income, <u>Five Monographs on Business
     Income</u>, pp 261-71; reprinted, Scholars Book Co, 1973.

1952 "Three Discussions of Financial Accounting and Inflation,"
     <u>Journal of Accountancy</u>, v.93 (Mar) pp 294-9.

     "Accounting In Time of Price Inflation," <u>Accountant</u>
     (England), v.127 (Oct 18), pp 442-6.

     "Limitations On the Significance of Invested Cost,"
     <u>Accounting Review</u>, v.27, pp 436-40.

1957 "Business Combinations, an Alternative View,"
     <u>Journal of Accountancy</u>, v.103 (April), pp 33-6.

     "Income Accounting and Social Revolution," <u>Journal of
     Accountancy</u>, v.103 (June), pp 36-41.

1958 "Generally Accepted Principles of Accounting," <u>Journal of
     Accountancy</u>, v.105 (Jan), pp 23-7.

1961 "Retrospect and Prospect," <u>Journal of Accountancy</u>,
     v.112 (July), pp 31-6.

NOTE: Twenty-Five Years of Accounting Responsibility: 1911-1936,
       ed., Bishop C. HUNT, Price Waterhouse, 1936; reprinted
       by Scholars Book Co, 1971. This book reproduces articles
       by May to 1936.

       Memoirs and Accounting Thought of George O. May, ed. Paul
       GRADY, The Ronald Press, 1962, includes a full bibliography.

REFERENCES

Book Reviews of Financial Accounting:
                  Journal of Accountancy, v.77, Feb 1944, pp. 158-61
                  (Staub, W A).
                  Columbia Law Review, May 1944, v.44 pp.467-68.
                  (Dohr, J L).
                  Accounting Review, v.21, 1946, pp.352-56
                  (Littleton, A C).
                  Harvard Law Review, July 1945, pp.886-04 (Baker, R J).
                  Journal of Accounting (A "Review Note"), v.76,
                  Oct 1943, p.
                  Accounting Review, v.48, 1973, pp.224-25 (W E Stone).

Book Review of Twenty-Five Years of Accounting Responsibility, Accounting
               Review, v.48, 1973, pp.224-5.

Edwards, J D & R F Salmonson, Contributions of Four Accounting Pioneers,
         (Digests), Michigan State University, 1961.

Grady, P (ed), Memoirs & Accounting Thought of George O May, Ronald Press, 1962.

Hart, A C Jnr, "George O May", Accounting Seminar, v.8, Dec 1953, pp.16-20,
         v.8, May 1954, pp.13-20.

Krane, R L, "Contribution to the Literature on Accounting Theory",
         Journal of Accountancy, v.89, Feb 1950, p.178.

Murphy, M E, "Seventy-Five Years Span of the AICPA: Pen Portraits of 15
         Members", The Author, (California), 1962.

Stabler, H F, A Study of Selected Contributions of George O May, (PhD
         Thesis), University of Alabama, 1962.

Stabler, H F & N X Dressel, "May & Paton: Two Giants Revisited", Accounting
         Historians Journal, v.8, 1981, pp.79-90.

Obituary Comments appeared in:
                  Journal of Accountancy, v.112, July 1961, pp.12,14,29-30.
                  The Accountant, v.144, 3 June 1961, pp.707-8.
                  Price Waterhouse Review, v.6, Summer 1961, pp.9-11;
                  Autumn 1962, pp.16-22.

FINANCIAL ACCOUNTING. A Distillation of Experience. By George O.
May.[1]   New York: Macmillan Company.   1943.   Pp. ix, 274.
$3.00.

Nearly ten years ago. Mr. May's partners published a large number of
his papers.[2]   The wide range of these papers in the interwoven areas of
accounting, law, regulation and government is indicated by the titles of
the parts.[3]   They disclose an experienced accountant and an acute mind
in action and in reflection, and go far to reveal to lawyers the methods of
thought and work of a leader of an affiliated profession.   Practicality and
philosophy are in admirable balance, and practice and principle are subjected to tests for social and economic significance.   Many lawyers in

---

[1] Lecturer on Accounting, Harvard Graduate School of Business Administration.
[2] MAY, TWENTY-FIVE YEARS OF ACCOUNTING RESPONSIBILITY (1936).
[3] The profession of accounting (including a discussion of the Kreuger & Toll and
the Royal Mail (Kylsant) cases) ; depreciation; valuation; regulation of securities;
taxation; the influence of accounting on the development of an economy; reviews
and criticisms (including numerous short writings, some quite informal).

corporate and tax practice have made good professional use of this book, and as students of the quarter century covered have had instruction and pleasure from its rich and varied content.[4] Nevertheless, it seems not to have been reviewed in any of the legal periodicals, and it is unfortunate that a large majority of the lawyers and judges in the country are probably not familiar with it. The 1911–1936 papers, together with his many published writings of the interval, have furnished the raw materials for the author's present book. Its subtitle is, very appropriately, " A Distillation of Experience." The two books are therefore the parts of one whole, and the better values of either are to be had by use of them together.[5]

Mr. May has undoubtedly written for his fellow accountants [6] and industrial and utility managers, and for legislators and those charged with administrative regulation. Moreover, it seems clear enough that he has written for lawyers; perhaps, particularly for lawyers.[7] One is grateful that he has done so. It is too often and too readily assumed that clear lines mark off the functions of accountants and lawyers. Concerning corporate finance and accounts, the supposed lines are non-existent ; decisions in the particular case and the ultimate working out of general principles (or " conventions ") call for joint contributions from the skills and judgment of both professions. It is fortunate, therefore, that an accountant, so entirely competent to do so, has undertaken to define and analyze so many of the more difficult phases of the ever-increasing complexity of corporate accounting, and to do so in terms the legal profession

---

[4] Many of the papers had important if not controlling significance in cases or proceedings for which they were currently prepared, or in which they are excerpts from Mr. May's testimony. Among them is a Memorandum (*id.* at 168), submitted November 1, 1927 in relation to the report in the then re-opened proceedings upon depreciation charges of steam railroad companies, ICC No. 15100, in which Mr. May discusses the original report of the Commission (see 118 I. C. C. 295 (1926), which includes telephone companies, ICC No. 14700). This is a carefully worked out comparison of the straight-line and annuity methods of depreciation in relation to valuation and the rate base. The report on rehearing, Depreciation Charges of Steam Railroad Companies, 177 I. C. C. 351, 409–13 (1931), written by the late Mr. Commissioner Eastman, indicates that Mr. May did not testify and that his Memorandum may not have been filed with the Commission. Whatever the practical merits of the straight-line method approved by the Commission, it is intellectually regrettable that Mr. Eastman was left in the position where he had to say: ". . . it may be that from a scientific and theoretical standpoint the annuity method is the soundest of all. We can not speak with assurance on that point, because of the fact that this method was not presented at the hearings where it could be subjected to the tests of analysis and cross-examination." *Id.* at 412. See c. IX of the present book and the Footnote thereto at p. 161, for further discussion of the alternative methods, and for analysis of these to show the nature of the annual charge and the relation of the different systems to the broad parts that cost and value should respectively play in accounting and regulation.

[5] Accounting writing is usually sparse in the use of footnotes and cross references. It would have been helpful if in the present book the author had provided reference more generously to appropriate parts of his TWENTY-FIVE YEARS OF ACCOUNTING RESPONSIBILITY and of his intervening papers.

[6] For reviews by accountants, see Hosmer, Book Review (1945) 35 AM. ECON. REV. 183, and the article-review, Sanders, *Government by " Accounting Principles"* (1944) 22 HARV. BUS. REV. 265.

[7] This flavor of the book suggests a second sub-title: Forensic Accounting.

can understand, and by clear and incisive writing.[8] It is as distinctly worthwhile as it is essential to bring the two professions into a close working association, and it is not entirely to the credit of the lawyers that the most significant efforts in this direction have been by accountants.

Corporation statutes are usually drafted by lawyers. There is evidence in the statutes of the last fifteen years that the draftsman reached certain dead-ends beyond which the language at his command seemed insufficient to carry him. Since most of these difficulties involved finances and finances seemed to the draftsman to be related to accounting and to be measured by its results, he borrowed a few accounting terms, put them in the bill and closed up his work, which the legislature thereupon adopted. It may be that no more could have been done, but the result in important areas is an illusory exactitude. The propriety of corporate action depends upon the interpretation of accounting terms which Mr. May makes very clear do not have certainty of meaning or content.

In at least three important statutes of the period,[9] " earned surplus " is made the primary and ordinary measure of funds available for dividends.[10] In the three statutes, the phrase stands stark, without definition,[11] and it seems to have been assumed that earned surplus was a thing subject to certain and almost automatic determination. Either the problem of definition baffled the draftsman or he was ignorant of the difficulties not only in computing annual operating income but in properly placing the burden among different surplus accounts of special debits and charges for write-offs, losses, or write-downs, or for premiums paid or unamortized discount on called securities, and the like. In these and other statutes, " paid-in surplus " is frozen against certain uses. Efforts are made to give the phrase a broad scope,[12] but the problem of where to place the special charges remains. The temptation is to put the burden on paid-in surplus and thus to absolve earned surplus as the freest source for dividends.[13]

---

[8] Mr. Dohr has accurately and felicitously appraised this contribution by the author. Dohr, Book Review (1944) 44 COL. L. REV. 467. And see Hosmer, *loc. cit. supra* note 6: ". . . though highly condensed, its style is clear and readable for those proficient in law, regulation, and the several branches of economics. One of the chief tasks of such a volume, which the author doubtless had in mind, is to clarify for those in related professions what financial accounting does, what its limits are, and the reasons for the position it takes."

[9] Those enacted in California, Michigan, and Minnesota. By prohibiting dividends from paid-in surplus except on preferred shares, Illinois and Pennsylvania reach or work toward the same result, although avoiding use of the words "earned surplus." § 12(c) of the Public Utility Holding Company Act authorizes the SEC to make rules, regulations or orders " to prevent the payment of dividends out of capital or unearned surplus." 49 STAT. 824 (135), 15 U. S. C. § 79l(c) (1940). See §§ 18–19 of the Investment Companies Act, 54 STAT. 817–22 (1940), 15 U. S. C. §§ 80a–18, 80a–19 (1940).

[10] And for the purchase by the corporation of its own common shares.

[11] Despite the seeming definitions in Minn. Stat. (1941) § 301.22(1), the earned surplus mentioned therein is not defined.

[12] *E.g.*, ILL. ANN. STAT. (Smith-Hurd, 1935) c. 32, § 157.2(1).

[13] Some statutes may permit many such charges to go against paid-in or reduction or other capital surplus, by-passing earned surplus, and thereby breaking down the concept of earned surplus that accountants would insist on. See CAL. CIV. CODE

The statutes frequently require that " proper allowance " be made " for depreciation and depletion sustained, and losses of every character," in the computation of funds available for dividends generally,[14] or as condition of the exercise of certain privileges.[15] But there is little or no attempt to define the measures of depreciation or depletion, or the losses required to be recognized,[16] or the time recognition must be given. Caselaw is almost non-existent.[17] These are problems that arise in the most usual corporate practice.

Some statutes also permit dividends from the net profits of a described fiscal period even though there may be no surplus of any kind. The assumption is that it is simple to ascribe income to a given period, although there is here no administrative process to determine or at least to compromise the matter as there is under the tax statutes.[18]

The parent and subsidiary relationship has its own special accounting questions, on which the state statutes are silent unless the prohibitions against dividends from unrealized appreciation apply. Are available earnings of subsidiaries not declared as dividends funds " available " to the parent? Conversely, are dividends received from subsidiaries current earnings of the parent without regard to the time they may have been earned by the declarant?[19] In this relationship and elsewhere is the question of proper accounting for share dividends, paid or received.

Utility regulation is reaching out more and more to control accounting. Not only are uniform systems of accounts prescribed, but accounting for particular transactions is vetoed or ordered. Security regulation, in connection with issue and exchange trading, reaches deeply into corporate accounts and finance. The same is true of bankruptcy and near-bankruptcy reorganization. It is probably in these fields and in tax practice that lawyers are brought into the most specialized accounting problems.[20]

(Deering, 1941) § 346c; ILL. ANN. STAT. (Smith-Hurd, 1935), c. 32, § 157.60(a); OHIO CODE (Throckmorton, 1938) § 8623–38; and cf. MINN. STAT. (1941) § 301.22(1).

[14] E.g., PA. STAT. ANN. (Purdon, 1938) tit. 15, § 2852–701B; MINN. STAT. 301.22.

[15] E.g., CAL. CIV. CODE (Deering, 1941) § 346; DEL. REV. CODE (1935) c. 65, § 34.

[16] Minnesota adds: " Whether or not realized."

[17] See Petroleum Rights Corp. v. Midland Royalty Corp., 19 Del. Ch. 334, 167 A. 835 (1933), as to computation of depletion.

[18] " The question ' when is income ' offers greater difficulty than the question ' what is income ' . . . ." May, *Improvement in Financial Accounts* in DICKINSON LECTURES IN ACCOUNTING (1943) 1, 19.

[19] This was the principal issue in Cintas v. American Car & Foundry Co., 131 N. J. Eq. 419, 25 A.(2d) 418 (V. C. 1942), aff'd on opinion below, 132 N. J. Eq. 460, 28 A.(2d) 531 (Ct. Errors and App. 1942). The problem arises under statutes permitting use of current earnings for dividends even in the absence of balance sheet surplus. Mr. May discussed the *Cintas* case in *The American Car and Foundry Decision* (1942) 74 J. ACCOUNTANCY 517; for summaries of the accounting affidavits, see (1942) 74 J. ACCOUNTANCY 380.

[20] Numerous utility plant accounting cases have reached the courts under the Federal Power Act (including licensee cases), the Federal Communications Act, and the acts administered by the SEC. See Kripke, *A Case Study in the Relationship of Law and Accounting: Uniform Accounts 100.5 and 107* (1944) 57 HARV. L. REV. 433, 693, and New York Tel. Co. v. United States, 56 F. Supp. 932 (S. D. N. Y. 1944), *appeal granted,* (1945) 13 U. S. L. WEEK 3398. New England Tel. & Tel. Co.

Labor and wage adjustments are more likely to involve the collection and use of statistics than the serious issues of financial accounting.[21]

One does not need to labor the point; it is obvious that modern law practice forces the bar to deal with the most difficult problems in the whole range of accounting, and that this compulsion will be greater rather than less if the present economic system prevails. Lawyers therefore welcome writing from accounting sources from which they may take learning the schools did not give them. There have been many useful books to supply this need,[22] but it is believed that Mr. May's book is the best of them for this purpose and makes the most significant contribution for lawyers. Substantially all the major questions arising in the legal-accounting fields suggested above are clearly defined and acutely discussed by the author.

The first four chapters are more clearly related to the accountants' profession, its history and growth, and the nature of the function it performs.[23] The next two chapters deal with the major choice between recording cost or value of permanent assets,[24] and the measurement of cost itself. Mr. May properly insists upon the need, for clear analysis, of recognition of changes in the value of the monetary unit in which assets and liabilities are recorded, as distinguished from other factors that may affect asset value. But a satisfactory " disentanglement of the elements " is probably impossible. Moreover, how can value be measured for property not intended for sale and for which normally no market exists? [25] Despite recognition of these difficulties, the author is unwilling to join the group who condemn all upward adjustments of cost to value, whether already made or proposed. He believes that many write-ups in the 1920's were sincere efforts to reflect the fall in the value of the monetary unit in charges thereafter made against income for depreciation in the belief that the price levels of, say, 1922 had become virtually permanent.[26]

---

v. United States, 53 F. Supp. 400 (D. Mass. 1943), involved the proper accounting under administrative regulation in connection with a pension and retirement plan that was only partially funded and included past services. Accounting issues appear in most stop-order or show-cause and delisting proceedings before the SEC under the 1933 and 1934 Acts. Accounts and the projection of accounts into the future are of great importance in reorganization.

[21] See, however, HOW CORPORATIONS CONCEAL PROFITS AND HOW TO UNDERSTAND YOUR CORPORATION'S FINANCIAL REPORT (1943) (prepared by the United Electrical, Radio & Machine Workers of America and printed privately), noted in (1944) 19 ACCOUNTING REV. 92.

[22] PATON, ADVANCED ACCOUNTING (1941) and GRAHAM & KATZ, ACCOUNTING IN LAW PRACTICE (3d ed. 1940) are among the most recent and useful.

[23] To ascribe these 85 pages to accountants is not to suggest that they do not contain much of interest to lawyers. They go far to show how much of an approximation accounts must be and to dispel the layman's conception of financial statements as representations of fact and of accounting as an exact science. See pp. 62–64, and 2 MAY, TWENTY-FIVE YEARS OF ACCOUNTING RESPONSIBILITY (1936) 79.

[24] This question " may be regarded as perhaps the central question of accounting."

[25] See the discussion of this question at pp. 90–100, and in the appendix to c. V, at p. 103.

[26] AMERICAN INSTITUTE OF ACCOUNTANTS, COMMITTEE ON ACCOUNTING PROCEDURE, ACCOUNTING RESEARCH BULLETIN No. 5 (April 1940) takes the position that, after such a write-up, future charges to operations for depreciation should be on

However, he concedes that today it is a fairly accepted rule that unrealized appreciation should not be recorded.[27] But a retroactive application of the present view is a different thing.

The difficult problem whether law or accounting principles require recording of values which, because of a decline in earnings for a considerable period, are deemed to be less than unamortized costs is seen in the light of the difficulty in determining whether the decline is temporary or relatively permanent, due to individual poor management or competitive inferiority or to deterioration in an entire industry. Mr. May indicates that if the cause is competitive inferiority of the particular corporation, principle requires the write-down, but that where the cause or causes are otherwise it is undesirable to lay down a rule of requirement, although " managements should, perhaps, be encouraged to give recognition to such declines through reorganization or quasi-reorganization." [28] The author takes a position which goes beyond that yet taken by the Committee on Accounting Procedure of The American Institute of Accountants, where write-downs are in fact made. " If a corporation has issued preferred stocks or bonds on the basis of a balance sheet, this may be regarded as implying an obligation to provide out of revenues for any decline in the useful value of such assets before making any distribution on junior securities. In such circumstances a corporation should not be permitted to reduce the book *value* of the assets to current value and thereafter compute depreciation on the basis of the reduced value, if that action would prejudice the position of the senior security which the corporation has a legal or a moral obligation not deliberately to impair. Subject to appropriate recognition of these equities, accountants should encourage corporations to deal through quasi-reorganizations with inheritances from the past which have lost their old significance." [29] In Accounting Research Bulletin No. 5 (April 1940), the Committee took the position noted above as to the basis for future charges for depreciation after a write-up but reserved the question in the case of a write-down.

---

the increased basis. Even where this practice is followed in the first instance, some of the related entries seem to a layman thereafter to lift the extra burden from income or at least from earned surplus under a theory of " realized " appreciation.

[27] Under New York Stock Corporation Law, § 58, it may be taken into account in determining funds available for dividends. Randall v. Bailey, 288 N. Y. 280, 43 N. E.(2d) 43 (1942). This is probably not true in any other important state; it is expressly prohibited in several.

[28] Pp. 100–01. The *Randall* case seems to impose the requirement where the condition is permanent, whatever the cause. For the principles governing such an accounting reorganization, see p. 207; see also AMERICAN INSTITUTE OF ACCOUNTANTS, COMMITTEE ON ACCOUNTING PROCEDURE, ACCOUNTING RESEARCH BULLETIN NO. 3 (Sept. 1939) ; SEC Accounting Release No. 1 (April 1, 1937), No. 7 (May 16, 1938) (items 2 and 3 under Surplus), No. 15 (March 16, 1940), No. 16 (March 16, 1940), and No. 25 (May 29, 1941).

[29] P. 101. This theory of the equities of senior securities is violated by the wasting assets doctrine and statutes where two-class situations exist. It may be violated by the privilege of paying dividends out of current earnings despite an existing capital impairment and absence of surplus. It bars a corporation from the benefit of reduced depreciation charges except at the price of refunding its senior securities.

Chapter VI on Cost deals with less controversial materials but none-theless with difficult and interesting problems. The choice of cost as the basis to record assets in the accounts is shown not to avoid the complex problems of valuation. This is especially so where non-homogeneous assets of a going concern are acquired for a lump sum payable in cash or securities. Assuming the fairness of the price (and ability to determine it if paid in debt or equity securities), it is practically necessary to allo-cate it to separate items of property acquired, tangible and intangible.[30] The more clearly engineering aspects of the valuation and allocation are pointed out, but the significant point is the author's insistence that the adoption of a low value, particularly for assets subject to depreciation, depletion or other amortization, is the reverse of its apparent con-servatism.[31]

The next three chapters deal with depreciation. The history of de-preciation, or substitutes therefor, is traced to and since 1918, in account-ing practice and regulation.[32] The basis and technique of depreciation accounting are explained in words chosen with great care and are con-trasted with other and competing systems, such as appraisal, replacement, retirement and retirement reserve.[33]

---

[30] *Inter alia*, the necessity arises from (a) the disallowance by the Treasury nor-mally of tax deductions for depreciation or obsolescence of intangibles; (b) the need for individual cost bases for property subject to allowable depreciation or depletion tax deductions; and (c) the need for such cost bases for all items to determine gain or loss on future disposition or retirement. Further, the allocation is necessary for purposes of management control through accounts.

[31] P. 112. The discussion of the point is worth very careful reading and con-sideration. The action of the Interstate Commerce Commission in *Reorganization of Chicago Great Western R. R.*, 247 I. C. C. 193 (1941), is set out at some length and praised. The Commission has since revised its accounting rules to include the principles adopted in this report, which recognize the original cost to a predecessor carrier as the basis for depreciation and retirement accounting (see *id.* at 200–02).

[32] A short summary of much that is in c. V and c. VI will be found in Mr. May's third lecture in DICKINSON LECTURES IN ACCOUNTING (1943) 36–38. This part of the book and particularly the historical part is essential to an understanding of the most serious issue for railroads and utilities relating to depreciation, that of retro-active application of a new view or policy. For Mr. May's views on the relation of straight-line depreciation to value and the rate base, see references in note 4 *supra*.

[33] Mr. May believes that retirement reserve accounting, as developed in the pub-lic utility field (exclusive of the major telephone companies), does not possess much theoretical merit, as being an illogical and incongruous combination of amortization and replacement theories, although having merit from the practical standpoint, par-ticularly under conditions of a rapidly expanding industry (pp. 128–29). The 1922 classification of the National Association of Railroad and Utility Commissioners (hereinafter designated NARUC) sanctioned the system and did not adopt deprecia-tion accounting (p. 131). The author's discussion in c. VIII of the significance of this action is essential to an understanding of the controversy that has arisen out of the reversal of policy by the Association in 1936–1938. See NARUC, PROC. 48TH ANNUAL CONVENTION (1936) 49, 69; *id.*, PROC. 49TH ANNUAL CONVENTION (1937) 460, 466; *id.*, PROC. 50TH ANNUAL CONVENTION (1938) 55, 425, 438–518. For fur-ther discussion of the differences between the systems, see Mr. Commissioner East-man in Depreciation Charges of Telephone Companies and of Steam Railroads, 118 I. C. C. 295, 301–13 (1926), and on further hearing in 177 I. C. C. 351, 382–97 (1931). See HOSMER, PROBLEMS IN ACCOUNTING (2nd ed. 1938) 412–24, for excerpts and data from annual reports of Detroit Edison Company at a time when it used and was one of the leading exponents of a retirement reserve system.

The discussion moves quickly into the area of debate. To lawyers, perhaps the most interesting point arises from the shift of many regulatory authorities since about 1935 to depreciation accounting from other systems theretofore used by many if not most utilities except the major telephone companies. Studies by the Federal Power Commission purported to show as of December 31, 1934, that reserves built up by utilities under retirement reserve accounting were 8.6% of the book cost of plant. With this was compared 27.3% for the Bell Telephone System at the close of 1937. By the end of 1941, the comparison was 14.23% and 28.51%.[34] Other studies of electric and gas companies revealed reserves which were low in comparison with reserves that would have existed had these companies followed depreciation accounting, and particularly straight-line, over the lives of their existing properties. As Mr. May points out, regulatory authorities were likely to say and did say that the existing reserves were inadequate, and despite the reversal of policy by these same authorities, to impute the failure to provide what they now consider to be adequate reserves to management and to call upon the companies to make good the deficit; [35] in other words, retroactive application of depreciation accounting. Increase of the reserves would deplete surplus (and it would be contended that it must be earned surplus that makes the contribution), or, for want of sufficient surplus, would require a capital reduction.

It may be that the statutes will be construed to permit the commissions, under their powers over accounting, to require retroactive application to be made,[36] and that, as so construed, such exercise of power will be sustained by the courts against constitutional objections.[37] But

[34] Report of Committee on Depreciation of NARUC, PROC. 50TH ANNUAL CONVENTION (1938) 438, 462; see also separately published report presented at 55TH ANNUAL CONVENTION (1943) at 135. Mr. May's general criticism of the latter report begins at p. 161. See also the letter noted in note 51 *infra*.
[35] P. 138.
[36] *Cf.* New York Edison Co. v. Maltbie, 244 App. Div. 685, 281 N. Y. Supp. 223 (3rd Dep't 1935), *aff'd*, 271 N. Y. 103, 2 N. E.(2d) 277 (1936).
[37] In United Light & Power Co. v. Grand Rapids Trust Co., 7 F. Supp. 511 (W. D. Mich. 1931), *modified and aff'd*, 85 F.(2d) 331 (C. C. A. 6th, 1936), effort was made to carry the insolvency back over the full period of the challenged dividends by setting up rates for straight-line depreciation on the property and accruing on them the reserve at the end of each fiscal year, in comparison with the small reserve the interurban railway had carried (seemingly on equipment only), being otherwise on non-reserve retirement accounting or replacement accounting. The effort failed. See 7 F. Supp. at 530, ns. 5–6. Effort was also made to show absence of true net income or surplus in the period by setting up charges against revenues on the basis of such straight-line depreciation, to establish that the dividends paid must have been out of capital. This also failed. See 7 F. Supp. at 528–29, ns. 3–4. The court was thus unwilling retroactively to apply depreciation accounting under the issue of liability of recipients after receivership to refund dividends received, as paid while insolvent or not out of earnings. But here of course there had been no administrative determination of a present inadequacy of reserves for a going concern.
Two cases have involved excessive accruals under straight-line depreciation accounting. In Board of Public Utility Comm'rs. v. New York Tel. Co., 271 U. S. 23 (1926), it was held that the utility could not be required to accept depressed rates for the present and for a period in the future because of such excess reserves accumu-

both accountants and lawyers are concerned with something that goes beyond the strict legalities of the issue. Even if the accounting provisions of the statutes are not so construed or a *direct* exercise of power thereunder is not sustained, the commissions may have means at their hand *indirectly* to force the same results, which means they will use. They may undoubtedly investigate the accounts and have their engineers and accountants examine the properties, books and records, and hold hearings concerning them. Based thereon, they may announce their conclusions as to the adequacy of existing reserves, predicated on a retroactive computation. It is not unlikely that in many instances the " inadequacy " will exceed existing surplus, earned or capital. What will be the effect? Some managements may be sufficiently sturdy to do nothing. Others may, in view of existing statutes relating to dividends, be sufficiently frightened to discontinue dividends, either until withheld earnings augment existing surplus to the point where a transfer to increase the reserve will bring the latter to the commission's declared standard of adequacy, or until other corporate and accounting steps can be taken to remove the fear by increase of the reserve. In many states, the cessation of dividends would include those on preferred shares.

In November 1940, the New York papers (and the financial services) reported that the directors of Brooklyn Union Gas Company had suspended dividends because of just such a development.[38] The state Commission had made no order; its staff had stated their judgment to be that the accrued depreciation on the depreciable property, on a retroactive application of straight-line depreciation accounting, was in excess of $21,000,000, whereas at the close of the previous year the reserve on the books was $13,600,000, and the surplus $2,345,000. The dividends were stopped, and the Company proceeded with the Commission to get an agreement upon the exact amount of the accrued depreciation so com-

lated in the past through charges against revenues. The Court answered No to the question " whether the company may be compelled to apply any part of the property or money represented by such [reserve] balances to overcome deficits in present or future earnings and to sustain rates which otherwise could not be sustained " *Id.* at 31. Admittedly the case does not reach to the present issue though it seems more nearly to do so than any other. Here, future rates are not concerned (at least directly), but past surplus accumulations or capital (through reduction) would be captured to set up a reserve in respect of a past period when neither law nor regulation required creation and maintenance of such a reserve, and during which it would be at least an assumption to say that rates collected carried " loading " for charges to establish the reserve and that such charges were diverted to distributions of income or accumulated in earned surplus. Lindheimer v. Illinois Bell Tel. Co., 292 U. S. 151 (1934), required refunding of the excess of rates charged over the period of litigation (since 1923) over lower rates then ordered by the state commission; the rates charged were deemed too high because they provided for excessive annual charges for depreciation, with the result of accruing an overly large reserve. But the effect of the decision was not truly retroactive in the sense here meant, since a condition imposed when the litigation began was that the company refund the spread between such rates and the lower rates then prescribed by the state commission if it failed to establish the confiscatory character of the latter. See *id.* at 154.

[38] In New York, *Randall v. Bailey, supra* note 27, indicates the reason for such caution. The opinion of Special Term had been filed on October 24, 1940. Similar reasons apply in other states.

puted.[39]   This done, and the necessary corporate and accounting steps taken to effect the accounting reorganization, dividends were resumed in 1942, from earnings subsequent to the date as of which the reorganization was made.[40]   Other means of indirect compulsion may be open to the commissions.[41]

The Brooklyn Company was fortunate; it had only one class of shares outstanding, and the necessary capital reduction could be made without threat of serious trouble with a preferred issue that might require a considerable cash payment.   Another New York corporation was not so fortunate.   The New York Water Service Company exhausted both its earned and capital surplus accounts on December 31, 1942, by transfers to " reserve for possible adjustments of utility plant and reserve for depreciation."   Thereafter, to provide accounting sources for augmenting this reserve, it was proposed that its parent surrender common representing $2,101,500 of capital; that capital be reduced by that amount, to be carried to the above reserve from which to be able to cover anticipated indications or findings of inadequacy of existing reserves.   But it was announced that " because of the decision of the Court of Appeals of New York in the Matter of Kinney, 279 N. Y. 423, the plan will provide that if any preferred stockholder objects to the proposed reduction of capital and demands payment for his stock, the plan will be abandoned." [42]   The adequacy of reserves, so tested, is an acute problem for many other companies.[43]

---

[39] The chairman of the Commission, in a report dated December 9, 1941 (Case No. 9225), said that the amount which should have been in the reserve at October 31, 1941, computed on the straight-line method of depreciation accounting, was over $22,143,000 on plant account of $91,474,000, based on " original cost."   From balance sheets presented, the existing reserve was $15,736,000.   To bring the latter up to the former would require an increase of $6,407,000, or over 40%.   The increase was " recommended.".   The existing surplus (earned) was then $5,275,000.   The Company accepted the recommendation.   By shareholders' vote, it reduced capital 20% or. $7,453,000; against earned surplus and this reduction surplus, it debited the increase in the reserve and $5,639,000 of net write-offs of other items, and came out with a capital surplus of $682,000 and no earned surplus.

[40] Prospectus dated September 20, 1944, at 46.   In the meantime, three issues of the Company's bonds (constituting all bonds publicly held) were removed from the legal list in at least two jurisdictions.   These issues were refunded in 1944.

[41] Many statutes require commission approval of numerous corporate steps, such as issue or refunding of securities, merger or consolidation, sale or purchase of assets, acquisition of shares of others.   N. Y. Herald Tribune, Nov. 13, 1943, p. 15, col. 6, reports adjournment of a hearing on the proposed consolidation of subsidiaries of Niagara Hudson Power Company, to obtain the ruling of the full commission of New York on the admission of evidence by its staff involving application of straight-line depreciation retroactively.   The report indicates that accounting adjustments to reflect the staff's position would result in a surplus deficit of nearly $40 millions.   Counsel has advised that the full Commission admitted the evidence.

[42] N. Y. Herald Tribune, May 22, 1943, p. 19, col. 6.   Query, whether the effect of the *Kinney* case can be avoided by an order of the SEC under the Holding Company Act. confirmed by the court.   *Cf.* Otis & Co. v. SEC, 322 U. S. 724 (1944).

[43] It becomes involved in proceedings before the SEC under the Holding Company Act (see, *e.g.*, Florida Power & Light Co., SEC Holding Co. Release No. 4791 (Dec. 30, 1943)), the Federal Power Commission, possibly but less frequently, the Federal Communications Commission.   In a Memorandum dated January 20, 1944, against retroactive depreciation accounting. submitted to the Committee on Depre-

The question is whether such a retroactive application of a newly adopted policy, to the extent of extinction of existing surplus accounts and wiping out large portions of capital, is necessary, wise, or fair and equitable.

The ICC, in extending depreciation accounting on a straight-line basis to carrier fixed property in 1926,[44] recognized the problem and said that the theoretically correct way of meeting the situation would be by a charge to profit and loss (surplus), as that account had profited in the past by the failure or partial failure to accrue depreciation charges.[45] But it was evident that, as to many if not most carriers, this method could not be followed for want of sufficient surplus. Therefore the Commission permitted the amount by which the reserves should be increased (or established) on account of computed accruals for the past to be set up in a suspense account on the assets side of the balance sheet, to be " gradually extinguished by charges to profit and loss over a maximum period of years or in such shorter time as the carrier might elect." [46] Mr. May has criticized the Commission for thus speaking of " failure " and " profiting," and has said that one of the principal objections to its proposals is the failure to provide an equitable plan for dealing with any depreciation attributable to the past, " having regard to the past history of railroad practice and regulation." [47]

In the present book he comes back to the theme, in terms of the new policy of NARUC. The change to depreciation accounting " creates the major problem of dealing with depreciation which under the new classification is deemed to have accrued in the past in so far as that sum exceeds, as it naturally will, reserves that were adequate under the previously existing classification." [48] He believes that neither the ICC nor the NARUC has presented adequate proposals for its solution in an equitable manner, although some commissions have dealt with it more or less satisfactorily in some specific cases. To effect a change of policy with retroactive effect at the expense of the companies would be a gross

---

ciation of NARUC by a committee of the American Gas Association, data for 72 companies as of December 31, 1942, show reserves at 15% of total fixed capital; and it is said that " straight-line depreciation computers usually produce a minimum of 28% for the accrued depreciation of a growing gas company." This would require an increase in the reserves of over $840 millions against total surplus (capital and earned) of $530 millions. See *id.* at 4. Hosmer publishes figures for the percentage in 1934 of reserves to total cost of all property for 28 gas companies in Massachusetts which range from 0.87% to 47.37%, and show 4.04% for the largest company. HOSMER, PROBLEMS IN ACCOUNTING (2nd ed. 1938) 404, 411.

[44] This extension was thereafter long postponed. With important exceptions, it became mandatorily effective on January 1, 1943. See ICC, 56TH ANNUAL REPORT (for period ending October 31, 1942) 52.

[45] This " profit " is debatable.

[46] 118 I. C. C. 295, 384 (1926). The precise method of handling the suspense account was left for later separate consideration. This leaves open the question whether charges to extinguish it are items of expense or income deductions.

[47] 1 MAY, TWENTY-FIVE YEARS OF ACCOUNTING RESPONSIBILITY (1936) 186–87, 189.

[48] P. 138; see also pp. 164–65, 169–70; and see pp. 247–48 as to the proper incidence of the charge " if it is to be made at all."

injustice; to impose on consumers of the future the burden of creating a reserve which it is now thought should have been created in the past might also be unjust; moreover, it has not even been made clear that a useful purpose would be served by setting up such reserves at this late date.[49] " Even if straight-line depreciation is to be adopted for the future, justice and practical wisdom would dictate that no effort should be made to require from either investors or customers the sacrifice necessary to bridge the gap between the retirement reserve and the theoretical depreciation reserve at the date of the change. What has occurred is in the nature of a change of rules in the middle of the performance of a quasi-contract." [50]

A committee of which Mr. May is a member has made public a letter it sent to the chairman of the NARUC Committee on Depreciation with respect to the report of the latter committee presented in September 1943. The Institute committee regards as the most important problem involved in the report the question of retroactive adjustment of reserves. Its letter suggests but does not fully work out the idea that there is a difference, not only in equity but in economic substance, between applying depreciation accounting, particularly on a straight-line basis, prospectively to a new enterprise and both prospectively and retrospectively to an enterprise that has reached maturity. On the whole, the committee was of the opinion that straight-line depreciation is the most desirable of the methods of accounting for consumption of capital assets to be employed in the case of a new enterprise. " However, at the present stage of utility development it is far from clear that there would be an advantage in substituting retroactive straight-line depreciation accounting for a system of reasonably generous retirement reserves. Dispassionate analysis might well lead to the conclusion that the change is not justifiable unless a fair and practicable method of effecting the transition is presented. The absence of any suggestions for a solution of this problem seems to us to be an outstanding omission that needs to be remedied in any revision of your report." [51]

The letter also suggests that, for the mitigation of unwarranted hardships, the problem be considered in relation to the new classification as a whole. The classification calls for capitalization of overheads and other expenses which many utilities have in the past charged to operat-

---

[49] As to the usefulness of so doing, the author points out at p. 124: " Depreciation accounting is one of those habits which is not really beneficial unless acquired in early youth. The time element is vitally important in regard to every aspect of the depreciation question. A scheme which would be manifestly desirable if adopted in the early stage of an enterprise, is of doubtful value when the enterprise has reached maturity, so that in terms of property units, replacements substantially equal exhaustion; and the doubt is greater if in the interval there has been a decline in the value of the monetary unit."

[50] P. 139.

[51] Letter on behalf of the Committee on Accounting Procedure of the American Institute of Accountants, dated January 28, 1944, and signed by Mr. Walter A. Staub as chairman, published in (1944) 77 J. ACCOUNTANCY 254. 258. For the official summary of the 1943 report of the NARUC Committee on Depreciation, see (1943) 76 J. ACCOUNTANCY 533.

ing expenses.[52] " There is no principle of accounting or of justice which would call for or permit retroactive adjustment of the treatment of depreciation without permitting the retroactive adjustment of other parts of capital asset accounting to conform to the new classification." [53]

The utility associations are, of course, very clearly aware of the problem.[54] It is evident that that part of American industry which comprises the steam railroads and most utilities other than telephone companies is presently confronted with a serious issue. It is one that may eventually have to be taken to the courts, where it can probably be settled only by a decision or a line of decisions [55] by the Supreme Court of the United States, except in so far as state courts may decide against administrative power to impose depreciation accounting, prospectively or retrospectively, as a matter of construction of state statutes.[56] Although the final solution may have to be at law, it seems the part of pessimism to believe or to assume that there is not enough statesmanship in our widespread system of regulatory commissions and among utility managements and their accountants, economists and lawyers to find means to compose the matter without invoking the authority of final court decisions. Certainly, the legal profession has no special competency to find the reasonable and equitable solution, and this is true also of the judges, even with the aid of our adversary system. An intransigent attitude on the part of either the administrative group [57] or the corporation group will serve only to increase the distrust which seems unfortunately to have recurred in recent years. Despite the charge that leaders of the accounting profession cannot be independent and impartial,[58] the accountants are probably able to contribute more to an equitable solution than any others. They are clearly best able to analyze the factors upon which the

---

[52] It is probable that, despite Treasury scrutiny and so-called uniform systems of accounts, operating expenses have also been charged in the past with substantial sums for betterments that now would be capitalized. Mr. May concludes that if revision is to be made, it should be complete *and bilateral* (pp. 116–17).

[53] For a suggestion for an equitable method of dealing with the retroactive issue, see Packman, *A Suggested Solution of the Depreciation Problem* (1944) 33 P.U. Fort. 737.

[54] See the Memorandum on behalf of the American Gas Association, *supra* note 43. The Memorandum quotes extensively from Mr. May's present book. In the meantime, accountants' certificates to utility statements follow the pattern: " In our opinion, subject to the adequacy of the provisions shown for depreciation, said financial statements present fairly. . . ." (1944 Report of New England Power Association).

[55] It is entirely possible the court may treat the legal problem as one dependent on the facts in each case, and so open up a wide range of litigation. *Cf.* the issue as to write-off of balances in Account 100.5, referred to below.

[56] Even so, there will be the difficulty of the over-lying or over-lapping jurisdiction of the federal commissions.

[57] The word " misrepresentation " is regrettable as it appears in some correspondence with the chairman of the New York Commission, in Editorials in (1944) 78 J. ACCOUNTANCY 5, 182.

[58] One regrets that Mr. Kripke felt called upon to imply this charge in his review of Mr. May's book. See Kripke, Book Review (1944) 53 YALE L. J. 825, 828–29. For an outstanding illustration of the independence of public accountants in dealing with their clients, see the excerpts from the 1943 report of the DuPont Company published in (1944) 77 J. ACCOUNTANCY 333.

solution depends. Mr. May's concept that financial accounting is not the product of a rigid mould and is purposeful should go far to indicate that each side can give and take where as here it seems that transition to a new policy is decreed. In such a case, the adoption of an *ex post facto* attitude should be tempered by recognition of the pains of the process.[59]

Accounting of industrials in this respect has for the most part been free thus far from public regulation. A disclosure of the depreciation policies followed is required in registration statements filed with the SEC. Possibly lurking in § 13 (b) of the 1934 Act,[60] there may be power as yet unexercised to reach companies under the Act in this respect. " The Commission may prescribe . . . the methods to be followed in the preparation of reports, in the appraisal or valuation of assets and liabilities, in the determination of depreciation and depletion. . . ."[61]

"Methods to be followed," as applied to appraisal or valuation of assets or determination of depreciation, is language that arguably goes beyond form and disclosure of what has been done; it may include power to say what shall be done and when. However, if Mr. May is right in believing that most important industrials have long used depreciation accounting (on a straight-line or modified straight-line basis), the risk of compulsory major changes in the accounts is not great.[62]

---

[59] Mr. May briefly touches upon an analogous problem at p. 248, relating to the present frequency of adoption of retirement pension schemes which confer benefits in respect of past services. Is the cost of launching the plan, so far as measured by past services, a proper charge to the present (as an expense to income) or to the past (surplus) ? The issue, in a rather specialized form, arose in New England Tel. & Tel. Co. v. United States, 53 F. Supp. 400 (D. Mass. 1943). It may be thought that the court, restricted by the narrow scope of review of administrative accounting orders, rather reluctantly allowed the element of past cost involved to fall in the accounts upon shareholders rather than consumers; it left open in no uncertain terms the incidence of the burden in any future rate proceeding. But at least the court was aware of the difference dependent upon the account charged, as the court in Pacific Power & Light Co. v. FPC, 141 F.(2d) 602, 605–06 (C. C. A. 9th, 1944) seems not to have been. Mr. Kripke clearly recognizes the significance of the difference, and indicates that counsel for the Commission took a position that misled the circuit court of appeals. See Kripke, *op. cit. supra* note 20, 447–48.

[60] Relating to periodical and other reports.

[61] If the registrant's methods of accounting are prescribed under any law of the United States, the rules and regulations of the SEC with respect to reports shall not be inconsistent with the requirements so imposed in respect of the same subject-matter, with a further qualification as to interstate carriers. See also § 15 (d), relating to filing of § 13 reports by issuers under the 1933 Act, not otherwise subject to the 1934 Act.

[62] Industrials commonly report depreciation reserves in relatively high ratio to plant accounts. General Electric Company, over the period 1937–1942 incl., reported reserves ranging between 75 and 80% of property, plant and equipment account. See MOODY'S MANUAL OF INVESTMENTS: INDUSTRIAL SECURITIES (1944) 2530. For 1937–1943 inclusive, Westinghouse reported a range of 46–51% (*id*. at p. 1270) ; Chrysler Corp., 40–49% (*id*. at p. 2739) ; American Chain & Cable Co., 52–58% (*id*. at p. 2190) ; American Chicle Co., 50–66% (*id*. at p. 2192) ; Crane Co., 39–45% (*id*. at p. 2372) ; Scott Paper Co., 36–46% (*id*. at p. 2174). It is not suggested that the figures are necessarily on a comparable basis; the methods followed are divergent. In later years, " certificate of necessity " amortization may draw the ratio upwards.

Another problem of special interest to utilities is discussed in Chapter IX under the caption " Writing-off Intangibles." [63] The introduction of a new concept of " original cost " in prescribed utility accounting systems in the past decade has required plant in service to be restated at the cost to the owner who first devoted it to public service. The spread between such original cost and the cost to the accounting corporation is to be recorded in a separate plant acquisition account. Mr. Kripke has previously explained the accounts and their background.[64] So far the sum of the accounts would reflect cost to the accounting corporation. But questions arise: (a) is all or some part of the amount in Account 100.5 subject to depreciation expense charges as part of the cost of tangible property, or is it wholly an account for intangibles not subject to ordinary depreciation; (b) if an intangible, may it remain permanently on the books or must it be written-off or amortized; (c) if to be written-off or amortized, at what time or over what period, and by charges against expense, income or earned or capital surplus? [65]

The Federal Power Commission seems broadly to regard the entire amount in the account as intangibles and, in purported reliance on accounting principles, to require it to be amortized over five or ten years by charges to income (*i.e.* to shareholders).[66] Mr. May is severely critical of the position that accounting principles require such a write-off or amortization, and of the Commission's use of accountants' statements as supposed support therefor, turning permissive action into mandatory action.[67] He rightly senses the court strategy of the administrative

---

[63] P. 153.

[64] Kripke, *op. cit. supra* note 20. The latter account of the Federal Power Commission is 100.5. We are not here concerned with company or system write-ups for which another account (107) is provided and which Mr. Kripke also discusses. There has been much writing on the subject. For others from the administrative staff point of view, see Morehouse, *Innovations in Public Utility Accounting Regulation* (1937) 46 YALE L. J. 955; CAHAN, ORIGINAL COST FOR UTILITY ACCOUNTING (1939).

[65] Substantial amounts may be involved. In Pacific Power & Light Co. v. FPC, *supra* note 59, the amount was $2,700,000 (required to be amortized over 10 years by charges to an income deduction account rather than to an expense account); in Florida Power & Light Co., SEC Holding Co. Release No. 4791 (Dec. 30, 1943), the amount was about $10,500,000 (required, pending final determination of the amount and the disposition to be made thereof, to be off-set by a contingency reserve created by appropriations out of earned surplus of at least $700,000 annually). The proceedings otherwise left the company no earned surplus, so this is equivalent to imposing a charge on shareholders' interest in future earnings to dispose of account 100.5. The order in the *Florida* case was appealed by the parent shareholder in American Power & Light Co. v. SEC, 143 F.(2d) 250 (C. C. A. 1st, 1944), where the petition to review was dismissed on grounds not relevant here, which action was reversed by the Supreme Court, 13 U. S. L. WEEK 4469 (June 4, 1945); and was appealed by Florida to the Fifth Circuit Court of Appeals, where it is pending.

[66] The SEC took the same position in the *Florida* case. This of course reaches deeply into the interesting question raised by the stipulation filed by the Government and accepted by the Court in American Tel. & Tel. Co. v. United States, 299 U. S. 232 (1936), involving similar accounts of the Federal Communications Commission. The latter accounts are involved in the *New York Tel. Co.* case (*supra* note 20).

[67] At p. 35 and elsewhere, Mr. May discusses the new concept of original cost. See also c. VI. Emphatically, it is not Mr. Justice Brandeis' prudent investment, however much some proponents may seek to foster that idea. See also p. 160. It

agencies: " If the procedure is challenged in the early stages the defense is that only methods of recording and no substantive rights are involved. But once the record is established it is made the basis of orders which affect rights but are in practice almost irreversible. In the *Telephone* case, the Supreme Court insisted on a stipulation designed to protect the utility from the practical effects of what was claimed and held to be only an order for classification of accounts. Later events have created doubts as to the effectiveness of such protection." [68] Many believe that the long-run strategy includes such elimination of part of the cost to the owning corporation, retroactive setting up of depreciation reserves on the basis of " original " cost, and persuasion of the courts to adopt such cost less such depreciation reserve as the rate base.

Chapters X and XI deal with inventories and commitments, accounts receivable and liabilities, and Chapter XII with income. The discussion is more confined to the special area of accounting than the preceding chapters. However, the problems of inventory valuation (closely related to the issue of unrealized appreciation), of the recognition of purchase commitments (especially those which have moved adversely to the buyer) and of accounting under long-term contracts and for accounts receivable (including installment sales, discounts and allowances for bad debts) have recurring interest for lawyers. They enter into the determination of income for a given period, which may be a source for dividends, and they relate to the accuracy of the income statement and the sufficiency of disclosures in connection therewith. The author wisely kept the text within small compass; the issues are more fully discussed in more general books on accounting,[69] and the purpose of the present book could not have been served by extended treatment of these subjects. Something of the same sort can be said about liabilities, but lawyers will find

---

may be a fair statement that Mr. May's mind is still not settled on the choice between enterprise accounting and corporation-now-owner accounting (or whether a free and clear cut choice is open), or on the definition of enterprise accounting (pp. 31–36). He has nothing but praise for the action of the Interstate Commerce Commission in the *Chicago Great Western R.R.* case, *supra* note 31, where the enterprise concept was applied to accounting of a reorganized railroad (pp. 113–14). But it is likely that he would reject the concept as applied to the distinctly new-ownership situations in the *Pacific Power & Light Co.* and *Florida* cases as to amounts in account 100.5. The *New York Tel. Co.* case lies between, ownership having passed between affiliates at prices not shown by the evidence to be excessive at the dates of the transactions, the Company's affirmative evidence tending to show them to have been fair and reasonable.

[68] P. 258. The scope of judicial review is very narrow even at the point where rights seem to be affected: Northwestern Electric Co. v. FPC, 321 U. S. 119 (1944); Pacific Power & Light Co. v. FPC, 141 F.(2d) 602 (C. C. A. 9th, 1944); New England Tel. & Tel. Co. v. United States, 53 F. Supp. 400 (D. Mass. 1943). Injection into the record of a little supporting accounting testimony (even if only from the Commission's own staff) seems sufficient at the present time to support the order, whether or not it is in accordance with good, prevailing or more widely accepted accounting. And the courts may not always distinguish accurately between the staff's views of accounting and of policy. See May. *Accounting in the Light of Recent Supreme Court Decisions* (1944) 77 J. ACCOUNTANCY 371.

[69] E.g., PATON, ADVANCED ACCOUNTING (1941), although Mr. May might dissent from some of the views of Paton.

more direct interest in the discussion of the tax and other effect of providing more or less permanent funds through interest-bearing securities as against shares; of the proper accounting treatment of debt discount, refunding by prosperous corporations,[70] and cheap own-debt purchases by non-prosperous corporations. The last of these operations appears to produce a gain, but it is a strange result that one's losses, which reduced the market for the security and opened the way to a cheap purchase, should produce gains.[71]

Capital, surplus and undivided profits are considered in Chapter XI, chiefly because these accounts appear on the liabilities side of the balance sheet as balances (sometimes in red) to be accounted for by the corporation. The author rightly says that legal capital as a substantial safeguard to creditors has in many states become little more than a legal fiction. Still it is recognized that legal theory and statutes maintain the concept of legal capital as of major significance, and therefore accountants are hampered in finding new and appropriate designations for the classifications into which the shareholders' interest falls. The matter is still under consideration by the Institute.[72] The subject of income is in many ways related, since the discussion is from the viewpoint of the recipient of the distribution and the importance to him of designation of its source and true nature.[73] The question of great present interest of the proper treatment of interest later received on bonds in default when acquired, and of dividends against arrearages on preferred when acquired, is discussed, with special reference to the tax problems.[74]

Chapters XIII and XIV deal with forms of statements and regulation of accounting. Mr. May warns against optimistic expectations from uniformity of accounts, and in the first of these chapters outlines the areas of accounting in which he thinks progress along these lines can be

---

[70] See, as to refunding, AMERICAN INSTITUTE OF ACCOUNTANTS, COMMITTEE ON ACCOUNTING PROCEDURE, ACCOUNTING RESEARCH BULLETIN No. 2 (Sept. 1939) and No. 18 (Dec. 1942). At p. 199, Mr. May points out that tax-savings should be taken into account in the event of a charge of the unamortized discount on called bonds to surplus. This is also true in the case of other direct charges to surplus which for tax purposes affect income, *e.g.*, when a pension plan is launched that includes past services (p. 248).

[71] See pp. 200–203.

[72] See the preliminary statement in AMERICAN INSTITUTE OF ACCOUNTANTS, COMMITTEE ON ACCOUNTING PROCEDURE, ACCOUNTING RESEARCH BULLETIN No. 12 (Sept. 1941), and the report of a sub-committee in (1942) 73 J. ACCOUNTANCY 451. One would have liked to have had Mr. May's view whether American statutes should adopt the English procedure to control capital reduction. For his views of the 1927–1929 amendments to the Delaware statute, see 1 MAY, TWENTY-FIVE YEARS OF ACCOUNTING RESPONSIBILITY (1936) 68, 2 *id.* at 331–32, 383.

[73] Our dividend statutes and practices being what they are. See also pp. 208–10 as to accounting for share dividends. For a recent further announcement on this subject by the New York Stock Exchange, see (1943) 76 J. ACCOUNTANCY 455; AMERICAN INSTITUTE OF ACCOUNTANTS, COMMITTEE ON ACCOUNTING PROCEDURE, ACCOUNTING RESEARCH BULLETIN No. 11 (Sept. 1941).

[74] Pp. 220–23. At p. 226, the subject of management compensation is brought in somewhat parenthetically, with emphasis on the personal tax aspects of special schemes of compensation, including pensions and share options, and on the corporate accounting.

made and in which he believes the goal is not obtainable or if thought
to be in hand would be illusory. But the outstanding feature of these
closing chapters (equally true of the opening ones) [75] is his forceful opposition to attempts by regulatory officials and staffs to drive accounting
into erroneous or as yet unaccepted or untried rules or paths, to introduce a rigidity which may become frozen beyond submission to new and
more enlightened thought and to changed conditions, to effect debatable
policy under the guise of accounting principles, and to destroy true
independence of accountants as professional men. The text carries
numerous illustrations of rulings and orders which Mr. May deems subject to one or more of these objections, and he feels strongly on the
subject.

One such instance is SEC Accounting Release No. 45 (June 21, 1943)
dealing with premiums paid on the redemption (or purchase) of preferred shares.[76] The theory is, in effect, that any sum paid to effect
the redemption in excess of the amount paid in on the shares redeemed [77]
must be charged to earned surplus, and no part of it may be charged to
a capital surplus paid in or created in respect of the contributions on
other shares of the same or another class to remain outstanding. Thus,
common shareholders who may contribute a paid-in surplus at the launching of a new enterprise, partly financed by high-dividend callable preferred, can later, when earning power has been developed, escape the
burdensome contract with the preferred by retiring or refunding it only
at the expense of a charge to earned surplus to the extent of the premium
component of the call price; this, even though, under state law, earned
surplus may be the only source of dividends for common. Whatever the
merits of the institution of paid-in surplus, so long as it is permitted
there must be some permissible uses for it in addition to investment in
plant or working capital. One such use frequently sponsored for paid-in
surplus on common is to avoid or keep down arrearages on cumulative
preferred in the early days of the corporation. If so, is it not equally
reasonable to regard paid-in surplus on common as a contribution that
may properly be used to buy the corporation out of a burdensome preferred contract through providing the necessary premium, and at the
same time preserving such earned surplus as there may be? If it be
thought that later statements would be deficient in reporting only the
balance of the contribution of economic capital by the common, it seems
relatively simple to make disclosure of its partial use in such manner
as not to be misleading. Or, as Mr. May points out, preferred may be
retired by an issue of common made for the purpose, at a premium equal
to or exceeding the call premium; " there would seem to be no reason

---

[75] See particularly c. IV.

[76] The release is printed in (1943) 76 J. ACCOUNTANCY 182.

[77] On the particular shares rather than the class, although averaging may be
permissible. The excess dealt with and deemed the premium is not the excess over
legal capital but over the economic capital paid-in or contributed.

to require the latter to be charged against earned surplus at any time." [78] He believes that accountants would favor a presumption, applicable in many situations, in favor of a charge being made to earned surplus, but he objects, and it seems rightly, to an accounting regulation that is rigid and seems to fail to recognize the impact of the facts of the case or the implications of what the parties had done and might expect.

To lawyers there may also seem to be too much rigidity in accounting releases by the SEC relating to accounting or quasi-reorganizations. [79] These releases seem to recognize no exceptions to the rule that the burden of all write-downs or downward adjustments in assets (or increases of reserves) must fall first on earned surplus to the point of extinction. The reversal of a write-up very likely ought to permit an exception. Paid-in surplus may have been initially created in the light of uncertainties about recorded figures for newly acquired assets and designed as the means of making later adjustments in the figures. SEC Accounting Release No. 10 (December 23, 1938) is another rigid ruling; even as a rule for general application subject to appropriate exceptions, there does not seem to be much to be said for it. [80]

Mr. May's objections to sweeping administrative regulation of accounting and especially to the resort to " accounting " to carry out policy have been well summarized and explained elsewhere. [81] On the other hand, they have been strongly and perhaps somewhat intemperately attacked. [82] One's own feeling is toward a strong sympathy with them, perhaps not strong enough to amount to a conviction, formulated perhaps by a dislike for the establishment of an ethic too rapidly and too much under the cover of a staff anonymity and for any form of *ex post facto* ethic untrammelled by responsibility for the hardships and problems of transition. This is especially so in the light of the narrow scope of judicial review, to which resort becomes necessary where the processes of consultation and equitable accommodation prove unavailing.

Lawyers have had the benefit and some will say the profit of the processes of the common law by which generalities arise out of cases decided one by one, and move slowly toward change as new conditions and thought produce new and modified decisions. The over-lay of statutes is not heavy. Lawyers may therefore have sympathy with an affiliated profession that asks somewhat of the same opportunity. Even if the profession operates, from the very nature of its function, in a more *ex parte* way, the difference does not seem sufficient clearly to justify denial of the opportunity. [83]

RALPH J. BAKER.*

---

[78] P. 213.

[79] See note 28 *supra*.

[80] See (1939) 67 J. ACCOUNTANCY 179.

[81] Sanders, *Government by " Accounting Principles "* (1944) 22 HARV. BUS. REV. 265.

[82] Kripke, Book Review (1944) 53 YALE L. J. 825.

[83] However, one is puzzled by a case such as appears in MOODY'S MANUAL OF INVESTMENTS: INDUSTRIAL SECURITIES (1938) 2955. In 1935, a New Jersey corpo-

(1)   What was the reason(s) cited by May   necessitating the use of
        conventions in accounting?

(2)   Whilst accepting the importance and usefulness of the valuation
        approach (as opposed to the cost approach) in accounting, May
        asserted that the valuation approach was impractical when business
        units become larger and more complex.
           - What was the basis to support this argument?

(3)   "Fixed assets by definition consist of property which is intended
        to be used and perhaps ultimately consumed in connection with
        business, and is not ordinarily offered for sale. Clearly there
        is no exchange value for such property in the sense in which the
        economist use that term, since no market for the property exists".
        (pg.88)
           - Consider the logic in the above quotation.
           (Does the second statement follow from the first?).

(4)   "It is undeniable - that books ... kept predominantly on a cost
        basis ... do not ... constitute evidence of either the enterprise
        as a whole or the separate assets thereof. This might be deemed
        a serious defect of accounting procedures but for two considerat-
        ions", (Pg.98)
           - What are the considerations May refers to?
           - How justified are these considerations?
           - How do these considerations fair in light of a statement in
             his memoirs (Pg.67) that "The only practical way in which an
             investor can today give expression to his conclusions in
             regard to the arrangement of the corporation in which he
             is interested is by retaining, increasing or disposing of
             his investment, and accounts are mainly valuable to him in
             so far as they afford guidance in determining which of these
             courses he shall pursue"?

(5)   What evidence is apparent in May's work of his concern for the
        usefulness of accounting information for decision purposes?
        Does May point to any use of depreciative historic cost account-
        ing information in financial decision making? Under what circum-
        stances might such information prove useful to decision makers?

111

■■

WILLIAM JOSEPH VATTER

The Fund Theory of Accounting

Biographical Chronology

1905	Born, 6 January, Cincinatti, son of John and Elizabeth (Rensenbrink) Vatter
1921-24	Student at the University of Cincinatti
1930	Married Rose H Schumacher, 2 August
1934	Awarded a BS, Miami University
1934-36	Instructor in Business, Miami University
1936	Appointed Research Assistant, University of Chicago; Became a CPA (Ohio); Consultant, US General Accounting Office.
1942-44	Director of Finance, Metal Laboratory, Manhattan Project
1947-57	Appointed Professor of Accounting and Production Control, University of Chicago. The Fund Theory of Accounting, published
1949	Consultant, Bureau of Naval Personnel
1955	Fullbright Professor of Accounting, University of Melbourne, Australia
1957-73	Appointed Professor of Accounting and Business Administration, University of California, Berkeley
1964	Fullbright assignemnt in Australia and New Zealand Survey of Accountancy Education in Australia, published
1966	Ford Foundation Visiting Professor, University of Chicago
1969-70	Vice-President, American Accounting Association (past chairman, committee on concepts and standards)
1971	Consultant, US General Accounting Office
1972	Emeritus Professor of Accounting, University of California, Berkeley.

Selected Bibliography

1937   "Depreciation Methods of American Industrial Corporations,"
        1927-35", Journal of Business of the University of
        Chicago, April, pp 126-46.

1945   "Limitations of Overhead Allocation", Accounting Review,
        v.20, April, pp 163-76.

        "Accounting Measurement of Incremental Cost," Journal of
        Business of the University of Chicago, v.18, July,
        pp 145-56; reproduced in Solomons, D (ed) Studies in
        Costing, 1952.

1946   "Cost in Economic Theory," Accounting Review, v.21, Jan,
        pp 90-92.

        "The Direct Method for the Preparation of Fund Statements,"
        Journal of Accountancy, v.81, June, pp 479-89;
        correspondence, v.82, Sept, pp 256-57.

1947   The Fund Theory of Accounting and Its Implications for
        Financial Reports, The University of Chicago Press;
        also Journal of Business of the University of Chicago,
        July, Suppl, v.17.

1950   "Accounting Education for Controllership," Accounting Review,
        v.25, July, pp 236-50.

1951   "Management Planning for Corporate Taxes," Controllership
        Foundation Inc (46 p. + app.).

        "Managerial Accounting," Proceedings, Ohio State Univ.
        Institution Accounting, pp 21-33.

1952   "The Control Function of the Accountant as an Indispendable
        Part of Management," Journal of Accountancy, v.93,
        June, pp 705-10.

1953   "Fund Flows and Fund Statement," Journal of Business,
        v.26, Jan, pp 15-25.

1954   "Tailor-making Cost Data for Specific Uses," N.A.C.A.
        Bulletin, v.35, Aug, sect.3, pp 1691-1707.

1955   "Accounting for Management," Australian Accountant,
        v.25, Nov, pp 461-73.

        "Controllership Stock Equities," in Backer Morton (ed)
        Handbook of Modern Accounting Theory, pp 361-423.

1958   "Contributions of Accounting to Measurement in Management,"
        Management Science, v.5, Oct., pp 27-37.

1959   "Does the Rate of Return Measure Business Efficiency?",
        N.A.A. Bulletin, v.40, Jan, sect.1, pp 33-48.

1960   "Misconceptions about Depreciation," <u>Hospital Accounting</u>,
v.14, Feb, pp 12-16.

"Capital Budget Formulae," <u>California Management Review</u>,
v.3, Fall, pp 52-68.

1961   "Accounting & Statistics," <u>Accounting Review</u>, v.36, Oct,
pp 589-97.

"Toward a Generalised Break-even Formula," <u>N.A.A. Bulletin</u>
v.43, Dec, Sect.1, p 5-10.

1962   "Another Look at the 1957 Statement," <u>Accounting Review</u>,
v.37, Oct, pp 660-69.

"Education for the Management Accountant," <u>N.A.A. Bulletin</u>,
v.44, Oct, Sect.1, pp 19-25.

"Fund-theory View of Price-Level Adjustments," <u>Accounting
Review</u>, v.37, April, pp 189-207.

1963   "Operating Confusion in Accounting - Two Reports or One?",
<u>Journal of Business</u>, v.36, July, pp 290-301.

"Postulates & Principles," <u>Journal of Accounting Research</u>,
v.1, Autumn, pp 179-97; also in <u>Journal of Accountancy</u>,
v.118, July 1964, pp 59-64.

$$"i = 22$$
$$\sum_{i = 1} (M_3)i \quad \text{An Evaluation}", \underline{\text{Accounting Review}},$$
$$\text{v.38, July, pp 470-77.}$$

1964   "The Accountant's Role in Business, 1975", <u>Australian
Accountant</u>, v.34, July, pp 353-8.

"Automobile Leasing and the Income Concept," <u>N.A.A.
Bulletin</u>, v.46, Oct, Sect.1, pp 23-9.

"Cost of Capital," <u>California Management Review</u>, v.6,
Sept 1, pp 19-30.

"Survey of Accounting Education in Australia - a Report,"
<u>Chartered Accountant in Australia</u>, v.35, Aug, pp I-XXXII;
<u>Australian Accountant</u>, v.34, Aug, pp 429-60; also
published separately (119 p).

1966   "Accounting for Leases," <u>Journal of Accounting Research</u>,
v.4, Autumn, pp 133-48.

"Income Models, Book Yield and the Rate of Return,"
<u>Accounting Review</u>, v.41, Oct, pp 687-98.

"Obstacles to the Specification of Accounting Principles,"
in <u>Research in Accounting Measurement</u>, AAA, pp 71-87.

"Critical Synthesis Conference Papers," <u>Empirical Research
in Accounting: Selected Studies</u>, pp 228-33.

"Corporate Stock Equities," in Backer, Morton (ed)
<u>Modern Accounting Theory</u>, pp 250-300.

1967	"Use of Operations Research in American Companies," Accounting Review, v.42, Oct, pp 721-30.
1969	Operating Budgets, Wadsworth Pub.Co. (Belmont, California) (162 p).
	"Progress in Pursuit of Principles," International Journal of Accounting Education & Research, v.5, Fall, pp 1-15.
	"Standards for Cost Analysis," Report to Comptroller General of the U.S., University of California, Berkeley (73 p).
1970	"Long-Term Liabilities," Chap. 22 of Davidson, S (Ed) Handbook of Modern Accounting, McGraw-Hill.
1971	Accounting Measurements in Financial Reports, Irwin (Illinois)(396 p)
	"Current Issues About Current Costs," in Sterling, R.R. (ed) Asset Valuation and Income Determination, pp 114-30.
	"Research in Accounting - 1970," Accounting Review, v.46, Jan, pp 184-206.
1972	"Percontatio Disciplinaque Inter Se Hortantur Conjuncte Crescendae Sunt," Proceedings, Third International Conference on Accounting Education, AAUTA, pp 1-15.
	"State of the Art (Books)," Abacus, v.8, June, pp 76-90.
1979	"State of the Art - Non-business Accounting," Accounting Review, v.54, July, pp 574-84.

REFERENCES

Book Review: Accounting Review, v.33, 1948, pp.440-41 (E C Moyer)

Goldberg, L, An Inquiry Into the Nature of Accounting, AAA, 1965, pp.146-51

Zeff, S A, A Critical Examination of the Orientation Postulate in Accounting, Arno Press, 1978, pp.173-76, 206-208

The published version of Vatter's doctoral dissertation,[1] which has generated surprisingly little comment in the literature, is an attempt to wed the English double-account form of the balance sheet with the ordinary funds statement. The results are not unlike those of the present-day accounting for institutions and governmental bodies.

The enterprise is divided into any number of "funds"

---

[1] William J. Vatter, The Fund Theory of Accounting and Its Implications for Financial Reports (Chicago: The University of Chicago Press, 1947); the author summarizes his "fund theory" in "Corporate Stock Equities--Part I," in Morton Backer (editor), Handbook of Modern Accounting Theory (New York: Prentice-Hall, Inc., 1955), pp. 367-70.

--the simplest division probably being the twofold breakdown into a "current fund" for current assets and current liabilities and a "capital fund" for fixed assets and all other right-hand items save retained earnings. Financial statements resembling a sectional balance sheet and typical funds statement are used to depict the status, and nature of changes in the residual equity, of each fund.

Each fund is devoid of personalistic attachments. A fund may relate to a particular purpose, activity, or situation. The assets and equities of each fund are viewed, respectively, as service potentials and restrictions thereagainst; in this respect governmental accounting is most closely approximated. The resulting financial statements may be rearranged, quite flexibly, to suit the specific purpose or purposes for which they are being used.[1]

Vatter's system includes no overt attempt at determining an "income." Indeed, the motive power behind Vatter's new mode of financial recapitulation is his dissatisfaction with both the "entity theory" and the "proprietary theory" (as well as with any single concept of "income," which will be discussed below):

> Neither the proprietary theory nor the entity theory is a wholly satisfying frame of reference for accounting. Each is vulnerable in that it adopts a personality as its focus of attention. The difference between them is mostly whether the person (for whom the books are kept and to whom the reports are made) is the 'proprietor' or proprietors in their

---

[1] For a concise summary of the anatomy of his fund accounts and the "theory," see Vatter, Fund Theory, pp. 94-95.

human selves, or whether real people must be viewed abstractly or in the guise of a fictional entity, corporate or otherwise. The weakness in these personalized bases for accounting is that the content of accounting reports will tend to be affected by personal analogies; and issues will be decided not by considering the nature of the problems but upon some extension of personality--to reach or to support conclusions that are for the most part mere expediencies. Dependence upon personality and personal implications in accounting theory, even as a convention, does not contribute to that objectivity toward which all quantitative analysis is aimed.[1]

He argues that "entity" data are no more "managerial" than are "proprietary" data--an obvious reference to Paton's "managerial point of view"--for "Management is concerned fully as much with what ought to be, or with what might have been, as it is with the actual events that occur."[2]

Furthermore, financial data that are oriented toward a personification inevitably fail to meet the needs of the major users of financial statements: management, social control agencies, and actual and prospective creditors and investors.[3] The solution, writes Vatter, is "to abandon entirely the notion of a 'general purpose' income statement and to force a reading of the entire financial report simply by abstaining from any reference or suggestion of an income computation in overt form."[4] The reader must therefore derive for himself a figure, or figures, that will suit his specific purposes. Gone is the general-purpose income figure which, according to Vatter, is practically valueless for application

---

[1]Ibid., p. 7. By his parenthetical phrase, does Vatter assume that the two parties are, of necessity, always the same?

[2]Ibid., p. 35.   [3]Ibid., pp. 8-9.   [4]Ibid., pp. 75-76.

to particular problems.

Vatter's Fund Theory contains a wealth of penetrating criticism of conventional concepts and conventional financial statements. But this writer must agree with Vatter's reviewer[1] who complains that the author presents many more questions than answers. And how many readers of financial statements will have the ability and patience to ferret out the figures that are most useful for them? For a large number of readers it might be more constructive to provide a general-purpose figure, such as income, which, although it may not be the optimal figure in most instances, will nonetheless act as a reference point from which they could estimate a more telling quantum. It is not consistent with the scope and object of the present study to evaluate at length the "fund theory" contribution.

Vatter's criticism of the general-purpose income is nonetheless meritorious, and will be reintroduced for further comment in Chapter VI.

---

[1] Eugene C. Moyer, Review of The Fund Theory of Accounting and Its Implications for Financial Reports, by William J. Vatter, The Accounting Review, XXIII, No. 4 (October, 1948), pp. 440-41.

Determination of the "Dominant" Beneficiary
in the Case of the Large Corporation

Probably the most influential cause of the multitude
of different conceptions of the orientation postulate is the
existence of diverse notions of the nature of business enterprise, particularly large corporations. The modern corporation has not become a static institution; it is constantly
changing and can today be found, as it were, in all shapes
and sizes. Inextricably related to this circumstance is the
question of who is the dominant personality for whom accounting reports should be prepared. Is there one dominant personality? If there is, should he be viewed as the only bene-
ficiary of accounting reports? Many decision-makers might
conceivably utilize some or all of the data in financial
statements: managers, common stockholders, preferred stockholders, bondholders, short-term creditors, prospective creditors and stockholders, employees, labor organizations, state
and federal regulatory agencies, courts of law and equity,
trade associations, legislatures, economic researchers, stock
exchanges, financial analysts, and taxing authorities, among
many others--and each group may have a multiplicity of purposes in using these data. Should one group be preferred over
the remainder? Yet can all interested parties be satisfied
by a single set of financial reports--such as those that are
contained in the typical annual report of a "listed" corporation? Inevitably, the questions raised in this paragraph
alone vitally affect each of the two orientation subpostulates.
Vatter would divide the enterprise into "funds." Suojanen
would view the enterprise in its societal context. Nammer
would envisage the enterprise as the locus of activities that
are directed toward the twin goals of survival and growth.[1]

One must agree with Vatter that the importance of
"income"--however it is calculated--has been seriously overstated. But there is no immediately available means of avoiding the selection of one or more indices of enterprise success.[2] Vatter's "fund" approach may be an acceptable answer,
but it will require--as would any major restructuring--a meth-
odical and purposeful initiation into, first, accounting lit-

---

[1]For a discussion of these writers' views, see Chapter
V, supra.

[2]For this writer's general recommendations to apply to
the longer term, see "Summary and Conclusions" in Chapter V,
supra.

119

erature, and, second, accounting reports. The "fund theory"
is still in incubation, although fourteen years have passed
since its birth. At the very least, it must be discussed,
developed, and adapted to specific business situations before
its usefulness can be fully appreciated. This study will
consequently be concerned with the need for a relatively
short-term, or temporary, solution. The term "income" being
imbedded in accounting literature and financial reports, its
use can hardly be avoided as a part of a near-term recommendation. Nevertheless, it should not be employed indiscrimi-
rately.

(The above has been reprinted from: Stephen A Zeff, A Critical
Examination of the Orientation Postulate in Accounting, 1961,
with permission of the author)

The Fund Theory of Accounting and its Implications for Financial Reports. William J. Vatter. (Chicago: The University of Chicago Press, 1947. Pp. v, 123. $1.50.)

As long as members of the accounting profession are able to view their efforts in a seriously critical vein, just as those outside the profession are bound to do, there are signs of progress in the field. Whether we agree with our own critics seems unimportant; what matters first is that the profession includes those with ability and inclination to analyze the accountant's role in society, match effort with expectation and point out shortcomings as the critic sees them.

Mr. Vatter's preface to the book refers to his efforts as a "little excursion into some untried and rather speculative areas of accounting thought" with an "attempt to set up a framework around which the ideas of accounting may have better and fuller expression and from which may develop a broader application of certain accounting techniques which now have but limited uses." Such comment introduces the reader into a series of criticisms leveled at present day financial statements.

The author devotes some space to an inquiry into the natures of proprietary and entity theories of accounting and concludes that neither theory solves the basic problems of accounting theory. This he attributes to the fact that both the proprietary and entity views are associated, intentionally or not, with a "person." Conventional financial statements, says Mr. Vatter, are viewed, unfortunately, as an expression of a person "to whom or for whom, or about whom, the accounting reports are made." Thus, he challenges whether accountants' statements provide all interested groups—the investor, the creditor, management, etc.—with useful data for answering questions peculiar to their individual interests. He thinks not. Partial support for this conclusion he finds in the "net income" figure of conventional financial reports. He points out the confusion among accountants who constantly are seeking agreement on definition of the term and the acknowledged fact that what may be designated as net income is not so all-important as some of us visualize. It is even suggested that the accountant should avoid stating net income as such. In addition, the author has some provocative thoughts on the concept of revenue. He develops two criteria for recognition of revenue: The existence of new service units (assets or service potentials) and the absence of restrictions (claims) against them.

It is suggested that what is needed for a more worthwhile evaluation of business events is a group of statements dealing with the units of activity of the business. Fund accounting statements are proposed, not necessarily to the exclusion of conventional financial statements but certainly as a necessary part of what accountants are trying to accomplish. Mr. Vatter thinks that the view of a fund as an accounting unit avoids what he considers the dangerous personal implications associated with modern statements; also the fund approach sidesteps other controversial questions concerning which accountants themselves disagree. It is admitted, however, the application of the fund theory in general practice may entail some differences—differences which he considers incidental. What seems important to the author is that the theory may be applied to situations other than government and institutions.

Mr. Vatter's treatise presents illustrations of fund statements applied to a manufacturing corporation. The areas of business activity (the author probably would say "fund activity") for which statements are illustrated are (1) Cash and Bank Funds, (2) General Operating Fund, (3) Investment Fund, (4) Sinking Fund and (5) Capital Fund. Other areas could be employed. Much is illustrated and more left unsaid for extensive discussion and disagreement. The first statement includes as assets "Cash on hand and in banks," against which is shown "Bank loans" as a specific equity and the balance is designated as "Residual equity." Perhaps few people will agree with a fund comprised as such, showing as it does only one specific restriction on cash. Or are bank loans necessarily a restriction on cash and nothing else? It is perhaps at this point that many who read this work will conclude that fund accounting applied in general practice uncovers new accounting pitfalls at least, if not more, dangerous than the ones from which we seek release with current practices.

The author leaves unsettled the questions arising in the reader's mind regarding classification for the different fund statements. And since the author proposes more statements, not less, will his thesis regarding fund accounting not multiply the many problems of account classification which we encounter today in fewer statements? He seems to open a wide field for this ever present problem. His book does not provide many answers in this direction.

Using Mr. Vatter's thought that statements prepared by accountants today do not adequately serve the peculiar needs of varying interests, it is appropriate to ask if fund statements will serve them better. Many readers will certainly agree with Mr. Vatter that statements of today are not always adequate for everybody. His objections to current practices in statement presentation generally are freely admitted. But if the fund theory is to be proposed as one solution, then it must answer these same objections. The writer offers some answers, not all. From a review of his fund statements one natural question would arise: To which of the statements (he presents five listed above) does the layman investor look as containing data of special service to him? This reviewer sees no one of them as filling this specified need. And there is challenge in the suggestion that the layman investor must use all the statements, or even two or more, put them side by side and extract from the assembled whole all that valuable information he seeks. There is doubt that such an investor exists. It seems, also, that educating the man in the street to the point where he can utilize such statements to advantage is a task surpassing by far that which accountants are now facing in respect to conventional statements.

So far as this reviewer is aware, Mr. Vatter's thesis is new and untried. It should not be judged by this alone, however, and then put aside with light consideration. It is a scholarly contribution that merits more practical attention. Further effort from Mr. Vatter in this matter should be welcomed by the profession as a whole. We must conclude, as does the author, that the work is an "excursion" into untried and speculative areas of accounting thought.

EUGENE C. MOYER

American University

(1) What is Vatter's view of theory construction? Is he consistent with it in developing his own analysis? Is the "fund theory" a "theory" or a practical manual?

(2) To what users of accounting data does Vatter direct his argument? (Has his approach influenced later writers?)

(3) What does Vatter mean by "the communication of ideas must have operational content" (p.14)?

(4) Vatter suggests in the Preface that he is venturing into some speculative areas of accounting thought. Are the definitions of assets and equities he develops/uses radically different from commonly discovered definitions?

(5) How does his concept of income differ from more conventional views?

(6) What is your opinion as to the format of the financial reports suggested by Vatter? Would they be more understandable than conventional reports?

(7) What reasons does Vatter provide for attempting to create a new theory of Accounting? How valid are his reasons today?

(8) The Fund Theory appears not to have had any considerable influence on later accounting theorists. What reasons can you (speculatively) suggest for this?

12

ANANIAS CHARLES LITTLETON

Structure of Accounting Theory

Biographical Chronology

1886	Born, Bloomington, Illinois, 4 December, the son of Robert and Mary (Sholtey) Littleton
1905	Graduated from Bloomington High School
1907	Matriculated at the University of Illinois
1912	Awarded an AB degree from the University of Illinois. Entered the public accountants firm of Deloitte, Plender, Griffiths and Co of Chicago.
1915	Joined the College of Commerce at the University of Illinois, serving as an instructor (1915-18), assistant Dean (1919-21), assistant professor (1920-1924), and professor from 1931 until his retirement in 1952. He was also assistant director of the Bureau of Economic and Business Research of the College of Commerce from 1921-1942
1916	Married Bonnie Ray, 21 August
1918	Awarded a master degree (AM) from the University of Illinois
1919	Certified as a CPA (Illinois)
1921	Drew up and offered the first graduate courses in accounting offered by the University of Illinois
1927	Began a two year term as National President of Beta Alpha Psi, founded by himself and Professor Scovill in 1919 at the University of Illinois
1931	PhD awarded (thesis used as basis for Accounting Evolution to 1900, 1933)
1934	Bestowed with the award of merit by Beta Alpha Psi for the most outstanding contribution to the literature of accounting for the year ended 1 May 1934. The work for which he earned the award was Accounting Evolution to 1900.
1936	Vice president of the American Accounting Association (AAA)
1938	Acting Director of Research, AAA; 1939-42, Co-Director
1939	Member of Committee on Accounting Procedure of the AICPA. Term lasted until 1941
1940	Director of Research of the AAA over the period 1940-42 Member of the Executive Committee of the AAA until 1947
1943	President of the AAA
1943	Began a four year term as Editor of The Accounting Review Member of the Selection of Personnel Committee of the AICPA (Term 1943-47)
1946	Member of the Accounting History Committee of the AICPA (Term 1946-47)
1952	Retired from the University of Illinois
1953	Structure of Accounting Theory published
1954	Received the Alpha Kappa Psi Foundation Accounting Award for significant contributions to accounting
1956	Elected to the Ohio State University's Accounting Hall of Fame
1967	Awarded the honorary Doctor of Laws degree from the University of Illinois
1974	Died 13 January

SELECTED BIBLIOGRAPHY

1920   "Adjusting Inventories," Systems (June), pp 1153-5.

1922   "Appraisal of the Balance Sheet Approach," Proceedings,
            American Association of University Instructors in
            Accounting (AAUIA), pp 85-92.

1923   "Discussion: Principles of Valuation as Related to the
            Function of the Balance Sheet," Papers and Proceedings.
            AAUIA, pp 14-5.

1924   "The Relation of Accounting to the Business Cycle,"
            Papers and Proceedings, AAUIA, pp 108-16.

1925   "The Development of Accounting Literature," Publications
            (Dec), pp 7-17.

1926   "The Evolution of the Ledger Account," Accounting Review,
            v.1 (Dec), pp 12-3.

            "Italian Double Entry in Early England," Accounting Review,
            v.1 (June), pp 60-71.

            "Research Work at the University of Illinois," Accounting
            Review, v.1 (Mar), pp 31-8.

            "2 to 1 Ratio Analysed," Certified Public Accountant
            (Aug), pp 244-6.

1927   "The Antecedents of Double-Entry," Accounting Review,
            v.2 (June), p.140.

            "Two Fables of Bookkeeping," Accounting Review, v.2
            (Dec), pp 388-96.

            "University Education for Accountancy," Certified Public
            Accountant, (Dec), pp 361-5.

1928   "Pacioli and Modern Accounting," Accounting Review, v.3
            (June), pp 131-40.

            "The Evolution of the Journal Entry," Accounting Review,
            v.3 (Dec), pp 383-96.

1929   "Value and Price in Accounting," Accounting Review,
            v.4 (Sept), pp 147-54.

1930   "Foreign Accounting Terms (German), Accounting Review,
            v.5, pp 262-3 (Sept), pp 320-2 (Dec), v.6 (1931),
            pp 645 (Mar), pp 147-9 (June).

1932   "Capital and Surplus," Accounting Review, v.7, pp 290-3.

1933   Accounting Evolution to 1900, American Institute
            Publishing Co, 368 p; reprinted, 1966, Artheneum Press;
            1981, University of Alabama Press.

            "Capital Flexibility," Journal of Accountancy, v.56 (Aug),
            pp 102-8.

"The Social Origins of Modern Accounting," <u>Journal of Accountancy</u>, v.56 (Oct) pp 261-70.

"Socialized Accounts," <u>Accounting Review</u>, v.8, pp 267-71; v.9 (1934), pp 69-74.

"Dividend Base," <u>Accounting Review</u>, v.9, pp 140-8.

"Dividends Presuppose Profits," <u>Accounting Review</u>, v.9, pp 305-11.

1935   "Auditor Independence," <u>Journal of Accountancy</u>, v.59, pp 283-91.

"Value of Cost," <u>Accounting Review</u>, v.10, pp 269-73.

1936   "Contrasting Theories of Profit," <u>Accounting Review</u>, v.11, pp 10-15.

"A Professional College," <u>Accounting Review</u>, v.11, pp 109-16.

1937   "Business Profits as a Legal Basis for Dividends," <u>Harvard Business Review</u>, Autumn, pp 51-61.

"Concepts of Income Underlying Accounting," <u>Accounting Review</u>, v.12, pp 13-22.

1938   "Tests for Principles," <u>Accounting Review</u>, v.13, pp 16-24.

"The Relation of Function to Principles," <u>Accounting Review</u>, v.13, pp 233-41.

"High Standards of Accounting," <u>Journal of Accountancy</u>, v.66 (Aug), pp 99-104.

1939   "Uses of Theory," <u>Accounting Review</u>, v.14, pp 227-33.

1940   "Integration of Income and Surplus Statements," <u>Journal of Accountancy</u>, v.69 (Jan), pp 30-40.

<u>An Introduction to Corporate Accounting Standards</u>, American Accounting Association (Monograph No.3), 156 p, (with W.A. Paton).

1941   "Genealogy of 'Cost of Market'", <u>Accounting Review</u>, v.16, pp 161-7.

"Questions on Accounting Standards," <u>Accounting Review</u>, v.16, pp 330-40.

"Inventory Variations," <u>Journal of Accountancy</u>, v.72 (July), pp 7-16.

1942   "Auditing Techniques," <u>Journal of Accountancy</u>, v.74 (Aug), pp 106-10.

"The Meaning of Accounting Education," <u>Accounting Review</u>, v.17, pp 215-21.

1943   "Examinations in Auditing," <u>Accounting Review</u>, v.18, pp 307-16.

1944 "Occupational Levels in Public Accounting," _Journal of Accounting_, v.78 (Dec), pp 470-6.

1946 "Guidance Tests for Accounting Students," _Accounting Review_, v.21, pp 404-9.

1947 "Three Audit Principles," _Journal of Accountancy_, v.83 (April), pp 280-2.

   "Fixed Assets and Accounting Theory," _Papers Presented at the Accounting Conference_, University of Illinois, pp 11-18.

1948 "Extension of Accrual Principles Would Help Depreciation Accounting," _Journal of Accounting_, v.86 (July), pp 21-2.

   "Inventory Disclosure," _New York CPA_, v.18 (Nov), pp 807-10.

1949 "Classified Objectives," _Accounting Review_, v.24, pp 281-4.

1950 "Inductive Reasoning in Accounting," _New York CPA_, v.20 (Aug), pp 449-55, 460; (Nov), pp 641-51.

   "Truth as an Objective," author, 16 p.

1952 "Characteristics of a Profession." _New York CPA_, v.22, (April), pp 207-11.

   "The Significance of Invested Cost," _Accounting Review_, v.27, pp 167-73.

1953 _Structure of Accounting Theory_, American Accounting Association, 234 p.

   "Variety in the Concept of Accounting," _New York CPA_, v.23 (July), pp 419-24.

1953 "Accounting Theory 1933-1953," _Accounting Forum_, v.24 (May), pp 11-15.

1954 "But is it Accounting?", _New York CPA_, v.24 (Nov), pp 688-92.

   Principles Under Challenge," _New York CPA_, v.24 (Jan), pp 24-8.

1955 "The Logic of Accounts," _Accounting Review_, v.30, pp 45-7.

   Prestige for Historical Cost," _Illinois CPA_, v.18, (March), pp 23-7.

1956 "Choice Among Alternatives," _Accounting Review_, v.31, pp 363-70.

   "Economists and Accountants," _Illinois CPA_, v.18, (Summer), pp 18-24.

"Evolution of the Journal Entry," in Studies in the History of Accounting, Richard Irwin, ed. Littleton, A.C. and B.S. Yamey, (392 p) pp 223-35.

1958   "The Search for Accounting Principles," New York CPA, v.28 (April), pp 247-56.

1961   Essays on Accountancy, University of Illinois Press, 637 p (a collection of extracts from the author's writing).

1962   Accounting Theory: Continuity and Change, Prentice Hall, 292 p (with V.K. Zimmerman).

1964   "Appraising the Knowns; Another Avenue for Accounting Theory Development," Illinois CPA , v.27 (Winter), pp 7-11.

1965   "The Continuing Importance of Basic Concepts," International Journal of Accounting Education and Research, v.1, pp 55-65.

1966   "The Significance of Interrelated Concepts in Accounting," International Journal of Accounting Education and Research, v.2, pp 25-34.

1970   "The Factors Limiting Accounting," Accounting Review, v.45, pp 476-80.

REFERENCES

Book Review of Essays:
        Accounting Review, v.37, 1962, p.381 (L J Buchan).

Bedford, N M & R E Ziegler, "The Contributions of A C Littleton to
    ·Accounting Thought & Practice", Accounting Review, v.50, 1975,
    pp.435-43.

Buckner, K C, "Profile: Ananias Charles Littleton", Accounting Historians
    Notebook, v.1 Spring 1978, pp.8,7.

_____ , Littleton's Contribution to the Theory of Accountancy,
    Research Monograph No.62, Georgia State University, 1975.

Chambers, R J, "Some Observations on Structure of Accounting Theory",
    v.31, 1956, pp.584-92.

_____ , "Details for a Blueprint", Accounting Review, v.32, 1957,
    pp.206-15.

Edwards, J D & R F Salmonson, Contributions of Four Accounting Pioneers
    (Digests), Michigan State University, 1961.

Farag, S M, "Littleton's Views on Social Accounting - An Elaboration",
    International Journal of Accounting Education & Research, v.2,
    1967, pp.123-32.

Ijiri, Y, "Review Article: An Introduction to Corporate Accounting
    Standards", Accounting Review, v.55, 1980, pp.620-8.

Vatter, W J, "Progress in Pursuit of Principles", International Journal
    of Accounting Education & Research, v.5, 1969, pp.1-15.

Zimmerman, V K, "The Long Shadow of a Scholar", International Journal of
    Accounting Education & Research, v.2, 1967, pp.1-20.

The Accounting Review

| VOL. L | JULY 1975 | No. 3 |

The Contributions of A. C. Littleton to Accounting Thought and Practice

Norton M. Bedford
and
Richard E. Ziegler

A. C. LITTLETON passed away on January 13, 1974, and the world of accounting lost one of the founders of its intellectual base. As a scholar and not a practitioner of the discipline to which he devoted his life, his presence on the University of Illinois campus for thirty-seven of his eighty-seven years assured students and colleagues alike that there was an intellectual underpinning to accounting practice. Ultimately, practitioners turned to theoretical studies for guidance, and his thinking—expressed in eight books, more than 100 articles, and numerous book reviews and published comments —did much to establish the view that accounting practice was to be guided by accounting principles and standards.[1]

In a historical perspective it seems reasonable to suggest that the impact of the efforts of Ananias Charles Littleton on accounting thought is particularly noteworthy because of the time period spanned by his work and because of the influence of his early academic thinking on subsequent organized accounting thought. His contributions in the area of accounting education, theory, and practice were continuous from the time he returned to the University of Illinois in 1915 to begin a teaching career until the mid-1960s, well past his retirement in 1952. An articulate and persuasive advocate of original cost-based accounting, his influence on the official pronouncements of the American Accounting Association endured for thirty years, and the thoughts expressed in his early writings even now are reflected in the official publications of the American Institute of Certified Public Accountants. Clearly, his views on accounting have influenced two

[1] For a factual description of Professor Littleton's life and his contributions, see V. K. Zimmerman, 1967, pp. 1–20.

Professor Bedford is the Arthur Young Professor and Head of the Department of Accountancy at the University of Illinois; Professor Ziegler is Assistant Professor of Accountancy at the University of Illinois.

generations of academicians and practitioners alike.

Several factors seem to have formed and shaped his thinking, but the particular environment of his early life and his intellectual interests seem to dominate. The son of a railroad worker, at the time of the industrial growth of the Midwest, in an area where livelihood centered around agriculture, he absorbed both the steadfastness and self-reliance of the farming community and the sense of progress accompanying the industrial growth. From that base, his intellectual interests developed. By the time he reached high school, he had become a voracious reader with a marked interest in English literature and composition. Perhaps it was this liking for reading and study that initially motivated his interest in attending college. In any even, by working in small Illinois towns as a railroad telegrapher, he accumulated funds for his education. This work experience apparently initially influenced him to study "railroad administration" when he entered the near-by University of Illinois. But when he returned to the University following his freshman year and after another period working with the railroad, his educational goal changed. A chance association with two students living in the same boarding house acquainted him with the relatively new Illinois CPA statute (1903) and the burgeoning public accounting profession in Chicago. He changed his program to the study of accounting, and employment in an accounting firm in Chicago followed his graduation in 1912. In later years his early experience in railroading was evident in effective analogies that permeated his speaking and writing.

It is difficult to determine why he entered academic life, but apparently it was the close personal relationship he developed with Hiram T. Scovill, who also worked for the Chicago accounting firm.

H. T. Scovill returned to the University of Illinois as a teacher and, when another instructor in elementary accounting was needed in 1915, A. C. Littleton was persuaded to fill this position. He found the experience challenging and started work towards a master's degree, which he received in 1918. Because teaching materials were sparse in those days, one of his first activities as a teacher was to write a text, *Introduction to Elementary Accounting*. It was published in 1919. In that same year, he also received an Illinois CPA certificate. He completed his formal education with a Ph.D. in Economics from the University of Illinois in 1931.

In 1933 Professor Littleton published what has become a classic in the field of accounting history, a prodigious volume entitled *Accounting Evolution to 1900*. Based on work done for his Ph.D. dissertation, this volume established his qualifications as a scholar of national reputation and formed the foundation for the wide acceptance of his writings. Also, the influence of this effort on his thinking is apparent in many of his subsequent writings. In Littleton's view accounting theory and accounting practice represented a single body of knowledge and were not separable. He firmly believed that practice reflected theory and that theory found its expression in practice. This is not to say that he believed all accounting practices were necessarily sound or that the theoretical justifications for particular accounting practices were necessarily valid. Rather, it was his discovery of anomalies in practice that could not be explained by any theoretical structure coupled with the existence of admittedly questionable practices supported by unsound justifications that spurred his search for the best practice and the best theoretical justification among many possible alternatives in accounting.

Littleton's greatest impact on the thinking of professional accounting bodies came in a period beginning in the late 1930s, the era to which the roots of much contemporary accounting practice may be traced. A review of the trend of developments prior to that time will help call attention to Littleton's influence in the 30s and 40s.

As early as 1917, pronouncements by the American Institute of Accountants, the predecessor organization to the present AICPA, and the Federal Reserve Board—prompted by the Federal Trade Commission—had tended to support increased uniformity of accounting practice. The passage of the sixteenth amendment in 1913, and succeeding revenue acts, particularly that of 1918, strengthened the cost-based notion of asset valuation. The widespread adoption of historical cost valuation and the point-of-sale realization rule, in fact, may have been caused more by the desire of businessmen to minimize taxes than to any developments in accounting theory. All of this Littleton, as a teacher, absorbed and taught to his students. By 1921, the point-of-sale realization rule was widely recognized as providing a conceptual justification for valuing current as well as fixed assets at cost. By the early 1930s, such foundations of present-day practice as the cost basis of accounting, the realization postulate, the doctrine of conservatism, and the necessity for consistency in accounting were well known. This too became a part of Littleton's thinking base, and many were the overconfident students who "marched in and crawled out" of his office as he calmly and relentlessly evaluated their attempts either to defend or to attack these somewhat imprecise guidelines for accounting practice. But the gap between the body of knowledge he had accepted and the accounting practice he observed was large. Companies listed on the stock exchanges continued to use a large variety of accounting and reporting methods, and departures from the cost basis of accounting

were frequent. To Littleton's impulse for order and harmony, this situation was intolerable and it called for a reconciliation or an explanation.

As a consequence of the disillusionment with the existence of uncontrollable valuation approaches to income determination in the post-1929 era, the view of measuring income by a matching of costs and revenues became the focus for the development of accounting thought. Littleton earlier had accepted this and contributed to its development. This change in the nature of the accounting income concept was further supported by the establishment of the Securities and Exchange Commission in 1933. The SEC sought objectivity in accounting measures and effectively served notice on the accounting profession that it must adopt or have imposed on it more systematic and comprehensive income-determination rules, and this development was compatible with the matching concept.

The Commission's requirement that the financial statements filed under the Act be accompanied by a certificate of an independent accountant gave the profession a great opportunity. To Littleton, this meant that accounting data would have to be based on objective evidence. In response to the SEC requirement, the American Institute developed the beginning of what now is known as the standard short-form audit report, a development that signaled the beginning of an extensive literature devoted to the matter of identifying "generally accepted principles of accounting" and to which Littleton responded.

At its meeting in December 1935, the American Accounting Association made a decision to participate in the development of accounting principles. According to Littleton this action was motivated, in part, by the decision of the American Institute to associate certification with generally accepted principles of accounting. The hope was that the AAA might be an effective force in improving reporting for the benefit of both the business community and the public at large. In 1936 the executive committee of the AAA, whose membership included A. C. Littleton and William A. Paton, produced the well-known report, "A Tentative Statement of Accounting Principles Underlying Corporate Financial Statements," and Littleton presented a report on this to the Association at its meeting in 1936. Up until that time, accounting procedures had been based primarily on specific rules and recommendations, and the 1936 Statement was significant because it was one of the first major attempts to develop a framework which might be regarded as representing a structure of the fundamental principles of accounting.

The 1936 Statement evoked a vociferous response in the accounting literature, but had little noticeable impact on the practice of public accounting. In common with businessmen, public accountants clung to the earlier view that financial statements were largely matters of individual owner, manager, or creditor concern, and since business was viewed as a private affair among these three groups, it seemed reasonable to conclude that principles might well vary according to the circumstances. To permit the disclosure of information relevant to various situations among these three groups, a permissible variety of accounting treatment was regarded as preferable to enforced compliance with universal and unalterable rules. The American Institute did encourage the efforts of individual firms to develop codifications of general purpose accounting principles. Littleton and others did write in practical terms attempting to explain the beneficial aspects of the 1936 Statement to accounting. In spite of the distinguished authorship of these attempts, they also had a negligible impact on efforts to establish an identifiable body of general purpose accounting standards. Since practice was already improving, some of the proposed desirable accounting standards were superceded before they were published with the result that their impact was unimportant.

A major step in the attempt to formulate accounting principles was taken by the American Institute in 1938. Its Committee on Accounting Procedures was reorganized and a research division was established with the charge of eventually formulating pronouncements on specific accounting procedures. The committee, which included A. C. Littleton, as well as William A. Paton and George O. May, soon issued three Accounting Research Bulletins dealing primarily with areas in which current practice had been subject to criticism. From this beginning, the committee adopted what came to be known as the "ad hoc" approach to the formulation of accounting principles—giving immediate help to accountants faced with special problems. In general, this Committee did not explain the relationship of its conclusions to any organized body of theory.

In contrast to the piecemeal approach being taken by the American Institute, the AAA continued working on the development of an overall framework of theory to support accounting practice. Undoubtedly this was due in part to the limited resources of the AAA but primarily it was due to the theoretical orientation of the majority of its members. It was under the auspices of the AAA that a most significant document, *Introduction to Corporate Accounting Standards*, was published in 1940. Authored by William A. Paton and A. C. Littleton, both of whom had served on the committee that had produced the 1936 Statement, this 1940 Monograph was intended to provide a framework of accounting theory underlying the 1936 Statement. At the time it represented, and in view of many still remains, the best available statement of ac-

132

counting theory applicable to the preparation of corporate financial statements in historic cost form. This result was somewhat surprising since it was a collaboration between men who began with very different premises.

Paton brought an economic point of view to the joint effort while Littleton provided an historical and philosophical background. To Paton cost was not important in its own right; rather it was important only as a measure of value of what was acquired. He would have preferred to restate acquisition cost for price changes before matching cost and revenue. Essentially, he thought the accounting measure of income should reflect the difference between the economic value of a business at the beginning and at the end of a period (allowance being made for investments and withdrawals), and he criticized accountants for taking it for granted that "cost" was always equivalent to "value."

To Littleton, income determination also was the heart of accounting, but he apparently was not as bothered as others by the absence of a close conceptual relationship between accounting practice and economic theoretical structures for the determination of income, as suggested by the following statement:

One of the keenest critics of accounting theory has said with much justification that "accountants have no complete philosophical system of thought about income." That statement is all too true. Accountants, like businessmen, are too deep in practical affairs to be philosophers. But that does not prevent accounting records from giving expression, piecemeal as it were, to definite concepts of profit and income (Littleton, 1937, p. 15).

Littleton recognized a dilemma between the wishes of the users of financial statements and what he considered to be the limitations of accounting. "The businessman, the banker, the investor, may have many occasions to 'evaluate' a property,

or prospect, or market, or stock of goods, but accounting never has" (Littleton, 1929, p. 153). To Littleton the primary function of accounting was a record-keeping and disclosure function, and secondarily, if at all, a valuation function. To him financial statements should aid users in evaluating one thing or another, but the financial statements were never really statements of values; because values were too momentary and too subjective to be clothed in figures. As a consequence, acquisition cost was important in its own right, as an expression of the investment in goods, but not as a surrogate for value. Littleton viewed profit as the end result of the efforts of management bent upon finding a profit out of acting as an intermediary between supply and demand. The accounting function was to serve primarily the supply, or cost, side. Its particular service lay, not in attempting to measure value, but rather in the individualistic function of recording capitalistic investments and advances, and of weighing these against the returns flowing from them under the influence of management.

Although these two scholars who produced the 1940 Monograph had differing conceptual notions of how the accounting measure of income should be approached, they did agree on the essential goal of accounting efforts:

The details of the process of measuring the rate of income are unsettled but there is no question as to the importance of this factor. Earning power—not cost price, not replacement price, not sale or liquidation price—is the significant basis of enterprise value. The income statement therefore is the most important accounting report (Paton and Littleton, 1940, p. 10).

Working together, the authors succeeded in developing theoretical support for contemporary, cost-based practice that was forward-looking and basic.

The authors shared compatible, although not identical, views concerning the methodology of accounting research. Paton was an advocate of the deductive, or postulational approach to determining accounting principles. To Littleton, there existed a mutual dependency between inductive and deductive approaches; if both approaches reached the same conclusion, "truth" was evident. Being primarily inductive, Littleton paved the way for the empirical approach to accounting knowledge. To him, there existed "fundamental truths" in accounting. These might be either generalized out of practical experience or deduced from stated premises which were accepted as truth in themselves. Accordingly, it was hoped that these "postulates" would not be subjected to refutation except perhaps as accounting evolved. Although the influence of the methodologies of both authors is apparent in the 1940 Monograph, the stronger impact appears to have been Paton's, for this was the first framework developed deductively rather than inductively derived from accounting practice. In the Monograph the concept of verifiable, objective evidence clearly reflects the thinking of Littleton. It provided a means whereby accuracy of the accounts could be tested by examination of the documentation supporting the original transactions. This emphasis upon objective evidence has never been weakened; in fact, it has become stronger as business activities have become more complex and as the separation of ownership and management has accelerated. Verifiable, objective evidence has become an important element in accounting and a recognized adjunct to the preparation of financial statements. It may well be that this postulate of "objectivity" had the greatest influence in gaining practical support for the substance of the 1940 Monograph.

The authors of the Monograph agreed that transaction price, or historic cost, should be the standard basis for measuring accounts on both sides of the balance sheet. The reasoning supporting this position was that carrying assets at acquisition cost would eliminate the heterogeneous results that had been found so often in corporate accounting. Past standards had been unduly lax in permitting periodic revaluation of resources, up or down, in accordance with changing prices and expected business developments. Similarly, liabilities, like assets, represented bargained prices, and the same was true of capital equity. These ideas represented a marked departure from the earlier thinking of Paton. Perhaps the issue of the cost amount to match against revenue was not as important to Paton in 1940 as it had been earlier because the price level problem was a dormant issue in the 1930s. Perhaps it was because of Paton's desire to formulate a theoretical underpinning for the 1936 Statement. For whatever reason, it was Littleton's conviction that accounting be cost-based that prevailed in the Monograph and gained for it the support of the practicing arm of the profession.

Overall, the impact of Littleton on accounting practice, through the vehicle of the 1940 monograph on corporate accounting standards, appears to include the following developments.

1. The wide recognition of assets as essentially deferred acquisition costs, as investments or effort applied to future objectives, rather than as measures of current values.
2. The reinforcement of the matching concept as a means for measuring income. It represents an operational definition of the concept of income only now being accepted in practice.
3. The clarification of the distinction between contributed equity capital and retained earnings, from which the all-inclusive income statement gained much support.

Subsequent to publication of the 1940 Monograph, Littleton's articles throughout the 1940s and 1950s dealt with the wide range of topics, including accounting education, the public accounting profession, accounting principles, and price level adjustments. In a sense he seems to have been explaining the implications of the 1940 Monograph to various areas of accounting and expanding certain aspects of the basic ideology of the Monograph.

Following his retirement from the University of Illinois, Littleton cast the framework of accounting thought into a broader scope. His monograph, *Structure of Accounting Theory*, published in 1953 under the auspices of the AAA, broadened the area of accounting concern to philosophical issues. This Monograph apparently was motivated by Littleton's view that there was far too little demonstration in the literature of theory as explanations, reasons, or justification of why accounting (technology and the profession) is what it is.[2] Essentially he was calling for rigor in accounting reasoning and may have contributed to the development of the use of modern research methods in accounting. The monograph also served as an aid to education so that students need not memorize rules:

Teachers of bookkeeping and later of accounting and auditing found it necessary to supplement the accumulated rules and descriptions of procedures by explanation and justifications. This was done in order that study should be something more than the memorizing of rules. (Littleton, 1953, p. 185).

The 1953 Monograph, and its successor, *Accounting Theory: Continuity and Change*, co-authored with V. K. Zimmerman, attempted to relate the practice of accountancy to a generalized thought structure broader than the "evolution" or "agreement" method used in developing propositions for the 1940 Monograph. An inductive approach, a departure from the earlier methodology of the 1940 Monograph, was used. While limited in scope to observations of the practice of accounting, the monograph demonstrated the need for an empirical approach to the development of accounting knowledge. The approach assumed an economic entity engaged in economic activities and defined the central purpose of accounting as making possible "the periodic matching of costs (efforts) and revenues (accomplishments)" (Littleton, 1953, p. 30). This concept was the nucleus of the theory and a benchmark that afforded a fixed point of reference for accounting discussion. The accounting principles in the 1953 Monograph were developed through the selection of generalizations about practice based on their coherence, according to Littleton's individual referent, with one another. Bad practices were to be distinguished from good practices on the basis of whether or not they fitted into the right arrangement of interrelated ideas that formed this "coherent" theory. While somewhat narrow in content, the methodology used opened wide the field of accounting research and, in time, the *Structure of Accounting Theory* may well become Littleton's greatest contribution.

In developing accounting principles and procedures, two major approaches may be recognized. One assumes that general purpose financial statements are prepared for a set of unknown multiple users with unknown multiple objectives. The focus of effort then is one of providing general information for the making of many types of economic decisions by many persons or organizations outside the reporting entity. The second approach sets as an objective the task of providing a means for developing information relevant to specific user decision models. This requires identifying users and information needs fairly

[2] For an elaboration on this early view, see Littleton, 1956, p. 363.

specifically and determining either what information the user wants or, by the use of normative models, what information the users should have. Littleton's efforts to develop principles and practices followed the first approach. His decision to rely on the "distillation of practice" to develop accounting principles in the early days probably was sound, partly because of the need to focus on a single set of financial statements for external use and partly because of a lack of knowledge regarding users and their specific needs. Significant as this effort was in calling to the attention of accounting scholars the need for empirical support for their conclusions and effective as he was in developing what is probably a most complete descriptive theory that attempts to explain the foundations and effect of current practice, the particular inductive approach on which his book rests commits the elementary fallacy of getting what *ought* to be from what *is*. Nevertheless, the 1953 Monograph did open the door to systematic research and, fortunately, the impact of his particular inductive conclusions was transient.

The second approach to the development of principles and procedures, where it is assumed that accounting is a measurement and communication process, results in a number of special decision models and may not permit the level of generalization sought by Littleton. Under this approach, current or proposed specific accounting reporting procedures are studied through the testing of hypotheses about such things as (1) the prediction of future objects, activities, or variables; (2) motivation and other behavior aspects of information; and (3) microeconomic activities. Littleton's work, of course, did not deal with the development of hypotheses about behavioral consequences which might be expected in specific situations from the employment of particular accounting-treatment rules. Rather he assumed that prevailing prac-

tice had, by the trial and error approach, solved the problem of accurate or inappropriate practices and that prevailing practice was, in a crude but effective way, the best practice possible and that it was possible to attempt to formulate a reasonably general theory of accounting inductively from such practices. Many now question the validity of his assumption about the effectiveness of practice in providing the most relevant information, and the issue of the proper approach to the development of accounting is unresolved. There are differences of viewpoint about whether a general theory of accounting can be formulated in advance of validated special theories developed from scientific research methods. Whether or not specific studies are likely to provide a complete basis for a theoretical approach to the development of a general theory of accounting, they may be very helpful in finding variables and relationships upon which accounting theory ultimately can be based and in providing a basis for testing hypotheses developed by the theory. Ultimately, the battle over theory may well have to be resolved at the level of abstraction identified by Littleton; well-formed arguments may have to be presented about what accounting ought to be in order to provide a basis for further empirical research.

While this perspective of Littleton's contribution has centered on the influence of his writings on accounting thought and practice, his direct impact on the profession also was substantial. Much of what he did is not reflected in publication. He was always very active in professional organizations. He was president of the American Accounting Association in 1943, director of research from 1940–42, and editor of THE ACCOUNTING REVIEW from 1943–47. He also served on several professional committees including the Committee on Accounting Procedures of the

American Institute of Certified Public Accountants.

His contributions to the field of accounting education also are exceptional. Under his direction a program leading to a M.S. degree in accountancy was developed in 1922, and ultimately the first Ph.D. program in accountancy in the United States was established, with the first degree being awarded in 1939. Eventually, his doctoral students carried his views of the scholarly aspects of accounting throughout the world.

It is difficult to attribute surviving accounting concepts to any one accounting scholar. But the following features of accounting practice, theory, and research seem to have felt the impact of Littleton's contributions:

(1) The inductive approach to the development of accounting knowledge.
(2) The historical method of relating accounting practice to its social and economic environment.
(3) The development of general purpose financial statements which permitted the initial development of an organized structure of accounting thought.
(4) The view of accounting theory construction as explanations of varying levels of validity of relations among concepts.
(5) The comprehensive view of accounting as one common interrelated body of knowledge to be studied and examined as a single discipline.

Other features could well be added and some of those associated with Littleton could also be attributed to others, but the foregoing will suffice to assure present day scholars and practitioners alike that we advance from the shoulders of a man who contributed to us a strong foundation for the further development of accounting. Even though we may from time to time repair, reject, expand, or restructure that foundation, we have had the advantage of a starting base for our thinking, and for this we salute Professor A. C. Littleton as an expression of our appreciation.

REFERENCES

Littleton, A. C., "Value and Price in Accounting," THE ACCOUNTING REVIEW (September 1929), pp. 147–54.

———, "Concepts of Income Underlying Accounting," THE ACCOUNTING REVIEW (March 1937), pp. 13–22.

———, Structure of Accounting Theory, Monograph No. 5 (American Accounting Association, 1953).

———, "Choice Among Alternatives," THE ACCOUNTING REVIEW (July 1956), pp. 363–70.

Paton, W. A., and A. C. Littleton, Introduction to Corporate Accounting Standards, Monograph No. 3 (American Accounting Association, 1940).

Zimmerman, V. K., "The Long Shadow of a Scholar," International Journal of Accounting Education and Research (Spring 1967), pp. 1–20.

(1)   "There are no immutable laws of accounting comparable to the
        immutable laws of Nature" (Pg.135).
            - What does the term 'immutable' refer to?
            - Are there, as Littleton states, immutable laws of Nature
              (consider the work of philosopher of science, Karl Popper)?
            - If so what are they?
            - Accepting the work of Popper is there any reason to expect
              that in accounting there are immutable laws?

(2)   "Hence it is appropriate to say that both the methods of practice
        and the explanations of theory were inductively derived out of
        experience" (Pg.185).
            - What does "inductively derived" mean?
            - Can a theory be purely inductively derived?
            - How does this idea of theory development contrast with that
              developed by Chambers?

(3)   "Trying to make financial statement figures tell of value would
        not produce a dependable basis for accounting. The data would
        lose their prior significance every few days" (Pg.212).
            - If valuations lose their significance every few days how
              much worse are historical valuations?
            - What does Littleton determine as the significance of
              valuations?
            - To what extent can Littleton be said to substitute
              usefulness of information for objectivity of information?
            - Are usefulness and objectivity necessarily substitutes
              for one another?

(4)   "Historical cost is an eminently logical basis for enterprise
        accounting in view of the objectives and limitations which attach
        to accounting" (Pg.210).
            - What does Littleton see as the function of accounting?
            - What are the limitations?
            - To what extent does his function ignore business survival?
            - How does an income figure containing depreciation (based
              on an allocation of cost) allow one to "... reach calculated
              judgements of the success of the enterprise"?

- To what extent does Littleton's reference to the income figure
as an approximation of success cover up the fundamental
question of how success is measured?

(5)   What does Littleton have to say about the introduction of some
system to account for price changes? What system (if any) does
he prefer? How useful (for what purpose) would income figures
be in this case?

(6)   To what extent are the principles which Littleton develops founded
on empirical testing? Are empiricism and observation the same
things? What does Littleton have to say on the matter? Are the
principles which he develops conceivably testable? If statements
are not testable how useful are they in the intellectual development of a discipline?
(Consider the work of Karl Popper).

(7)   Littleton fails to define assets/liabilities/income.
- What explicit and implicit reasons lie behind this fact?
- To what extent is measurement possible without definition?
- Is Littleton justified in talking about the "Structure of
Accounting Theory" without defining these terms?
- What justification is there for a re-titling of Littleton's
book to "A Structure of Accounting Theory"?

13

MAURICE MOONITZ

The Basic Postulates of Accounting

Biographical Chronology

1910	Born 31 October, in Cincinnati, Ohio; son of Samuel David and Eva (Wittstein) Moonitz.
1927-29	Student at the University of Cincinnati.
1933	Awarded a BS, University of California, Berkeley.
1934	Married Ruth Helen Lubin.
1936	Awarded a MS, University of California, Berkeley.
1937-42	Employed as an instructor in business administration, University of Santa Clara, California.
1942-44	Employed as an instructor in economics, Stanford University, California.
1944-47	Joined the firm of Arthur Andersen and Co, San Francisco, as a staff accountant.
1947	Appointed Associate Professor of Accounting, University of California, Berkeley.
1953	Appointed Professor of Accounting, University of California, Berkeley.
1954-59	Associate dean of graduate school of business administration at University of California, Berkeley.
1958	Vice-President of the American Accounting Association.
1958-9	Chairman of AAA Committee on Accounting Theory.
1959	Married Lee Cynthia Daniels, 25 June.
1959	Editor of the California Management Review.
1960-63	Served as the director of accounting research of the AICPA.
1963-66	Served on the Accounting Principles Board of the AICPA.
1966-68	Founding Director and Professor, Lingnan Institute of Business Administration, Hong Kong.
1968	Erskine Visiting Scholar, University of Canterbury, New Zealand.
1978	President of the American Accounting Association.
1979	Inducted to Ohio State University's, Accounting Hall of Fame.

Selected Bibliography

1942   The Entity Approach to Consolidated Statements,
     Accounting Review, v.17, pp 236-42.

1943   Inventories and the Statement of Funds, Accounting
     Review, v.18, pp 262-66.

1944   The Entity Theory of Consolidated Statements, American
     Accounting Association, Monograph No.4, 102 p; reprinted
     by The Foundation Press (Brooklyn, NY) in 1951.

1946   The Entity Theory of Consolidated Statements - Rejoinder,
     Accounting Review, v.21, pp 96-8.

     Accounting for Present Company's Investments in Subsidiaries,
     New York CPA, v.16 (May) pp 227-36.

1948   Adaptations to Price-Level Changes, Accounting Review,
     v.23, pp 136-47.

1952   Accounting - An Analysis of its Problems (2 Volumes),
     Foundation Press (Brooklyn, NY) (with Charles C.
     Staehling) 712 p; 618 p.

1953   The Case Against LIFO as an Inventory - Pricing Formula,
     Journal of Accountancy, v.95 (June), pp 682-90.

     How Realistic are Modern Accounting Procedures in the
     Valuation of Business Capital?, Journal of Accountancy,
     v.96 (July), pp 86-9.

1956   Reporting on the Flow of Funds, Accounting Review,
     v.31, pp 375-85.

1957   Income Taxes in Financial Statements, Accounting Review,
     v.32, pp 175-83.

1960   The Changing Concept of Liabilities, Journal of Accountancy,
     v.109 (May) pp 41-6.

     Recent Developments in Accounting Theory, Accounting
     Review, v.35, pp 206-17. (With Carl L. Nelson).

1961   The Basic Postulates of Accounting, AICPA (Accounting
     Research Study No.1), 61 p; conclusions in Journal
     of Accountancy, v.112 (Nov), pp 71-2.

     Direct Costing and Public Reporting, NAA Bulletin,
     v.43 (sect. 1, Oct), pp 45-6.

1962   Should We Discard The Income Concept? Accounting Review,
     v.37, pp 175-80.

     A Tentative Set of Broad Accounting Principles for
     Business Enterprises, AICPA (ARS No.3) (with Robert
     J. Sprouse)

The Nature of Research in Accounting, Proceedings, International Conf. on Accounting Education, University of Illinois, pp 83-86.

1963   Why Do We Need "Postulates" and "Principles"?, Journal of Accountancy, v.116 (Dec), pp 42-6.

Some Critical Areas in the Development of Accounting Principles, Florida CPA, v.3 (Nov) pp 15-21.

1964   The Development of the Accounting Research Program - Past, Present and Future, Texas CPA, v.36 (Jan) pp 3-10.

Accounting: An Analysis of its Problems, v.1 (1963); v.2 (1964), Holt, Rinehart and Winston, 588 p. and 521 p. (with Louis H. Jordan).

1967   Chambers on the Price Level Study, Abacus, v.3, pp 55-61.

1968   Why is it so Difficult to Agree Upon a Set of Accounting Principles?, Australian Accountant. v.38 (Nov), pp 621-31; Chartered Accountant in Australia, v.39 (Nov) pp 439-49.

1970   Price-Level Accountancy and Scales of Measurement, Accounting Review, v.45, pp 465-75.

Three Contributions to the Development of Accounting Principles Prior to 1930, Journal of Accounting Research, v.8, pp 145-55.

Accounting Principles - Some Lessons from The American Experience, Journal of Business Finance, v.2, pp 51-64.

1974   Obtaining Agreement on Standards in the Accounting Profession, American Accounting Association (SAR No.8), 93 p.

Restating the Price-Level Problem, Canadian Chartered Accountant, v.105 (July) pp 26-31.

Accounting Principles - How They Are Developed, in Institutional Issues in Public Accounting, ed., R.R. Sterling, Scholars Book Co., pp 143-71 (followed by Comments by S.A. Zeff).

Changing Prices and Financial Reporting, Accounting Lectures, Stipes, 59 p; also ICRA, University of Lancaster, Occasional Paper No.3.

1976   Market Value Methods for Intercorporate Investments in Stock, AICPA, Accounting Research Monograph No.2, 75 p. (with Reed K. Storey).

Auditing Standards, Emanuel Saxe Distinguished Lectures in Accounting, 1976-77, (NY), pp 49-66.

1978   International Auditing Standards, Prentice-Hall, 159 p. (with Edward Stamp).

REFERENCES

Reviews of <u>The Basic Postulates, ARS 1</u>:
                    <u>Accounting Review</u>, v.37, 1962, pp.602-605 (A C Littleton).
                    <u>Accounting Review</u>, v.39, 1964, pp.16-21 (R W Metcalf).
                    <u>Accounting Review</u>, v.41, 1966, pp.458-63 (H R Givens).

Review of ARS3:   <u>Accounting Review</u>, v.38, 1963, pp.220-22.

Briloff, A J, "Needed: A Revolution in the Determination and Application
        of Accounting Principles, <u>Accounting Review</u>, v.39, 1964, pp.12-15.

Chambers, R J, "The Moonitz & Sprouse Studies on Postulates & Principles",
        <u>Proceedings</u>, Australasian Association of University Teachers of
        Accounting Conference, Canberra, Jan 1964, pp.34-54; followed
        by, "Comments" by W P Birkett, pp.55-59.

Gordon, M J, "Postulates, Principles & Research in Accounting", <u>Accounting
        Review</u>, v.39, pp.251-63.

Philips, G E, "The Revolution in Accounting Theory", <u>Accounting Review</u>,
        v.38, 1963, pp.696-708.

Schattke, R, "Evaluation of AICPA Research Study No.1 - The Basic
        Postulates of Accounting", <u>Proceedings</u>, 10th Annual Inst on
        Accounting, 1963, pp.30-43.

Comments on "The Basic Postulates of Accounting"

This is the second in the series of summaries of comments received on Accounting Research Studies issued by the Research Division of the American Institute of CPAs. These summaries are prepared by members of the Institute staff, and are reviewed by the chairman or another member of the Accounting Principles Board. The first such summary, dealing with comments on "Cash Flow Analysis and the Funds Statement," appeared in the September 1962, JOURNAL.

IT is difficult to generalize about the substance of the comments made on this research study. The large number of letters received ranged in length from one sentence to detailed remarks comparable to article length. Some of the longer comments which raise significant new issues or present alternative proposals will be published in article form in THE JOURNAL OF ACCOUNTANCY.

Interest is widespread. The letters are as diversified in their reaction as they are in geographical origin. Several comments have been received from professional accountants and accounting groups from other nations. Members of all facets of the profession as well as nonaccountants have responded. All of the letters have been carefully studied by Maurice Moonitz and the research staff. Some of the comments received are illustrated in this summary. They have been presented in roughly the same manner as the postulates study itself is structured. In accordance with the policy outlined in the editorial in the September issue of THE JOURNAL, the anonymity of the writers has been respected.

Prior to illustrating by category some of the more cogent comments made on the postulates study, it might be useful to indicate some of the general characteristics of the letters. The subsequent comments on specific portions of the study may then be viewed in proper perspective.

There were fifty-two letters which formed the basis for this summary. As a matter of interest, these fifty-two letters contained 147 typewritten pages. Of the fifty-two, only nine expressed an unqualified over-all opinion on the study. Two of the nine letters indicated general disapproval of the over-all study; two additional letters contained objections to specific portions of the study and, based on these objections, disapproved the entire study. The remaining five endorsed the report without qualification.

Thirteen additional letters commented on the over-all study, but were either noncommittal or sufficiently lukewarm to warrant classification as nonapproval. However, nonapproval represents tentative reluctance to express an opinion either for or against the study, and should thereby be distinguished from disapproval.

The remaining letters contained comments ranging from suggestions for minor wording changes to objections to, or endorsements of, specific portions of the study.

In summary:

Over-all Comments:	
Endorsements	5
Disapprovals	4
Nonapprovals	13
Specific comments on portions of the study	30
	52

144

There was a definite reluctance among practitioners to express an over-all opinion on the study. Of the nine letters received which did this, six were from educators, one from a controller, and two from practicing certified public accountants. As might be expected, educators were more prone to endorse the work than were other interested readers. A comment from a chairman of one study panel is characteristic of the nonacademic reader group:

> The responses received, and inferentially those not received, clearly indicate a lack of desire on the part of the panel to take any strong position upon the study.

The two practicing CPAs who expressed an opinion on the study offered a conservative compliment and stated a fairly complete disenchantment:

> ... the task of formulating a set of basic accounting postulates is a major undertaking. Though I am about to be quite critical of some of the postulates offered, nevertheless, I feel Dr. Moonitz has done an excellent job in setting forth many basic observations and conclusions about accounting and the environment in which it exists.

> Usefulness is dismissed early in the work as a criterion for formulating postulates, but I imagine that I may use it as a test in judging the work itself. By this test, the work does not seem to me to score high. The problem-oriented approach, the heavy reliance on deductive reasoning, the separation of problems and solutions from the people who have to recognize and solve them—all these seem to leave us still a long way from the reality which the AICPA research program and the APB must face.

Four brief quotations taken from letters from teachers will serve to illustrate the general reception from the academic community. Three of the four teachers are members of the Institute.

> Accounting Research Study No. 1 is certain to take its place as a landmark in the development of accounting theory. It is a carefully considered, well-organized, soundly reasoned expression of accounting theory. Its excellence is a quality which the accounting profession has come to regard as characteristic of the contributions of Professor Moonitz.

> If every accountant were completely familiar with the ideas expressed in this monograph, we would have better accountants and better financial statements.

> Many thanks for the copy of "The Basic Postulates of Accounting." I think you have done an excellent job of bringing together the underlying ideas in accounting. The postulates are so fundamental that I can't see any basis for a quarrel with them.

> I wish to communicate to you at this time my

support of the position taken in the monograph, "The Basic Postulates of Accounting," by Maurice Moonitz. I hope that the Accounting Principles Board will adopt these statements of postulates as the basis upon which to build accounting principles. The work is succinctly written and evidences logical and clear thought throughout. It is, in my opinion, the most significant contribution to the literature of accounting on this vital subject.

Accounting teachers were more prone to examine the study from a theoretical viewpoint and minimize any transitional problems of implementation. Practitioners, conditioned by a different environment, were more predisposed to emphasize the possible departures from current practice.

As an example of how an individual's environment serves to condition his reaction, note these two short comments:

> The study is too theoretical, impractical, and does not provide for necessary flexibility in a growing profession such as ours.

> It seems to me the entire bulletin smacks of practical influences. Concepts have been developed because they are adaptable to what is currently being done by one or more practicing members of the profession. We need a statement of what should be done which can stand the test of rigorous investigation and analysis.

In addition, these two different opinions should serve to illustrate that it is an impossibility to please everyone. Further examples of "poles-apart" expressions of opinion will be given later in this article.

One thing must be remembered when reading the comments on this study. Those persons agreeing in whole or part with the work would tend to be either silent or submit brief notes of commendation. On the other hand, individuals tending to disagree with the study would feel a much greater obligation to react in depth to the work. For that reason it should not be concluded that the proportion of respondents choosing to comment on any controversial theoretical issue are truly representative of the population of readers.

The stated objectives of accounting

In the comments by Leonard Spacek at the end of the postulates study there appears the following statement:

> The essential prerequisite to the establishment of a sound framework of accounting theory must be a clear definition of the purposes and objectives of accounting. . . .

It is obvious from reading the letters received regarding the study that this is an area where many persons agree with Mr. Spacek. Although the objectives may be read into the study by a careful perusal of its arguments, it is obvious that a more definitive statement of the goal(s) or objective(s) of accounting would have been welcomed. Some of the comments received along these lines are as follows:

. . . much more must be done to clearly set forth the purpose or purposes of accounting.

The monograph in itself seems to exist in something akin to a vacuum, having neither a clearly defined starting point nor an obvious sequel. To put the study into a proper perspective, it would have been better if it had started off with a concise but thorough explanation of the purpose and objectives of accounting. This information is actually provided in the course of the various discussions but it is not given the proper degree of emphasis nor highlighted as the basic foundation from which the study develops.

. . . it seems possible that between the author of the monograph and Leonard Spacek there may be an area of misunderstanding. The preface of the monograph clearly states that the "Special Committee" proposed "a study of the *basic postulates* underlying accounting principles generally," whereas Leonard Spacek, who was a member of this Special Committee, states, "the essential prerequisite to the establishment of a sound framework of accounting theory must be a clear determination of the purposes and objectives of accounting." Are "basic postulates" and "purposes and objectives" the same? I think not, and if they are not the same, then it seems clear that a "determination of the purposes and objectives of accounting" should come first, to be followed by a determination of basic postulates, and then finally by a determination of principles and rules. However, the assignment for the monograph was only the second of these, and possibly the Special Committee erred in not starting at the beginning.

It seems to me that among the "group A" postulates should be included some reference to objectives. Perhaps this could be accomplished by adding "and objectives" to Postulate A-1.

Somewhere in the postulates there should be a statement to give direction to accounting processes. Income determination presumably is based on an assumption that profit is an important objective of enterprise activity. If an individual were in business for some reason other than profit, there would seem to be little justification for preparing a conventional income statement for his use.

I cannot see that these postulates—fourteen in total number—point to or lead to a fundamental objective or purpose in accounting, even though they may be descriptive. It is my belief that we in accounting should have a fundamental purpose or aim in our accounting process, and I was hoping that this study would provide that aim. A mere observance of such things as quantification, exchange, entities, time period, unit of measure, financial statements, tentativeness, and so forth, does not provide us with a goal in accounting.

Few comments were made on the approach taken to postulate formulation. A great deal of the criticism received regarding individual postulates resulted from the fact that the correspondents analyzed the proposed postulates within their own concepts of what the method of attack should have been. Occasionally this was recognized by writers in their expressions of discontent with the definition of postulates used as a basis of the study. One writer specifically acknowledged this problem:

Dr. Moonitz recognizes in the introduction to the study that there is no general agreement on what the term "postulates" means. Therefore, I suspect, although my criticisms deal specifically with the individual postulates, that in actuality the real difference of opinion lies in our interpretations of the term "postulates" and in what such postulates are to accomplish in the over-all field of accounting pronouncements. In formulating my own concept as to what the postulates are or should be, I lean heavily on the wording used in the report to the Council, ". . . the basic *assumptions* on which principles rest," and the further wording that they are ". . . to provide a meaningful foundation for the formulation of principles and the development of rules or other guides for the application of principles. . . ."

Two letters commented on the approach taken to formulation of the proposed postulates, but without expression of great personal desire for any given method of attack:

. . . the author points to the limitations of observation as a means for collecting data. With this I completely agree, for I believe every observer sees according to what he has been conditioned to see and by the environment in which he observes. It is literally impossible to state anything as a fact. After having made this valid statement and calling for "heavy reliance . . . on deductive reasoning in the development of accounting postulates and principles," the author proceeds to adopt the problem-oriented approach as a means of developing postulates. While I personally prefer the pragmatic approach, particularly that set forth by C. S. Peirce, I could also accept the ethical approach quite readily. I fail to see any justification for the problem-oriented approach. It provides no systematic method for the recognition of postulates and I think the thing will get us into more trouble. It seems to me essential that accounting research be directed toward scientific methods of research, if this profession of ours is to realize its potential. I am unsympathetic with any improvised statements, aimed at meeting a special problem of the profession, which gives the implication that such is the complete substance of the field.

The study indicates that the procedure is to first recognize and define the problems to be solved, then move to their solution by careful attention to what "ought" to be the case. I have no quarrel with this procedure, but it does seem that it is somewhat inconsistent with the rejection on page 3 of the ethical approach. Whether you start with the problem and then consider the "ought," or start with "ought" and then consider the problem, would not the relation between them be the same? If not, I think the proposition could well be worked out in greater detail.

Over-all comments on the postulates

Prior to illustrating the comments received on the individual postulates, note should be taken of eight individuals who expressed an opinion on the postulates as a whole. Of these eight, three comments pertained to whether the study satisfied its purposes, and two commented on the number of postulates.

Two of the three letters which dealt with the problem of satisfying purposes indicated that the study had not done so. The third letter argued that insufficient basis exists for evaluating the proposed postulates.

In my opinion, the fourteen postulates as listed in the monograph cannot be stated to be basic assumptions or axioms on which accounting principles can be based, and I agree with Mr. Spacek's statement that "the so-called postulates . . . are self-evident observations that cannot serve as the basic foundation on which sound accounting principles can be established." It further appears that basic "ground rules" for determining accounting principles have not been set forth and the proposed postulates are based on opinions of individuals or committees, as reflected in publications issued in the past.

The purpose of conducting an inquiry into the basic postulates of accounting, as established by the Special Committee, was to provide a foundation from which reasonable men can deduce in a logical fashion accounting principles or guides to action. The postulates suggested by Dr. Moonitz, while true in themselves, provide no such springboard for further reasoning. Many of them are really axioms or facts rather than basic assumptions on which accounting principles rest.

A major criticism of the monograph as it now stands is the lack of attention to the nature and function of postulates in a system of theory. This is an oversight similar to the one in the Andersen monograph, *The Postulate of Accounting.* In each case the author contends he has accepted the Special Committee's use of the term "postulate." Yet the two monographs differ in their interpretations. Actually, the Special Committee did not give extensive study to this term and its appropriate use; rather it suggested that such study would be appropriate. In the quotation from the Special Committee's report on page 1 of the Moonitz monograph, we find: "The profession, however, should make clear their understanding and interpretation of what they are, to provide a meaningful foundation for the formulation of principles and the development of rules or other guides for the application of principles in specific situations."

I take this to mean that the profession should not only attempt to state specific propositions as postulates, but should also make clear its understanding of what postulates are in general and where they fit into a system of theory for accounting. Without such a statement, how can we judge whether any given proposition meets the tests of a postulate? How can we determine whether any given set of propositions constitutes a system of postulates?

Because the Moonitz monograph does not give this basic issue adequate attention, one cannot tell whether the proposed "postulates" meet even the author's standards, much less whether they meet the requirements of those who write authoritatively about the organization of knowledge in general.

Two correspondents commented on the number of postulates, one tending to believe that there must be less than fourteen, and one arguing that there is no basis for knowing at the outset of an inquiry how many postulates there are.

One obvious comment is that this study winds up with no less than fourteen basic postulates. It somehow seems extremely doubtful if there are that many propositions which are entitled to this rather pretentious designation. This suggestion is perhaps reinforced by considering the extraordinary range in "basicness" between Postulate A-1 and Postulate C-5, at the other end of the line. The former makes the broad assertion that "quantitative data are helpful in making rational economic decisions" (one wonders why "helpful" should not have been replaced by "essential"). The latter asserts that "accounting reports should disclose that which is necessary to make them not misleading." This is surely not a proposition which is in the same logical category as A-1, true and useful though it may be. It borders perilously close on being an accounting principle, a lower order of creature, according to the report of the Special Committee on Research Program.

Incidentally, how did the Special Committee *know* that the postulates are few in number or that they are necessarily derived from the economic and political environment, etc.? This seems to me to be the sort of proposition one might put forward at the conclusion of an inquiry, rather than at the beginning where it seems almost like restrictive terms of reference.

Of the three persons suggesting that there may be specific additional postulates, one person voted for communication and one for materiality. The third party felt that there should be some postulates of "limitation."

I believe that the communication (reporting) element is an essential part of accounting. To say otherwise is to suggest that accounting is self-contained—self-regulating—an end in itself. That, of course, is not the case. Accounting's sole reason for existence in the scheme of things is communication: the transmission of information of a certain type to someone. And circumstances surrounding the transmission and the parties thereto can and should have an important influence on the antecedent steps within the function of accounting.

I am not sure, but I believe materiality is a postulate because it is the root of much misunderstanding and I believe an important function of adopted postulates is clarification of misunderstandings. A balance sheet that balances conveys to many people an impression that the financial statements have meticulously accounted for every penny. Also many people have the idea that accountants allow themselves to be lengthily involved in tasks of accounting for nickels and pennies.

I have one suggestion which probably is not worth very much because I am sure it has been thought of many times before. I could, however, wish that there were a page or two devoted to the limits of the whole accounting and auditing procedure and the relationship of these limits to the function of management. I find too many people in all walks of life who think "it must be honest and it must be efficient because the accounts are audited by reputable auditors." In short, am I wrong in thinking that some of the postulates should be those of limitation?

The "A" group postulates

For each of the three groups of postulates, a brief restatement of content will be made. The five group "A" postulates are as follows:

Postulate A-1. Quantification. Quantitative data are helpful in making *rational economic decisions,* i.e., in making choices among alternatives so that actions are correctly related to consequences.

Postulate A-2. Exchange. Most of the goods and services that are produced are distributed through exchange, and are not directly consumed by the producers.

Postulate A-3. Entities (including identification of the entity). Economic activity is carried on through specific units or entities. Any report on the activity must identify clearly the particular unit or entity involved.

Postulate A-4. Time period (including specification of the time period). Economic activity is carried on during specifiable periods of time. Any report on that activity must identify clearly the period of the time involved.

Postulate A-5. Unit of measure (including identification of the monetary unit). Money is the common denominator in terms of which goods and services, including labor, natural resources, and capital are measured. Any report must clearly indicate which money (e.g., dollars, francs, pounds) is being used.

This group of postulates was generally well-re-

ceived. Only two writers took issue with the group as a whole, feeling that the postulates were "obvious truths" and "trivial."

In reading the summary of the postulates on pages 51-53, I am impressed by their apparent unevenness of quality and significance. Some seem to have the general characteristics of postulates; others do not. For example, Postulate A-1 appears to me to be concerned with an idea that is definitely at the postulate level. Postulate A-2, however, is merely a recognition of an obvious truth. Postulates A-3, A-4 and A-5 recognize obvious truths of our present economic system and out of these practices draw rather obvious conclusions. It stretches my imagination to see any of these last four propositions as productive of concepts or principles. And if they are not productive, they are not postulates.

The suggested "A" postulates are trivial and are not a good basis for formulation of principles. In any event, the last sentence in postulates A-3, A-4 and A-5 should be omitted because it belongs in the related "B" postulates.

The following are representative of the letters supporting the "A" group.

Whether the postulates proposed are "postulates" (which Mr. Spacek questions), seems to be of no great importance. Statements A-1 to A-5 may not be "propositions" taken for granted but they constitute a comprehensive list of those phenomena which create the requirement for accounting processes.

The group "A" postulates (except as related to disclosure) are basic observations of practice or fact. Therefore, I do not feel they fit the Council's definition of a postulate and probably do not have to be restated as official accounting pronouncements. However, I do not take any particular exception to the content of these postulates.

The first five postulates are true postulates; that is, they are self-evident statements about the environment in which accounting is found and which it cannot change. They are not subject to formulation but to recognition and statement, for they exist whether or not we recognize them. Although (as the monograph points out) many others could be found and stated, the special virtue possessed by the five specifically stated in the monograph is that they have a direct relationship on the second group of postulates which are directly concerned with accounting.

. . . I cannot find any basis for disputing the "A" group of postulates. I agree with the author that "there may be more than the five," but I doubt that anyone can take serious issue with the five that *are* given.

If it is correct to regard a postulate as a self-evident truth, there is no reason to quarrel with the five group "A" statements. . . .

Very little specific comment was received with respect to the individual postulates in the "A" group. There seemed to be some discomfort with postulates A-3, A-4, and A-5, not because of any disagreement as to substance, but because these three were felt to be somewhat different in nature from A-1 and A-2. The first quotation cited above in this section is one example of this; another is as follows:

It seems to me that the implied conditions that you attach to your propositions A-3, A-4 and A-5 are rather more of the nature of "imperatives" (as you use the term) and represent "C" class propositions or perhaps something between your "B" class and "C" class. I agree that reports "ought to" conform to the conditions you stipulate, but I doubt whether all such reports do so in fact (as I think is implied in the use of "must"). . . . There is also the logical point that an "ought" proposition cannot—at least so far as I can see—be derived solely from "is" propositions without the interposition of some other "ought" proposition. For example, in your statement of Postulate A-3 on page 52, it seems to me that before we can say that the second sentence is derived from the first, we need another proposition. Thus:
(a) Economic activity is carried on through specific units or entities.
(b) These units ought to be readily identifiable.
(c) Any report on the activity ought to identify clearly the particular unit or entity involved.
Proposition (b) is necessary, I think, to complete the reasoning.
There is the further point that the references to reports in these postulates relate to accounting rather than to the environment itself and for that reason ought not to be in the "A" group.

The other comments received regarding the "A" group postulates related specifically to A-4 and A-5. Two individuals suggested rewording A-4:

The "time period" Postulate (A-4) would to me sound less rooted in natural laws (which it isn't) and more in keeping with reality if it read: "It is useful to divide into specified intervals of time the period during which economic activity is carried out."

Expenditures of funds or other assets shall be prorated over the periods of time benefited thereby, provided however, that no amount shall be deferred beyond such time as remaining benefits can be objectively ascertained to exist.

Two parties objected to Postulate A-5, primarily because of the restriction of the unit of measurement to money. The following statement from one letter summarizes the argument:

I strongly disagree with the concept that accounting should be confined to quantitative data expressed in monetary terms. It is true that the common denominator of money is extremely useful. It is also true that the double-entry system and the trial balance have been confined to monetary

equivalents, that they also are useful and should continue to be so. However, even at the present time, nonmonetary data such as shares authorized, outstanding, optioned, etc., are considered an integral part of accounting data; some financial statements of promotional ventures do not even assign monetary equivalents to some important assets.

The "B" group postulates

Postulate B-1. Financial statements. (Related to A-1.) The results of the accounting process are expressed in a set of fundamentally related financial statements which articulate with each other and rest upon the same underlying data.

Postulate B-2. Market prices. (Related to A-2.) Accounting data are based on prices generated by past, present or future exchanges which have actually taken place or are expected to.

Postulate B-3. Entities. (Related to A-3.) The results of the accounting process are expressed in terms of specific units or entities.

Postulate B-4. Tentativeness. (Related to A-4.) The results of operations for relatively short periods of time are tentative whenever allocations between past, present, and future periods are required.

The "B" group postulates were also well-received. Of six letters which commented on the group as a whole, five tended to express satisfaction with these four proposed postulates. The one letter stating dissatisfaction did so in this manner:

The "B" group of postulates are descriptive in nature; they describe selected features of current accounting practice. Almost any principles one might want to propose could be claimed to rest on—or at least not conflict with—such a group of propositions. If stated differently, Postulate B-4 might hold real promise, but the others fail to meet my understanding of the requirements of a postulate. A careful study of the nature of postulates, as suggested above, might have eliminated these propositions from consideration as well as some of those in the "A" group.

The five remaining letters commented as follows: (As can be seen, two felt that the "B" group were corollaries of the "A" group.)

The second group of four postulates (group "B") are, with the exception of part of the first, corollaries of group "A"; if the postulates of group "A" are accepted, those of group "B" must be accepted because they logically follow and there are no alternatives.
. . . The one exception to the statement that this group constitutes corollaries to the first group is found in the requirement of articulation in Postulate B-1. This requirement is not a necessary consequence of Postulate A-1, but is an "impera-

tive." It is nevertheless valid, and no harm is done if for the sake of convenience it is stated as a part of Postulate B-1. These four postulates are valid because those in group "A" are valid.

The set of postulates in "B" and "C" are more specific. As such they seem more like corollaries of "A" rather than separate postulates. This, however, is a matter of semantics.

The "B" postulates are the ones of most value as postulates. However, under rules governing the use of postulates, one postulate should not be dependent on another postulate.

As to the supplementary propositions (the "B" group) it would also follow that, "there could be more." However, I see no conflict as between those that are expressed in this group and our present economic environment as I see it.

Statements B-1 to B-4 may be claimed to be only statements of existing practice but criticism on that basis would have difficulty in finding substitutes to support it. It seems to me, however, that financial statements and market prices are so essential to the accounting process that it might be appropriate to accentuate it by adding to the verb the words "and must be." The results of the accounting process are not only expressed in financial statements but *must be* so expressed.

As far as the specific postulates of group "B" are concerned, only B-2 drew any comment. Two persons felt that this postulate offered too much leeway for interpreting pertinent accounting measurements.

> Postulate B-2 should be expanded to offer some basic criteria for distinguishing between past, present, and future exchanges since all three cannot be equally valid in the formulation of accounting principles.

> To set up a postulate, such as B-2 dealing with market prices, so broadly as to encompass past, present, and future exchanges, establishes no postulate at all. To me this postulate states that accountants can record transactions at any amount they believe is suitable.

Of course, it must be kept in mind that at the time these letters were written, Accounting Research Study No. 3, "A Tentative Set of Broad Accounting Principles for Business Enterprises," had not yet been published. Therefore, it is likely that a large proportion of the reading audience did not realize that Postulate B-2, if accepted, would provide a basis for reducing the traditional accounting emphasis on historical costs. If this had been anticipated, it is quite possible that more comments both for and against B-2 would have been received.

The "C" group postulates

Postulate C-1. Continuity (including the correlative concept of limited life). In the absence of evidence to the contrary, the entity should be viewed as remaining in operation indefinitely. In the presence of evidence that the entity has a limited life, it should not be viewed as remaining in operation indefinitely.

Postulate C-2. Objectivity. Changes in assets and liabilities, and the related effects (if any) on revenues, expenses, retained earnings, and the like, should not be given formal recognition in the accounts earlier than the point of time at which they can be measured in objective terms.

Postulate C-3. Consistency. The procedures used in accounting for a given entity should be appropriate for the measurement of its position and its activities and should be followed consistently from period to period.

Postulate C-4. Stable unit. Accounting reports should be based on a stable measuring unit.

Postulate C-5. Disclosure. Accounting reports should disclose that which is necessary to make them not misleading.

The "C" group of postulates received by far the most comments. A large number of those persons reacting to this group felt that classifying these five statements as postulates was seriously open to question. Some felt that C-1 and C-2 might deserve such classification, but not the remaining three. Typical of comments expressing both these views are the following quotations:

> I consider C-1 and C-2 to be appropriate assumptions upon which to build accounting principles and C-3, C-4, and C-5 constitute essential prerequisites in reporting practice.

> Postulates C-1 and C-2 appear to be valid postulates, although of course final judgment on this cannot be given until their usefulness in providing a base for valid concepts and principles been established. The last three in this group, however, are more in the nature of standards for the presentation of accounting reports than postulates. The fact that they are reasonable statements of important requirements does not in itself constitute them as postulates.

> It was pointed out that such things as materiality and conservatism are not postulates of accounting, but, rather, they refer to the way accountants report or should report information. Thus, it was somewhat surprising to find that he had included objectivity, consistency, and disclosure as accounting postulates. All of these, but particularly consistency and disclosure, refer solely to reporting and not to accounting theory. What information should be disclosed is simply a matter of someone's judgment, not an explicit assumption.

> The propriety of describing the "C" group as postulates seems open to question. These statements seem to be more in the nature of working rules or propositions that have been, or should be, adopted for various reasons. (I think that applying the designation "Imperatives" to the statements in the "C" group is entirely proper. Per-

haps B-1 and B-2 might be added to that list after substituting "should be" for "are" in each case.)

The "C" postulates are not postulates. They are accounting principles to be developed from postulates.

If we are guided by the definition that postulates are the basic assumptions on which principles rest, it appears that the statements listed in groups "A" and "B" are actually "postulates" or assumptions as bases for the imperative principles contained in group "C."

One person disagreed with these views:

The five postulates in group "C" are different from the others. This difference lies in the fact that they are chosen alternatives rather than self-evident statements or corollaries of such statements. In spite of the fact that they are formulations rather than statements of existing conditions, they are no less valid than the postulates of groups "A" and "B." Their validity lies in the fact that they are truly "imperatives"; that is, although there are alternatives which make them choices or assumptions, these alternatives are not acceptable for accounting even though they may be acceptable in other fields. The alternative to continuity is limited life, an assumption that is valid only under certain limiting circumstances; the alternative to objectivity is subjectivity, an assumption that cannot provide useful measurement in accounting; the alternative to consistency is inconsistency; the alternative to disclosure is concealment. Partial consistency and partial disclosure are merely degrees of inconsistency and concealment. The "imperatives," wherein accountants have to make the assumption they do for want of an acceptable alternative, can be contrasted with a rule such as realization, where there are several acceptable alternatives among which choice may be made.

Postulate C-2 was criticized by several correspondents because it was phrased in a negative manner. The following two quotations summarize this criticism:

. . . I have a question with respect to the negative approach in Postulate C-2. It seems to me that the provision that "changes . . . should not be given formal recognition . . . earlier than the point of time at which they can be measured in objective terms" invites reliance on the cliché of "cut short the losses, let the profits run on" and on "conservatism"—a practice that is without logic as is pointed out on page 48, and too often leads to misleading reports. It does nothing to avoid Sidney Alexander's criticism of accountants which is quoted on page 42. I would prefer the positive approach. . . .

Postulates C-2 and C-5 are phrased in the negative. The question of the use of the positive versus the negative is discussed on pages 41 and 42 and the statement is made that "the basic

(negative) form of this proposition does not rule out the 'positive,' " etc. Nevertheless, this negative postulate, while not ruling out the positive, does not necessarily include it, and, therefore, recognition of changes in assets and liabilities is permissive when "they can be measured in objective terms" but neither compulsory nor advisory. This permits a wide latitude of interpretation and a wide variance of practice. I suggest that this subject needs much more consideration, and I would favor the positive approach. Certainly, Alexander's view which is quoted at the bottom of page 42 would argue for the positive.

In addition to this problem of presentation, several individuals suggested changes in substance:

Proposition "C-2" is difficult in terms of the wording. We are continually using various assumptions in attempting to measure business alternatives. The significance of the particular phrases used is hard to follow.

I should think changes in assets, etc., should be recognized as soon as a change is apparent rather than waiting until a method of objective measurement can be developed.

Postulate C-2 should be amended to cover subjective as well as objective elements. Knowledge, judgment, moral values may be more important than objective factors.

Some aspects of objectivity have a place in the theoretical structure of accounting, although it is also a standard of reporting. I would have preferred to see this postulate more narrowly defined just in the area of revenue recognition. Surely, the same concept of objectivity is not used in recording assets as it is in recording liabilities, as in recording losses versus recording gains. I believe the degree of objectivity should be the same in all cases. Perhaps the author intended that more specific "principles" would be derived from this postulate for each of the specific areas.

Postulate C-3 was on the receiving end of comments from four letters. All four endorsed the idea of consistency, but doubt was expressed about classifying consistency as a postulate. One particularly interesting comment is representative of this group.

I have felt for some time that "Consistency" (Postulate C-3) should be the consequence of a scientific attitude on the part of each accountant as he et li es "scientific methods" in performing accounting functions. A careful consideration of relevant factors by a competent accountant should lead him to the same conclusions each time he faces essentially the same problem. For example, if income is generated by enterprise activity, then the accountant ought to approach income measurement in the same fashion as a scientist approaches the task of reading a gauge or some other measuring instrument. He should attempt to measure the results of business actions as objectively as possible. Methods should be selected which are suitable to the purpose of obtaining a dependable measurement. The consequences of this type of approach will be consistency.

I would delete "and should be followed consistently from period to period" from Postulate C-3.

As one might expect, Postulate C-4, dealing with a stable measuring unit, drew substantial comment. The supporters of a stable measuring unit were brief in their endorsement.

I am especially pleased to notice that a strong case has been made for a postulate on a stable monetary unit, since this should aid in getting some action on the price-level problem.

With respect to the unit of measure, I believe accountants should energetically strive to implement the proposals of the Study Group on Business Income and of the American Accounting Association's Committee on Accounting Standards.

Of those persons disagreeing, two did so because they felt that there is no such thing as a stable monetary unit.

I think this is fine and sometime I would like to see somebody's definition of a stable measuring unit. I do not see much purpose to this proposition unless you feel there really is such a thing as a stable measuring unit.

. . . on page 27 it is suggested that accounting could be made to supply data such as factory buildings stated in constant dollars or at replacement costs. As to constant dollars, there is no such thing. Accounting is in an environment, like the physical universe, where nothing is fixed. To measure anything we must choose a frame of reference. Whether we choose the monetary unit or a quantity of butter and eggs in stating factory buildings, we are choosing a frame of reference which, itself, is not stable. It is misleading to talk of "constant dollars." As to replacement costs, they are generally so far in the future that any attempt to reflect them currently would violate Postulate C-2, even if it could be assumed that old buildings would be replaced in kind. . . .

One correspondent objected to the logical development of the argument for a stable measuring unit:

Dr. Moonitz's recommendation for recognition of price-level changes rests entirely on his assertion that failure to do this is inconsistent with Postulate C-4: "Accounting reports should be based on a stable measuring unit." In my opinion, his recommendation does *not* follow logically from Postulate C-4. Obviously, money is not a stable measure of *purchasing power*, but Dr. Moonitz gives no argument, either in this section or anywhere else in the study, in support of the idea that accounting should seek to measure purchasing power.

It is perfectly clear that money can be used to measure an attribute other than purchasing power, and, when used for this purpose, it is stable (except in those rare cases, as in France in 1960 and USSR in 1961, where the definition of the monetary unit changed). A promise to pay $1 million twenty years from now, or twenty years ago, means just that. Changes in purchasing power affect the relative importance of this promise, but do not in any way change the fact of the $1 million.

Or, to disentangle this from accounting, consider the measure of distance. The airline distance from New York to Chicago is 724 miles. In the sense of the time sacrificed in going from one city to the other (which is roughly analogous to purchasing power in accounting), this distance keeps shrinking in importance as airplane speeds increase, and we often see references to this shrinkage. "Hours required" is *one* measure of distance, but would anyone seriously argue that it is the *only* valid measure and that we should therefore do away with mileage as a basis for our measurement system, on the grounds that it is not a stable unit?

Comments received on definitions

In the postulates study an attempt was made to define accounting, cost, and to distinguish between income, earnings and profit. The definition or distinctions proposed were as follows:

Accounting (page 23): The function of accounting is (1) to measure the resources held by specific entities; (2) to reflect the claims against and the interests in those entities; (3) to measure the changes in those resources, claims, and interests; (4) to assign the changes to specifiable periods of time; and (5) to express the foregoing in terms of money as a common denominator.

Cost (page 30): In the interests of precision in meaning and in analysis, "cost" should be given a single meaning. Otherwise, those characteristics of "cost" which are valid in one of its meanings may easily be attributed incorrectly to its other meanings. For example, "cost" is often urged as a basis in accounting because it is objective, or easily measured, or verifiable. These characteristics are usually valid if cost means "actual price, in money, paid or promised." They are not so valid, however, in cases where the consideration given is in a form other than cash or a promise to pay cash. Preferably we should restrict "cost" to those resources acquired for money, e.g., the purchase of materials and their subsequent transfer to work in process and finished goods. The "non-cash acquisitions" should then be called by other names, such as "market price," "fair value," "estimated value," etc. It will then be crystal clear that accounting is not and cannot be restricted to "cost" (cash-price), and the whole problem of basis will come into sharper focus.

Income, earnings, and profit (page 13): . . . entities produce, consume, spend; business or business-types entities concentrate mainly on producing goods and services. This distinction is widely recognized in the separation of business and personal affairs (e.g., the use of separate records for each distinctive venture under common ownership in proprietorships, partnerships, and other forms of unincorporated associations). We propose to use this distinction as the basis for suggesting that "income" is a term that should not be applied both to natural persons and to business entities. Mainly because the economic theory of income is primarily a theory of the income of natural persons and not of accounting entities, we should restrict the term "income" to personal income. The terms "earnings" or "profit" are then available to describe the related concept when applied to accounting entities.

It is interesting that only three comments were received concerning the definition of accounting, and were noteworthy by the brevity of remarks. The observations were as follows:

The definition of the function of accounting does not stress the importance of analyzing and interpreting the results of recording, classifying and summarizing transactions. It is believed this function should be included.

The brief attention to the definition of accounting hardly seems adequate in a work of this type.

An accountant is one skilled in the art of accounting—why say more?

On the other hand, the definition of cost suggested prompted considerable reaction. The majority of correspondents disagreed with restricting the meaning of cost to cash consideration. The following two quotations are representative of this group:

My only other comment of significance deals with the recommendation relating to the term "cost." While I would agree that some narrowing of this concept may be necessary, I believe the cost concept is and must remain much broader than the "cash consideration" suggested. I believe some term must exist which means "valuation based on consideration given upon acquisition" as distinguished from a gift or a value based on appraisal which would reflect appreciation for which no consideration was given, or depreciation from which no apparent value was received. None of the terms offered carry with it such connotation. Further, I cannot see any valid basis for distinguishing between the payment of consideration in cash or in some other equally valuable asset, so long as the value can be objectively measured. To follow the suggestion as to the term "cost" further, no manufacturing inventory could be described properly as being valued at cost if depreciation or other allocated costs were included therein, particularly if the fixed assets had been acquired in exchange for capital stock. It seems to me the implications of the suggested revision of the definition of cost are much broader than the problem itself. While I have no objection to clarifying

the term "cost," I do not believe we can eliminate the broad concept in which it is usually used.

The usefulness of this restriction of the meaning of "cost" should be demonstrated before the restriction is accepted. If U.S. Government bonds are the consideration given, for example, "cost" could not be used. Is this helpful? Perhaps a more important problem would arise with plant, equipment and inventory acquired for, say, stock. These become commingled in the production process with purer "costs." How is the resulting output remaining in inventory to be described?

Ten persons reacted to the suggestion that the term "income" be restricted to natural persons. Three favored the proposal, seven did not. Those favoring the proposal did so because of a general feeling that this would improve understanding by various user-groups. Those disagreeing with the suggested distinction generally felt that no useful purpose would be served by making such a change. The following quotations are representative of both sides of the issue:

. . . the more I think about the limitation of the word "income" to natural persons, the more I am inclined to agree with Moyer. I see no useful purpose in establishing the limitation recommended in the bulletin.

I like the reasoning which has led to your suggestion that the term "earnings" should be used only to describe the enhancement in worth resulting from business type activities and restricting the use of "income" to describe "personal" income. However, the average investor will have difficulty in understanding the reason for the difference, and I agree with Professor Moyer that the difference in the connotation of the two terms hardly justifies an attempt to change a usage that has been so widely accepted. In any event, I would avoid any suggestion of continuing the use of the word "profit."

I applaud the restriction of "income" to natural persons. "Profit" has an advantage over "earnings" in relation to businesses because of its antonym "loss." I can't readily think of an appropriate antonym for "earnings." I don't agree with Moyer's objections; after all, "profit" was there first and "income" in this sense is a relatively recent interloper in accounting literature. However, the really important issue, to my mind, is to distinguish between two different concepts, whatever names might ultimately be attached to them.

It appears to me that the decisions to restrict the use of the term "income" was a very good one. Despite Professor Moyer's dissent, I think the term "income" has been used in so many other ways, such as—gross income, marginal income—that the words "earnings" or "profit" are best used to describe the end result.

At the end of the postulates study a fairly lengthy comment appears by Leonard Spacek. In this comment Mr. Spacek presents a strong appeal for consideration of a proposed postulate of "fairness," the rationale of which has been developed in depth elsewhere in the literature. Since Mr. Spacek's comment was included as an appendix to the postulates study, it also received some comment.

Ten individuals discussed the fairness concept, three endorsed it, six did not favor it, and one attempted to reconcile the differences between Mr. Spacek's comment and the postulates study. The comment which attempts to reconcile the differences is as follows:

The view that there are less than fourteen postulates is expressed (with a vengeance) by one member of the project advisory committee, who filed a minority report supporting the view that there is only one basic postulate, namely, fairness. His disagreement with the author is founded in principal part on adherence to a different definition of the word postulate. Webster's Unabridged gives five definitions. The author of the monograph seems to accept the number two definition (though he does not say so) which roughly identifies "postulate" with "axiom" or "assumption." According to this definition a postulate "provides the first premise in a train of reasoning or for a philosophical system. . . ." This definition seems to correspond closely to what the Special Committee on Research Program had in mind. The project committee dissenter prefers definition three, which is, simply, "a condition; an essential prerequisite." His fairness postulate is essentially authoritarian rather than merely logical or philosophical.

The three comments which favored classifying the concept of fairness as a postulate are:

I wish to urge reconsideration of the basic principle of usefulness so cavalierly dismissed on page 4 of the monograph. The two questions: useful to whom and for what purpose, have already been answered. Usefulness "must be judged from the standpoint of society as a whole" (see quotation from ARB 43 on page 5). The purposes are varied, and this appears to be recognized in the monograph at the top of page 28. I think the concept of usefulness is not greatly at variance with that of fairness urged by Leonard Spacek. I prefer usefulness because it avoids the implications of ethics which, though important, do not belong in the category of postulates. In this I am in agreement with the comments on pages 3 and 4 of the monograph. It would follow from fundamental emphasis on usefulness that principles or practices could be determined, not by deductive reasoning, but rather by an inductive process guided by studies of their individual effect in the current environment. Admittedly this is a difficult, not to say painful, and possibly never-ending undertaking but it shuns the fallacious quest of an easy answer where none exists. It is also recognized that my recommended approach nullifies the attempt to provide the foundation type of postulates, and therefore, the announced objective of the study.

In the process of interpreting economic events,

accountants apply certain standards. If these standards had to be summarized in one word, it would probably be "pragmatism." That is to say, any accounting principle must meet the pragmatic test that it should be useful (in the light of the needs of the users of accounting information), and it must be possible (i.e., the average accountant must be able to understand and apply the principle). There would be no objection to the inclusion of "fairness" among the interpretive standards for the development of accounting principles, as is desired by Mr. Spacek, but one must agree with Dr. Moonitz that this ethical concept is subjective and "itself needs standards to be capable of application."

Three of the six letters received which disagreed with the concept of fairness are as follows:

Fairness is at best an ethical concept related to the existing sociological environment and at all times is a subjective judgment. Is something made more fair by Government support, a court decision, a unanimous vote, or an agreement between opposing parties? Will such an evaluation be lasting? I think not.

. . . a principle which may be fair for one purpose is not necessarily fair for all purposes. An example might be carrying assets at present value vs. carrying them at cost. I suppose it is true that any information which does not tell lies or mislead (which implies its purpose is understood) is fair to everybody.

The point of dissent appears to be that of a different mental approach. The monograph emphasized "objectivity"; the dissenters substitute a "subjective" approach. Throughout the monograph our author has warned against subjectivity and on page 4 he asks, quite pointedly, ". . . useful to whom? and for what purpose?" The same inquiries are germane with respect to "fairness."

When it is stated that we must be fair "to all segments of the business community" (with the connotation that each and all of these segments will agree on the fairness), how can one seriously hold that "management, labor, stockholders, creditors, customers and the public" will accept as wholly fair a decision which may be adverse to the particular interest of those persons or groups?

Surely, our aim is to be fair. Justice, truth, and fairness are the goals toward which we aim. With Pontius Pilate we ask "What is Truth?" Lacking omniscience, we try to base our aim on what we know (or think we know).

Method of presentation

Somewhat anticlimactic, but nevertheless worthy of mention, are several comments received from correspondents regarding the general method of presentation and the length of the discourse. Unfortunately, about the only conclusion which can be reached from reading these remarks is that no matter what is done, some persons will be unhappy. Witness the following four comments on the character of the presentation:

... the erudite manner in which the monograph is written detracts from its usefulness as an effective exposure vehicle. The intricate discussions of the various factors tend to obscure the real purpose of the study and make it difficult reading.

The breakdown of Dr. Moonitz's monograph into six chapters is clear and logical. The concise framing of his chapters enables the reader to absorb the contents easily and to keep a clear conception of his ideas.

I am not enthused about the author's style of presentation. The material appears to have been presented in too heavy a manner and, as a consequence, is uninteresting and slow reading. I also note that in many instances he abounds with excessive examples related to a single circumstance or thought.

... the monograph is a very well-written document which presents basic problems of accounting and business in an orderly manner. It develops fourteen so-called postulates which are clearly written and concise statements of underlying and accepted bases for accounting.

Comments on the length of the study were similarly inconclusive:

"... we found that the document tended to be philosophic in approach and tone which resulted in its seeming to be discursive, vague, and indirect. The preliminary build-up hardly seemed necessary to support the self-evident conclusions which resulted.

... although the monograph was very well-written and the material ably presented, it is altogether too lengthy and too cluttered with notes to serve as a final document.

The brevity of the entire treatment is such that a reader has very little basis for determining the nature or reliability of the author's method in arriving at the postulate presented. So little in the way of explanations is offered that a reader is unable to determine even the author's own standards for acceptance of propositions as postulates. One cannot tell how he will interpret the propositions he has selected nor how they will be used in developing a comprehensive theory of accounting.

I have no doubt that the author has given a great deal of thought to his subject, yet the monograph itself gives the reader little more than an outline or summary.

QUESTIONS

(1)   What is a postulate? What (if any) is the relation of a postulate
       to an axiom, to a principle and to an imperative?

(2)   What does Moonitz mean by "the a priori part of accounting" (p.3)?

(3)   Is there a "fundamental pervasive limit in the field of account-
       ing research" (p.7)?

(4)   The five functions of accounting are intended to be derived from
       the five "A" postulates. To what extent are they successfully
       related?

(5)   Is money "a common denominator" (Postulate A-5)? Are there any
       qualifications to the postulate needed in order to make it
       relevant to economic activity?

(6)   Do the statements listed as Postulates-B and Postulates-C com-
       prise true postulates (in relation to your answer to question 1)?
       What relationship between the three groups of postulates
       - is necessary?
       - is sufficient?

(7)   What basic problems did Moonitz attempt to solve in ARS 1?

(8)   Is Spacek fair in commenting (p.56) that
                "this study illustrates that the historic and
                customary approach to the formulation of a
                basic foundation and framework of accounting
                theory is not adequate and that a completely
                new approach is needed,"?

(9)   ARS 1 & ARS 3.
       "The principal task of accounting is to measure the history of
       the resources held by an economic entities". (ARS 3, pp.11-12).
       Is the use of the term 'measurement' in both studies (especially,
       ARS 3) consistent with conventional (theoretical) usage?

(10)   ARS 3 is "the companion" study to ARS 1. How are they related?

156

14

EDGAR OWEN EDWARDS

The Theory and Measurement of Business Income
(with P W Bell)

Biographical Chronology

1919	Born, 20 December, Fox borough, Massachusetts, son of John Owen and Winifred Beatrice (Roberts) Edwards.
1937-39	Attended Green Mountain College.
1939-41	Employed by Telescope Folding Furniture Company, production controller, 1940-41.
1942-46	Military service, infantry US Army, attaining rank of captain.
1946	Married Jean Elizabeth Lotz, 27 April.
1947	Awarded BA, Washington and Jefferson College.
1949	Awarded MA, Johns Hopkins University
1950-53	Instructor (Richard Stockton preceptor) in economics, Princeton University.
1951	Awarded PhD, Johns Hopkins University.
1953-56	Assistant Professor of Economics, Princeton University.
1953-54	Awarded Guggenheim Fellowship, Sweden.
1956-59	Associate Professor of Economics, Princeton University.
1959-69	Hargrove Professor of Economics, Yale University.
1959-64	Chairman, Department of Economics, Yale University.
1961	Recipient, Distinguished Alumni Award, Washington and Jefferson College.
1961	The Theory and Measurement of Business Income, published.
1963-68	Appointed principal economic advisor to the Ministry of Economic Planning and Development, Government of Kenya.
1968-69	Awarded Fellowship, Economic Growth Centre, Yale University.
1969-74	Economic Advisor on Asian and Pacific Programme, Ford Foundation.
1974-	Economic Advisor, Government of Kenya.
1977	Appointed Henry Gardiner Symonds Professor of Administrative Science and Economics, Rice University.

PHILIP W BELL

Biographical Chronology

1924	Born.
1941-45	Pilot, US Air Force.
1946-47	Correspondent, New York Times.
1947	Awarded BA, Princeton University.
1949	Awarded MA, University of California, Berkeley.
1949-50	Research Assistant, US Government, Council of Foreign Relations.
1951-52	Research Associate, Institute for Advanced Study, Princeton University.
1952-56	Assistant Professor of Economics, Haverford College.
1954	Awarded PhD, Princeton University.
1956-57	Associate Professor of Economics, Haverford College. Awarded Social Science Research Council Post-Doctoral Fellowship, London.

1957-60	Associate Professor of Economics, University of California, Berkeley.
1959	Ford Foundation Professorship, University of California, Berkeley, Spring and Summer.
1960-67	Appointed Associate Professor of Economics, Haverford College. Promoted to Professor in 1962.
1961	The Theory and Measurement of Business Income, published.
1961-63	Consultant, US Treasury Department.
1962-63	Consultant, Rockefeller Foundation.
1963-64	Visiting Professor, University of Pennsylvania, Spring.
1963-65	Professor and Head, Department of Economics, Makerere University College (Uganda). Appointed Dean of Social Science Faculty in 1964.
1965-66	Professor and Acting Head, Department of Economics, Fisk University.
1965-67	Associate Director of Humanities and Social Sciences, The Rockefeller Foundation. Consultant, US Treasury Department.
1966-67	Professor and Head, Department of Economics, Lincoln University.
1966-68	Consultant, US State Department on African Affairs. Member, Technical Assistant Panel, President's Scientific Advisory Board.
1968-78	Professor of Economics, University of California, (Santa Cruz).
1968-72	Provost, Merrill College, University of California (Santa Cruz).
1972-74	Director, Nairobi Study Centre, University of California Education Abroad Program.
1977	Visiting Professor, Jesse H Jones Graduate School of Administration, Rice University, Fall.
1978	William Alexander Kirkland Professor of Administrative Science and Accounting, Rice University.
1980	Economic Theory (with M P Todaro), published.
1981	May-June, Visitor, Inflation Accounting Research Project, University of Waikato, Hamilton, New Zealand; June-Aug, Visiting Fellow, Australian National University, Canberra, Australia; presented annual endowed/research lectures of Australian Society of Accountants.

SELECTED BIBLIOGRAPHY - EDWARDS

1952   "Funds Statements for Short and Long-run Analyses,"
            Journal of Business, v.25, pp 156-74.

1954   "Depreciation Policy Under Changing Price-Levels."
            Accounting Review, v.29, pp 267-80; reprinted in
            Zeff S. and T. Keller (eds) Financial Accounting Theory,
            McGraw Hill, 1964, pp 167-82.

1961   "Depreciation and the Maintenance of Real Capital,"
            in Meij J.L. (ed) Depreciation and Replacement Policy,
            pp 46-140.

            The Theory and Measurement of Business Income, University
            of California Press, 323 p (with Bell P.W.).

1974   "An Indifference Approach to Profit-Volume Analysis,"
            Accounting Review, v.49, pp 579-83 (with L. Todd
            Johnson).

1975   "The State of Current Value Accounting," Accounting Review,
            v.50, pp 235-45.

1978   "Primacy of Accounting Income in Decisions on Expansion:
            An Exercise in Arithmetic," in van Dam C., Trends in
            Managerial and Financial Accounting, Leiden, pp 45-62.

1979   Accounting for Economic Events, Scholars Book Co.,
            692 p (with P. Bell and L. Todd Johnson).

                            BELL

1951   "Cyclical Variations and in Occupational Wage Differentials,"
            Review of Economics and Statistics, v.33, pp 329-37.

1956   The Sterling Area in the Postwar World, Clarendon Press,
            434 p.

1961   The Theory and Measurement of Business Income, University
            of California Press, 289 p. (with E. Edwards).

1962   "Taxation on Private Investments Abroad - Economic Aspects,"
            Proceedings of Southwestern Legal Foundation, pp 235-47.

1963   "Discussion - the Balance of Payments Issue," Journal of
            Finance, v.18, pp 214-16.

1966   "The Measurement of Business Income,Part 2: Price Changes
            and Income Measurement," Chapter 4 in Modern Accounting
            Theory, ed, Backer M., Prentice-Hall, pp 91-7.

1971   "On Current Replacement Costs and Business Income,"
            Asset Valuation and Income Determination, ed, Sterling R.
            Scholars Book Co., pp 19-32.

159

1975   "Optimizing Inventory Acquisition and Holding Policy in the Face of Price Changes," Proceedings, AAA Annual Meeting (Tucson, Arizona), pp 435-51.

1976   "Current Replacement Costs: a Qualified Opinion," Journal of Accountancy, v.142 (Nov) pp 63-70 (with L. Todd Johnson).

1977   "Security Portfolio Reports for Client and Manager," Financial Analysts' Journal, v.33 (May/June), pp 56-61.

1979   "Current Value Accounting and a Simple Production Case: Edbejo and Other Companies in the Taxi Business" (with L. Todd Johnson), in Accounting for a Simplied Firm, ed, Sterling R.R. and A.L. Thomas, Scholars Book Company, pp 95-130.

              Accounting for Economic Events, Scholars Book Co., 692 p (with E.O. Edwards and L.T. Johnson).

1980   "Economic Theory and Development Economics: Where do we Stand?", Social Research, v.4 (Summer), pp 235-47.

1982   "CVA, CCA and CoCoA: How Fundamental are the Differences?", Accounting Theory Monograph No.1, Australian Accounting Research Foundation, 59 p.

REFERENCES

Review: Accounting Review, v.37, 1962, pp.596-7 (Schlatter, W J). Journal of Accounting, v.113, Jan 1962, pp.91-2 (Bedford, N). Journal of Business, v.35, 1962, pp.221-2 (Johnson, C E).

Anderson, J A, A Comparative Analysis of Selected Income Measurement Theories in Financial Accounting, AAA (SAR No.12), 1976.

Catlett, G R, "Response to 'On Current Replacement Costs & Business Income'"in Asset Valuation & Income Determination, Sterling, R R (ed), Scholars Book Co, 1971, pp.33-41.

Chambers, R J, "Edwards & Bell on Business Income", Accounting Review, v.40, 1965, pp.731-41.

_____ , "Edwards & Bell in Income Measurement in Retrospect", Abacus, v.18, 1982.

Drake, D F & N Dopuch, "On the Case for Dichotomizing Income", Journal of Accounting Research, v.3, 1965, pp.192-205.

Revsine, L, "The Theory of Measurement of Business Income: A Review Article", Accounting Review, v.56, 1981, pp.342-54.

Wright, F K, "Depreciation & Obsolescence in Current Value Accounting", Journal of Accounting Research, v.3, 1965, pp.167-81.

Edwards and Bell on Business Income

R. J. Chambers

W̲E̲ WISH to examine some elements of the proposals of Edwards and Bell for the measurement of business income.[1] Let it be said at the outset that we accept the general tenor of their scheme. In particular we accept the necessity of taking into account the effects of variations in specific prices and of variations in the price level in any computation of income which shall indicate improvement in well-offness. The points with which we shall be concerned are in part matters of principle and in part matters of effective communication, which in an important sense are matters of a different principle. The two will inevitably be intermingled. If any reader should suppose, when we begin to discuss particular terms or phrases, that we are engaging in mere verbal quibbles, we ask him to reflect at the outset on the fact that words and numbers are the stock in trade of all men who must trade ideas with others. This applies to the messages that accountants transmit to others every bit as much as it applies to those who discuss what messages should be transmitted and by what signs. It bears as much on the process of evaluating business behavior as on the process of assessing the merits of proposals for reform of accounting practices.

The Emphasis on the Income Account

We accept that Edwards and Bell have chosen to deal with income and with nothing else. They are certainly not primarily concerned with balance sheets or other financial statements; the treatment falls back on balance sheets for illustrative effects of the devices used only.

However, even accepting the emphasis, it is still a matter of direct concern to specify the function of a balance sheet or of the financial position it does or may disclose. At the very least, the balance sheet specifies the balances to be carried forward from one period to another, however those balances have been derived. The position represented must therefore have some meaning at the point of time as for which it is drawn. The financial position of a firm may be discovered quite independently of the records it may have kept; and indeed it should perhaps be so discovered from time to time, as a check against the distortions which may arise from the mere manipulation of figures as well as from deliberate misbehavior. Sprague seems to have been entirely correct when he suggested that a balance sheet could be obtained in two ways, by inspection and by inference from records, and that ideally the results from both methods would be identical.[2] In the intervening half century

---

[1] Edgar O. Edwards and Philip W. Bell, *The Theory and Measurement of Business Income* (University of California Press, 1961). References hereafter are given by page numbers in the text.
[2] Charles E. Sprague, *The Philosophy of Accounts* (New York: Ronald Press Company, 1907), p. 27.

R. J. Chambers is a Professor in the Department of Accounting at the University of Sydney, Australia.

we seem to have forgotten that as between the figures appearing in balance sheets and income accounts only the former can be authenticated by reference to facts beyond the firm, and that such facts are the only facts relevant to its dealings with others. Figures in income accounts can only be authenticated by a less direct, inferential process, which in any case depends on the discovery of many matters not already in the books of account at the end of a period. We will return to this matter at a later point.

Evaluation

A great deal is made, and very properly, of the role of accounting information as a basis of evaluation. What is meant by evaluation is something akin to appraisal or judgment; it does not relate to putting a number representing a measure on any thing or class of things.

But evaluating what? Business decisions: " . . . a principal function of accounting data is to serve as a fundamental tool in the evaluation of past decisions. . . ." (*pp. 3–4*) Now, if we contemplate the simple firm which economists often use in discussions of business behavior, it is not difficult to imagine that a single past decision can be appraised when its effects have worked themselves out. But there are few, if any, such simple firms making one homogeneous product, making one decision at a time, and waiting until its effects have become apparent before making the next. The typical firm has a whole series of specific acts, the consequences of specific decisions, in the course of execution at any and every point of time. And they are all in some respect interdependent. Which of all the past decisions can accounting "data" be used to evaluate? Which past decision, if any, can be said to have been in error, when so many past decisions are commingled? How are we to disentangle the effects of one decision from the effects of others? And even if there were only two choices open at the outset, how can we know, after the event and with the knowledge of its consequences, whether the consequences of the alternative would have been more advantageous? For, in experiencing the event we have modified our capacity for choice between the alternatives, and in bringing about the event we have changed the environment against which the assessment is made. "You maintain that you are free to take either the right- or the left-hand fork in the road. I defy you to set up a single objective criterion by which you can prove after you have made the turn that you might have made the other."[3]

There seems to be only one sense in which the evaluation of past decisions can have any meaning in the typical case. And that is evaluation of the complex of initial decisions and all intervening modifications (strictly new decisions) between the dates of initial decisions and the date of evaluation. But again, decisions are not made by any individual or small number of individuals constituting the "management" of a firm. Perhaps Edwards and Bell (*p. 2*) mean by "management" all the persons who have positions of authority. But decisions are also made by others who have no authority in the formal sense: by workers who may work more or less assiduously, by suppliers who may or may not deliver as and when required, by investors or creditors who may or may not influence the availability of funds, and so on. Of none of these possibilities, even for such a term as one year, can management have any exact foreknowledge. It is therefore difficult to see how "accurate" can be applied to expectations. (*p. 2*)

The kinds of specific decision which Edwards and Bell use as illustrations rep-

[3] P. W. Bridgman. *The Nature of Physical Theory* (New York: John Wiley & Sons, Inc., 1964, first published 1936), p. 12.

resent the obvious major choices which confront many firms from time to time. But they leave aside all questions about methods of securing coordinated action, methods of adapting to changes in external circumstances, methods of inspiring the best efforts of all personnel, and a host of similar organizational questions. Every one of these has a bearing on the results which accounts show at the end of a period. The accounts simply do not show unequivocally whether an achieved degree of success was due to any singular decision or any limited number of distinctive major decisions. All they can show is the *general* effect of all decision-making and decision-changing behavior—in brief the quality of the *adaptive* behavior as a whole—of a firm in an interval. Edwards and Bell recognize this (*p. 38*), but in shifting from the evaluation of specific decisions to the evaluation of performance in general they fail to develop the full sense of general evaluation.

This becomes apparent in two ways. The first is the isolated nature of the test of success. "The test of success, and therefore the logical criterion for the evaluation of business decisions, is the extent to which the achieved increments in market value approximate the increases originally anticipated." (*p. 48*) This test of success is purely internal to the firm, and because one element of it is internally manufactured (the anticipated increases) the test is far from satisfactory. Suppose a firm sets out to earn, say, 30 per cent on its sales; and that a general rise in demand during the period for which the expectation was formed makes it possible to earn 50 per cent. Would the firm then have *failed* if it earned 50 per cent? Or would it have kept its margin to 30 per cent for the purpose of *succeeding*? The logical criterion for the evaluation of business decisions can only be how well they work out by comparison with other firms. Success,

efficiency, and similar attributes are judged comparatively by outsiders, and therefore must also be so judged by insiders, with reference to other firms. This introduces the second point.

We are told that "accounting data must serve internal functions first." (*p. 5*) Perhaps first in time. But the relevance of accounting information to stockholders and creditors and its role in the allocative function of the securities market is very much played down; it receives brief mention on pp. 5, 59, 265, 279. Now the actual rate of return on capital, one would suppose, should be the prime test of those investing in business generally, so that it is not a mere sideline of the argument. The judgments of external users of accounting information have direct effects on the survival of firms. Stockholders and creditors may well wish to decide, and often do decide, that to liquidate a firm is preferable to its continuation. They cannot decide in an informed manner unless they know at least what could be obtained by disposal of the assets piecemeal (in a careful manner, not in a straight "knock-down" liquidation), for that is the minimum sum they could invest otherwise. Knowledge of financial position on this basis is a necessary factual premise of the choice; and the rate of return is a necessary factual premise of choice between alternative investments even if piecemeal disposal is not in contemplation.

One thing is left quite out of the picture of decision-making. We are told that "the successful management is one that acts upon expectations that are relatively accurate." (*p. 2*) We are not told anything about the facts that expectations are based on. One thing beyond doubt influences the expectations that come to be entertained and adopted. This is the *relative* advantage of one course over alternative courses employing *given* means. Decision-making is nothing more than choosing. At any point of time we must suppose that a firm has a given collection of resources and associations and potent¹·ls for making possible the attainment of the goals expected by its supporters. In particular, the collection of resources limits the alternatives; only some are feasible. Unless therefore the extent of the collection and the monetary equivalents of each item in the collection are known, it is impossible to compare the expectations entertained about alternatives and, therefore, impossible to choose. Contemporary knowledge of the *given* means is a prerequisite to choice. It provides the factual basis both of expectations and of future actions.

It should be apparent therefore that evaluation is only one of the functions which accounting may serve. A second is the continuous provision of statements of fact in contemporary terms, statements of the contemporary cash equivalent of the assets and equities; hence our earlier remark on the necessity of paying more than passing attention to the derivation of, and the meanings of the measures incorporated in, balance sheets.

Exit Prices or Entry Prices

The principal contribution of Edwards and Bell towards the elucidation of the problem appears to lie in Chapters II and III. Chapter II sets up a scheme based on opportunity costs which is said to be apposite in the short run. Chapter III "extends" the analysis to the long run, choosing "current cost" as the basis of valuation.

To begin, we state the differences in the two bases. Opportunity costs are the "values [presumably prices] that could currently be realized if assets . . . were sold . . . outside the firm at the best prices immediately obtainable." (*p. 79*) Current cost is "the cost currently of acquiring the inputs which the firm used to produce the asset being valued." (*p. 79*) As the former

is an "exit" price and the latter an "entry" price, it seems rather strained to call the long-run analysis an "extension" of the theory developed for short-run analysis. It is in fact an entirely different theory. We have therefore to inquire why quite a different basis is adopted for the so-called long-run analysis than that so strongly argued for the short run. The reason for the switch appears to lie in the manner in which the authors conceive the long run and the short run.

Now the short run and the long run are part of the same "run"; this includes all intervals from the time of choice to the effective horizon of expectations. Every such interval will in the course of time become a short-run interval on the expiry of its antecedent interval. Unless the long-run expectation is equal to the sum of all short-run expectations there would be a difference in expectations. No such difference is described, nor is there any discussion about the possibility of there being a difference. We therefore presume that the long-run expectation *is* equal to the sum of the short-run expectations. If, then, any course of action is taken in the short run which is less ambitious than would be taken if only a short run were in contemplation, the limitation would be predicated on the recovery of the short-run "sacrifice" in some period in the future when that period itself becomes the short run. Every short-run expectation is thus part of a long-run expectation; the two are not different things. We act here and now with the idea of being somewhere else later; if we wish to walk a mile we must first make steps; the one is part of the other. That we must do first things first is unchanged even if in the course of doing first things we change our goals. If we do not get through the short run, there will be no long run.

The distinction made by Edwards and Bell leads them to some curious assertions. Current operating profit, we are told, "is essentially the long-run profit associated with the existing process of production carried on under existing conditions." (*p. 99*) It is difficult to see what this short-run "long-run profit" is; at least it is difficult if the short run is regarded as part of the long run. Again current operating profit "does not indicate . . . the excess of what is obtained from one outflow of resources over what could be obtained from another outflow of resources." (*p. 99*) But if it does not do so, of what use is it in choosing between the present deployment of resources and alternative deployments? Of what use is it in decision-making?

Again, we are told that a positive realizable profit (based on opportunity cost) "indicates only that the firm should be operated in the short run." (*p. 100*) Of course it does no such thing. It indicates the surplus arising on the footing that the firm *may* do the same *or* other things in the succeeding period, and that the market prices of the goods and services available at the end of the period are necessary knowledge in making the choice between doing the same or other things. Again, we are told that "realizable operating profit has been constructed essentially on the basis of the theory of a single investment . . . and . . . on the assumption that the only alternative to operating the business in the way in which it is being operated is to discontinue the business." (*pp. 100–101*) We have not found any explicit adoption of the stated position. It is certainly not inconsistent with the conception of opportunity cost, as defined by the authors, to contemplate "replacement and chains of replacement" on an opportunity cost basis. (*p. 70*) The definition says "if assets were sold"; it does not say "if *all* assets were sold and the business were discontinued." Replacement is in a very real sense no different from any other investment. With given resources, it is necessary to know what means are available for the acquisition of a new asset, whether it is a replacement or an innovation.

We are told that "realizable profit [i.e., on the opportunity cost base] may indicate when the assets themselves should be abandoned by the firm, but the abandonment of a particular use of those assets can better be determined on the basis of current operating profit. So long as there is some use to which the assets can be put within the firm and which will yield a positive current operating profit (in excess of interest), the measurement of realizable profit serves a secondary purpose." (*p. 101*) The entrepreneur in this case seems to be a rather short-sighted fellow. He is apparently quite unconcerned with any better use of the funds obtainable by abandoning their use, so long as the present return exceeds the rate of interest. He is clearly not a maximizer in any sense, except of ineptitude or inertia.

The additional justifications of current operating profit which occur in pages following those cited are of the same kind. They leave a clear impression that the authors have found themselves on the horns of a dilemma: " . . . it is our feeling that a strong case can be made for the incorporation of both sets of data [i.e., on opportunity cost and current cost bases] in the accounting records." (*p. 97*) In the end they say they have chosen on the basis of purposes with the highest priority and "upon certain practical considerations such as the wide acceptance of traditional accounting principles." (*p. 98*)

This dilemma goes to the very heart of the matter. At an early stage the authors after discussing internal and external users say: "It should not be surprising then if the same set of accounting principles can be used to develop data suitable to external as well as to internal users." (*p. 5*) Notice that this does not suggest that the two users require different data, and that the same set of principles can produce different data; the context of the passage is a discussion of similarity of evaluation processes, even though the evaluators may be different. At page 110, however, it appears that they countenance a number of concepts of profit. "The fact that accounting data can serve many purposes suggests that it may be a serious mistake to restrict accounts to the kind of data from which but one profit concept can be developed." And then at the end: "The information that real capital is or is not being maintained is perhaps good to have, but it is not relevant to profit-maximizing decisions." (*pp. 264–5*)

We cannot escape an uneasy feeling that several critical difficulties are being passed over. Suppose we wish to know the amount by which a tree has grown in height between two dates. This involves an exercise in lengths. We can imagine a number of different kinds of persons who might have use for the information in respect of any given tree; tree cultivators, foresters, lumber merchants, lumber carriers, and so on. Each of these has a set of premises specific to his own interests; each applies to his own set of specific premises the information relating to the growth of the tree; and each reaches his own set of conclusions. Notwithstanding that all the parties have different specific premises, the additional premise is common to all. None is free to say length or the increment in length is for him a concept different from what it is for the others. Nor does the surveyor, or whoever it is that measures the height of trees, know or care about the specific premises of potential users of the information that he produces.

The measurement of income is exactly the same in principle. If all kinds of users may have some use for the measurement, it seems a matter of the clearest moment that the concept shall be unequivocal. We may, if we wish, show the components, but that can in no way modify the concept. Now, as income is an increment, it is only necessary

to decide of what it is an increment. It is an increment of residual equity. But if residual equity is measured according to different scales (units of different purchasing power), the original measurement in the earlier scale must first be converted to the prevailing scale at the date of income measurement. The difference between this converted measurement and the measurement of residual equity at the closing date is the measure of income.

To be quite unequivocal and quite objective in taking the measure of residual equity (by measuring the difference between assets and liabilities in a contemporary scale), it is necessary to disregard the fact that at one point of time the management of the firm committed the firm to a certain collection of assets with certain expectations in mind. On the discovery of the present position, any or all of those expectations may be revised. It would be circular or contradictory to allow the possibility of any such revision on the basis of figures which imply continuation without revision. We reach the conclusion that opportunity cost, and not the authors' current cost, is the appropriate asset measurement basis. *Opportunity costs (market resale prices) are relevant to the firm always.*

In stating this conclusion we are asserting a principle. If in any particular circumstance market resale prices are unobtainable, it seems not unreasonable to take an entry price as an approximation; it is the best available. But entry or replacement prices are not thereby elevated to the rank of principle. They are expedients only; necessary, but expedients only to be adopted when superior indications of opportunity cost are just not available.

Some Constraints

Edwards and Bell have adopted several explicit contraints in devising their solution. The first is that the system required is one which adheres closely to existing conventions and procedures. They leave the reader in little doubt that accounting profit is a meaningless or useless number; yet their solution is tied to methods which yield accounting profit. This can lead only to confusion. If the term "accounting profit" persists, readers will almost certainly try to attach some meaning to it; and if the methods of Edwards and Bell were to prevail as accepted accounting methods surely their "business profit" would become the "accounting profit" of the future. There seem to be no realistic grounds for the retention of the term if it denotes a meaningless quantity. Tax considerations are no criteria; a major reform can be expected to evoke some changes in tax laws; it is unlikely to occur if its supporting arguments are allowed to be whittled away by concessions to existing taxation rules.

Again, they adhere strongly to the notion of realization. More than anything else, the consequences of this contribute to the complexity of their solution. It gives rise to a whole crop of distinctions and new accounts—realizable, realized, and unrealized cost savings; realized and unrealized surpluses; realizable, realized, and unrealized fictional gains; and in Chapter VIII, even more complicated terms. The whole demonstration has its logic, of course, and it is not beyond the comprehension of the patient and painstaking. But it gives rise to grave doubts about the communicability of the results. It is difficult to imagine what answer an accountant would give to an innocent question like "What is a fictional realizable cost saving?" put to him by a manager who thinks he understands business and the vernacular language.

Year-End Adjustments

Again, they appear to have adopted as one of the principal desiderata of their system that the necessary adjustments to traditional accounting statements shall be capable of being made in one set of operations at the end of each period. We wish now to challenge the propriety of this.

If year end adjustments on the authors' pattern are to suffice, some quite heroic assumptions have to be made about uniformities of changes.

Consider first some physical changes. The example used when dealing with inventories shows an increase in physical inventories during a year. (*pp. 144-5*) For the purpose of the exercise it is assumed that the growth in the inventory occurs at a constant rate. (*footnote 9, p. 144*) Using the result, a certain sales pattern is deduced, purely formally, on the assumption that sales were on the dates of purchases and "were equal to 95 per cent of purchases on the dates when purchases were made." (*p. 145*) The process of deriving the dates and quantities of sales is quite unnecessary; in practice they would be data. These dates and quantities, based on the stated uniformity of growth in inventories, are then used to obtain the amount of the realized cost savings. But the assumption is quite unreal. The solution given is not the only solution to the question, "What sales and at what prices will aggregate 380 units and yield $4,000?" Quite different results can be obtained if this unreal assumption is not made. Indeed, if the units are indivisible, the authors' solution does not fit the facts; it yields halves of units. Some similar calculations occur on page 241.

Consider, now, some price changes. When dealing with inventories, it is said that the current cost of materials used can be obtained by taking the weighted-average purchase price during the period in question. (*p. 144*) Now, having already assumed that the increments to physical stock occur at the dates of purchases, spread through the whole year, it is assumed that the realizable cost savings on the increment may be computed by applying the difference between year average and year-end prices to the physical increment in inventories. By implication the physical increment occurred in the second half of the year, whereas the figures given show that only half of the physical increment occurred in the second half. The two assumptions seem to be incompatible. This discrepancy may be regarded as a triviality; it may, however, also be regarded as a warning against multiplying hypotheses.

The real point of criticism is the gross assumption of uniformities and their treatment by averaging. In the simple example given it is quite possible to make easy assumptions about regularities. But the realities are much harder to live with. Suppose that inventories had in fact been run down and then up, or vice versa, during the year; suppose there were one hundred or one thousand items in the inventory moving at different rates and whose prices were moving at different rates and in different directions; suppose there were initially large mark ups followed by mark downs, or vice versa. What then would averages, supposed to fall mid-year, mean? Added to that, the calculations for a homogeneous inventory are complicated enough; a heterogeneous inventory would require a computer, putting the process beyond the reach of all but a small proportion of firms. Further, the reduction of opening and closing figures to average price figures, and the restoration of these eventually to closing price figures by the use of price indexes, increases the possibility of errors through the averaging process; for even if the calculations are done with impeccable accuracy, indexes are approximations only, to be used as sparingly as possible.

Edwards and Bell admit that their method contains and yields approximations. There can be no question that every such method includes and requires approximations. But it seems to be unnecessary to make approximations when the facts are available. They describe the accounting problem as "one of recording and relating to each other these particular price changes *as they occur*." (*p. 17*, emphasis added) They refer to the possibility of using the perpetual inventory as a vehicle for introducing inventory valuation adjustments as they occur, so that inventory is always carried on a contemporary price basis. (e.g., *p. 144, note 9*) But, notwithstanding this, they dismiss the suggestion in the belief that a single year-end adjustment will suffice. Such a view, however, overlooks the fact that contemporary information about costs and about the amount invested in holdings is always relevant to action. Action cannot be continuously informed if adjustment is deferred until the year's end. Deferring the adjustment is tantamount to saying that what is going on during the year is irrelevant during the year; it is as if one were to say, "We will not make up the accounts until the year's end." If some kind of adjustment is necessary, for evaluation of performance or any other purpose, at the year's end, it is no less necessary during the year; the year's end may well be too late.

An Alternative Solution

We have indicated elsewhere the basis of our own solution to the problem.[4] Simply as an exercise in comparison we use the figures of the Edwards and Bell examples without some modifications which our solution might require. (We omit 000's in each case.) We assume, for example:

(a) a rise in the general level of prices to be indicated by the change in the index from 98 to 102. (E. and B., *p. 237*)

(b) the contemporary cash equivalent of the inventory at the beginning to be

[4] "Measurement in Accounting," *Journal of Accounting Research*, Spring 1965. The argument is fully developed in our *Accounting, Evaluation and Economic Behavior*, in course of publication.

168

$515, and at the end to be $690. (E. and B., *Ch. V*.)

(c) the contemporary cash equivalent of the fixed assets at the beginning to be $1,650, and a rise to have occurred during the year in the index of fixed asset prices from 180 to 204. (E. and B., *Ch. VI*) In our case this would give a gross balance at the end of the year of $1,870 (i.e., 1,650×204/180) and a depreciation change of $170 (i.e., one eleventh of the gross amount, leaving ten elevenths to be recovered over the next ten years.

(d) the amount payable on the bonds to be $600 at the end as at the beginning, no repayment having been made.

(e) the wages and miscellaneous costs ($1,536), interest ($24), dividends and taxes ($244) to be as given by Edwards and Bell.

(f) the timing of purchases and sales assumed by Edwards and Bell. Their adjustment of $71 (*p. 145, note 11*) would be augmented under our method by $6, the result of applying to 120 units the rise of 5 cents between November 20 and December 31.

The balance sheets as they would appear on these assumptions would be stated in terms of the prices currently prevailing, at each year end, as follows:

Assets	1959	1960
Net money claims..............	$ 100	$ 126
Securities......................	272	248
Inventories....................	515	690
Fixed assets (net).............	1,650	1,700
	$2,537	$2,764

Equities		
Bonds payable.................	600	600
Capital (opening balance).......	1,937	1,937
Capital maintenance adjustment...		79
Retained income of year........		148
	$2,537	$2,764

The income statement for 1960 would be prepared along the following lines:

Receipts from sales of goods.............		$4,000
From sale of securities................		30
Total revenues........................		4,030
Less:		
Contemporary costs of materials used or sold (opening stock, $515, plus purchases, $2,200, less closing stock, $690, plus inventory price adjustment, $77).........		2,102
Contemporary cost of securities sold......		30
Wages.................................		1,536
Interest...............................		24
Depreciation...........................		170
		3,862
		168
Plus: Price adjustments		
Inventories.....................	$ 77	
Plant...........................	220	
Securities......................	6	303
		471
Less: Capital maintenance adjustment (4/98×1,937)...............		79
Income of the year....................		392
Less: Dividends and taxes..............		244
Retained Income......................		$ 148

It would perhaps be odd if, in working from assumptions so similar, our own method should yield an income figure materially different from that of Edwards and Bell. And indeed it does not. Edwards and Bell, taking their figures to two decimal places, obtain a real business profit of $399.82; our own, omitting decimals, is $392. We have not attempted a reconciliation of the two; nor would it be profitable since the methods are materially different. But we may compare the two for interpretability.

The above method shows the revenues actually obtained and the cash outlays actually made. The final statement of Edwards and Bell shows neither. (*p. 254*) It is difficult to see how the firm can be evaluated on the footing of sales at $4,080 when actual sales were $4,000. It is not difficult to foresee incipient confusion if a historical cost statement showing $4,000 and a supplementary statement showing $4,080 were tendered together—to anyone.

The above method shows, as well as the data can show, the origin of the various

169

components of the income figure, the only explanations required being of the price adjustments and the capital maintenance adjustments. The statement of Edwards and Bell resorts to a variety of complicated terms in describing the components; and the meanings of the individual magnitudes are by no means easy to describe. The balance sheet of Edwards and Bell (*p. 263*) is even more complicated, with its notations, cost, adjusted historic cost, price-level adjustments, mixed dollars, current dollars, and fictional elements. (It is notable that, on returning to evaluation, Edwards and Bell make no attempt to carry out a little exercise or two in financial statement analysis to illustrate how their figures aid in the process of evaluation.)

The above method holds closely to the principle of recording nothing that is not observable or calculable from observation, and to the exclusion of any of the effects of events in other periods (a principle which Edwards and Bell avow). But Edwards and Bell require to assume a variety of "average" movements and changes, most of which would not be corroborated by observation; the results are therefore unlikely to be readily interpretable by any person who is himself an observer, especially if he were told how the figures were obtained.

Conclusion

There are other specific points of the exposition of Edwards and Bell to which attention could be drawn. But perhaps enough has been said to raise some questions. We set out some of our own views, without much in the way of argument, on just a few points not dealt with above.

We believe that the notion of realization should be applied more strictly—to revenues only. Income is the result of a calculation, an inference; it seems hardly correct to apply the term realized or realizable to it. In commercial usage generally, to real-ize means to convert into monetary assets; "realization" has a definite usefulness as describing this event, which it loses if it is also used in relation to income or profit.

We believe that it is unrealistic to attempt to find the specific impacts of price changes and price-level changes item by item, and then to add all the pieces together to get a total effect. The complex of assets and obligations is a complex in which changes, in respect of some items, in one direction are automatically accompanied by changes, in respect of other items, in another; it is not therefore reasonable to dissect the effects as if they were the consequences of quite separate decisions. It seems quite sufficient to discover the gross effects. Analysis of a continuously interacting set of variables can be expected to yield no more than this.

We believe that it is unnecessary, confusing, and potentially misleading completely to convert the figures of one period's statements into equivalents of the succeeding period's price level. Comparisons of specific magnitudes in successive periods yield little of help in the evaluation process. The only useful comparisons which can be made between successive periods are comparisons of ratios, and these of course can be derived without completely transforming the prior period's statements.[5]

We believe that business investments are made for gain, or for avoidance of loss, of any and every kind, and sometimes for all kinds simultaneously. It therefore does not seem to be realistic to suppose that holding gains or cost savings are a class apart from sellers' margins. They all, if positive, make the firm better off, that is, able to command more goods and services than before.

In conclusion, we repeat our opening

[5] See R. J. Chambers, "Measurement and Objectivity in Accounting," THE ACCOUNTING REVIEW, April 1964, p. 267.

remarks. We do not disagree with the argument of Edwards and Bell insofar as it relates to the underlying incidents affecting the investments of firms and the necessity of bringing into account the effects of events other than transactions. We disagree in principle with the entry-price criterion; it is a concession to the historical-cost idea which Edwards and Bell disparage and it is at variance with the practical necessities of the users of financial statements. We reject the hypotheses of uniform change so lavishly built into their system. These are at odds with commercial experience, and can scarcely be useful in situations of the common kind. They are, as it seems, necessitated by the objective of year-end adjustment which is inconsistent with the premise of recording changes as they occur. (*p. 17*) We regard changes in the prices and costs of non-monetary assets as perennially useful and necessary information. Their recognition during the course of any regular fiscal period is a prerequisite of informed action during that period.

(1) What, according to E & B, are the two 'principal functions' of accounting?

(2) E & B distinguish between estimating short-run and long-run profit. For the former the authors favour opportunity cost (defined as market resale price). For the latter they favour current cost.
   - What is their basis for this distinction?
   - Accepting that the short-run is part of the long-run how justified are E & B in referring to entry prices as being an extension of the theory of exit prices?

(3) In choosing between realizable and business profit E & B state that,"So long as there is some use to which the assets can be put within the firm and which yield a current operating profit (in excess of interest) the measurement of realisable profit serves a secondary purpose" (Pg.101). The apparent consequence of this is that as long as the present return exceeds the rate of interest the entrepeneur is unconcerned with any better use of funds obtainable by abandoning their use.
   - How valid is the inference above?
   - To what extent do each of the above income figures make use of traditional accounting principles? (Consider the realisation principle in particular).
   - What does this suggest to you?

(4) Given the definition of opportunity cost on page 79, is it poss-ible to contemplate "replacement and claims of replacement"on an opportunity cost basis? What affect would this have on the two concepts of income developed?

(5) Realizable profit and business profit are two concepts of profits developed to suit two different decision environments.
   - What are these?
   - What is (are) the justification(s) for the existence of different decision environments?

(6) "... a principle function of accounting data is to serve as a fundamental tool in the evaluation of past decisions" (Pg.3-4).
   - Are E & B referring to decisions plural or decision singular?
   - To what extent is it possible to evaluate singular a post decisions in a complex business organisation?
   - How would the substance of E & B change in the know-ledge that accounting data provides information to he make business decisions?

(7) How did the idea of supplementary statements figure in E & B book?

15

RICHARD VICTOR MATTESSICH

Accounting and Analytical Methods

Biographical Chronology

1922	Born, 9 August, Trieste, Italy; son of Victor (a ship purser) and Gerda (Pfaundler) Mattessich.
1936-40	Qualified as a Mechanical Engineer after attending Engineering College, Vienna, Austria.
1942-44	Accountant with K Ladurner Import,Vienna .
1944	Engineering and construction manager, Wagner and Biro, Vienna.
	Awarded an MBA, Vienna School of Economics & Business Administration.
1945	Awarded a Dr rer pol (econ), Vienna School of Economics & Business Administration .
1945-47	Research associate, Austrian Institute of Economic Research.
1947-52	Instructor, Rosenberg College, Switzerland.
1952	Accountant, Prudential Association Co, England, Montreal, Quebec.
	Married Hermine, 12 April.
	Granted Canadian citizenship.
1953-58	Professor and Head of Department, Mount Allison University New Brunswick, Canada.
1957-67	Certified public Accountant with NB Association of Certified Public Accountants.
1958-67	Took up a concurrent appointment as Associate Professor in Accounting, University of California, Berkeley .
1961	Ford Foundation Fellow.
1965	Visiting Professor, Free University of Berlin and University of St Gallen .
1966-67	Professor of Accounting, Ruhr University, Germany.
1967-	Professor of Accounting, University of British Columbia, Canada.
	Concurrently appointed Professor and Chairman of the Institute of Industrial Administration and Methodology, Technical University, Vienna.
1970	Erskine visiting scholar, Canterbury University, New Zealand .
1972-3	AICPA Literature Award.
1973	Received International Literature Award, American Institute of Certified Public Accountants .
1978-	Member, Board of Nomination, Accounting Hall of Fame.
1980	Elected to National Academy of Italy.
	Mattessich currently holds Arthur Andersen & Co Alumni Chair in Accounting, University of British Columbia.

173

Selected Bibliography

1956   "The Constellation of Accountancy and Economics,"
            Accounting Review, v.31, Oct, pp 551-64.

1957   "Towards a General and Axiomatic Foundation of Accountancy:
            with an Introduction to the Matrix Formulation of
            Accounting Systems," Accounting Research, v.8, pp 328-355.

1958   "Mathematical Models in Business Accounting," Accounting
            Review, v.33, July, pp 472-81.

1961   "Budgeting Models and System Simulation," Accounting
            Review, v.36, July, pp 384-97.

1963   "Opportunities for Research in Accounting - Mathematical
            Applications," Proceedings, International Conference
            on Accounting Education 1962, Illinois, pp 100-6; also
            in Illinois CPA, v.26, Autumn 1963, pp 38-42.

1964   Accounting and Analytical Methods, R.D. Irwin (Illinois),
            552 p; reprinted, 1978, Scholars Book Co (Houston).

            Simulation of the Firm Through a Budget Computer Program,
            R.D. Irwin (Illinois), 194 p.

1966   "Impact of Electronic Data Processing and Management
            Science Upon Accounting Theory," in Backer, M. (ed.)
            Modern Accounting Theory, Prentice-Hall (NJ) pp 511-
            34.

1967   "Accounting and Analytical Methods: a Comment on Chambers'
            Review, Journal of Accounting Research, v.5, Spring,
            pp 119-23.

1970   "On the Perennial Misunderstanding of Asset Measurement
            by Means of 'Present Values'", Cost & Management,
            v.44, March-April, pp 29-31.

1971   "On Further Misunderstandings about Asset 'Measurements'
            and Valuations: a Rejoinder to Chambers' Article,"
            Cost and Management, v.45, March-April, pp 36-42.

            "Market Value according to Sterling: a Review Article,"
            Abacus, v.7, pp 176-93.

            "Asset Measurement and Valuation - a Final Reply to
            Chambers," Cost and Management, v.45, July-Aug,
            pp 18-23.

            "Some Thoughts on the Epistemology of Accounting,"
            Proceedings, 2nd Internal Conf. on Accounting
            Education, London, pp 46-53.

1972   "Methodological Preconditions and Problems of a
            General Theory of Accounting," Accounting Review,
            v.47, July, pp 469-87.

1974   "The Incorporation and Reduction of Value Judgements
in Systems," Management Science, v.21, Sept, pp 1-9.

1975   "Information Economics and The Notion of 'Management
Information System'" in Grochla, E and N Szyperski
(eds) Information Systems and Organizational Structure,
Walker de Gruyter (New York), pp 342-54.

"Epistemological Consequences of Artificial Intelligence
and Systems Research," Contributed Papers, 5th
International Congress of Logic, Methodology and
Philosophy of Science, London, Ontario, pp V-85 to
V-86.

1976   "Normative vs Positive Systems: On the Relation between
Normativity, Teleogy and Mentalistic Aspects,"
Proceedings, 8th International Congress of Cybernetics,
Namur.

1977   "Systems Methodology and Accounting Research,"
Collected Papers, AAA Annual Meeting, 22-24 May 1977,
Florida, pp 270-86.

1978   Instrumental Reasoning & Systems Methodology, D.
Reidel Publishing Co (Dordrecht/Boston), 396 p.

1980   "On the Evolution of Theory Construction in Accounting -
a Personal Account," Accounting & Business Research,
v.10, no.37A, pp 158-73.

1982   'Axiomatic Representation of the Systems Framework:
Similarities and Differences Between Mario Bunge's
World of Systems and my Own Systems Methodology,"
Cybernetics and Systems: An International Journal, v.
13, pp 51-75.

REFERENCES

Book Reviews: Choice, v.2, June 1965, p.254.
                 Southwestern Social Science Quarterly, v.46, 1965-6,
                   p.316 (P W Henderson).
                 Accounting Review, v.41, 1966, pp.201-5 (W W Cooper).

Chambers, R J, "Review: Accounting & Analytical Methods", Journal of
Accounting Research, v.4, 1966, pp.101-18 (Mattessich's reply,
v.5, 1967, pp.119-23).

(Review of Instrumental Reasoning in Accounting Review, v.55, 1980, p.365)

175

Reviewer's Corner

Accounting and Analytical Methods:
A Review Article*

R. J. CHAMBERS†

The exponential rate of increase in knowledge is the subject of frequent comment. On almost every established front of inquiry, the last century has witnessed major revisions, reformulations of principle, and technical developments on a remarkable scale, either as antecedents or as consequences of advances in knowledge. In accounting the advances have been modest, certainly not spectacular, unless we include the development of high-speed data processing as an advance. But this, in any case, is an advance in a different field; it may as well be allied to mathematics as to accounting, but we do not hear of mathematicians claiming it as an advance in their knowledge or art.

The advances in accounting have been principally in the direction of elaborating upon existing themes, or applying techniques formerly used with relatively simple problems to increasingly complex ones. It may be alleged, however, that this is no advance at all. By analogy, it might be supposed that, inasmuch as large organizations are not only larger than but also materially different from smaller organizations, a new and different kind of accounting may be apposite; for, in other fields, it is now known that larger phenomena may not be regarded or supposed to behave as smaller phenomena, and that the concepts applicable to the smaller are not necessarily applicable to the larger. It may even be alleged that accounting has retrogressed; while the present century opened with a modest set of generalizations and rules, new rules have sprung up in profusion and disputes over them cloud the main issues to a point where the notion of systematic knowledge has virtually no place.

The debates of the last decade may be considered the beginning of the

* Richard Mattessich, *Accounting and Analytical Methods* (Homewood, Ill.: Richard D. Irwin, Inc., 1964).

† Professor of Accounting, The University of Sydney.

end of this, particularly if accounting comes to be regarded as a technique and a subject of study upon which other fields of inquiry and the methods of those fields may be expected to shed some light. Many fields closely related to accounting have only recently developed; many others are old enough to have long since influenced accounting but have had little or no influence. In the former class are studies in the theory of organizations and in communication and information; among the latter are the basic disciplines of language, logic, economics, and mathematics. Some may say there is ample evidence of the impact of some or all of these on accounting, but on closer examination the impact will be seen to be superficial. The appropriate words have been freely borrowed, but the absorption of significant elements from the fields mentioned is not evidenced merely by a larger vocabulary.

Professor Mattessich's book is directed towards an integration of the study of accounting with other studies bearing on similar subject matters, and an integration of the practice of accounting with the practice of other informative and appraisive arts. To shake loose our attitudes towards accounting from old-fashioned and deeply ingrained habits, he suggests that "knowledge of the achievements of modern logic, the philosophy of science, measurement theory, management and behavioural science, systems simulation, etc." is urgently needed. His objective is to attempt such a synthesis. The relevance of this knowledge can scarcely be overstated.

Much of the book is ostensibly devoted to accounting. The "analytical methods," to which the second part of the title refers, are methods of simulating the changes of state of an entity anticipatively, as in budgeting. It is not categorically stated that accounting is a distinctly different activity from budgeting and similar calculations, but there is evidence suggesting that these two activities are not regarded as distinctly different by the author. When dealing with budget models he suggests that as the basic accounting frame is retained, the use of the expression "accounting for the future" in respect to budgeting "seems to be well justified" (p. 334). Other examples of the closeness of Mattessich's conception of both are given below, because the concept raises some difficulties.

The Definition of Accounting

A crucial point in any discussion of accounting and its relationship to similar arts is the meaning ascribed to accounting. Before introducing his own definition or description, Mattessich notes two others. One, of the A.I.C.P.A. Committee on Terminology, is an enumerative description of a class of operations limited by three factors: (a) representation in terms of money, (b) transactions and events which are, in part at least, financial, and (c) a time interval extending from the past to the present. The time limitation is implicit in the words "transactions and events" and the absence of any qualifier such as "future" or "expected." This definition may have limitations. Mattessich's principal observation on it is an attempt to make it more comprehensive than it is. The definition, he says, "does not exclude the recording of future transactions and events, leaving open the door for incorporating periodic budgeting and other projections of *future* ... events" (p. 17). This extension seems to be unwarranted; we can make little use of definitions if we are free to interpret them as embracing things not specifically excluded. The only justification for attempting to stretch the definition seems to be to give some authoritative color to Mattessich's own definition. The terms of the A.I.C.P.A. definition are quite straightforward; taken at face value, the definition has the power of demarcation which is said to be the chief criterion of a good definition (p. 18). Curiously, after stretching the definition to make recording include valuation and projection, it is said "the shadow of this advantage creates a certain vagueness that is open to criticism" (p. 17). Apparently, in the process the power of demarcation has been lost! The defect of too broad a definition is thereafter lost to sight, for Mattessich's definition suffers from exactly the same disadvantage.

The second definition noticed is functional, orienting the design of the process to the provision of "financial information as a guide to future action in markets." Mattessich observes that a purely functional definition that reflects "essential, *generic* features proves inadequate for our purpose" (p. 18). What these essential generic features are we are not told, but a functional definition is not wanted. Now, whether we accept one definition or another, it seems impossible to do without a statement of function which provides a rationale for its invention and persistence. As Mattessich rightly points out, a description of a dog in terms of what it can do would not be regarded as a satisfactory definition in biology. We need not specify why hydrogen, mice, or pterodactyls exist or existed in the course of describing them. But an invented process cannot be understood without laying its foundation in some need or want not satisfied or satisfiable by naturally occurring things. Unless the need or want is specified we have no way of focussing our inventiveness on a device which will satisfy it.

Mattessich's definition lacks this necessary connection with the exigencies of men. "Accounting is ... concerned with the quantitative description and projection of the income circulation and of wealth aggregates by means of a method based on [eighteen specified basic assumptions]" (p. 19). It is said that these assumptions, on being tested, may be regarded as necessary and sufficient conditions. But they are not sufficient to explain why such descriptions and projections are, or may be, made. No part of the definition and the subsequent description of the assumptions give a clue to the behavioral assumptions which are unquestionably implicit in the processes described. In Chapter 5 and other places, there is an examination of the maximization principle. But neither this nor any other principle or context of behavior is referred to as the conditions which necessarily give rise to "quantitative description and projection, ... etc." Why then, are we to consider accounting to include "projection"? And why refer to income and wealth rather than to some other concepts? In his attempt to avoid every suspicion of teleological argument, Mattessich appears to have deliberately avoided laying a foundation for much of his subsequent discussion of purposes and their pursuit.

Form or method rather than function appears to be adopted as the characteristic which distinguishes accounting from non-accounting (pp. 18–19). But it is not easy to reconcile this choice with the observations on purpose which seem to have stimulated the attempt to clarify the field. We are told that "the traditional financial and cost accounting systems [are] multipurpose devices ... [which are] not very satisfactory and may occasionally be harmful"; and that "it is likely that in the future several interrelated 'monopurpose' accounting systems will replace one multipurpose establishment" (p. 9). These remarks in the early pages establish the expectation that the exploration will begin with an analysis of the purposes to be served or the functions to be performed by accounting information. But the widespread occurrence of assertions to the effect that different information is required for different purposes seems to have been taken as adequate proof of the validity of the proposition. And when, in a later chapter (pp. 215–17), a series of problem situations is used to show what information is relevant, in certain of the cases the viewpoint of the substantive decision-maker is taken while in others the viewpoint of the accountant as informant to the decision-maker is taken. The inconsistency of treatment seems to be directly attributable to the lack of a clear statement differentiating accounting information from other information and from mere speculative calculation in terms of their different functions or contributions to the pursuit of ends.

Difficulties of a similar kind emerge from the wish to embrace within the one framework the accounting of singular and aggregative entities. We are told "one of the important tasks of accounting theory is the formulation of various alternative sets of hypotheses required for specific purposes" (p. 45). In its context, this remark appears to allude to the devising of different (not strictly alternative) hypotheses for the design of accounting systems for such divergent entities as business firms, governmental agencies, and economics as wholes. Although the accounting systems of these different entities may have a common form, the products of those systems enter in quite different ways into the pursuit of ends; their functions are quite different. Businessmen may use the products of accounting processes in assessing both inputs and outputs; governmental agencies are frequently unable to use such information in assessing outputs; and national accounts are strictly statistical, their products having no direct bearing on choice, though they may have some indirect bearing on the administrative regulation of the choices of members of a community. The similarities are formal, the differences are substantive. If we fail to see this, we may be led to depend on false analogies. Mattessich describes certain of his broadly stated assumptions as "place-holders" for a set of empirical hypotheses adapted to a particular purpose (p. 31); but he provides no motivational "place-holder," no opportunity to design an accounting system appropriate to particular classes of entity on the basis of the stated objectives of the user of its products.

The Basic Assumptions

Mattessich's assumptions do not define a particular kind of accounting. That is not his intention. His aim is to state in broad terms, so that they may be defined by inserting further propositions apposite to a specific entity or type of entity, the principal components of all kinds of accounting. What he proposes is an abstract general theory of accounting (p. 8). This is, in principle, a valuable thing to do. If a series of particulars can be brought within one framework, even at the most general and abstract level, the generalizations which emerge will have correspondingly great power as principles, predictors, or guides. The task is by no means simple, and Mattessich properly disclaims belief in the perfection of the result (p. 32).

First of all, some comments on generality. Although he seeks to formulate the assumptions in the most general terms, all the illustrative and explanatory comment on the assumptions, with one or two minor exceptions, has reference to business entities. It would have been of interest to have some illustration of the counterparts of the examples given, or specific examples of the interpretation to be given to the assumptions and their component terms, in the case of service organizations and economics as wholes. One may well suspect that the absence of illustration is evidence that, after all, private accounting and national accounting may not be considered as of the same class.

The generality of the statements of the assumptions is indicated in each case by the formula "There exists ..." or some equivalent indicative. Thus, the assumption of monetary values reads: There exists a set of additive values, expressed in a monetary unit; this set is isomorphic to the system of (positive and negative) integers plus the number zero (p. 32). And to take an example of the class of assumptions which are described as place-holders: There exists a set of hypotheses determining the value assigned to an accounting transaction (p. 42). A system built up on such pure postulates escapes many of the difficulties which arise if the postulates are to be tied to statements of function. A hypothesis is itself functional; we formulate hypotheses to serve our ends. It seems insufficient to assert that "there exists a set of hypotheses..." without indicating why, for example, the value assigned to an accounting transaction is to be determined. How we may choose between alternative hypotheses or sets of hypotheses on any particular issue is not indicated, yet this seems to be a crucial issue. For example, the traditional hypotheses relating to the assignment of monetary magnitudes to assets and obligations differ from the hypotheses of those who would take direct account of changes in prices of goods held by a firm. Mattessich refers to original evaluations and evaluation adjustments (p. 42) but adduces no argument indicating why the implied set of hypotheses should be adopted rather than the traditional set. This difficulty pervades the whole of the "place-holding" assumptions. We are left wondering whether the whole of the eighteen assumptions is necessary or sufficient to "define" the accounting which the author envisages.

Consider now some more specific points. Income and wealth are major elements of the definition proposed. Income is defined as "the flow of goods and services, within a well-defined period between the production side and the consumption side of an entity" (p. 21). First, it seems difficult to envision two "sides" of an entity, such that a flow of goods and services between them can constitute income in any ordinary sense. Income surely means inflow, not crossflow. The absence of any reference to inflows implies something like a Robinson Crusoe economy in which one is better off only by doing things for oneself. Nor does income defined as a flow of goods and services have any of the attributes usually associated with the term. The definition does not refer to utilities, to gains in monetary terms, or to the maintenance of capital.

Again, the notion of an "accounting transaction" is used. The term is novel and, in the absence of definition, we look to the context for aid in interpreting it. It seems to mean an operation on an account. It might be supposed that the function of the accounts of an entity is to represent economic effects on its position, and that, in particular, accounting transactions would correspond with, or be isomorphic with, economic transactions of the entity. Not so, however. Mattessich asserts that "there need not be a one-to-one correspondence between [an economic transaction and an accounting transaction]" (pp. 40–1). If this is so, then we have been deluded by those who hold that it is the function of accounts to represent transactions. The conclusion appears to have arisen from the ambiguity of Mattessich's position. He alludes to two entities within the same context, dealing with one part of the time and with the other the rest of the time. His duality assumption, presumably the foundation of the double-entry practice, is described thus: For all accounting transactions it is true that a value is assigned to a three-dimensional concept consisting of two accounts and a date (pp. 33–4). But this is followed by a statement, "The two accounts of a transaction need not belong to the same entity. They may belong to different entities in which case a superentity comprising both entities may be envisaged" (pp. 34–5). On the basis of the former statement the double-entry principle *for every entity* has escaped. It is retrieved by the second sentence, but the shift from one entity to the other between the two sentences falsifies the first sentence! Other examples of this type of ambiguity are mentioned below.

We make no attempt here to discuss all of the basic assumptions; that task deserves more elaborate analysis than is possible. But one of the most noticeable features of the definition and assumptions is the absence of definitions for a full series of necessary terms. We do not ordinarily expect the definition of a field to supply definitions of all the terms necessary for its development. Mattessich, however, by incorporating so much in his definition of accounting, is obliged to spell out the development. But we find no definition of asset, equity, liability, financial position; no reference to markets as determinants of "values" to be assigned; no reference to prices as the sources of "original valuations." The process of abstraction has been pushed to a stage such that the result is free of many of the characteristics which are commonly and, as we think, necessarily associated with accounting.

Measurement

The paucity of work on metrological features of accounting makes any attempt to elaborate on it worthy of attention. Chapter 3 is devoted to this. Following a discussion of Stevens' classification of scales of measurement, it is suggested that all four classes—nominal, ordinal, interval, and ratio scales—have applications in accounting. The application of the first three classes is not germane to what has always been the principle problem in accounting—the assignment of numbers of monetary units to represent some property of assets, equities, income, and costs. The relevant scale is the ratio scale, in particular, the scale of positive natural numbers (including zero), for we reckon numbers of monetary units specified in this scale. An example is given of the possibility of transforming measures in units of one such scale into measures in units of another such scale (dollars to pounds sterling) by the use of the rate of exchange as a transformation rule. But at this point the discussion breaks off. This, however, is the very point at which the argument could have become interesting.

Mattessich notes that "event" implies a time dimension "which must not be neglected" (p. 74). Two observable things occur with the passage of time; both deserve but do not get attention. Measures of the monetary properties of objects and of equities change; and the significance of the units in which those measurements are made changes. Put in a less metrological way, prices of given goods change and the purchasing power of money changes. On these *events*, and their effects on the representation of some monetary property of objects and equities, Mattessich has nothing to say. This seems odd indeed, for the substantial introduction of "modern measurement theory" gives rise to expectations that these very questions will be broached.

The failure at this point appears to derive from two directions. Scarcely any attention is given to the property to be measured in the monetary scale. Passing reference is made to the "magnitudes of 'properties' (values) ... measured ... in the scale of dollar-values" (p. 75). Confusion arises from the use of "value" in two senses here, as it does in other places to be mentioned. For if the parenthetical "values" refers to "magnitudes of 'properties,'" we are not told what the property is, nor the rule for assigning numbers; and if the parenthetical "values" refers to "properties," we do not know whether to interpret "values" in the compound "dollar-values" in the same way or not; and if "values" means numbers representing preference orderings (e.g., pp. 144, 221), we are confounded. But the main point is that, whereas the valuation assumption (p. 42) refers to value changes, no reference is made to the implications of these changes in the treatment of the measurement problem.

The failure arises, secondly and more importantly, from Mattessich's almost complete disregard, in this chapter, of prices and the price mechanism as a generator of measures in the monetary scale. "We might measure the value of an asset by its purchase price (historic cost basis), by its discounted expected net revenues, by the potential of its liquidation yield, or many other variations and combinations" (p. 79). The treatment of measurement, however, gives no warrant for the application of the term to estimates of the future or predictions. We may measure a property of something that has occurred or something that is present, but not something which does not exist and has not existed. Of the possibilities referred to in the quoted passage, only initial purchase price qualifies as a measurement. There are, of course, prices of the asset subsequent to the date of purchase, including the resale price at the date of measurement, but there is no reference to these and hence no discussion of the manner in which a choice should be made among these possible prices in the process of accounting. The avoidance of market price is strongly indicated by the observation that "most of the economic and accounting measures belong in the category of measurement by fiat" (pp. 79, 143), presumably by the will of the measurer. This view is held notwithstanding a subsequent specification of a useful measure; namely, that it "must be able to enter into a great number of relations with other variables" (p. 79). Of course, the place where monetary measures enter into a great number of relations with other monetary measures is the market place; and the measures of the market place (money prices) are not at all the will of the measurer, nor of any single buyer or seller. If prices were arbitrary, if measures in the monetary scale were measures by fiat, business operations and planning would be impossible and economists who concern themselves with market processes would be wasting their time. It is said, "this quest [for a useful measure] will restrain us from carrying to an extreme the conversion of a multiple-purpose into a limited-purpose accounting measure since then the [requirement that it must be able to enter into a great number of relations with other variables] ... might not be fulfilled" (p. 29). Very true, but this strongly suggests market prices as appropriate measures rather than subjective magnitudes such as discounted expected net revenues; and it is quite inconsistent with the earlier prognostication that "in future several monopurpose accounting systems will replace one multipurpose establishment" (p. 9).

The variability of prices and the purchasing power of money through time entails that measures taken in one context at one time are not necessarily the same in significance as measures of the same objects at a different time. The fact that the monetary scale is a ratio scale enables transformations to be made from measures in units of one purchasing power to measures in units of a different purchasing power. The fact that the market is continually generating new prices makes possible the discovery of magnitudes presently assignable for the purpose of considering future alternatives. Though both of these facts are implicitly recognized in the discussions of valuation in economics and accountancy (Chap. 5), they are not brought to bear on Mattessich's scheme in the chapter on measurement or in Appendix A, which presents a set-theoretical or an axiomatic formulation of accounting. In essence, the latter is based on the assumption of invariance both in the monetary scale and in the measure assigned to the monetary property (or price) of any object in that scale.

Value

There have been many critics of the suggestion that accounting can or should represent values; the criticisms are not all irrelevant, for the term "value" has been used so freely that it has created considerable confusion. Mattessich senses some of the difficulties and apparently has made the attempt to elucidate this problem an important part of his task. But the confusion persists.

The term first appears in the assumption of monetary values: There exists *a set of additive values*, expressed in a monetary unit ... (p. 32). Here value is used in the sense of mathematical values in the scale of numbers of monetary units; the implication of the proposition is that the monetary scale is a ratio scale. Assumption 6, economic objects, posits "*a set of economic objects*, whose values and physical properties are subject to change" (p. 36). Value is used here as the measure of a quantity, that is, in the same sense as has been mentioned before. Assumption 11, valuation, posits "a set of hypotheses determining the value assigned to an accounting transaction" (p. 42). Here value again seems

184

to be interpretable in the same way as before. But there follows an explanatory statement: *"Original evaluations* of economic objects are based on a preference order among those objects at the time of transaction within the frame of reference of a specific entity and purpose" (p. 42). Evaluations are presumably assignments of values in the above-mentioned mathematical sense. Difficulties begin when it is asserted that these valuations "are based on a preference order among those objects"; for it is hard to imagine how a preference ordering can yield a value in the monetary scale.

The difficulties mount when the matter is taken up at length in Chapters 5 and 6. Here valuation is defined as "a procedure by which numerals are assigned to objects or events according to rules (to be developed) in order to express preference with regard to particular actions" (p. 144). Valuation thus defined is described as "the central theme of accounting." It is taken up again in Chapter 6 where the definition is repeated (p. 220). But now it becomes complicated. "The numeral which usually expresses this preference order is called the *value*.... A *value scale* is a standard of measurement (normally a ratio scale, occasionally merely an ordinal or interval scale) for evaluating an object, event, or state in terms of another object" (p. 221). Now, we find it impossible to conceive valuation as a procedure "assigning a preference order to an object" (p. 220); a preference ordering entails that there shall be *a number of objects* to be ordered, two at least. A preference ordering arranges a series of objects in the order in which they are preferred. It says something about the person who does the ordering, but it says nothing about the magnitude of any property of the object or objects. A man may prefer a pound of cheese to a pound of butter, and a pound of butter to a pound of bread; but the assignment of the numeral 3 (in the scale of preferences) to the pound of bread does not mean that in the scale of weights a pound of bread is three times as much, or one-third as much, as a pound of cheese. The question is whether the function of the numerals assigned is to express preferences of the assignor (that is, to say something about the assignor) or to express magnitudes of a property of the objects in question.

Mattessich clearly asserts the former (pp. 144, 220), and just as clearly switches immediately to the latter. Manifestly there is no value scale in the preference-ordering sense which is standard. A man who prefers a pound of cheese to a pound of butter in one set of circumstances may have the reverse preferences in another set of circumstances; preference ordering is a variable ordering, there is nothing standard about it. But, we are told, the numerals assigned in accounting express units of currency (p. 144); and it seems clear that the reference to evaluating an object in terms of another object in the definition of value scale (p. 217, and p. 221 cited above) contemplates units of currency as the other object. This interpretation would make the two passages consistent. Why, then, introduce the parenthetical "normally a ratio scale, occasionally merely an ordinal or interval scale," when the monetary scale is admittedly a ratio scale?

Again, we are told that use is made of a number of different valuation models (pp. 215–20, 224). Given the definition of valuation as a procedure assigning a preference order (p. 220), a valuation model would be a scheme or device for assigning numerals which represent preference orderings. This is not, however, the meaning of valuation model in the passages cited. Those "models" are the historical cost basis, the current value basis, the present value basis, and the marginal value basis (p. 224). The discussion switches from numerals representing preference orderings to numerals representing quantities of monetary units which have no ostensible connection with preference orderings, while the same terms "value" and "valuation" are applied to both. The difficulties become apparent if we substitute the definition of value (p. 221) in the first assumption, which then reads: There exists a set of additive numerals which express preference orderings, expressed in a monetary unit. Now, preference orderings are not expressed in a monetary unit, nor are they additive. In any case, measures in ordinal and interval scales are not additive; if additivity is stipulated as a necessary property of a value scale, it is impossible to assert that the value scale "is normally a ratio scale, occasionally merely an ordinal or interval scale" (p. 221). It can only be the first.

Intuitively, it seems, Mattessich has sensed that somehow preference ordering is related to measures expressed in a monetary scale. In this, his intuition has not played him false. But he does not specify the mechanism which relates them. Briefly, assuming that the entity in question is a business firm, it is this: the agent or manager envisages a series of alternative courses of action, each having an expected outcome and an expected cost. Insofar, and only insofar, as these outcomes and costs are prices to be received and paid can they be quantified in terms of the monetary scale. The alternative courses of action will be assigned a preference order in the light of the expected net outcome in monetary terms, appropriately adjusted for non-pecuniary outcomes and costs; the ordering is obviously subjective, as different persons will value differently the various combinations of pecuniary and non-pecuniary outcomes and costs. Given the preference order, every course of action which involves expected costs beyond the present capacity to command resources in the market place will be eliminated. Ascertaining this present capacity is a measurement problem. The measure of the cost of the chosen course of action does not represent the value assigned to that course, for if the outcome of that course were not preferred above (or valued more highly than) the sacrifice necessary to attain it there would be no cause for action. Thus valuations or preference orderings enable us to understand how particular courses of action are chosen; but only market processes give measurements of costs or outcomes in the monetary scale.

Chapter 5 discusses the problem of valuation in economics as well as in accounting. On the basis that "every measurement process commands the establishment of a one-to-one correspondence between the object or event to be measured, and a scale," the value of an object is said to be derived "from the purchasing power of that quantity of legal tender which the *agent considers equivalent to the object* in question" (p. 145). We find it difficult to imagine how a quantity of legal tender may be considered to be equivalent to another object; but more importantly, if the value of a given quantity of legal tender were equivalent to the value of the object, we find it hard to imagine why the object would be preferred, for preferring is surely based on inequality or non-equivalence. Be that as it may; the market is, at this point, introduced as the medium which enables us to substitute "for the value judgment of an individual the value judgment of a social aggregate" (p. 145), giving us the opportunity of "establishing a relatively objective 'subjective value'" (p. 145). This juxtaposition of contradictories does not help. What the market does is reveal prices, not values in any other sense than prices. If the term "price" had been introduced the confusion would have been avoided. Prices themselves are not value judgments, individual or social. A man who chooses to buy at a given price certainly expresses a value judgment, but both the price and the good are the objects of his judgment. He prefers to have the good rather than the amount of money designated by the price. It would be as true to say that a good is subjective as to say that its price is subjective.

Part of this chapter seems to be directed to criticism of the basic views of economists on values and valuation. But they seem to be economists of the author's own invention. It is said that "the economist's assumption that every person is endowed with *one and only one* preference function may be unrealistic" (p. 147). There may be some economists who make such a loose assertion, but what economists assert more commonly is that there is *one* preferred ordering of alternatives at a given point of time and in the circumstances of the person at that time. Mattessich himself asserts such a proposition (p. 163) but he does not, at that point, give the credit to any economist. Again he speaks of "the conviction of some economists that there exists only one true value, namely that which expresses the pertinent marginal utility" (p. 147). But again, economists only assert that the value relevant to choice at a particular point of time and in particular circumstances is the marginal value of a commodity; the statement referring to "one true value" is so truncated a version of the proposition as it is commonly stated that it glosses over the implications of the economist's notion of varying marginal values as holdings of a given commodity's rise or fall.

The author's attachment to values leads him to other pseudo-questions.

He appears to have no patience with "the belief [which] lingers on that there must exist ... one way of assigning values ... that is *neutral* to all purposes" (p. 147, see also p. 205). This view is ascribed to accountants. There may be some accountants who make such a loose assertion, but what is properly asserted is that there exists one way of assigning a monetary measure which is neutral for all purposes. The reference to values seems to have led to the oversight of a proposition already quoted, that to be useful a measure must be able to enter into a great number of relations with other variables (p. 79). This capacity is of the essence of neutrality, and market prices alone of monetary measures have this capacity. Mattessich comes to market price by way of the Edwards and Bell and the Sprouse and Moonitz studies. But, true to his disbelief in the possibility of there being one neutral and pertinent monetary measure, market price appears to rank equally with other traditional formulae.

On the whole, the source of confusion over values and valuations may well be in the underlying characteristics of Mattessich's notion of accounting, and it probably stems from the widespread but loose usage of those terms in accounting discourse. As we have noticed, Mattessich includes in his definition of accounting both quantitative description and projection, or, in different terms, history and prognostication. One may drive an automobile backwards as well as forwards; the actions are not materially different. But time is irreversible. The same processes cannot be applied to the past and the future. By diligent effort we can learn more about the past, describe it more fully, measure its measurable events. But no amount of effort will give us knowledge about the future; indeed a remark of Devine is quoted, with approval, to the effect that no one has ever learned anything from the future (p. 238). Nothing of the future is present here; no aspect of it can be measured. We can only speculate about it and about the probable magnitudes of the events which we expect to occur in it. Those magnitudes are probable or expected magnitudes; they are not measurements.

Anti-Legalism

There has been a tendency on the part of many who are seeking to give a new and "more practical" orientation to accounting to suggest that the flaw in traditional financial accounting lies in its legalistic foundations. It is implied that these conflict with or cut across the functions of providing financial information for other purposes. For example, Mattessich speaks of the "compromise enforced by systems designed to satisfy concurrently legal, administrative, as well as managerial purposes. These goals apparently are too diverse to be combined in the *stem* of a single system" (p. 84). Again, "an accounting system based on purely legal principles will always supply a meaningless profit figure" (p. 166). The observation that "traditional accounting has always stressed pure *custodial control* [and] it neglects too much the *control of efficiency*" is followed by speculation on "whether or not some kind of split between financial-legalistic accounting and managerial accounting will occur (perhaps in the form of a scientific information system)" (pp. 166–7).

The law, however, is not to blame for the inadequacy of traditional accounting. The law provides the framework within which members of society contract between themselves, buy and sell goods, acquire property rights. The so-called "cost basis" of accounting may have had its origin in, and still has application to, trusts in respect of nominated moneyed funds. It strictly has no application to business ventures which are not trusts of this kind. The fact that the "cost basis" is now condoned under S.E.C. regulations is an aberration from the law; for the Securities Acts themselves contemplate that investors and the public shall have meaningful information on which to base their judgments. As Mattessich rightly points out, "the value of an object is bound to time and circumstances" (p. 163); and this is true whether we refer to value in the sense of preference ordering or to prices. But the basic legislation is not in violation of or in opposition to this.

Insofar as managers must arrange their affairs within the law, and insofar as they seek to preserve and develop the enterprises they manage through legally enforceable contracts having moneyed magnitudes established in the market place, managerial purposes and the legal prescriptions ensuring accountability must be reconcilable. If managerial choice is predicated on present facts and present preference-orderings, contemporary information as to the facts is indispensable. The same applies to the choices of investors. And the law seeks to ensure that contemporary information is made available. References to the cost basis being more objective "legalistically speaking" (p. 163), objective legal evidence (p. 164), legally objective (p. 217), as if there were distinctive kinds of objectivity, seem irrelevant, for there is no definition of legal objectivity in the law. All references in the law to fair presentation are meaningless unless fair means information which is *equally fair to all as information*, and that implies factual information of a contemporary kind.

Mattessich misses the opportunity to produce a fully integrated conception of valuation (as monetary measurement) by giving so little attention to the legal side of the matter by comparison with his lengthy disquisition on views from economic, accounting, and management science standpoints. This is unfortunate. The law is not culpable for the generation and persistence of the defect of cost-based accounting. But it is doubly unfortunate because it has led to some rather quaint discussion of the duality principle.

The duality or double-entry principle takes on an almost mystical aura at the hands of the author. We are asked to accept "the idea of subjecting certain economic events to the abstract, mathematical notion of a transaction. The essence of the latter lies in a fundamentally two dimensional property that permits double classification within one set of classes" (p. 26). Why, when accounting is primarily concerned with an ostensibly legal or commercial notion of transactions, we should resort to an abstract mathematical notion, is puzzling. Likening it to the Cartesian system of coordinates (p. 103) does not resolve the puzzle, nor does the assertion "one may subject certain economic data to a dual classification, thereby imposing upon these data a preconceived structure that lends added meaning to the information transmitted" (p. 103); for whence does the "preconceived structure" arise? If, on the other hand, we take the observable and far from abstract notion that every transaction changes the legally enforceable rights of one entity vis-a-vis the rest of the community, the significance of double entry is apparent. A transaction of a given entity brings about a change in the composition of the resources, of the equities, or of both, vis-a-vis the rest of the world. The consequence of every such change is a change in the capacity for action. If we see the transaction as having simultaneously brought about a change in legal rights and a change in the resources over which those rights exist, both being measured in monetary terms, the duality principle has an immediate and perceptible justification; credit balances represent the distribution of legal equities, debit balances represent the distribution of investments of the entity. No abstract mathematical notion and no preconceived structure need be invoked.

If the parallel between the duality principle and the Cartesian system of analytical geometry had been extended to indicate that the double entry principle gives a means of representing economic entities in an "economic-legal" space, its function would have been clearer. But reference to it as a dual classification, rather than as a classification of two properties of economic events, leaves it with a metaphysical or mystical character which is properly subject to the criticisms which Mattessich, with some distaste, notices (pp. 103–4).

Empirical Hypotheses

Chapter 7, "Empirical Hypotheses in Accounting," is concerned with some methodological matters. At the beginning a distinction is drawn between scientific and pragmatic hypotheses. The distinction is drawn on the basis of the process by which each type of hypothesis is rejected or rejectable. A scientific hypothesis, we are told, is invalidated by instances which testify reliably to its falsity; an invalid scientific hypothesis is "not acceptable because not true." A pragmatic hypothesis is invalidated "by demonstrating (or believing) that, *in the long run* or *on the average*, the actions based on it yield results that are *less* satisfactory than the results of actions based on another hypothesis" (p. 235). The distinction seems empty. It seems to rest on a notion that we can know what is true in an absolute sense, so that we can reject any proposition which is inconsistent with what is true. If hypotheses are the basis of science, this is just not a tenable position. Testing a scientific hypothesis consists of taking action on the basis of it and of alternative hypotheses, and discovering which yields the most satisfactory results, which is the most useful; but this is the same as the above-quoted prescription for testing a pragmatic hypothesis.

It is unfortunate that after the repeated postulation of sets of hypotheses (unspecified) in the statement of basic assumptions, Mattessich does not give some examples in this chapter to illustrate what he means by the title of the chapter. There is some discussion of error in accounting measurements; it would have been most instructive to find a discussion of one of the common hypotheses which underlie contemporary practice, namely, that it is possible to add expenditures made at diverse dates (and therefore at diverse prices and price levels) and to obtain a meaningful aggregate by the process. Instead we are exhorted to think "in terms of empirical hypotheses instead of legalistic rules" (p. 251), as if the rules of law were not themselves based on hypotheses which are continually open to testing and supersession by more useful hypotheses.

The tendency to denigrate the importance of related disciplines and their findings is characteristic of other accounting literature. Instead of synthesis we are treated to arguments for separateness. Instead of finding a way in which legal notions may be interpreted so that they are illuminating, we are asked to disregard them. Instead of attempting to show that the processes of thought and inquiry in scientific fields are just as pertinent in the development of accounting theory and practice, we are offered grounds for supposing that they are not. And all this, notwithstanding the author's avowed intention to synthesize, and notwithstanding his quotation, with apparent approval, of a view of Davidson that "the notion of managerial analysis and financial reporting as separated, fragmented, and even opposing activities should . . . be soon supplanted by the view which emphasizes the basic unity of the accounting function" (p. 410).

If we are to make use of empirical hypotheses in accounting, and we must if our conclusions are to be useful in the world of experience, we need to be sure of their nature and their role. Mattessich poses the question: "Accounting rules: hypotheses or constraints?" (p. 251). This seems to be an improper question, for in no direct sense can a rule be a hypothesis. A hypothesis may be one of the bases of a rule; and the application of a rule may provide the evidence upon which a hypothesis may be confirmed, tentatively accepted, or rejected. But the two are not one and the same thing. Nor is it proper to suggest that rules are logically anterior to hypotheses, as when it is said that presently accepted rules "will help to determine the boundaries within which the ultimate accounting hypotheses have to be formulated" (p. 252).

Empirical hypotheses in accounting will represent an understanding of the relationship between information and choice. They will be based on observation statements about information and choice, but they will be inferences from such statements. Thus, we may observe that people use aggregative financial statements and the aggregates which appear in them in the process of choice. We cannot observe how these aggregates enter into the process of choice; we have to generate a hypothesis about the precise relationship, perhaps on prior hypotheses about the process of choice itself. As choice implies alternatives, the hypotheses relating information and choice will have something to say about the kinds of aggregates which bear on choice from among alternatives. On these hypotheses we may then base rules for obtaining those aggregates, rules which will be consistent with all other rules for aggregation. If, on application of the rules, we obtain information which is demonstrably pertinent to choice (if, on the closest examination, the information is found to be used), the hypothesis is confirmed and the rules are justified. The process is not, of course, well illustrated in the literature. One cannot help feeling that after a tentative sally in the direction of scientific rigor, the reactionary element of Mattessich (and we all have a reactionary element) asserted itself; for the chapter winds up with a long reproduction of a digest of the Accounting Research Bulletins of the American Institute.

On the following two chapters on planning and budgeting models we have little to say. As is the case with all anticipatory calculation, the presentation bristles with hypotheses. But there is little in the way of justification of the resulting pieces of information in terms of their relevance to particular or overall decisions.

The final chapter is directed to the discussion of accounting as a management science. As a goal or an ideal, the notion of accounting as a scientific process of inquiry and discovery has everything to commend it. But in the end there seem to be so many open questions, so many points of uncertainty about the relation between positive knowledge and expectation and judgment, that the present status of accounting can scarcely be described as scientific. Mattessich stoutly defends the specialist nature of accounting, but we are not left with a feeling that any claim to such rigor as other processes of inquiry may have, could yet be well supported.

In Sum

Mattessich accepted a weighty brief. His acquaintance with the immediate and peripheral literature is extensive. He well recognizes that its unruly mass of argument and counterargument, fact and hypothesis, clarity and confusion, imposes heavy burdens—"this book is plagued with all the shortcomings of a pioneering attempt" he warns the reader on his final page. This kind of modesty is commonly found only among those who, to their credit, have ventured beyond safe waters. The task of a synthesizer demands the temporary suspension of judgment over every field related to the synthesis, for only in such a fluid state is it likely that superficial distinctions will disappear and that critical differences will emerge. That the work has many vestiges of the author's commitment to a number of positions well-established in the literature is evidence of the difficulty of breaking with old habits, even when one sets out to be an iconoclast. The points discussed in this note are only a selection from those which Mattessich challenges and from those on which one might wish to challenge him; there is, for example, no discussion at all of the problem of communication, of financial signs, symbols and statements as signals. But the very number of the points which his work opens or leaves open for discussion is perhaps the great merit of his exercise. He does not necessarily think we will be convinced, but he would like us to join him in the enterprise. It may well have been for him, and it may be for his readers, more pleasant to travel hopefully than to arrive.

QUESTIONS

(1) "The purpose of this study is to present a <u>unified frame</u> of
accounting, and to acquaint the reader with new significant
developments in this discipline" (p.ix).
- How compatible are these two aims in a theoretical work?
- What "frame" of accounting does Mattessich attempt to provide?

(2) Mattessich provides his rather lengthy definition of accounting
on p.19. It includes 18 assumptions all of which have to be
elaborated upon. Is this a satisfactory basis for a definition?
What essential features should a definition have? Is Mattessich
consistent with his definition in the rest of his analysis?

(3) To what extent does Mattessich build his argument around definitions from or concepts of economic theory - for such notions as
income, wealth etc?

(4) Does Mattessich present a theoretical argument, or does he merely
synthesise and describe (and quote) arguments of others?

(5) Why does Mattessich claim that valuation has to be "measurement
by fiat" (p.143)?

(6) What is meant by:
    "... the accounting model imposes legal and
    economic dualities upon a host of otherwise
    instructured commercial data" (p.424)?

(7) Are the "empirical hypothesis"of chapter 7 in fact empirical?

(8) What problem was Mattessich attempting to solve?

16

R J CHAMBERS

Accounting, Evaluation and Economic Behavior

Biographical Chronology

1917	Born, 16 November, Newcastle, New South Wales, Australia. Attended Newcastle High School.
1938	Awarded Bachelor of Economics, University of Sydney.
1939	Married Margaret Scott Brown, 9 September.
1943-45	Joined Australian Prices Commission.
1945-52	Lecturer, School of Management, Sydney Technical College.
1947	Financial Management, published.
1953-54	Senior Lecturer in Accounting, University of Sydney.
1955	Function and Design of Company Annual Reports, published.
1955-59	Associate Professor of Accounting, University of Sydney.
1957	Accounting and Action, published.
1959	US Relm Foundation Fellow.
1960-	Appointed Professor of Accounting, University of Sydney.
1960-61	President, Australian Association of University Teachers of Accounting.
1962-	Visiting Professor, University of Chicago.
1963-70	Chairman, Appointments Board, University of Sydney.
1965-74	Editor, Abacus.
1966	Accounting, Evaluation and Economic Behavior, published. Visiting Professor, University of California, Berkeley.
1967	Awarded American Institute of Certified Public Accountants' Gold Medal. Visiting Professor, University of Washington. Director, The Nestle Co (Aust Ltd).
1970	Visiting Professor, University of Kansas, University of Florida. Citation for Meritorious Contribution to Accounting Literature, Australian Society of Accountants.
1971	Leverhulme Foundation Fellow, Waseda University, Japan.
1973	Securities and Obscurities, published.
1975-76	President, NSW Division, Australian Society of Accountants.
1976	American Accounting Association, Distinguished International Lecturer. Alpha Kappa Psi Award.
1977-78	National President, Australian Society of Accountants.
1978	Chairman, NSW Government, Accounting Standards Review Committee.
1980	Price Variation and Inflation Accounting, published. Visiting Professor, University of Illinois.
1982	Visiting Professor, University of Cape Town, South Africa. Retired, University of Sydney.

Selected Bibliography

1947   Financial Management, Law Book Co. (Sydney), 442 p;
       revised ed. 1953; 3rd ed. 1967.

1948   Accounting & Management, Australian Accountant,
       v.18 (Dec.), pp 417-20.

1949   Accounting and Shifting Price Levels, Australian Accountant,
       v.19 (June), pp 313-20.

       The Spice of Accounting, Australian Accountant, v.19 (Nov),
       pp 398-401.

1950   The Relationship Between Accounting & Financial Manage-
       ment, Australian Accountant, v.20 (Sept), pp 333-55.

1952   Accounting and Inflation, Australian Accountant, v.22,
       (Jan), pp 14-23.

       Accounting and Business Finance, Australian Accountant,
       v.22 (July and Aug), pp 213-30, 262-66.

       Effects of Inflation on Financial Strategy, Australian
       Accountant, v.22 (Nov), pp 391-98.

1955   Blueprint for a Theory of Accounting, Accounting Research,
       v.6 (Jan), pp 17-25.

       The Function and Design of Company Annual Reports, Law
       Book Co (Sydney), 322 p.

       A Scientific Pattern for Accounting Theory, Australian
       Accountant, v.25 (Oct), pp 533-35.

1956   Some Observations on Structure of Accounting Theory
       (Littleton), Accounting Review, v.31 (Oct) pp 584-92.

       The Formal Basis of Business Decisions, Australian
       Accountant, v.26 (April), pp 155-74.

1957   Details for a Blueprint, Accounting Review, v.32 (April),
       pp 206-15.

       Accounting and Action, Law Book Co (Sydney), 248 p,
       rev., 1965.

1958   Asset Revaluations and Stock Dividends, Journal of
       Accountancy, (Aug), pp 55-68.

1960   Measurement and Misrepresentation, Management Science,
       v.6, (Jan), pp 141-48.

       The Conditions of Research in Accounting, Journal of
       Accountancy, v.110 (Dec), pp 33-39.

1961   Towards a General Theory of Accounting, Australian
       Society of Accountants Annual Lecture, (2 August),
       48 p (published 1962).

1962   Changes in Accounting Theory, Proceedings of Illinois
        Conf. on Accounting Education for Collegiate Teachers
        of Accounting (Chicago), 23 p.

1963   The Resolution of Some Paradoxes in Accounting,
        University of British Columbia, Occasional Paper No.2,
        33 p.

        Why Bother with Postulates? Journal of Accounting Research,
        v.1, pp 3-15.

        Measurement in Accounting, (Mimeo: private circulation)
        48 p.

        Conventions, Doctrines and Common Sense, Accountants'
        Journal, v.43 (Feb), pp 182-87.

        Measurement and Objectivity in Accounting, Accounting
        Review, v.39 (April), pp 264-74.

        The Role of Information Systems in Decision-Making,
        Management Technology, v.4 (June), pp 15-25.

1965   Measurement in Accounting, Journal of Accounting Research,
        v.3, pp 32-62.

        The Complementarity of Accounting and Economics,
        Calculator Annual, v.3 (1964-65), pp 76-86.

        Edwards and Bell on Business Income, Accounting Review,
        v.40 (Oct), pp 731-41.

        The Development of Accounting Theory in R. Chambers,
        L. Goldberg and R. Mathews (eds) The Accounting Frontier,
        Cheshire (Melbourne), pp 18-35.

1966   Accounting, Evaluation and Economic Behavior, Prentice-Hall,
        388 p.

        Accounting and Analytical Methods by Mattessich, Journal
        of Accounting Research, v.4, pp 101-18.

        A Matter of Principle, Accounting Review, v.41 (July),
        pp 443-57.

        A Study of a Price-Level Study, Abacus, v.2, pp 97-118.
        (see reaction of Moonitz and Chambers's response in
        Abacus, v.3 (1967), pp 62-73).

1967   The Foundations of Financial Accounting, Berkeley Symposium
        on the Foundations of Financial Accounting (Univ. of
        California) pp 26-44.

        Price Variation Accounting - An Improved Representation,
        Journal of Accounting Research, v.5, pp 215-20.

        Continuously Contemporary Accounting - Additivity and
        Action, Accounting Review, v.42 (Oct), pp 751-77.

        Uniformity in Accounting, New York CPA, v.37, pp 747-54.

        The Mathematics of Accounting and Estimating, Abacus,
        v.3, pp 163-80.

197

1968 Measure and Values - A Reply to Professor Staubus, Accounting Review, v.43 (April), pp 239-47.

Accepted, Better or Best? - One Goal of Inquiry in Accounting, Singapore Accountant, v.3, pp 27-33.

Tax Allocation and Financial Reporting, Abacus, v.4, pp 99-123.

1969 The Linked Logics of Pedagogy and Practice, Australian Accountant, v.39 (June), pp 267-75.

Accounting, Finance and Management, Arthur Andersen and Co and Butterworth's (Sydney), 762 p; collection of 50 articles, 1948-68 plus a bibliography.

The Missing Link in Supervision of the Securities Market, Abacus, v.5, p 16-36.

Financial Information Systems, Australian Accountant, v.39 (Aug), pp 364-68.

1970 Methods of Accounting - series of articles for The Accountant (UK): 26 Feb, 5 Mar, 19 Mar, 2 April, 16 April and 30 April.

Accounting from a Logical Point of View, Singapore Accountant, v.5, pp 13-18.

Second Thoughts on Continuously Contemporary Accounting, Abacus, v.6, pp 39-55.

1971 The Commercial Foundations of Accounting Theory, in Williard E. Stone (ed), Foundations of Accounting Theory, University of Florida, pp 59-77.

Evidence for a Market Selling Price Accounting System, in R.R. Sterling (ed), Asset Valuation and Income Determination Scholars Book Co, pp 74-96.

Income and Capital: Fisher's Legacy, Journal of Accounting Research, v.9, pp 137-49.

The Validation of an Accounting Theory, Waseda Business and Economic Studies, v.7, pp 1-21.

1972 The Anguish of Accountants, Journal of Accountancy, v.133 (March), pp 68-74.

Accounting Theory, Practice and Policy, Singapore Accountant, v.7, pp 39-43.

Measurement in Current Accounting Practice, Accounting Review, v.47 (July), pp 488-509; a critique of Ijiri, whose reply is in the same issue, pp 510-26.

1973 Accounting Principles or Accounting Policies? Journal of Accountancy, v.135 (May), pp 48-53.

Securities and Obscurities, Gower Press, 243 p.

Accounting Principles and the Law, Australian Business Law Review, v.1, pp 112-29.

Observations as a Method of Inquiry - the Background of <u>Securities and Obscurities</u>, <u>Abacus</u>, v.9, pp 156-75.

1975 Stock Market Prices and Accounting Research, <u>Abacus</u>, v.10, pp 39-54.

The Objectives of Accounting, <u>Singapore Accountant</u>, v.9, pp 39-45.

Third Thoughts, <u>Abacus</u>, v.10, pp 129-37.

1975 NOD, COG and PuPu: See How Inflation Teases, <u>Journal of Accountancy</u>, v.140 (Sept), pp 56-62.

<u>Accounting for Inflation</u>, University of Sydney, 120 p.

1976 The Possibility of Normative Accounting Standards, <u>Accounting Review</u>, v.51 (July), pp 646-56.

Accounting Principles and Practices - Negotiated or Dictated? <u>Proceedings of Accounting Research Convocation</u>, University of Alabama, pp 1-22.

1977 <u>An Autobibliography</u>, Occasional Paper No.15, ICRA, University of Lancaster, England, 70 p.

The Delusions of Replacement Cost Accounting, <u>Financial Analysts Journal</u>, v.33, (July/Aug), pp 48-52.

1978 The Use and Abuse of a Notation: A History of an Idea, <u>Abacus</u>, v.14, pp 122-44.

1979 The Myths and the Science of Accounting, <u>Accounting, Organisations and Society</u>, v.5, pp 167-180.

Usefulness - The Vanishing Premise in Accounting Standard Setting, <u>Abacus</u>, v.15, pp 71-92.

1979 "The Hard Core of Accounting", in <u>Essays in Honor of William A. Paton</u>, edited by Zeff S.A., Demski J. and Dopuch N., University of Michigan, pp 73-92.

1980 <u>Price Variations and Inflation Accounting</u>, McGraw Hill, 174 p.

<u>The Design of Accounting Standards</u>, University of Sydney Accounting Research Centre, Monograph No.1, 93 p.

1981 The Search for a System in Financial Calculation, <u>Abacus</u>, v.17, pp 68-72.

1982 Edwards & Bell on Income Measurement in Retrospect, <u>Abacus</u>, v.18

REFERENCES

Book Reviews of AEEB:

    Accounting Review, v.42, 1967, pp.207-8 (A R Cruse).
    American Economic Review, 1967, pp.297-9 (G Benston).
    Journal of Business, v.40, 1967, pp.211-3
      (E J Hendriksen).

Anderson, D & R Leftwich, "Securities & Obscurities: A Case for the
    Reform of the Law of Company Accounts", Journal of Accounting
    Research, v.12, 1974, -p.341-7 (Chambers's reply, pp.348-54).

Iselin, E R, "Chambers on Accounting Theory", Accounting Review, v.43,
    1968, pp.231-8.

Larson, K D & R W Schattke, "Current Cash Equivalents, Additivity &
    Financial Action", Accounting Review, v.41, 1966, pp.634-41
    (Chambers's reply, v.42, 1967, pp.751-7).

Leftwich, R W, "A Critical Analysis of Some Behavioural Assumptions
    Underlying R J Chambers', Accounting Evaluation & Economic
    Behavior", Queensland Papers, Department of Accounting,
    University of Queensland, v.1, No.7 (Chambers's reply, "The
    Canons of Criticism" was sent to the author but not published).

McKeown, J C, "An Empirical Test of a Model Proposed by Chambers",
    Accounting Review, v.46, 1971, pp.12-29.

Ma, R, "On Chambers' Second Thoughts", Abacus, v.10, 1974 (Third
    Thoughts - a response - v.10, pp.129-37).

Most, K S, "Chambers' Continuously Contemporary Accounting", Singapore
    Accountant, v.6, 1971, pp.64-7.

Staubus, G J, "Current Cash Equivalents for Assets: A Dissent", Accounting
    Review, v.42, 1967, pp.650-61 (Chambers's reply, v.43, 1968,
    pp.239-47).

Wright, F K, "Capacity for Adaptation and the Asset Measurement Problem",
    Abacus, v.3, 1967, pp.74-9.

Waikato University Inflation Accounting Research Project, Manual for
CoCoA, Allen Craswell, 1976, 50p; Project Work Manual, 1976.

Accounting, Evaluation and Economic Behavior. By RAYMOND J. CHAMBERS. Englewood Cliffs: Prentice-Hall, 1966. Pp. xii, 388. $7.50.

There are few basic works in the literature of accounting that undertake a thoroughly theoretical approach. Indeed, most writing by accountants or about accounting is concerned with applications of existing rules of practice to specific situations, the tracing of precedents for or against some procedure, or with teaching the methods and techniques currently used by professional accountants. Scattered throughout the articles and textbooks, one finds protests by a few academicians and practitioners against the inconsistent body of rules that are known as "generally accepted principles of accounting." These protests have sometimes contrasted accounting with economics in order to develop a structured system of accounting definitions and rules (e.g., J. G. Canning, *The Economics of Accounting,* 1929); have been concerned about the effects of price level changes and called for and described a system of constant dollar accounting (e.g., H. W. Sweeney, *Stabilized Accounting,* 1936); have presented a plea for meaningful accounting reports (e.g., K. MacNeal, *Truth in Accounting,* 1939); have presented a system of accounting based on "practical" considerations, such as cost-based measurements that can be readily audited (e.g., W. A. Paton and A. C. Littleton, *An Introduction to Corporate Accounting Standards,* 1940); and have sought to develop and describe a system in which trading income and capital (or holding) gains are reported separately (e.g., E. O. Edwards and P. W. Bell, *The Theory and Measurement of Business Income,* 1961). Professor Chambers' book is one of the most recent of this genre.

On the jacket Chambers' book is described as "A thorough and literate foundation for a system of accounting, developing the many facets of the function of accounting as an aid to the efficient management and development of the economic institutions of an industrial society." This foundation is built of propositions that are ". . . admitted only because their premises are believed to be acceptable or demonstrable and because they comprise a consistent system" (p. 10). The propositions are drawn from the theory of signs and language, measurements, logic, social structures, communication, etc. The belief in their acceptability is based on copious references to authorities in these fields. (The economist quoted most often is von Mises.)

The system of argument is predominantly deductive. Statements about human behavior, perception, needs, institutions, etc. are made and supported by many references to the assertions and conclusions of authoritative writers in many fields. Each chapter is followed by an outline, in flow-chart form, and a list of numbered definitions and assumptions, from which inferences and conclusions are drawn and also numbered. After each conclusion, one or more numbers are given that refer back to a previously drawn conclusion or assumption on which it is based or related in some way. The net result of this form of argument is a carefully built up, apparently logically consistent system, upon which a theory of accounting is to rest. (I use the word "apparently" because, despite the heroic efforts of the author to provide schematics and cross-referenced statements, I find it extremely difficult to keep track of the basis for the multitude of assertive statements made. Perhaps a reason for my problem is that Chambers uses philosophical terminology that prevented my fully understanding the points being made.)

The first three chapters (about a fifth of the book) construct, from basic assumptions, the milieu in which an accounting system functions. Chambers begins with statements and definitions about the behavior of people: their capacity for perception, motivation for action, reaction to stimuli, and capacity for and method of reasoning, learning and belief. His following discussion on the achievement of desired ends is based on these statements. "Actors" are said to choose among alternative means to the desired ends by discovery and evaluation of the consequences and marginal utilities of their actions. The "environment of action"—natural and social, legal, and economic—is considered next. The conclusion drawn from these introductory chapters is that an entity must be able to choose among alternative causes of action and adapt to changing conditions in order to survive.

Chapter 4, "Monetary Calculation," contains Chamber's conclusions about the function and method of accounting. He argues that the ability of an entity to adapt by engaging in market exchanges is measured by ". . . the simple financial property which is uniformly relevant at a point of time for all possible future actions in markets . . the market selling price or realizable price of any or all goods held" (p. 92). "We therefore define accounting functionally, as a method of retrospective and contemporary monetary calculation the purpose of which is to provide a continuous source of financial information as a guide to future action in markets" (p. 99).

The remaining two-thirds of the book presents useful elaborations of the conclusion—an illustration of the effects of not making price level adjustments, a discussion of the application of current market prices to different types of assets, a consideration of accounting for trading ventures, corporations, and nonprofit organizations, as well as additional statements about behavioral problems and some basic and often irrelevant observations about such subjects as double entry bookkeeping and epistemology.

Chamber's key conclusion, that assets should be measured at contemporary market prices and income measured as the change in these asset amounts (adjusted for changes in general price levels and investments in the entity), differs from the present value approach favored by most economists. He rejects present value because the calculations are not based on current market "facts," but rather on expectations about the future. Considering that Chambers believes that financial statements should show the short-term ability of the entity to adjust by selling or buying individual assets, his rejection of present values may be justified. However, his valuation rule requires that the assets of an entity always be stated at the lower of exchange or use values. It is difficult, for me at least, to conclude (even granting Chambers' premises) that this is or might be the sole function of accounting data. To give just one example, consider that the cost of a specialized machine would be shown as an expense in the period of its purchase, if it has no resale value (net of transaction costs), even though it has high use value. If managers and/or owners view the accounting statements seriously, what might the effect of this procedure be on their decisions to acquire assets?

A different type of problem that one encounters with this book, perhaps because of the theoretical approach that Chambers takes, is that he does not consider adequately the practical problems of measuring asset values in terms of current market prices. Chambers asserts that ". . . whether or not [a person] chooses to discover his financial position, that position is discoverable" (p. 81), in terms of the current cash equivalent of his assets. But the amounts that may be received for assets differ when they are sold singly or in groups, even when unambiguous market prices exist for specific assets. (This fact violates the principle of additivity about which Chambers is very concerned). Nor is the market price of manufactured goods known until they are sold. (Interestingly, in the brief paragraph or two in which he considers the problem of manufactured goods, Chambers seems to suggest that traditional cost allocations be made, with the exception that original costs be restated at current market prices.) Indeed, the essential problem for accountants, in my opinion, is that of measurement. I believe that it behooves the proponent of a theory of accounting to spell out, in detail, how his concepts can be made operational.

It would seem, given the as yet unsolved problems of valuing assets, either in terms of current market price, present value or in some other way, that Chambers would favor accounting statements in which assets are valued on several bases. But he rejects this notion emphatically, on the grounds that only one method can be correct.

At the conclusion of his book, Chambers likens his work to that of Copernicus; he envisions a similar Copernican revolution in accounting thought. As he notes, others have complained about the inconsistencies and meaninglessness of much accounting practice. Considering the pragmatic orientation of accountants, it is doubtful if Chambers' formal axiomatic presentation, with its limited consideration of methods of measurement and recording, will be as effective as he hopes. Nevertheless, Chambers has provided us with a rigorously constructed system that attempts to integrate accounting theory with other disciplines. In so doing, he has prepared a strong foundation upon which additional research into the measurement and reporting techniques of accounting can proceed.

GEORGE J. BENSTON

University of Rochester

(1)   To what extent was Chambers concerned with methodological arguments in accounting?

(2)   "The objective of the process of observation and reasoning ... knowledge ... consists of propositions of two kinds, empirical statements and formal statements... The gap must be bridged between the emprical and the formal ... The bridging is done by rules of correspondence ..." (Pg.34).
- To what do "rules of correspondence" refer?
- To which discipline is this term associated?
- What is the context in which it appears in that discipline?
- What degree of acceptance does the explanation (of which the above term is part) hold in the discipline to which it belongs?
- What does this imply about use of the term by Chambers?

(3)   Chambers is at pains to point out that accounting information is important for decision-making.
- Does he indicate the sort of decisions needed to be made?
- Is the system of information which he proposes sufficient for decision making?
- What are his claims in this latter regard?

(4)   What is Chambers's view of supplementary financial statement disclosure? Is his view a common one? What reasons does Chambers cite in support of his view? Are there other reasons which might lend support to Chambers' view?

(5)   "... goodwill is not an asset of a firm" (Pg.212).
- What arguments does Chambers present in support of the above statement?
- Are the arguments consistent with his definition of assets?
- What other authors have come to the same conclusion?
- How (if at all) have the latters arguments differed from Chambers's?

(6)   'Solvency' and 'profitability' are the cornerstone concepts of the accounting system predicted by Chambers.

- How true is this statement?
- Assuming it is true how they do they differ from the cornerstone concepts of traditional accounting?
- To what extent might we be justified in assuming that Chambers's system is quite different because it does not give into expediency and accepted accounting conventions. (Consider in particular the works of Gilman, May, MacNeal and Paton).

(7)   Chambers, although not adopting most of the conventions of traditional accounting can be found making a number of references to the "going concern".
- Is his use of the term an inconsistency in his work or does he adopt a particular idea of going concern? If so, what is it? And how is it different from the accepted understanding?

(8)   What is Chambers's view in regard to conservatism in accounting?

(9)   What is Chambers's view on the valuation of assets which are not readily marketable? Contrast his view with that of MacNeals. To what extent is Chambers's view based on the value in use/value in exchange distinction?

(10)   How does Chambers ₃ account for price level fluctuations in a period? To what extent are price level changes accounted for in income? To what extent do the income components of the Chamberian and Edwards and Bell systems correspond? How do they differ?

17

YUJI IJIRI

The Foundations of Accounting Measurements

Biographical Chronology

1935	Born, 24 February, Kobe, Japan
1956	Awarded LLB degree, Ritsumeikon University, Japan
1957-59	Auditor, Price Waterhouse and Co
1960	Awarded MS degree, University of Minnesota
1961-	Appointed Management Consultant, Gulf Oil Corporation
1962	Married
1963	Awarded PhD (industrial administration), Carnegie Institute of Technology
1963-67	From Assistant to Associate Professor of Business Administration, Stanford University
1965	Management Goals and Accounting For Control, published
1967-	Professor of Industrial Administration, Carnegie-Mellon University
1967-68	Visiting Professor, Aoyama Gakuin University and Tokyo University, Japan
1967	The Foundations of Accounting Measurements: A Mathematical, Economic and Behavioural Inquiry, published
1968	Awarded, American Institute of Certified Public Accountants, Gold Medal
1972-74	National Science Foundation Fellow, Carnegie-Mellon University
1974-75	Vice-President, American Accounting Association
1982	President, American Accounting Association

Selected Bibliography

1960	"CPA Practice in Japan," CPA of Minnesota, v.9 Jan, pp 4-5; also in Ohio CPA, v.19, pp 124-5.
1963	"A Linear Programming Model for Budgeting and Financial Planning," Journal of Accounting Research, v.1, Autumn, pp 198-212, with Levy, P.K. and R.C. Lyon.
1964	"Business Firm Growth and Size," The American Economic Review, v.54, 2, March, pp 77-89, with Simon, H.A.
1965	"Axioms and Structures of Conventional Accounting Measurement," Accounting Review, v.40, Jan, pp 36-53.
	Management Goals and Accounting For Control, Rand McNally and Co (Chicago), 191 p.
	"The Effect of Inventory Costing Methods on Full and Direct Costing," Journal of Accounting Research, v.3, Spring, pp 63-74, with Jaedicke, R.K. & J.L. Livingstone.

1966   "Mathematics and Accounting," in Backer, M (ed) <u>Modern Accounting Theory</u>, Prentice-Hall (NJ), pp 535-53.

"Reliability and Objectivity of Accounting Measurements," <u>Accounting Review</u>, v.41, July, pp 474-83, with Jaedicke, R.K.

"Physical Measures and Multi-dimensional Accounting," in <u>Research in Accounting Measurement</u>, AAA (edited Jaedicke, R.K., Ijiri and O. Nielsen), pp 150-64.

"The Effects of Accounting Alternatives on Management Decisions," in <u>Research in Accounting Measurement</u>, pp 186-199, with Jaedicke, R.K. and K.E. Knight.

1967   <u>Foundations of Accounting Measurement</u>, Prentice-Hall (New Jersey), 235 p.

1968   "Application of Input-Output Analysis to Some Problems in Cost Accounting," <u>Management Accounting</u> (NAA), v.49, sect 1, April, pp 46-61; reprinted in <u>Management Accounting</u> (Eng), v.46, Sept, v.50, pp 367-77.

"On Budgeting Principles and Budget-Auditing Standards," <u>Accounting Review</u>, v.43, Oct,

"On Budgeting Principles and Budget-Auditing Standards," <u>Accounting Review</u>, v.43, Oct, pp 662-7.

"Integrated Evaluation System for Budget Forecasting and Operating Performance with a Classified Bibliography," <u>Journal of Accounting Research</u>, v.6, Spring, pp 1-28, with Kinard, J.C. & F.B. Putney.

1969   "Probabilistic Depreciation and its Implication for Group Depreciation," <u>Accounting Review</u>, v.44, Oct, pp 743-56.

1970   "Application of Mathematical Control Theory to Accounting and Budgeting," <u>Accounting Review</u>, v.45, April, pp 246-58.

"Sequential Models in Probabilistic Depreciation," <u>Journal of Accounting Research</u>, v.8, Spring, pp 34-46, with Robert S Kaplan.

"Four Objectives of Sampling in Auditing: Representative, Corrective, Protective and Preventative," <u>Management Accounting</u>, v.52, Dec 1 pp 42-4; also in <u>Accountants' Journal</u>, v.49, May, pp 360-2.

1971   "Axioms for Historical Cost Valuation: A Reply," <u>Journal of Accounting Research</u>, v.9, Spring, pp 181-7.

"Critique of A.P.B. Fundamentals Statement," <u>Journal of Accountancy</u>, v.132, Nov, pp 43-50.

"A Defense for Historical Cost Accounting," in Sterling, R.R., <u>Asset Valuation and Income Determination</u>, Scholars Book Co, pp 1-14.

"Logic and Sanctions in Accounting," in Sterling, R.R. and Bentz, W.F. (eds.) Accounting in Perspective, South-Western Publishing Co (Cincinnati) pp 38-50.

1972 "Approximations to Interest Formulas," Journal of Business, v.45, July, pp 398-40.

"Measurement in Current Accounting Practices: a Reply (to Chambers)," Accounting Review, v.47, July, pp 510-26.

"The Nature of Accounting Research," in Sterling, R.R., (ed) Research Methodology in Accounting, Scholars Book Co., pp 59-69.

1973 "Quadratic Cost-Volume Relationship and Timing of Demand Information," Accounting Review, v.48, Oct, pp 724-37, with Hiroyaki Hami.

1974 "Improving Reliability of Publicly Reported Corporate Financial Statements," in Prakash, P., Public Reporting of Corporate Financial Forecasts, Chicago, pp 161-188.

"Problems of Implementing the Trueblood Objectives Report," Studies on Financial Objectives, (Conference on Research in Accounting, Chicago), pp 29-42, with Richard M Cyert.

"A Model for Integrating Sampling Objectives in Auditing," in Dickinson, J.P., Risk and Uncertainty in Accounting and Finance (Lexington, Mass.) pp 41-58, with Robert S. Kaplan; also "Sequential Models in Probabilistic Depreciation," (Ijiri and Kaplan), pp 3-17.

1975 Theory of Accounting Measurement, Studies in Accounting Research, No.10, A.A.A. (Florida), 210 p.

1976 "The Price-Level Restatement and its Dual Interpretation," Accounting Review, April, pp 227-243.

1977 "From Accounting to Accountability: Steps to a Corporate Social Reporting," Accountancy in the 1980's, Arthur Young Roundtable (1976) University of Illinois, pp 105-57, with Cooper, W. Co.

Skew Distributions and the Sizes of Business Firms, North-Holland Publ. Co. (Amsterdam/New York), with Herbert A. Simon.

1978 "Cash-flow Accounting and its Structure," Journal of Accounting and Finance, v.1, Summer, pp 331-48.

1979 "Oil and Gas Accounting - Turbulence in Financial Reporting," Financial Executive, v.47, July, pp 42-6, 48.

Eric Louis Kohler: Accounting's Man of Principles, edited, Reston Publishing (Va), with William W. Cooper, 248 p.

1980   "Recovery Rate and Cash Flow Accounting," _Financial_
        Executive, v.48, March, pp 54-56, 58, 60.

        "Multi-dimensional Accounting and Distributed Data
        Bases: Their Implications for Organisations and Society,"
        Accounting, Organisations and Society, v.5, No.1,
        pp 115-123, with Edward C Kelly.

        Stein's Paradox and Audit Sampling," _Journal of_
        Accounting Research, v.18, Spring, pp 91-108, with
        Robert A. Leitch.

1981   _Historical Cost Accounting and its Rationality_, The
        Canadian Certified General Accountants' Research
        Foundation, Research Monograph 1.

REFERENCES

Book Reviews of _Foundations_:
                Accounting Review, v.43, 1968, pp.199-201
                (T R Dyckman).
                American Economic Review, v.58, 1968, p.280
                Choice, v.5, Nov 1968, p.1182.
                Journal of Accountancy, v.127, Jan 1969, pp.90-1
                (T H Williams)

Book Reviews of _Theory_:
                Accounting Review, v.52, 1972, p.289.
                Journal of Finance, v.31, Dec 1976, p.1539.

Anderson, J A, _A Comparative Analysis of Selected Income Measurement_
        Theories in Financial Accounting, AAA (SAR No.12), 1976.

Bedford, N M, "Review: _The Foundations of Accounting Measurement_",
        Journal of Accounting Research, v.6, 1968, pp.270-82.

Chambers, R J, "Measurement in Current Accounting Practice: A Critique",
        Accounting Review, v.47, 1972, pp.488-509 (followed by Ijiri's
        reply, pp.510-26).

Wells, M C, "Axioms for Historical Cost Valuation", _Journal of Accounting_
        Research, v.9, 1971, pp.171-80 (followed by Ijiri's reply).

The Foundations of Accounting Measurement

NORTON M. BEDFORD*

An evaluation of a scholarly representation may be favorable or un-
favorable depending upon the criteria of success established by the reviewer. Presumably, a "fair" reviewer should accept as criteria the objectives of the author in presenting the material to his academic
associates and then evaluate the contribution in terms of the stated objectives. However, in the case of *The Foundations of Accounting Measurement* which Professor Ijiri has submitted to accounting academicians,
the objectives are not well specified. One is not certain whether Ijiri's
book should be measured by its new contributions to basic accounting
concepts or in terms of the insights gained from a formal representation
of the fundamental propositions of accounting. If the criterion is a contribution to basic accounting concepts, one finds few to evaluate. But if
the criterion is the insight into the nature of established accounting propositions, the opposite prevails. On balance, it seems appropriate to review
Professor Ijiri's contribution in terms of both criteria with an emphasis
on the process which he provides as a means for gaining insight into the
nature of the basic propositions of accounting. More precisely, we shall
consider his contribution primarily in terms of its effectiveness in laying
bare the essence of accounting's basic propositions.

Surrogates and Principals

The cornerstone of *The Foundations* is the proposition that accounting
representations are surrogates of underlying economic reality. While deci-

---

* Professor of Accountancy and Business Administration, University of Illinois.

sion makers are interested in the underlying reality, the accounting measurement provides only a surrogate or symbolic representation of that reality. Designating the symbols used to represent other things or phenomena as surrogates and the things or phenomena represented by the surrogates as principals, Professor Ijiri suggests that the principal-surrogate relationships used in accounting, which are rather complicated ones, are the basic blocks in the foundations of accounting measurement. This proposition seems to be accurate and rather obvious. No one questions the assertion that an accounting representation of "Merchandise ... $3,000" is anything more than a description of the physical asset, merchandise. The advantage in recognizing that the surrogate-principal relationship exists is that it raises immediately the question as to how accountants go about selecting the surrogates or representations of economic reality.

Measurement Characteristics

In order to understand the methods by which surrogates are developed and processed in accounting, one must understand the basic characteristics of measurement. Such an understanding necessarily constitutes a prefoundation block of the accounting measurement. In Ijiri's terms, "Measurement is a special language which represents real-world phenomena by means of numbers and relations among numbers that are predetermined within the number system." There is nothing particularly new about this description of measurement as a language, but we may benefit from a review of the nature of predetermined relations within the number system. Possibly, the most commonly accepted relation in the arabic number system is the relation of ordering. Thus, the symbols 1, 2, 3, 4, 5 imply the relation that 5 follows 4 which follows 3 and so on. Also, to most members of society, these symbols have built in such relations as "greater than," "equal to," and "addition." Of course, there are many other predetermined relations commonly accepted or capable of being in the arabic number system. Conceptually, it is not necessary to use arabic numbers; however, accounting measurements have used this set of arabic numbers and their built-in relations as symbols useful for revealing economic activity. The significance of this disclosure is that it calls attention to the nature of the numbers used by accountants. From this knowledge, it becomes apparent that any special set of symbols could be called numbers if a relation or relations among numbers were established. With the predetermined relations built into the number system, a number could be assigned to an object "as if the object had a property represented by the number which is independent of the properties that other objects have. This assignment of numbers to objects is called measurement."

Relations

The intent of a measurement is to represent a given relation(s) among objects by predetermined relation(s) among the numbers. For example, if one object is greater than another object, this relation among the two objects could be represented by the numbers 200 and 100 respectively. We may also assume that the predetermined relation among the numbers in the set of real numbers is such that the 200 and 100 representations disclose not only that one object is greater than another but also by how much. The main point, however, is that "a simple assignment of numbers to objects does not convey anything unless it is specified which relation among numbers is used to represent which relation among objects." Furthermore, once it is understood that the nature of the built-in relations among numbers in the number sets is man-made, interest then focuses on ways of building in new relations in an improved number set. The objective of such interest is the establishment of predetermined relations among numbers in such a way that various relations among the set of underlying objects or principals can be described.

This study of number systems is an integral part of *The Foundations of Accounting Measurement*. Accounting research should include methods of developing relations among symbols known as numbers; the most useful mathematics for developing such relations appears to be set theory. Since a binary relation is merely a set of ordered pairs and a relation among more than two elements is merely a set of ordered n-tuples, the foundations of accounting measurement could be presented in terms of set theory. Set theory is also appropriate because accounting measurements deal with the development of such set theory concepts as model homomorphism and isomorphism between a relational system of principals and a relational system of surrogates.

Scope of Measurement

Significant as Ijiri's description of the nature of measurement is, one cannot help but feel that he stopped short of the more fundamental description of measurement as a unit of information. Since he refers to Churchman's discussion of the teleology of measurement, apparently his decision to adopt a less fundamental concept of measurement was intentional. But the ironic point is that classification, which Ijiri apparently views as part of the object identification process, is an accounting problem that can be included in the broader functional notion of measurement as an information development process. Failure to include identification (classification) as part of the measurement process results in a somewhat unsatisfying treatment of the way objects are identified in the continuum of an entity's economic activity. Starting with the basic identification question—"How, then, do we become able to identify objects in a continuous whole?"—Ijiri contends that we "sense the independence of a subshape" in the whole. But the way this sensing should be done for compiling accounting information is not well developed. In fact, he states that "we must arbitrarily pick out some portions of it (the whole), identify them as objects, and then describe their properties." This arbitrary manner by which objects are to be distinguished in the continuous whole is an unsatisfactory element of Ijiri's identification process. The feeling persists throughout that the abstract description of methods appropriate for a breakdown of the continuous whole into discrete parts may not provide a realistic base for the development of the foundations of accounting measurement.

Also inherent in the restricted definition of measurement is the implication that the foundations of accounting measurement are to be constructed in terms of physical science, rather than social science measurement methods. This may be undesirable since accounting has a closer association with the social sciences than the physical sciences. Ijiri evidently considered a broader measurement base because his bibliography includes a number of references which deal with social science measurement methods. But his rejection of a broader base is definite. He contends "the measurement problem is often confused with the problem of comprehending phenomena in the real world. . . . The measurement problem is strictly a representation problem which comes after the relations among objects are clearly understood." This is confusing from a social science point of view because the very process of labeling two distinct objects creates the relation of "different from." Thus, the comprehension of phenomena can hardly be distinguished from their classification which is a measurement process. It may be that the only social science measurement method not included in Ijiri's notion of measurement is that of classification, but it would be more assuring if the actual measurement base were clarified. A similar criticism applies to his failure to recognize explicitly that a significant part of existing mathematics was developed to further the advancement of physical science measurements. We can only infer that the same mathematics may be used as a foundation for accounting measurement. If the inference is intended, and evidence is available to indicate that the foundation of accounting measurement should be confined to such a mathematical framework, it would be well to have a definite assertion that such is the case.

Substance of Accounting

In addition to its methodological base, *The Foundations of Accounting Measurement* includes a consideration of the substance of that which is measured by the accounting process. Although Ijiri recognizes that in the future the substance of accounting may encompass more than the communication of economic events, he concludes in chapter two that economic activity is now the conventional substance of accounting. This restriction of substance necessarily limits in some ways the scope of his study. Since he is concerned only with the foundations of accounting measurement as they now exist, it may be appropriate to restrict his conception of the substance of accounting in developing the initial foundations. But the rapid development of the technology of accounting in recent years, which has tended to encourage an expansion of the accounting function into all areas where that technology is useful, raises some question as to the proper scope of the substance of accounting. Some have proposed that the substance of accounting should not be limited at all. Removal of the substantive restriction would leave the foundations of accounting measurement with a somewhat universal applicability but without a standard substance. Such proposals are unconventional at this time; nevertheless, they call attention to the limitations of any statement of the long-run foundations of accounting measurement which is confined to contemporary views of the substance as economic activity.

Ijiri's description of the economic events which form the substance of accounting is based on a purposefully oversimplified discussion of the concept of values and valuation. He confines his description to three main features of values and valuation:

(1) the duality of values
(2) the transformation from a utility differential to a monetary differential
(3) the treatment of valuation as a representation of causal networks.

One is inclined to be critical of this abbreviated description of economic activity even though the boundary was purposefully adopted. Moreover, one must question the introduction of the notion of the economic events of an entity without specifying which of the on-going activities of an entity represent events. The concept of events is not at all clear, although Ijiri indicates they are "identified in accounting by economic resources which the entity controls and by their changes." From this somewhat crude identification, he describes economic resources as "things that benefit us and that we must make a sacrifice to obtain" and thus arrives at the notion that value is a dual concept of benefit and sacrifice whose difference triggers economic activity. This hedonistic explanation is not placed in perspective but is accepted as one of the underlying rocks on which the substantive foundations of accounting measurement may be placed. It is interesting, in view of the limited explanation of human motivation which he accepts, that in a footnote (page 37) Ijiri observes that psychology may offer other explanations of human behavior. However, he then proceeds to ignore them without further comment. This is bothersome because it raises the doubt that the assumptions used have been adopted mainly to permit a fairly rigorous exposition of certain foundations of accounting measurement that may not be universally pertinent for professional application.

The difference between the sacrifice value of economic resources and their benefit value is defined as the utility differential of the goods. The manner in which this utility differential is transformed into a monetary differential is the second main feature of Ijiri's description of the nature of accounting values. Using a somewhat involved analysis, he expands the personal utility differential concept through the process of exchange into the notion of a monetary differential which—in its realized form as a profit—motivates economic activity. While the analysis is a somewhat elementary discussion of economic price theory and avoids the details of the bargaining process between buyers and sellers and the planning over time by which prices are actually set, it may be a satisfactory assumption for purposes of constructing a simplified structure of the meaning of accounting measurements.

The third main feature of Ijiri's conception of accounting values is his treatment of valuation as a representation of causal networks rather than as a direct cause and effect line. The causal network is held to exist because of the joint cost problem which may preclude the determination of both sacrifice value and benefit value of a product in a meaningful manner. If one views the flow of a common product to a group of joint products which are then used as separate products in combination with other products, the geometric representation of a network emerges. The contribution of such causal methods allows Ijiri to illustrate three major problems which make accounting valuation difficult and ambiguous:

(1) the *inseparability* of elements (common product) in a causal network

(2) the *multiplicity* of a causal network involving a particular element

(3) the *instability* of a causal network over time.

If one steps back to take an overall view of Ijiri's three main features of values and valuation, a quite familiar but hazy picture of the accounting problem of developing useful information for decision making takes shape. Essentially, no new features are revealed and one develops a slight dissatisfaction with the description. However, a closer examination indicates that the description of the three features of accounting values and valuation permit a rigorous analysis of the accounting problem. And Ijiri's analysis is rigorous.

Illustrative is his development of the "similarity" assumption of human behavior. Relating benefit and sacrifice to utility and disutility respectively and attributing these to goods, he recognizes a causal relationship between the need to sacrifice in order to obtain goods and the need to consume goods in order to realize benefits. Recognition of this causal relationship, which has no greater validity than that the relationship has held in the past or in a similar situation, permits him to propose a space-time inference rule which is defined as the similarity assumption of human behavior. This assumption is stated in terms of regularity, which may be deterministic or probabilistic, in the sense that "the regularity that has been observed in known phenomena will also be observed in unknown phenomena." This logical support for the role of descriptions of past activities reinforces a considerable amount of intuitive support for the informational contribution of accounting data on past activities.

Ijiri's discussion of the valuation concept departs from traditional theories. He contends, from his findings that goods have both utility (benefit value) and disutility (sacrifice value), that goods have dual values and should be measured in terms of "a pair of numbers representing utility and disutility." Thus, while the concept of economic value is considered to be the substance of accounting, the various aspects of value make the substance a somewhat involved concept. Specifically, four kinds of valuation are distinguished as follows:

Time	Sacrifice value	Benefit value
Past	Historical cost (1)	Realized value (3)
Future	Replacement cost (2)	Realizable value (4)

While recognizing no one value is "best" for all uses, Ijiri suggests "there is one valuation which is unique in terms of its practicality in measurement, i.e., the valuation method based on historical costs."

In a sense, Ijiri's development of the four kinds of valuation is a step in the direction of operational measurement. But he stops short, failing to recognize that the definition of a substance depends considerably on the way it is measured. He seems to accept the notion that one must know the thing to be measured before starting to measure it, rather than adopting the view that the purpose in making a measurement will indicate both the properties to be measured and the method of measuring them. His approach will not provide precise measurements since a verbal description of such a thing as value is necessarily so imprecise that multiple measures of it could be developed. The proper description of value can be provided only by stating the operations involved in measuring it—an operational description. In fact, there are an infinite number of uses to which a measurement of value could be put, and the restriction of accounting valuations to the cited four does not serve effectively as a description of the substantive foundations of accounting measurement. It would have been more accurate, though possibly less satisfying, to recognize the multiple foundations of accounting measurements and refer to the four kinds of valuation as expediencies or reasonable approximations for most of the desired accounting measurements. In this way, Ijiri could have drawn attention to the omission from the accounting discipline of a clear recognition that cost (or sacrifice) is the cost of an action and not the cost of a thing at all. The accounting reference to the cost of merchandise rather than to the cost of acquiring the merchandise (an action) or to the cost of using the merchandise (another action) could be explained as being roughly or approximately correctible through the use of one of the four variables.

Axioms of Accounting

After examing the methodological and substantive foundations for accounting measurement, Ijiri then turns to the axioms of accounting essential for performing the accounting function of communicating the economic events of an entity. He does this without stating the reservations to the axiomatic method, although certain institutional mathematicians are somewhat opposed to it. Subject to this criticism, and assuming brevity is desired, one must appreciate his selection of the axioms of control, quantities, and exchanges. The control axiom is used to designate the resources of an entity, including both positive and negative (liability) assets, to be measured. The axiom of quantities is used to classify and quantify resources in terms of class names and quantity measure. The axiom of exchanges is used to recognize "a cause-and-effect relationship" between "things foregone and things obtained." The latter provides a basis for determining the amount of resources exchanged and this "makes it possible for us to develop a value measure as an aggregation of the set of quantity measures."

The three axioms and a set of valuation rules are then used to develop for historical cost valuation an axiomatic system that approximates accounting practice. Though oversimplified, the resulting model of accounting practice is excellent in that it can serve as a basic model to which modifications could be attached in order to develop a realistic axiomatic structure of practical accounting information systems. The three axioms are stated in the following manner:

Axiom of Control: There exists a method by which resources under the control...of a given entity at any time t are uniquely determined at that time or later.

Axiom of Quantities: There exists a method by which all resources are uniquely partitioned into a collection of classes so that for each class a nonnegative and additive quantity measure is defined and so that we are indifferent to any two sets of resources in the same class if and only if their quantities are the same.

Axiom of Exchanges: There exists a method by which all changes in the resources controlled by a given entity up to any time t are identified at that time or later and are partitioned uniquely into an ordered set of pairs of an increment and a decrement, where the increment belongs to one and only one class.

Using the three axioms, a set of valuation rules is developed as follows. The axiom of control identifies all assets and liabilities (negative assets) of an entity and the axiom of quantities identifies the quantities of each asset and liability, so the only remaining problem is to place a homogeneous value measure on the quantities. For this valuation process, the following rules are proposed.

Basic Rule 1: The value of any set of...resources in the basic class (cash) is defined to be equal to its quantity as determined by the quantity measure for the class.

Basic Rule 2: The value of an empty set is defined to be equal to zero.

Value Allocation Rule: Allocate the value of all resources in each class before the exchange to outgoing resources in the class and remaining resources in the class in proportion to their quantities. The sum of values allocated to outgoing resources in each class is the value of the decrement. Decrease the value of resources in each class by the value allocated to outgoing resources in the class.

Value Imputation Rule: If the resources in the increment belong to a nonbasic class, set the value of the increment equal to the value of the decrement. Increase the value of resources of the class by the value of the increment.

Value Comparison Rule: If the resources in the increment belong to the basic class, calculate a value gain or loss by subtracting the value of the decrement from the value of the increment.

A particular advantage of the axiomatic structure of the conventional historical cost valuation accounting system is that the system can be extended to multidimensional accounting where multiple rather than single values are placed on resources. Prior to explaining the extension into multidimensional accounting, Ijiri attempts to show that double-entry was developed to provide for historical cost valuation. To do this, he indicates there are two distinct types of double-entry which he calls *classification double-entry* and *causal double-entry.* By classification double-entry, he refers to double-entry as the recording of the same thing twice but looked at from two different points of view. By causal double-entry, he refers to the belief that the two entries describe two different objects looked at from the same angle but tied together by a causal relationship between them. The assertion with which most accounting theorists will possibly take greatest issue is his contention that causal double-entry is the proper description of the double-entry system. Because the nature of the causal relationship to which he refers is not clearly defined, his support of the position is not very strong. Also, accountants who believe that the purpose of accounting is to develop information for multiple uses may be inclined to question his belief that causal double-entry provides more information or that classification double-entry is unsatisfactory. Logicians may even question the idea of intuitive causal relations on which the causal double-entry concept appears to rest.

Using causal double-entry, Ijiri suggests that the essential element in accounting is not the increment or decrement in the assets of an entity but the causal relationship between them. This search for the causal relationship to determine which accounts to debit and which to credit results in the conventional historical cost bookkeeping practice. Classification double-entry, Ijiri contends, cannot be used to describe conventional double-entry bookkeeping practices.

The ability to extend his axiomatic structure of double-entry into multidimensional bookkeeping is one of Ijiri's more significant contributions. Essentially, he points out that his axioms of control and quantities provide for a valuation of resources in physical terms and that the valuation rules for conventional double-entry recording is merely one set of valuation rules which could be applied. Multiple sets of valuation rules would permit multiple valuations of the quantities of resources. This would insert into accounting measurements a degree of flexibility in the development of information for different uses. A more complete multidimensional bookkeeping system seemingly could be developed by aggregating assets and activities into appropriate very small classes or groups which would permit aggregations of data in such a variety of ways that almost any information need could be satisfied.

Ijiri goes even beyond multidimensional bookkeeping by suggesting that valuation is a linear aggregation of quantities—a sum of quantities weighted according to different prices. As a result, different sets of prices would give different valuations from which different incomes could be computed. Recognizing that no aggregation of quantities—no set of price-weighted quantities—is appropriate for all uses and that for each use there must be a particular relation between a set of quantities and an aggregate (set of weights), the inquiry turns to means of representing, by a surrogated relation among accounting values, the most appropriate principal relation between a set of quantities and an aggregate. Since the conventional accounting aggregation is seldom a perfect representation of a principal relation between quantities and an aggregate which is desired by a user at any one time, the question turns to means of determining the nearness or extent to which an accounting aggregation approximates various principal aggregations needed by users. An answer to the question is attempted by seeking to determine a function which relates the accounting aggregation w to the principal aggregation y in such a way that $y = f(w)$. That is, a rule is sought which will permit a translation of an accounting aggregation into the desired aggregation. Normally any such functional relation cannot be perfect in that it cannot predict perfectly values of y (the principal aggregation). Nevertheless, it may provide a better prediction of Y—the desired aggregation—than merely using the average of y's which have prevailed in the past. To illustrate, assume a user wants to know the total variable costs for a period. Assume an average of variable costs of past period $(\bar{y})$ is \$6,380. Although the user does not have total variable costs for this period (y), he may use the average of past periods as an approximation of them. Assume, however, the user does have the accounting aggregation of total cost for the period (w) which amounts to \$12,000. Assume the functional relationship between Y and W has been determined to be $Y = h(w) =$

$w/2$. Using this functional relation, the variable costs are valued at $6,000 which is held to be a more realistic measure of y than the $6,380 average of past periods. Ijiri uses an "aggregation effectiveness coefficient," which is the same thing as the linear correlation coefficient of statistics, to measure the contribution made by the accounting aggregation w for predicting the principal aggregation desired by the user or decision maker. This coefficient may be used to measure the extent to which conventional accounting aggregations provide the measurements desired by users.

The objective sought in developing an aggregation effectiveness coefficient is much needed in contemporary society, but one must be skeptical about the effective use of Ijiri's coefficients for many purposes in the future. This skepticism exists because of the difficulty of the task of establishing a suitable functional relation between accounting aggregations and principal aggregations for specific purposes. Nevertheless, Ijiri has posed an area for empirical research of some promise, and this research apparently is now in process in various places.

Having suggested this improvement in basic accounting measurements, Ijiri next turns to the task of quantifying the degree of objectivity and reliability of accounting measurements. The development of such a quantification technique would, of course, add significantly to the tools of accounting measurements. Ijiri's technique relies on the statistical concepts of variance and mean-squared error.

Defining objectivity in a manner somewhat similar to that used in the physical sciences as the "consensus among a given group of observers or measurers," Ijiri describes how the degree of objectivity of a measurement can be measured. He proposes that a group of measurers be asked to measure an object such as the income of a firm. Taking the average of these measurers, he computes the statistical variance from the average and uses it as an indicator of the degree of objectivity of the measurement. A measure which is inherently highly objective (has a small variance) will be relatively free of personal bias and a "decision maker can use the measure without being concerned about who the measurer was." However, we should recognize that income measurements take place in a highly dynamic environment and that a measure of its objectivity in one time and place may be quite different than in another time and place. However, there may be limits within which all such measures of objectivity would fall, and this would be of use to users of measurement.

The objectivity of an accounting measurement is only one aspect of its reliability. Ijiri introduces the notion that users develop a functional relationship between accounting measurements and resulting acts. (For example, a shareholder may develop the functional relationship that a company's dividends are one-half of the accounting measured income.) The concept of reliability is then related to the extent subsequent accounting measurements of income confirm this function. The reliability measurement is the average of the square of the difference between the value of the accounting measurement and the value inferred by the user after observing action. For example, the user may infer income of $8 per share if a dividend of $4 is paid and if the accounting measured income is $10 per share, the accounting measurement is not completely reliable. Over a period of time, the reliability can be measured as the mean-squared error in the manner noted as

$$R = (X_1 - X^*)^2 + (X_2 - X^*)^2 + \ldots + (X_n - X^*)^2,$$

where X^* is the user's inferred value of the object being measured.

The significant aspect of the attempt to develop a measure of reliability is that it calls attention to the need to understand the thinking and understanding of users before the usefulness of accounting information can be predicted. The need for a measure of the reliability of accounting measurement is forcefully put in the following terms: "The degree of reliability (which encompasses objectivity) is the important criterion, and it will ultimately determine the extent to which the decision-making public will accept and use accounting measurers."

In his concluding chapter, Ijiri turns to the question of the conditions under which variations in accounting methods will induce different decisions. The answer, Ijiri contends, depends upon both empirical studies and a "theoretical clarification of the mechanism by which an accounting process and a decision process are related." He examines the theoretical issue and indicates that the factors involved in a decision process are (1) an environment where various situations may prevail, (2) a variety of possible decisions which can be made, and (3) a payoff resulting from various environmental situations and decision alternatives. Defining an accounting process as one of receiving and recording as surrogates observations of the environment (the recording function) and transmitting analyzed surrogate information to cause decisions to be made, Ijiri directs our attention to the "ill-structured" nature of decision-making problems and suggests that accounting measurements may be used by managers to develop a structural situation. He contends that in ill-structured problems accounting measurements are assigned as goals of managers and influence their decisions. Although changes in the accounting process may not result in rapid changes in the decision process, ultimately some adaptation occurs.

It is difficult to evaluate the contribution of *The Foundations*. An immediate reaction after reading the book is that Ijiri went to great lengths to explain the obvious. Most of the facts brought out by Ijiri in weaving his ideas on measurement are fairly common knowledge. The value of this book seems to be the well structured and mathematical approach to accounting measurement. Presenting existing material in a different way may not be a trivial contribution. If his new way of looking at accounting opens new areas for research and facilitates

future development of the accounting discipline, the contribution will
be significant. Time will provide the answer.

It is clear that calling attention to the surrogate nature of accounting
measurements and explaining the implications of such a fact represents a
contribution of highest order. In addition, associating accounting
theory and analysis with basic measurement methods is fundamental.
On the other hand, efforts to measure objectivity and reliability, to
explain the behavioral aspects of accounting measurements, and to
interpret accounting representations by a linear aggegration coefficient
are proposals which will have to be developed substantially before they
can be implemented to any extent. The rather interesting axiomatic
structure of historical accounting supports other efforts in this direction, and the attempt to throw a new light on value concepts is most
refreshing. The most realistic conclusion is to consider *The Foundations
of Accounting Measurement* as a significant contribution to the objective of broadening the scope of accounting research and practice.
History discloses no cases where a discipline has suffered from an
infusion of mathematics, and Ijiri has forcefully thrust set theory and
functional analysis into the development of accounting theory.

QUESTIONS

(1)   "Accounting is a system for communicating the economic events
        of an entity" (p.3). How satisfactory is this as a definition
        of accounting? Is it complete? Does it permit exceptions?

(2)   What does Ijiri mean by claiming his book (Foundations) may be
        "classified as meta-accounting or accounting sociology" (p.x)?
        Does it really describe accounting as it is (or was when written)?

(3)   What is a surrogate? How does Ijiri use the notion of surrogate
        in his book?

(4)   Measurement is obviously a crucial part of Ijiri's analysis. How
        consistent is he in the use of the concept in his book?

(5)   What meaning does Ijiri attach to "assets"? Having indicated
        what they are does he qualify his notion of assets?

(6)   What place do his axioms have in this analysis?

(7)   If theories are to explain practice why does Ijiri try to provide
        a theoretical framework for conventional accounting?

(8)   Is the analysis in Foundations, clarified or extended in Theory?

18 ROBERT R STERLING

The Theory of the Measurement of Enterprise Income

Biographical Chronology

1931	Born, 16 May, Bugtussle, Oklahoma; son of R(oland) P(omeroy) (a farmer) and Lillian (Newman) Sterling.
1945-47	US Military Service.
1950-52	United States Navy.
1954	Married Margery Stoskopf, 2 May.
	Teaching assistant, England, Denver.
1955-57	Instructor in Economics, University of Denver.
1956	Awarded BS degree, University of Denver.
1957-62	Accountant, Florida.
1958	Awarded MBA degree, University of Florida.
1958-60	Ford Foundation Fellow, University of Florida.
1960-61	Ford Foundation Grant, Florida.
1962-63	Assistant Professor of Accounting, University of Southern California.
1963	Awarded PhD(Econ), University of Florida.
1963-66	Assistant Professor of Social Science, Harpur College (now State University of New York At Binghamton).
1965-66	Ford Foundation Faculty Fellow of Business, Yale University, New Haven
1966-67	National Science Foundation, Faculty Fellow, Yale University.
1967-69	Associate Professor of Business Administration, University of Kansas, Lawrence.
1969	Awarded American Institute of Certified Public Accountants Gold Medal for best research published in English, 1968, for "The Going Concern: An Examination".
	Department Editor, The Accounting Review.
	Coordinator and Chairman, Arthur Young Colloquia.
1969-70	Appointed Professor of Accounting, University of Kansas.
1970-72	Arthur Young Distinguished Professor, University of Kansas.
1970	The Theory of the Measurement of Enterprise Income, published (essentially his PhD dissertation).
1972-74	Director of Research, American Accounting Association.
1972-74	Jesse Jones Distinguished Professor, Rice University, Houston.
1974	President, Fellow Accounting Researchers International Association.
1976	Bicentennial Distinguished International Lecturer, Europe.
1976	Dean, Graduate School of Administration, Rice University.
1979	Hoover Distinguished International Lecturer, University of New South Wales, Australia.
1979	Towards a Science of Accounting, published.
1980	Appointed as Windspear Distinguished Professor, University of Alberta
1981	Appointed to FASB as Simon Fellow (full-time).

Selected Bibliography

1962 The Determination of Goodwill and Bonus on the
    Admission of a New Partner, Accounting Review, v.37,
    pp 766-68.

1966 An Operational Analysis of Traditional Accounting,
    Abacus, v.2, pp 119-36.

1967 Elements of Pure Accounting Theory, Accounting Review,
    v.42, pp 62-73.

    The Case of Valuation and Learned Cognitive Dissonance,
    Accounting Review, v.42, pp 376-8.

    Conservatism: The Fundamental Principle of Valuation in
    Traditional Accounting, Abacus, v.3, pp 109-32.

    A Statement of Basic Accounting Theory - A Review
    Article, Journal of Accounting Research, v.5, pp 95-112.

1968 The Going Concern: An Examination, Accounting Review,
    v.43, pp 481-502.

    A Glimpse of the Forest, Accountant's Magazine, v.72
    (Nov), pp 62-73.

1969 A Valuation Experiment, Journal of Accounting Research,
    v.7, pp 90-5 (with Raymond Radosevich).

    A Test of the Uniformity Hypothesis, Abacus,
    v.5, pp 37-47; also in Accountancy, v.81, (July),
    pp 508-13.

1970 The Theory of the Measurement of Enterprise Income,
    University of Kansas Press, 384 p.

    On Theory Construction and Verification, Accounting
    Review, v.45, pp 444-57.

1971 Conflicts in Income Measurement, Accounting Papers,
    University of Talsa (Oklahoma), pp 21-41.

    Costs Versus Values: An Empirical Test, Australian
    Accountant, v.7 (June), pp 218-21.

    The Roll of Liquidity in Exchange Valuation, Accounting
    Review, v.46, pp 44-56 (with Richard E. Flaherty).

    An Explication and Analysis of the Structures of
    Accounting, Abacus, Part One: v.7, pp 137-52;
    Part Two: v.8, pp 145-62 (1972).

1972 Accounting Power, Oklahoma CPA, v.11 (July), pp 28-41;
    also in Journal of Accountancy, v.136 (Jan), pp 61-7.

    Exchange Valuation: An Empirical Test, Accounting Review,
    v.47, pp 709-21 (with R. Flaherty and J. Tollefson).

    Decision Oriented Financial Accounting, Accounting and
    Business Research, v.2, pp 198-208.

1973	Accounting Research, Education and Practice, _Journal of Accountancy_, v.136 (Sept), pp 44-52; also in _International Accountant_, v.44 (March, 1947), pp 3-8; also in _Journal of Business Administration_, v.4 (1973), pp 15-30.
1975	Relevant Financial Reporting in an Age of Price Changes, _Journal of Accountancy_, v.139 (Feb), pp 56-62.
	Toward a Science of Accounting, _Financial Analysts Journal_, v.31 (Sept-Oct), pp 28-36; note also paper of same title presented at a seminar and reproduced in _Stanford Lectures in Accounting_, Stanford University, 1975, 20 p.
1976	The Nature and Verification of Theories in _Bridging the Gap_, Accounting Research Convocation, University of Alabama, pp 15-37.
	Accounting at the Crossroads, _Journal of Accountancy_, v. 142 (Aug), pp 82-87.
	Accounting in the 1980's in _Accountancy in the 1980's - Some Issues_, ed, N.M. Bedford, University of Illinois, pp 225-68.
1979	_Toward a Science of Accounting_, Scholars Book Co (Texas), 247 p.
	Sterling has edited several volumes of scholarly essays. For some of these he has written Introductions and these are significant contributions to the accounting literature.

REFERENCES

Book Reviews: _Accounting Review_, v.45, 1970, p.822-24 (R W Schattke).
                     Choice, v.8, Sept 1971, p.878.
                     Journal of Accountancy, v.131, Mar 1971, pp.90-1
                         (L L Vance).

Anderson, J A, _A Comparative Analysis of Selected Income Measurement Theories in Financial Accounting_, AAA (SAR No.12), 1976.

Nichols, D R & J E Parker, "An Alternative to Liquidity as a Basis for Exchange Variation", _Abacus_, v.8, 1972, pp.68-74.

Petri, E & R Minch, "Contemporary Inflation Accounting Proposals: An Analysis & An Alternative", _Abacus_, v.11, 1975, pp.182-92.

Mattessich, R V, "The Market Value Method According to Sterling: A Review Article", _Abacus_, v.7, 1971, pp.176-93 (Sterling's reply, v.8, 1972, pp.91-101).

Stamp, E, "Why Can Accounting Not Become a Science Like Physics?", _Abacus_, v.17, 1981, pp.13-27.

RICHARD MATTESSICH

The Market Value Method According to Sterling:[1] A Review Article

Introduction

The so-called market or current value undoubtedly is one of the most important values for accounting and economics — perhaps it is *the* most important value. But whether it is the best and only acceptable value for measuring entrepreneurial income, is a very different and much more controversial issue. Professor Sterling's book might easily be interpreted (or misinterpreted) as a defence of the unique validity of the market value method. Thus Sterling, after Professor Chambers, would seem to be the second major proponent of this extreme point of view. Of course, there are many other scholars in favour of the market value method and in the face of an excessive application of the acquisition cost method in actual practice, this enthusiasm for market value can only be welcome. But these other authors would hardly be so radical as to banish other valuation methods; most of them would be willing to supplement the market value, or even abandon it, wherever the information purpose calls for other valuation approaches. Sterling obviously opposes this view; but the boundaries of this opposition are somewhat vague. Originally and officially he raises his claim of the market value only for a highly simplified situation (a trading firm operating in a perfect market free of price level fluctuations and under the silent assumption of a single information purpose), but by extension and by further implication this claim is spread to a much wider area. But is it not dangerous to chop off so much of reality until a narrow pattern emerges satisfying a particular view, and then suggesting that these results may hold by analogy in a much broader context? Yet this issue is quite complex and, in order to avoid misunderstandings, must be discussed in detail; before this is done, some introductory words may be opportune.

Academic accountants interested in foundations and theory construction are not in great abundance. And those of them having the philosophic flair and background indispensable for engaging in such enterprise are even rarer. Professor Sterling's book is evidence that its author is endowed with these important qualities. Indeed, the major merit of this book seems to lie in the attention it devotes to fundamental questions and to many details and problems of measurement, information and communication theory, decision making as well as to related philosophic issues. Even those disagreeing with the somewhat narrow frame of premises

1. Robert R. Sterling, *Theory of the Measurement of Enterprise Income*, University of Kansas Press, Lawrence 1970.

RICHARD MATTESSICH is a Professor of the Faculty of Commerce and Business Administration in the University of British Columbia, Vancouver, Canada.

and the conclusons of Sterling's book, will recognize that it is a highly stimulating contribution in theory construction. *The Theory of the Measurement of Enterprise Income* is based on a doctoral dissertation, most of which was written many years ago.[2] This fact entails several limitations. First of all, a dissertation by its very nature is not expected to be a fully matured work. Indeed, a comparison between this book and Professor Sterling's more recent publications might indicate that his dissertation only foreshadows his present reputation. Secondly, the points of gravity of his thoughts seem to have somewhat shifted, but above all, thirdly, such important works as Professor Ijiri's *Foundations of Accounting Measurement*, Professor Chambers's *Accounting, Evaluation and Economic Behavior*, as well as other books on accounting theory were admittedly not taken into consideration. It is regrettable that Sterling decided not to up-date his original work and failed to incorporate ideas from, and reactions to, this modern struggle towards firm foundations of accounting theory. All this, of course, does not infringe upon his own genuine contributions to this search.

But, as we have already hinted, our critique is not limited to these items — it extends to the breadth and direction of Sterling's approach as well as to several details. And at this stage it is only fair to the reader as well as to our colleague to point out that a good deal of this critical attitude is the result of our own, perhaps for an accountant strongly synthetic, tendencies on this particular point. Therefore, we should like to review Sterling's book in the spirit of constructive criticism. Even if our criticism is occasionally harsh, it is not designed to destroy but to help towards a broader synthesis. Perhaps this was the reason for inviting me (whose opposition to the exclusive market value method is only too well known) to write this article.

Market value versus the teleologic (purpose-oriented) approach of valuation

At the very outset Professor Sterling reveals to the reader that his book is concerned with the search for the *correct* or *best* method of measuring income:

> We intend to argue that one method of calculating income is superior to others. The difference is that we have tried to make all the assumptions explicit, insofar as we are aware of them, and we have tried to set down the reasoning in meticulous detail. (p. 4)[3]

To achieve this task it appears at first that Sterling engages a method widely used in analytical economics. This method consists of starting the analysis under highly simplified assumptions and then to progress, step by step, to more complicated or more realistic situations. Although this method does not always lead to realistic and satisfactory solutions, it has great merit and may, indeed, not have been employed to a sufficient extent in traditional accounting. Thus Sterling begins in Part I with a wheat trading company operating in a perfect market under stable-price-level-conditions. While Part II is concerned with the discussion of

---

2. In his Preface Professor Sterling mentions that the first version was written eight years before publication of his book and the final version appeared five years before in manuscript form (hence in 1962 and 1965 respectively).

3. Quotes without further indication are taken from Sterling's book under review.

competing valuation models, Part III is reserved for the essential business of developing the simple model, introducing less restrictive assumptions, making the model more and more realistic and sophisticated. Alas, this progression is only sketchy, merely relaxes somewhat the assumptions of stable price levels and perfect market and devotes hardly ten per cent of the entire book to the introduction of refinements of the actual model. At the end we are still left with a simple trading enterprise. Although these are severe enough limitations, they would be acceptable were it not for Sterling's fatal flaw of underrating the argument that different entrepreneurial purposes need different income definitions or at least different ways of measuring income and wealth. He is by no means unaware of this argument, but he disparages it and side-steps the crucial issues while devoting considerable space to problems of much lesser significance. As a result the market value method emerges triumphantly as the only correct method for measuring entrepreneurial income. Let us study his concluding remarks:

> In short, the Present Market method of valuation is (1) relevant to all receivers, because it specifies the currently available alternatives and the ability to perform current obligations; (2) veritable, in the sense that all observers would agree to the value; (3) a measurement of an empirically meaningful dimension; (4) additive, in the sense that the sum of the parts is equal to the independent measurement of the whole; (5) temporally consistent, in that the measurement is made at a point in time as opposed to an event and as opposed to a prediction; (6) a valuation, in that we can infer that the trader prizes his selected position more than the other available positions; and (7) more informative than any other single figure, because it indicates the direction of the trader's expectation.
>
> When the market is imperfect, there will be disagreement among observers, and there will be questions about the additivity of the parts. When the price level is unstable, the measure will not reflect the changes in the command over goods and sacrifice (although it will still reflect the sacrifice and command-over-goods at a point of time) and the procedures for correcting this are imperfect. Despite these limitations, the Present Market is the superior valuation method. It still meets the criteria better than the other suggested valuation methods. Therefore, for this type of firm, we conclude that the periodic reports ought to show the current (exit) values at the time the report is prepared, and the subsequent reports should adjust the previous reports by the Consumer Price Index.
>
> These conclusions are restricted to the trading assets in a trading firm. Given that restriction, we think the conclusions of this study are incontrovertible. We invite the reader to demonstrate that they are not.
>
> We also think that these conclusions can be extended with minor modifications to other types of firms. However, since we have not demonstrated their extensibility and since Braithwaite (p. 93) has warned that 'the price of the employment of models is eternal vigilance', we will offer the extension of these conclusions to other firm models as an unsupported conjecture that requires further research. (pp. 360-1)

Sterling refers to the incontrovertibility of his conclusion and challenges the reader to demonstrate the contrary. What does he have in mind? Does he mean that his conclusion inevitably follow from his premises or that his premises too are indisputable? Should he refer to the second meaning, one might confidently accept this challenge. Let us first examine his response to Boulding's warning that different purposes need different ways of measuring income. Sterling is fully aware of this view (for which Boulding is only one of several major spokesmen) and even quotes the following statement:

> The concept of profit [income] will quite rightly differ depending upon the purpose for which we need it. The definition of profit for tax purposes, for instance may differ considerably from the definition which is required for other forms of decision making. What we need here is not a single definition of profit applicable to all cases, but a spectrum of definitions, in which the relationship of the various concepts is reasonably clear and in which the definition is fitted to the purpose for which it is to be used.[4]

But nowhere in Sterling's book can we find a thorough treatment and refutation of the above view. At times he seems to confuse this view with what he calls Boulding's 'arbitrary valuation constant' to which he does pay more attention. But these are two different issues which are not properly kept apart. The above mentioned problem seems to be brushed off with such observations as:

> The notion of different incomes for different purposes is quite the vogue in this day and age, but, surprisingly enough, income definitions derived for different purposes do not necessarily vary. (p. 9)[5]

Unless different strata of income definitions are distinguished, it is hopeless to disentangle the underbrush of this issue. Without doing so confusion is inevitable. But this point ought to be illustrated in detail. Suppose one accepts the well-known Hicksian income definition[6] for the following three purposes:

(1) Financial statement presentation (and income determination) for creditors and public investors (minority shareholders).

(2) Income determination for taxation purposes (i.e. minimizing legally the firm's tax-obligation).

(3) Income determination for deciding whether to continue the operation of the enterprise or whether to liquidate.

There is no reason why the Hicksian definition cannot be accommodated to all three of these purposes. But this holds because such a definition belongs to a comparatively high stratum which comprises a series of interpretations or sub-definitions. Since Hicks's definition does not specify how wealth or well-offness should be measured, every possible evaluation method provides a different inter-

4. Kenneth Boulding, 'Economics and Accounting: The Uncongenial Twins', *Studies in Accounting Theory*, W. T. Baxter and S. Davidson (eds.), Homewood 1962, p. 45.

5. This statement is the result of a cursory comparison of the income definitions by John R. Hicks, Robert M. Haig and Henry C. Simons. The statement quoted can of course not be denied, because of the escape clause 'not necessarily'. But it is disturbing that such self-evident, yet by far too vague propositions are used to build up a case for one specific valuation method. The philosophers of science are well aware of such dangers: 'A . . . trick for eluding empirical test is to maximize *vagueness*. Certain qualifying phrases such as "under certain circumstances", "in favorable conditions" and "*mutatis mutandis*", can produce facile truths, i.e. truths so insensitive to empirical details that they come close to logical truths.' M. Bunge, *Scientific Research I*, Springer-Verlag, New York 1967, p. 263.

6. 'We ought to define a man's income as the maximum value which he can consume during a week, and still expect to be as well off at the end of the week as he was at the beginning.' J. R. Hicks, *Value and Capital*, 2nd edition, Clarendon Press, Oxford 1946, p. 172.

pretation and thus strictly speaking a different definition (sub-definition).

Let us accept for the first purpose (at the moment at least) Sterling's argument that the market value method is the only correct method of measuring wealth and thus income. But how about the second purpose, assuming a situation in which market values would indicate a higher income figure than cost values? Then undoubtedly the cost value and not the market value would be the appropriate choice (provided the tax law permits both methods or the cost-or-market value whichever is lower) for minimizing the tax obligation. With regard to the third purpose a good case can be made for the argument that the correct method for measuring income for the purpose of determining the correct rate of return is the present value method and not the market value method.

The following simple example (fully in accord with Sterling's assumption of a trading company with only trading assets in a perfect market without general price level fluctuations) seems to us sufficient to refute the thesis that the market value method is the only correct method for measuring entrepreneurial income. The following symbols shall be used: MV for market value of net assets (owners' equity), AV for acquisition cost value, PV for present value (or any other subjective value appropriate for the case), IM for income (net profit) under market value method, IA for income under acquisition cost value method and IP for income under present (subjective) value method. The subscript b refers to 'beginning of period', the subscript e to 'end of period'. We assume that no addition (except profit) to and no withdrawal from owners' equity has occurred during the current period, and that the following data (in dollars) hold:

$$MV_b = 500,000 \qquad AV_b = 500,000 \qquad PV_b = 500,000$$
$$MV_e = 600,000 \qquad AV_e = 530,000 \qquad PV_e = 400,000$$

Then the income figures under the three valuation methods or sub-definitions would be as follows:

$$IM = 100,000 \qquad IA = 30,000 \qquad IP = 100,000$$

Let us now examine which income concept is the appropriate one for which purpose. For the first purpose we have already agreed to the market value method and no dispute is necessary. Thus the income concept to be accepted is IM and the numeral ascribed to it would be $100,000. One only must point out that this purpose is not identical with 'legalistic statement presentation' in all those countries the commercial laws (common or codified) of which prescribe 'acquisition cost' or 'cost-or-market-whichever-is-lower' methods for this specific purpose (a problem to be discussed in more detail at the end of this section).

For the second purpose (minimization of income tax) we may assume, in conformity with most tax laws in the western hemisphere, that the cost or the market value methods are permissible. If neither of these methods is obligatory, management would have the choice between IM = 100,000 and IA = 30,000. But since the purpose is minimization of the tax obligation, any consultant advising that the market value is the only correct way of measuring income for this purpose has hardly much chance of being called upon again, since this advice would lead to unnecessary tax payments on an additional amount of $70,000. Obviously the income concept IA and not IM should here be chosen.

The third purpose (deciding to liquidate or continue the business) requires some preliminary remarks. The model here presented of course assumes that only economic factors influence this decision and all of them are reflected in the subjective value. In accord with this economic theory no purchase or sales decision ought to be made without comparison between market value of the commodity and the corresponding subjective value attributed to it by the buyer or seller on the basis of long-run considerations. Thus comparing the figures

$$MV_e = 600,000 \text{ with } PV_e = 400,000,$$

it is easily inferred that for some reason the market evaluates this enterprise much more optimistically than the owners. Of course, it is to be understood that this subjective evaluation by the owners (e.g. in form of the present value of all expected and discounted future net revenues or any other acceptable method) is not haphazard but based on thorough soul-searching. Thus if all the above-mentioned conditions hold, a consultant, again, would fail grossly if recommending the owners to base their decision on the market value method. The respectable profit and rentability based on market values may be due merely to the speculating forces and misconceptions of a bullish market, which, were it in possession of the inside information of the owners, would also assign a value of $400,000 instead of $600,000. The objection that the owners too might err is valid, but does not help at all Professor Sterling's case. If an *ex post* examination should reveal that the owners' judgement was incorrect, then a consultant (whose responsibility we have assumed to lie with the recommended income and valuation model, but not with the procurement of the data) can legitimately point out that the incorrect action was not due to the model but due to the owners' judgement. Whereas in the reverse case, in which the *ex post* examination proves at fault, the consultant would be blamed for the losses of failing to recommend liquidation if the ultimate decision of using the market value model was based on his erroneous recommendation in spite of the correct judgement-data supplied to him by the owners.

The above examples and many others are such obvious evidence of the need for different valuation methods and income definitions for different purposes that an inevitable question arises: how is it possible that some eminent scholars fail to recognize this evidence? This question may be difficult to answer in general, but in Sterling's case we have the benefit of a recent personal conversation with him.[7] According to this, he would not deny that in the previously quoted example of accounting for three different purposes, the acquisition cost method and the present value method are just as important as the market value method. He would further assert that this is no contradiction to his book, since the latter deals neither with tax accounting nor managerial accounting but exclusively with financial accounting.

7. Professor Sterling addressed the Accounting Faculty and PhD students of the University of British Columbia on 31 May 1971. The ensuing debate centred around the above mentioned problems.

To Sterling's credit it must be pointed out that his book repeatedly emphasizes the focus on financial accounting but by doing so he falls into a trap that also caught many another accounting academician. On one side one claims to be concerned with financial accounting only, but on the other one behaves as if accounting consisted of nothing else but financial accounting. The passages quoted above and many other passages of Sterling's book are evidence of this. There, most of the time he speaks only of 'accounting' whereas he should speak of his comparatively narrow brand of 'financial accounting'. We claim that this usage has a most dangerous psychological impact, not only upon the reader but even on the author himself. It suggests that all other non-financial accounting is a side-issue of no or very little relevance to accounting. This brings us to what we deem the most crucial issue in contemporary accounting, namely the question whether it is possible to solve the theoretical and foundational problems of our discipline and of modern management information systems by concentrating in isolation on specific and narrow areas like financial accounting, without first searching for an over-all theory that comprehends all areas of accounting and perhaps other management information systems as well. Before discussing this question at the end of the next section some further remarks on Sterling's book may be required.

In Chapter II (The Definition of Income and the Competing Schools of Thought), Sterling shortly discusses the Fisherian tradition, the accounting tradition, the market value approach, as well as Boulding's extreme approach. Nowhere does he seriously take issue with what seems to be the most natural attitude, namely the purpose-oriented or teleologic approach to income measurement. This is all the more surprising since he expressly states:

> Several authors take the position that the purpose of the income measurement will determine which of the methods of valuation should be used and that there is no single correct method. Thus, the 'different incomes for different purposes' notion in which more than one valuation method may be used concurrently. The extreme form of the argument that there is no single correct method is presented by Boulding. He argues that the selection process is so arbitrary that a constant valuation ratio might be used.

To our mind, a decisive flaw of Professor Sterling's book lies in the fact that he deals only with this extreme version proposed by Boulding, identifying it with the teleologic approach in general. If Sterling admits that Professor Boulding seems to be in a class by himself in his suggestion for the use of a constant then we cannot let Sterling get away with implicitly treating Boulding's argument as representative for the general argument of what he calls the ' "different incomes for different purposes" notion'. This general argument — of what we might call the teleologic (purpose-oriented) theory of valuation — denies that the value to be chosen is arbitrary, but asserts that for certain purposes the correct value basis is the acquisition cost, for others the market value, for others the present value, etc. and for some purpose two or more values derived from different bases have to be employed and juxtaposed.[8]

If Sterling points out that Boulding's valuation coefficient is 'arbitrary' and 'the "proper" or "correct" valuation coefficient is not immediately apparent' and 'is the subject of much debate', then this may be true for the specific theory of Boulding (although we suspect that Sterling interprets Boulding's argument in too narrow a way), but it should not be generalized. The general set of rules for identifying the appropriate valuation method for a specific purpose may concisely and roughly be expressed as follows:

(1) If income measurement or valuation serves a purely legalistic or other dogmatic purpose, then any valuation approach permitted within this legal (or dogmatic) framework may be chosen.

(2) If the purpose of income measurement or valuation is maximizing or minimizing a goal function within a certain framework (legalistic or non-legalistic) an optimal value must be chosen from all alternative value bases available within this framework.

(3) If the purpose of income measurement or valuation is a managerial investment (including disinvestment) decision, then a dual valuation juxtaposing the current 'objective' evaluation of the market with the subjective valuation of the investor is required. If the (complete) subjective evaluation yields a higher value than the market value the investment object should be acquired or kept, if it yields a lower subjective value than the market value, it should be sold or not acquired.

(4) The rules 1 to 3 may be generalized and extended to further cases by the following summary: Income measurement and valuation serve many economic and quasi-economic objectives; as purpose-oriented activities they require specific teleologic models. A valuation model must be able to generate all those values relevant to the objective under consideration.

We have demonstrated previously that the 'exclusive market valuation model' (even under the highly simplified circumstances assumed by Sterling) does not give a measure of income which leads to the minimization of income tax obligations, and does not enable correct investment decisions to be made. A study of the legal requirements in many countries will further reveal that the exclusive market value method will not satisfy those (common and codified) laws and thus cannot fulfill the pertinent legalistic purposes. Furthermore we maintained previously that a strict distinction ought to be made between 'financial accounting for serving stockholders and investors', on one side, and 'financial accounting for satisfying

8. This point of view has been defended by us for a long time and on many occasions. *See* R. Mattessich, *Accounting and Analytical Methods*, Homewood 1964, pp. 224-6, 250; *Die wissenschaftlichen Grundlagen des Rechnungswesens* (Bertelsmann Universitaetsverlag, Duesseldorf 1970), pp. 77-94; 'On the Perennial Misunderstanding of Asset Measurement', *Cost and Management*, March-April 1970, pp. 29-31; 'On Further Misunderstandings About Asset "Measurement" and Valuation — A Rejoinder to Chambers' Article', *Cost and Management*, March-April 1971; 'Asset Measurement and Valuation — A Final Reply to Chambers', *Cost and Management*, July-August 1971.

the commercial law' on the other. Two separate goals are here involved, which only under ideal circumstances would coincide. The goal of the first accounting system is to supply sufficient or even optimal information to investors, the goal of the second is to satisfy a minimum requirement of disclosure enforced by law. Even if the purpose of this law is to serve the investor and broad public, which might be regarded as the *de jure* lawgiver, there is no warrant that the *de facto* lawgiver (e.g. the professional accounting bodies adhering to certain standards and issuing principles, opinions and recommendations) pursues this very goal. In our experience the accounting goal of the *de facto* lawgiver usually deviates considerably from that intended by the *de jure* lawgiver (e.g. the common people or their political representatives). We know several countries in which the *de facto* lawgiver pursues the objective of minimizing the workload and valuation risk of the accounting profession, while the *de jure* lawgiver intends to fulfill a very different purpose, for example to offer relevant information to shareholders for their investment decisions. But as long as the *de jure* lawgiver condones the purpose of the *de facto* lawgiver and fails to enforce a change in law accordingly, the purpose of the *de facto* lawgiver is actually pursued and thus has to be fulfilled by law-abiding citizens. To do so is a legalistic accounting matter; the other problem, that of changing the law and forcing the *de facto* lawgiver to conform with the wishes of the *de jure* lawgiver, is a political-legal matter, but not a problem of accounting theory. These subtleties are rarely clearly distinguished and their disregard has created much confusion in accounting circles.

Some aspects of Sterling's premises and conceptual scheme

Professor Sterling's book contains many assumptions, not all of them systematically listed or made explicit; but on p. 34 he offers us a summary which may suffice as a starting point for examining critically major aspects of some of his arguments. There he states:

> In summary, we assume:
> 1. The trader's maximand is utility.
> 2. The *raison d'être* of the enterprise is to maximize the trader's maximand.
> 3. Utility varies in the same direction as the ability to command goods and services.
> 4. Money is the appropriate expression of the ability to command goods.
> 5. Therefore, the prime maximand of the enterprise is money (or ability to command money), and the correct valuing agent is money. (p. 34)

This is neither an exhaustive statement of assumptions nor are all of its items premises. Item 5 is meant to be a conclusion inferred from preceding items. The message of the first two premises is to accept as the enterprise goal (*raison d'être*) the *maximization of utility*. Yet after all the economic insight one has gained in recent decades most economists would consider this a meaningless statement. The literature overflows with warnings against such expressions:

> Is there something called 'utility' — something like weight, height, wealth, or happiness — that people are really trying to maximize? No. The term originated

during the early history of economic analysis. At a time it was popular to think that goods provide utility or usefulness in some objective, psychological, and measurable sense. But although that erroneous psychological conception has been abandoned, the name 'utility' has stuck. It is now simply an *indicator* for comparing options and showing preferences among them. Thus, it is now a matter of convention to say that if a person chooses option A rather than option B, option A has more utility for him. Saying that a person "maximizes utility" may seem an elaborate camouflage of our ignorance; for it would appear that whenever a person voluntarily does anything, he can be said to be maximizing his utility.[9]

Such statements span the modern literature, from elementary introductory texts, as the preceding quote showed, to fairly sophisticated books, as the following concise quote demonstrates: 'The concepts of utility and its maximization are void and of sensuous connotation'.[10]

As the reader is well aware, the modern literature restricts the usage of this word either to the *Neumann-Morgenstern utility* (and its relatives) or to *utility functions* (preference orders), and Professor Sterling is no exception. He mentions his compunctions, yet in spite of it, proceeds to employ such dangerous propositions. But even if the old-fashioned utility concept would be acceptable, confusion would arise. The classical utility concept obviously is a *subjective* concept, as the most renowned traditional textbook of economics attests: 'Utility is taken to be correlative to Desire or Want'.[11]

But if utility is a subjective concept (thus referring to an individual or, at most, to a small group of people, but certainly not to the market), then it can obviously not be represented by the market price, only by accident will the latter coincide with the subjective valuation. Not even when buying an asset do we have warrant of such a coincidence. All we then may assert is that the market value (and the utility of its monetary amount for us) is *not higher than* the utility of the commodity expressed by our subjective value.

In looking at Sterling's assumption 4 the reader may conclude that by giving up the ability to command goods and services (e.g. in the process of consumption) the trader loses utility. This is hardly what Sterling means, since he assures us previously that: '. . . we assume that there are two (relevant) sources of utility (1) consumption and (2) command over goods' (p. 30).

Most disturbing, however, is item 5 which, through the word 'therefore', is designated by Sterling as a conclusion rather than a premise or original assumption. We not only fail to see how this proposition should follow from the preceding ones, but find it in gross contradiction to propositions 1 and 2. Economists and management scientists have taken great pain to demonstrate that maximizing a utility function is something very different from maximizing a function based on monetary values. Since the utility function is in most cases non-linear but the monetary value function is linear, one can hardly expect that these two maxima

9. Armen A. Alchian and William R. Alchian, *University Economics*, Belmont 1964, p. 18.

10. James M. Henderson and Richard E. Quandt, *Microeconomic Theory — A Mathematical Approach*, New York 1958, p. 6.

11. Alfred Marshall, *Principles of Economics*, 8th edition London 1956, p. 78.

coincide. The mere fact that both utility as well as monetary value 'move in the same direction' (something we do not at all consider a necessity)[12] does not ensure that the maximum of the latter coincides with the maximum of the former.

Apart from such queries about the underlying premises, there looms the more incisive question as to the appropriateness of the boundaries set explicitly and implicitly by Professor Sterling to accounting theory.

Sterling seems to stake the boundaries of accounting theory in such a narrow way that at best it would serve only the investor, or potential investor, interested in buying, selling or keeping shares of the pertinent enterprise. To serve such a goal is a meritorious task, the more so since none of the existing accounting systems do serve this goal properly. As the reader well knows, rarely can investors rely on the published financial statements and hardly ever can they forego procuring *additional* financial information. The *de facto* purpose of present financial and legalistic accounting is rather to minimize risk and responsibility of accountants, something well evidenced by the strong emphasis on the acquisition cost method by public and other practising accountants as well as by their flagrant neglect of the market value method. Yet, this unfortunate situation must not lead us into the extreme of believing that financial accounting should no longer serve *de facto* purposes and that entirely separate accounting theories ought to be devised for minimization of tax obligations, for liquidation purposes, for managerial decision making etc.

We cannot accept the argument that the tax regulations are only 'incidental' to accounting and that it is not the task of financial accounting to generate financial statements (within the confines of the tax laws) that would minimize the corporation's tax obligation. Nor can we accept the notion that the subjective value (the indispensability of which Professor Sterling also admitted in private conversation) is not a part of accounting and thus is eliminated from competing with the market value. In a time when actual practice is about to broaden its accounting systems, when they are converted to or incorporated into management information systems, such subjective values as 'present values' constitute one of the most important input data for financial and investment decisions of management. The separation between tax accounting, financial accounting and managerial accounting may have proved useful in the past for classroom-teaching and setting boundaries to text books. But for the evolution of a practically useful theory of accounting and management information systems, this fairly artificial separation proves disastrous. It may well constitute the major reason why a general theory of accounting and management information systems has not as yet been completed and why it will have difficulties of initial acceptance.

All this does of course not mean that subjective values should be made public. Normally this would give away by far too much confidential information; but sub-

12. We think of a situation where the market price of a painting by a renowned artist has increased during a time when its owner got to dislike it more and more so that he takes the opportunity of a favourable price of finally selling it. In this case obviously the utility of the painting (not of its money-worth) and that of the monetary value it commands moved in *opposite* directions.

236

jective values of top management as well as those of managerial sub-groups must be available to the entrepreneurial information system and must be utilized in it for investment and managerial decisions. Accounting theory of our age can no longer limit itself neither to the description of legalistic dogmas nor to the sole purpose of serving the speculator and investor in marketable securities, it must provide scientific criteria for judging which managerial information system is adequate or even optimal for which purpose. Such a theory has two prerequisites: (1) It must be truly general hence comprising propositions of validity for all accounting purposes alike and (2) it needs specific or auxiliary propositions valid for the individual purposes pursued. But in contrast to a series of separate and independent little theories for each accounting area, the auxiliary propositions tailor-made to each purpose would be closely connected to and would directly evolve out of the basic propositions. In such a theory there is no place for a single purpose dominating the general theory (as did financial accounting in the past), nor would there be a single valuation method (like Sterling's market value) superior to other valuation methods. The theory would rather draw impartially upon all kinds of valuation methods depending on the specific need.

Information, measurement and related problems

This paper concentrates on such major issues as 'market valuation versus teleological evaluation', 'specific accounting theories versus general accounting theory' etc. Therefore it cannot do full justice to many interesting details dealt with in Professor Sterling's book. However, further aspects of this work, those of information and measurement, shall shortly be discussed here. In his fourth chapter, devoted to the problems of 'Information and Communications', Sterling postulates the following series of information and communication propositions:

I.P. 1: 'Messages must be veritable. Verity is judged by agreement among qualified observers' (p. 46).

I.P. 2: 'Messages must be relevant. Relevance refers to a particular (specific) problem' (p. 48).

I.P. 3: 'The theory concerning the solution of the problem specifies the relevant information' (p. 50).

C.P. 1: 'The locus of the relevance criterion is at the transmission sources' (p. 54).

C.P. 2: 'The transmitter must choose the appropriate theory' (p. 56).

C.P. 3: 'Education has a high priority in the allocation of channel capacity' (p. 61).

Information Proposition 1 (I.P. 1) is worth noting for several reasons. Its first sentence is an *imperative* one and is thus not a proposition in the sense in which traditional philosophy defines this term. Besides that, we all know there are many messages (in present day accounting as well as other information systems) that are not true. And yet they may still be messages and may even be useful.[13] Most of

13. From Sterling's comment to his propositions the reader may conclude that the intended meaning of I.P. 1 and I.P. 2 is expressed much more correctly in his sentence on p. 40: 'If a message is to be useful there are two prerequisites: (1) verity and (2) relevance'.

us have encountered these strange cases where somebody benefited more by acting upon an incorrect message than had he acted upon a true message. We do not think that truth and usefulness of an individual message are critical correlates, but rather that high probability of truth and usefulness as long-run characteristics of messages in general (not individual ones) ought to be correlated. Furthermore the reader must note that Sterling's operational definition of 'verity' is in marked contrast to science and philosophy where it is defined in terms of confirmation and refutation.

His I.P. 2 and I.P.3 we consider extremely important for the theory of modern management information systems and thus have no objections to raise. Had Sterling consistently applied these propositions to accounting in general, something would have evolved which is much closer to our notion of what a theory of measurement of enterprise ought to be.

Communication Propositions 1 to 3 (C.P. 1 to 3) deserve special attention, because they tie the relevance criterion and model choice to the transmission source instead of the receiving end. We do not object to this approach, but some experts point out that it should be the consumer and not the producer of information who should determine which model or system is relevant and should be chosen for a specific information purpose. From a practical point of view this suggestion is difficult to materialize in accounting.

> To understand this properly, however, a distinction should be made between the construction of a standard system for one among several standard purposes, on one hand, and the application of a standard system to a specific (non-standard) purpose, on the other. In the first case obviously the model builder and no one else must apply the relevance criterion. Yet, in the second case when it comes to the application of a standard system to a specific purpose (which may somewhat deviate from the standard purpose) it will be the task of the information consumer to determine the degree of relevance involved. Only where the goal for which the theory is constructed is perfectly identical with the goal of the information user can his tie to the relevance criterion be neglected.[14]

Two full chapters (V and VI) of the book under review are devoted to measurement problems. Here too we find ourselves in disagreement on several items with Professor Sterling's view. But these discrepancies are mainly based on semantical issues and are thus of lesser import than those mentioned previously. Thus we fully agree with Sterling's assertion that:

> The term 'measurement' is defined and used by physicists and psychologists in strikingly different ways. Anyone who expects to find a single, well-established definition of measurement is due to disappointment. (pp. 65-6)

Sterling also distinguishes clearly between what he calls the 'broad' and the 'narrow' schools of measurement, but he seems to overlook the concept of

14. This problem is further illuminated in Section VII item 5 of 'The Report on the Foundations of Accounting Measurement' by Y. Ijiri, R. Mattessich, A. Rappaport, E. Summers and A. Thomas, *The Accounting Review, Supplement to Vol. ⌐LVI*, p. 45.

'*measurement by fiat*'[15] which to our mind is indispensable for understanding measurement in accounting and economics.[16]

Sterling's rejection of Stevens's nominal scale as a measurement scale is an example of the semantical issues we referred to above. With this rejection, he is forced to renounce Stevens's definition of measurement as 'the assignment of numerals to objects or events according to rules'. For measurement too he develops a set of five propositions, but under consideration of the much more rigorous propositional frameworks nowadays available for measurement (e.g. the work by Pfanzagl quoted in footnote 11) we shall abstain from going into details.

Another semantical issue, and Sterling's conservative attitude towards the meaning of the word 'measure', finds manifestation in such sentences as:

> Thus all measurements are of past dimensions . . . The original purpose of making the measurement may be to predict a future condition or retrodict a past condition, but this does not negate the fact that measurement concerns an existing condition and that predictions are of a fundamentally different nature.

Readers not acquainted with 'measure theory' developed in modern mathematics and with the more recent measurement literature in statistics and the social sciences will not hesitate to agree with the above quote. But those familiar with the pertinent literature and the reasons for the preference of a less conservative terminology, might hesitate to accept Sterling's view. Nowhere in mathematical measure theory will the reader find definitions of 'measure' and 'measurement' restricting these concepts to past or present events. And W. W. Roozenboom in his work *Foundations of The Theory of Prediction* (Homewood 1966) develops prediction as measurement. In the accounting literature too one has become aware that the separation between measurement and prediction rests on too arbitrary a criterion and the recent 'Report of the Committee on Foundations of Accounting Measurement'[17] indeed abandons this distinction for 'measurement in the broad sense of the word'. As to be expected all this created,[18] and will continue to create, reaction with the

---

15. This concept, referring to measurement the rules of which are not based on scientific laws but on assumptions of much lesser reliability, seems to have been introduced by Warren S. Torgerson in his *Theory and Methods of Scaling* (New York 1958) and has since been used widely. Cf. the most recent standard work on measurement by J. Pfanzagl's *Theory of Measurement* (Wuerzburg: Physica, 1968).

16. He also asserts that "All (schools) agree that weight and length can be measured but that shape and color cannot". To our knowledge there seems to be a general agreement that colors can be measured with great precision by the length of the light waves they reflect.

17. By Y. Ijiri, R. Mattessich, A. Rappaport, E. Summers and A. Thomas, *The Accounting Review — Supplement to Volume XLVI*, pp. 1-50.

18. With regard of this and the controversy between non-teleologic and teleologic valuation, the reader may consult the following controversy between Professor Chambers and this author: R. Mattessich, 'On the Perennial Misunderstanding of Asset Measurement by Means of "Present Values"', *Cost and Management*, March-April 1970, pp. 29-31. R. J. Chambers, 'Asset Measurement and Valuation', *Cost and Management*, March-April 1971, pp. 30-5. Mattessich, 'On Further Misunderstandings about Asset "Measurement" and Valuation: A Rejoinder to Chambers' Article', *Cost and Management*, March-April, pp. 36-42. Chambers, 'Measurement and Valuation Again', *Cost and Management*, July-August 1971. Mattessich. 'Asset Measurement and Valuation — A Final Reply to Chambers', *Cost and Management*, July-August 1971.

more conservative members of our profession and thus will not be generally accepted by accountants as long as the arguments for and subtleties of such a novel point of view are not fully digested.

Sterling also devotes several pages (pp. 100-5) to the important subject of value additivity but neglects the distinction between linear and non-linear additivity. This might not seem to be a grave omission, since traditional accounting is based exclusively on the assumption of linear additivity, but if one introduces the notion of classical utility (the additivity property of which is non-linear)[19] this distinction might no longer be dispensable.

His book also contains (pp. 105-15) profound thoughts on the problems of 'objectivity' and 'objective versus subjective measurement'. We agree with several of Sterling's pronouncements but must emphasize that in our view the distinction between subjective and objective measurement is a matter of degree which shifts with the sophistication of science and measurement techniques, whereas for Sterling this distinction seems to be more clear-cut and permanent.[20]

Summary and conclusion

Chapter VII bears the title 'The Theory Constructed' (pp. 117-56) and ought to constitute the core of Sterling's book as well as theory. It consists of a set of the following six valuation propositions (V.P.) with elaborate comments, as well as of his 'decision theory of the trader'.

V.P. 1: 'Valuation arises only when we are forced to sacrifice one good in order to obtain or maintain another good.'

V.P. 2: 'Valuation is a continuous activity that is being performed at all instants of time.'

V.P. 3: 'The current choice, the selected alternative, is prima facie more valuable to the chooser than all rejected alternatives.'

V.P. 4: 'The value of a good may be measured ordinally by comparing it to the measure of the next best alternative.'

V.P. 5: 'The temporal modifier of value must coincide with the temporal modifier of the sacrifice.'

V.P. 6: 'Current value may be measured ordinally only by measuring current sacrifice.'

Apart from minor considerations concerning the content of these propositions, we have difficulty in comprehending the structure of Professor Sterling's theory. Are all these formal propositions (including those of information, communication, measurement etc. mentioned previously) meant to be premises only? If yes, why

---

19. Unless one approaches the non-linearity of the utility function by several *segmented* linear functions and thus tries to solve the additivity problem of accounting by introducing particles of positive and negative good will, as we have done in pp. 224-31 of *Accounting and Analytical Methods*.

20. Measurement of temperature for example remained a predominantly subjective measurement until the thermometer was developed which enabled objective measurements. Yet more often than not, for our everyday purposes, we measure temperature subjectively. When we look at the thermometer it is frequently enough to confirm our subjective measures or to make them more precise and reliable.

are the major conclusions not likewise expressed in formal propositions? If no, which of those propositions are premises, which are conclusions (one might ask in addition which are his primitive and which his defined terms)? These questions might seem unfair since Sterling's intention obviously was not to present a completely formalized axiomatic system. Yet we ought to be aware that formalization is a matter of degree, and the mere fact that Sterling lists sets of propositions, indicates that at least a minor degree of formalization was pursued; furthermore, it is generally accepted that even an informally presented theory has its hidden primitives (basic terms and premises) and derivatives (defined terms and conclusions). We also find it difficult to trace the points of tying together various propositions which lead to the ultimate conclusions of the book. Especially the introduction of Sterling's valuation proposition obviously must lead to the conclusion that the subjective value is no less important and no less dispensable than the market value for the trader's decision making.

As to the second part of Chapter VII it has to be pointed out that in spite of its subtitle 'Decision Theory of the Trader' it has nothing to do with 'Decision Theory' as developed by statisticians and management scientists. Sterling is here rather concerned with information needed by managers and 'other interested receivers' relevant to their problems, hence with what traditionally is called managerial accounting in the broad sense. This could have been the place for developing accounting models for all kinds of purposes, giving recognition to the equal importance of valuation methods beyond the market value approach. Indeed, some steps in this direction are made in this section, but only cursorily and without developing a teleologic theory of accounting that provides a series of different models each tailor-made for a specific standard purpose. Thus it hardly surprises if the conclusion of this section too stresses the superiority of the market value method, pointing out that 'one bit of information is relevant to all these decisions: the present price'.[21]

However, the method employed in this section as well as in the ensuing Chapter VIII ('The Theory Applied') is not without merit and deserves the attention of all those engaged in serious accounting research. Sterling interprets the various states, positions, prices and values as information bits and examines which bits are relevant for which decision. If the results are biased in favour of one valuation method, it is not the fault of the method employed but lies in a one-sided and merely partial application of this method.

In Chapter VIII the plea for the market value is further reinforced by the argument that

> the consideration of the additivity requirements leads to the rejection of past (purchase) and future (sale) prices as valuation coefficients. Both prices and quantity need to be temporally homogenous in order to express an existing, as opposed to a hypothetical, sacrifice. All measurements are made in the present and this leads to the

21. 'Present price' here obviously means 'current market price'. Occasionally Sterling employs the expression 'present (market) value' to mean 'current market value' which is especially disturbing in face of the customary usage of 'present value' for 'discounted future net cash flows'.

use of a present price. The difficulties of observing a price in the absence of exchanging the particular good held were considered; and although difficulties do exist, it was argued that those difficulties were less than those encountered in the determination of the past (purchase) price and also less difficult than determining the future (sale) price.

Thus, from a measurement point of view, the present price is the appropriate valuation coefficient. (p. 187-8)

Apart from the fact that we have difficulties in comprehending Sterling's opaque argument that 'consideration of the additivity requirements leads to the rejection of past and future prices as valuation coefficients', we must disagree with the notion that a valuation method is inappropriate simply because it yields less reliable measurement, although it may be the only relevant method available. In our example of three purposes and three valuation models (*see* Section 2), we assumed in the second instance (minimization of tax obligation) a situation in which the acquisition cost value yields a smaller tax obligation than the market value. A consistent treatment of Sterling's argument just mentioned would insist on using here the market value method, and thus paying higher taxes, merely because it is the appropriate valuation method from a measurement point of view (which may be doubtful for a second reason, namely in all those cases where the acquisition cost can be measured more reliably than the market value).

The remaining chapters are reserved to a discussion of 'Boulding's Constant' (Chapter IX), 'The Fisher Tradition' (Chapter X), 'The Accounting Tradition' (Chapters XI and XIII), 'The Assumptions Relaxed' (Chapter XIII) and an 'Epilogue' (Chapter XI) offering an excellent summary of Sterling's book. We have little to add to Chapter IX beyond our previous remark that Boulding's approach must not be identified and confused with the teleologic approach which we have defended for many years. As to Chapter X the following quote is characteristic for its conclusions:

In short, even under conditions of certainty, even on Fisher's own ground, we find that for purpose of valuation, the discounting process is, at best, superfluous — yields identical results to other more direct methods — and, at worst demonstrably wrong. (p. 228)

Again we encounter Sterling's perennial vacillation between accounting in general and financial accounting in the most narrow sense, without ever being sure to which of the two his arguments pertain. But as to his conclusion we can only refer to our previous demonstration that the determination of subjective values is an indispensable enterprise, just as the 'present value method' has proved in theory and praxis (in the majority of cases) the most convenient and reliable method of determining subjective values. We do *not* assert, however, that it is the only method for evaluing an asset subjectively, nor do we assert that it is always the best method for this purpose.

Concluding we should stress again that this paper has selected particular but major conclusions of Professor Sterling's book and expressed our reaction to it. The article may not have done full justice to the entire structure of this work and thus we deem it advisable to commend to the reader Sterling's 'Epilogue' summarizing this work in his own words. As regards structure, we do not find in it the same logical necessity which characterizes, for instance, a work of very similar title, namely Edwards and Bell's *The Theory and Measurement of Business Income* (Berkeley 1961). Whereas the structure of the latter may be compared to that of a Gothic cathedral in which every element fulfills an indispensable architectonic function, Sterling's work rather resembles a Baroque building, endowed with rich ornamentation, often fascinating, but not always contributing to the support of the major structure.

Epilog 1982

More than a decade has passed since this article was published, and a good deal of research has meanwhile come forth from either side. Obviously, Professor Sterling did not agree with my review article of his first book and gave expression to it in a rejoinder[22] the evaluation of which I confidently leave to the reader's judgment. Later on Sterling published a series of pertinent articles, and finally sharpened and reiterated his view on the market or exit value method in his book *Toward a Science of Accounting*.[23] As far as my own research is concerned, I continued and will further continue my efforts towards *an instrumental or teleological theory of accounting*[24] in which different accounting models (and hence different valuation hypotheses) serve different information objectives. To solve the complex problem of matching certain means of accounting to specific financial and managerial information purposes, it was first necessary to clarify on a more general epistemological and methodological plane, the issue of means-end relationships or "instrumental

[22] R R Sterling, "The Market Value Method According to Sterling: A Reply" *Abacus* June 1972, pp.91-101.

[23] R R Sterling (Houston, Tex.: Scholars Book Co., 1979).

[24] e.g. R Mattessich "Methodological Preconditions and Problems of a General Theory of Accounting" *The Accounting Review*, Vol.47, No.3 (July 1972): *idem*. "Instrumental Aspects of Accounting" in R R Sterling and A L Thomas (eds.) *Accounting for a Simplified Firm* (Houston: Scholars Book Co., 1979) pp.335-351; *idem*. "Instrumentelle Bilanztheorie: Voraussetzungen und erste Ansätze" in *Zeitschrift für betriebswirtschaftliche Forschung*, Vol.30, No.10/11, Oct/Nov 1978b pp.792-800; *idem*; "On the Evolution of Theory Construction in Accounting: a Personal Account" in *Accounting and Business Research*, Spring 1980, No.37A Special Accounting History Issue, pp.158-173.

hypotheses", as I called them in accord with Lowe (1965) and Machlup
(1969)[25]. I attempted such a clarification in a comprehensive book under
the title *Instrumental Reasoning and Systems Methodology -- An Epistemology
of the Applied and Social Sciences,*[26] and I hope that these insights
will not be lost to accounting theory. The area of inflation accounting
is one of the simplest situations to demonstrate the relationships
between particular information objectives and specific accounting models
(e.g. the *nominal current cost accounting model* serving income measurement under physical capital maintenance, the *general purchasing power
model* serving real financial capital maintenance, the *real current cost
accounting model* serving equally well the real financial capital maintenance and, with minor re-arrangements, also serving physical capital
maintenance,[27] etc.). And the *current cost accounting* legislation
(*supplementary* to the traditional *historical cost valuation*) in the UK,
the USA and other countries is excellent evidence for the *public need of
multiple evaluation bases,* and is thus a strong counterargument against
the exclusive use of the market or exit value basis. By no means have I
confused premise (or "approach" as Sterling calls it) and conclusion,
but for me the information purpose, is the premise, while *the basis of
valuation* (as well as of classification, or realization, of aggregation,
etc.) *is the conclusion.* I regard either the action goal or the
information purpose as given. If the former is given, the latter should
be desirable, but in either case will the valuation basis be derived
from the information purpose. Our scientific task must be limited to the
inference of instrumental hypotheses and consequences, but does not
extend to the choice of the goal or purpose. As social and applied
scientists we have to respect the information needs of the public, and
must not impose our own value judgments upon them; we merely may argue
our case as one among many possible *norms.* Thus, contrary to Sterling's
assertion, I do not consider his theory as incorrect, merely as being
onesided and a potential attempt of imposing a certain value judgment
upon others.

This research during the last decade strongly reinforced my previous
outlook that a purpose-oriented hence instrumental view of accounting is
needed, and that *"the degrees of reality and accuracy are here not
decisive, and are overruled by the degrees of efficiency and effectiveness at which the stipulated or derived information purposes are fulfilled
... Thus the criteria of acceptance of an instrumental theory are fundamentally different from those of a cognitive theory, and any attempt to
apply the latter criteria to accounting must lead to confusion and misunderstanding ... The first major difficulty ... lies in the inference
of the accounting hypotheses from the information purposes ...* Most
importantly, I emphasized that it cannot be the task of the theoretician
to provide a specific accounting system for a manager (or group of shareholders) if the preference and belief-functions of this manager (or group

[25] Adolf Lowe, *On Economic Knowledge* (New York: Harper & Row, 1965), and
Fritz Machlup, *Methodology of Economics and Other Social Sciences*
New York: Academic Press, 1978).

[26] (Dordrecht-Holland/Boston, USA: D Reidel Publishing Co., 1978a).

[27] R Mattessich, "Major Concepts and Problems of Inflation Accounting,
Part II, General Purchasing Power, Capital Maintenance and the
Canadian CCA Exposure Draft" CGA-Magazine (Canada), June/July 1981,
pp.20-27.

of shareholders) is not known to him. *The best the theoretician can do is to provide certain accounting systems standardized for different information purposes.*"[28]

In the face of these results, I conclude that the major objections against the market value as the *predominant* valuation basis of accounting *expressed a decade ago in this review article are still eminently valid.* Of course, the ultimate explanation for this conclusion has to be sought in the following three assumptions:

1. That. academic accounting is at best an *applied science* but not a pure science.
2. That academic accounting *cannot be based exclusively on the principles of neoclassical economics* (which among other things neglects the crucial difference between renewable and non-renewable resources), but requires a broader basis that includes the behavioural and ecological sciences as well as the information and systems sciences.
3. That *neopositivism is not an adequate philosophic basis* for accounting and ought to be replaced by an approach that gives better recognition to implicit as well as explicit value judgments.

QUESTIONS

(1)   Is Sterling's method of argument ("Structure of the Argument") a suitable vehicle for theoretical exposition? Does he follow it consistently? Does the use of simplifying assumptions create the basis for an artificial theoretical argument?

(2)   What is Sterling's notion of information? Is it consistent with modern theoretical (especially accounting) usage?

(3)   "Income is a concept bounded by time; it is a phenomenon that occurs within a time interval". To what was Sterling referring? Is this notion found elsewhere in the accounting literature?

(4)   What is the "ordinal measurement of value" (p.155) referred to by Sterling?

(5)   The book is entitled, Theory of the Measurement of Enterprise Income; is it a theory of accounting (in general)?

(6)   What theoretical argument does Sterling advance to support the use of exit prices (selling prices) for the measurement of assets?

(7)   Is part 2 necessary to the argument? How different, to Sterling, is the accounting tradition from that of the economists?

---

[28] R Mattessich "Instrumental Aspects of Accounting" (see present footnote 24), pp.350-351.

245

19

TREVOR ELLISON GAMBLING

Societal Accounting

Beyond the Conventions of Accounting

Biographical Chronology

1929	Born, 7 November, Newton Abbot, Devon.
	Married, June Mary.
1950	Bachelor of Commerce, Durham University.
1953	Admitted as Chartered Accountant (ICAEW).
1957-61	Lecturer, City of Birmingham College of Commerce, Commerce, Birmingham, England.
1961-69	Lecturer, University of Birmingham.
1964	Houblon-Norman Fund, research award to study accounting in USSR.
1966-67	Visiting Associate Professor, University of California, Berkeley.
1969	Appointed Professor and Head of Department, University of Birmingham.
1969	PhD awarded.
1968-70	Consultant major chemical company.
1970-71	Deputy Dean, School of Commerce & Social Science, University of Birmingham.
1971	Acting Dean.
1972	Visiting Professor, University of Illinois, Urbana.
1971-78	Advisory visits to Ahmadn Bello University, Nigeria and Nanyang University, Singapore; Chairman, Faculty Computer Services, University of Birmingham.
1974	Societal Accounting published.
1974-77	Principal researcher, SSRC project into human resource accounting.
1975	Modern Accounting (edited text of his doctoral thesis) published.
1978	Beyond the Conventions of Accounting published.
1980	Distinguished Visiting Lecturer, Griffith University, Queensland, Australia.

Selected Bibliography

1958 "New Outlook on Professional Training," The Accountant, v.138, 22 March, pp 335-36.

1961 "Flaw in the Jewel? Does the Concept of Double-Entry Need to be Re-examined?" The Accountant, v.144, 11 Feb, pp 150-1.

1962 "On a Teaching Vocation," The Accountant, v.146, 12 May, pp 595-6.

"Variation on the Balance Sheet Theme," The Accountant, v.147, 10 Nov, pp 598-602.

1963 "The Making of an Accountant," Accountants Journal (UK), v.55, Nov, pp 403-6.

"'New Frontiers' for Accountancy," The Accountant (UK), v.148, 8 June, pp 741-4.

1964 "Training Accountants in 1984," Accountants Journal (UK), v.56, Oct, pp 397-8.

1965 "Accounting and Management in the Soviet Union," The Accountant, v.153, 18 Dec, pp 801-5.

"Some Observations on 'Breakeven Budgeting & Programming to Goals,'" Journal of Accounting Research, v.3, Spring, pp 159-65.

1968 "LIFO vs FIFO under conditions of 'certainty'", Accounting Review, v.43, April, pp 389-9.

"Technological Model for Use in Input-Output Analysis and Cost Accounting," Management Accounting, (N.A.A.), v.50, pp 33-38.

1969 "Accounting Theory and Inter-Related Processes," Abacus, v.5, pp 78-87.

"Model Building and the Accountant," Accountancy, v.80, pp 416-419.

1970 "Note on Input-Output Analysis: its uses in Macro-economic and Micro-economic", Accounting Review, v.45, Jan, pp 98-102 (with A Nour).

The Accountant, the Computer and the Abacus, University of Birmingham, U.K.

1971 "Towards a General Theory of Accounting," International Journal of Accounting Education and Research, v.7, Fall, pp 1-13.

"National income accounting and the accountant," Accountancy, v.82, July pp 376-380.

1973 "Negotiation of Budgets," Chartered Accountant in Australia, v.44, Aug, pp 20-26.

1974	Societal Accounting, George Allen & Unwin (London), 230 p.
	"A Systems Dynamics Approach to Human Resource," Accounting Review, v.49, July, pp 538-46.
1975	Modern Accounting: Accounting as the Information System for Technological Change, Macmillan (London), 208 p.
1976	"Societal Accounting Meets the Sandilands Report," Singapore Accountant, v.11, pp 25-35.
	"Systems Dynamics and Human Resource Accounting," Accounting Organisations and Society, v.1, pp 167-174.
1977	"Magic, Accounting and Morale," Accounting, Organisations and Society, v.2, pp 141-151.
1978	Beyond the Conventions of Accounting, The Macmillan Press (London), 182 p.
	"Too Much of a Good Thing or Not Enough?", Accountancy, v.89, June, pp 58-9.

Gambling has also written several Discussion Papers, Conference Papers and Invitation Lectures. He has also written a two volume accounting text entitled, A One-Year Accounting Course (Pergamon Press) 1969; 138 p, 136 p.

REFERENCES

Book Reviews of Societal Accounting:
    Journal of Economic Literature, v.12, Dec 1974, p.1406.
    Chartered Accountant in Australia, v.45, Apr 1975, pp.39-40 (L Gregory).
    Management Forum, v.1, 1975, pp.72-73 (E J Evans).
    Accountancy, v.86, Jan 1975, p.86 (T Buckland).
    Accounting Review, v.51, 1976, pp.457-8 (R Estes).

Book Reviews of Modern Accounting:
    Accounting & Business Research, v.6, 1976, pp.153-4, (J Arnold).

Beyond the Conventions of Accounting - A Review

Trevor Gambling has the reputation of being an unorthodox accounting writer. The publication of his latest book, Beyond the Conventions of Accounting [10] (hereafter referred to as Conventions) is likely to reinforce this belief. In fact the title (let alone some of the chapter headings) is likely to dissuade those who prefer a more traditional approach to accounting from reading it. This is unfortunate because, although his approach may not be that commonly found in accounting texts, his concern with improving the discipline is genuine. This paper examines the main ideas contained in that recent publication. The book, however, cannot be considered in isolation as it is a continuation and refinement of much of the author's previous work so the broader framework into which it fits is first examined.

The Gambling Triptych
Modern Accounting
Conventions, can, in fact, be viewed as the final panel in a triptych. The central aspect would be his, Societal Accounting [6] (SA) and it would be flanked on one side by Conventions and on the other by his Modern Accounting: Accounting as the Information System for Technological Change [8] (MA). This metaphor is used because SA contains the genesis of the central and dominating theme of the three books: accounting as a major economic information system of society. The title of MA is fairly indicative of its content - it examines technical and technological considerations, Conventions examines human considerations.

MA was written prior to SA (it is referenced there) but published later. The book is, in fact basically the author's doctoral thesis. It is, as its title suggests, concerned with information systems, technology and change. Accounting is seen as 'an exercise in commercial systems engineering' (p.vii). That it is an earlier work is also suggested by the fact that some notions are stated which in the other two works were refined or disappeared. An example is the statement, 'The objective of any business is to maximise its "profits" '(p.8).

Accounting and Culture

The first half of the 1970's witnessed an upsurge in the interest in
examining the societal orientation of accounting. Although there was
substantial overlap, the discussion evolved around three subject
concentrations: accounting as a socially responsible profession, accounting
for socially responsible business firms and accounting as aid to
macro socio-economic planning. The Canadian journal, Cost and Management,
devoted the major part of an issue to the subject (September-October
1976) and in it these themes are evident.

Gambling's approach in SA is difficult to classify however as it is
quite original. In the book he has argued for a reappraisal of the basic
premise of accounting. Anomalies in the discipline exist because
accountants have failed to see that in assessing an organisation's
success in achieving certain goals, they were overlooking the fact that
those goals were dictated by the culture of the society in which the
organisation existed. After examining 'traditional' macro and micro-
accounting systems, his answer was to first develop a theory of
societal accounting which could then be extended to a generalized
theory of accounting. In order to examine questions of culture, he
has turned to the work of social psychologists and anthropologists.

If accounting is to be the product of and be able to respond to the
needs of culture it will be subject to a variety of human values.
Gambling acknowledges this when he states that accountants are
'faced with the the task of making objective measurments, which, in the
final analysis, are to be judged subjectively' (SA, p.215). While
this is obvious, it does highlight the fact that human values impose
constraints which an accounting information system model will need to
consider.

Gambling's solution in SA is to require more information to be disclosed.
That is, more information than mere summaries of the direct flows;
information which has been described in the literature as 'externalities'.
The human environment to which data relates, however, also imposes severe
constraints so much so that Gambling has felt the need to extend this
aspect of his theory of (societal) accounting. This is done in
Conventions, as discussed below.

In $\underline{SA}$ it was argued that there exist three levels of accounting theory:
1. mini: that of individuals
2. micro: that of the firm
3. macro: that of the economy

However because accounting is cultural the only effective accounting theory is that which results from the co-incidence of the various inner theories of all citizens, the Weltanschauungen of the people. Accounting theory is to be representative of a society's culture and this has no existence outside these Weltanschauungen.

Extending The Argument

Theory Construction

The first chapter of $\underline{Conventions}$ elaborates on the theme of $\underline{SA}$ and offers a framework for understanding the Weltanschauungen of the citizens: their attitudes to life. This framework would look thus:

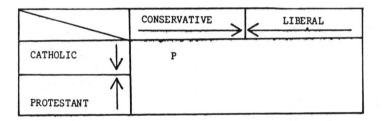

Gambling had earlier discussed this framework [9] but its inclusion in this book is important for an understanding of the argument. The liberal-conservative dichotomy is, as its name implies, on the basis of breadth of vision, whereas the catholic-protestant distinction is on the extent of reliance on opinions of authorities (experts). The more catholic, the greater the reliance on opinions of established experts. A society such as Poland would be an obvious example of a catholic-conservative society (Gambling [9] p.27) (somewhere near P in the matrix).

If Accounting theory and culture are interrelated then by determining the 'catholicity' (or not) and the conservativeness (or not) of a society it will be easy to know the accounting theory that will be acceptable. This certainly requires a broad definition of accounting

theory. It is interesting to compare Gambling's conception with a
more conventional one. Watts and Zimmerman [15] also define accounting
theory very broadly (p.273) but their conclusion is very different.
To these writers,

> not only is there no generally
> accepted accounting theory to
> justify accounting standards
> there will never be one (p.301)

Gambling is more optimistic; what is needed is more research by
accountants in areas not normally investigated by them. This will lead
to acceptable theories.

On the other hand there is a similarity in that both works acknowledge
that accounting will be subject to external pressures: to Gambling
these are social, to Watts and Zimmerman they are purely political.

Unconventional Accounting

The title of Gambling's book is Beyond the Conventions of Accounting
and, as already indicated above, much of it is in fact unconventional.
Its theme is the effect of human values on the accounting information
system. It contains seven chapters and an extensive general appendix
on human resource accounting (HRA). The first three chapters set the
scene, by defining the problem, the next three offer some solutions
(Gambling's and others') and the last, a concluding overview.

It is Gambling's approach and style which is particularly unconventional.
To those used to more orthodox approaches to accounting problems his
style could be described as sensational; to those bored with orthodoxy,
a welcome palliative.

His first footnote (p.162) acknowledges that 'a serious minded American
reviewer' took him to task over the jovial tone of many of the
footnotes in SA. Gambling's answer is to offer one which will, he says
(p.162) 'rot his (that reviewer's) socks'. His first chapter is
entitled 'Accounting and the Pursuit of Happiness'. Subheadings include,
'Magical Accounting', 'Accounting for Ideals' and 'The Rationale of
Superstition.' Nevertheless his concern is very real and it is worth
examining some of the ideas in this unconventional accounting book.

Accounting and Science

How Scientific is Science?

It is difficult to ascertain Gambling's concept of science. Like many
others (for example, Peasnell [12]) he argues that the so-called
'social sciences' are methodologically inferior to those subjects
described as 'natural sciences'. Accounting and the social sciences
are in a 'prerenaissance state' (p.105). If he means that accounting
is, to use a more contemporary expression, 'preparadigmatic' (that is,
unstructured and without a single unifying theoretical foundation) then
he has chosen an inappropriate term for prerenaissance implies prebirth.

It is ironic that, in this context, he has (again like Peasnell) quoted
Sterling [14] for that writer was making the very point that science is
a process of rigorous study and not the determination of imaginary
immutable laws. Accounting therefore is capable of being studied
scientifically as are any of the other social sciences. Gambling's
scientific method which has not 'spilled over into the social sciences'
(p.105) is as imaginary as the immutable natural laws. He had earlier
admitted that for him, 'accounting seems to be one of the most interesting
scientific fields left to man'. ([5], p.1).

It is difficult to know just what Gambling means when he claims that
'natural science is the study of structure rather than properties'
(p.105). Assuming he means the physical sciences to be natural
sciences it is certainly true that researchers in those fields often
have the advantage of relatively stable states with which to experiment.
But does it mean that scientists such as Roentgan, Becquerel and Thomson
researching, what we now know of as, X-Rays were not true natural
scientists?

It may be argued that much of the discussion little affects
Gambling's overall theme. However it should be pointed out that he is
concerned with articulating a theoretical structure. How, for example,
can one determine in which position a society would fit on the
attitude matrix? Gambling has attempted to gauge where Britain
stood by an empirical study (reported in Chapter 1). However he does
acknowledge that such an answer is unlikely to have statistical validity.

This is probably because it was a small sample (100) of a fairly
narrow interest group ('mortgage borrowers at a local building society')
with a 30% (usable) response rate. Gambling confesses that 'too much
should not be read into the result' (p.20). His hypotheses which were
borne out, he argues, were that the problem of inflation is now
reasonably well understood (p.15) and that useful replies to questions
which affect the determination of accounting principles can be answered
by average citizens (p.20).

Even a superficial examination of the trend of accounting literature
in the last decade would show that empiricism is seen as the panacea for
all research problems. This seems to arise from the misguided notion
that empiricism gives scientific respectability. Philosophers of science
have expended considerable effort in the last thirty years to demonstrate that there are inherent structural weaknesses in empiricism.

Scientific Theory Construction

In dealing with disciplines dependent on human action, empiricism has
certain immediate appeal. It is both illuminating and useful to
determine human action in response to certain data. However herein
lies the first type of problem for empiricism: that which can best be
described as methodological. Empirical methodology relies on
induction and can therefore only provide probable answers. Empirical
methodology relies on observations. Observations will always be theory
laden: presuppose the theory. There are other problems associated with
observation - it is a vague concept (see Achinstein [1] for an analysis).

The second type of problem can be described as philosophical. In any
theoretical situation there are going to be problems which are
non empirical in character - conceptual. Alternatively these may be
described as foundational assumptions. Too often these are merely
stated as primitives and their relation to the empirical problems
overlooked. In Gambling's situation these conceptual problems are evident
in his notion of the average citizen.

In light of this, the only conclusion that can be drawn is that insofar
as providing the material for theory construction pure empiricism is quite
inadequate. Nevertheless this is in no way meant to deny that the aim of

science is to maximize the scope of solved empirical problems.
It is suggested however that many theoretical researchers in accounting
overlook the conceptual problems.

In view of the size and nature of the sample, Gambling's claims are
not at all substantiated, in the scientific sense. Moreover the
survey and result should not have been reported in the book. It
adds nothing to the argument except raise doubts as to the author's
appreciation of scientific research methodology. His other
'conclusion' that accounting principles can be determined in the
manner described is even more dangerous - on methodological and
conceptual grounds, as suggested above.

While this appears to be the case for much of the reported recent
accounting research Gambling's concept of science and scientific
theorizing is elusive. He seems to be aware that such processes
cannot be separated from our Weltanschauungen yet his faith in
unbridled empiricism often gets free rein.

It is also interesting to note, as an aside but in this context, that
Gambling sees accounting containing elements of 'prescientific
thought: magic, scholasticism....and above all humanism...'
(Conventions, p.44). His individualistic approach is similar to the
methodological anarchism of American philosopher of science, Paul
Feyerabend who, by coincidence, is a believer in the view that
theory choice in science should be determined solely by empirical
considerations. Paradoxically he promotes magic as a very acceptable
scientific activity (Feyerabend [4]).

Systematic Considerations
Behavioural Considerations
The point was made several years ago (Stenhouse and Gaffikin [13])
that if accountants are going to extend their research interests
into areas in which other scientists are working then it is well
they have a full appreciation of the 'state of the art' in those
areas. This was particularly made in respect to the behavioural
fields. Conventions is very much concerned with behavioural studies
and the question is to what extent is Gambling aware of current

ideas in areas such as social psychology?

> ... research in behavioural accounting,
> if undertaken on an appropriate basis
> and by the right people, can be
> expected to provide an appreciable
> likelihood of significant advance in
> the understanding of human behaviour,
> social institutions, and behaviour
> theory generally.
>> (Stenhouse and Gaffikin [13]10)

The treatment afforded in <u>Conventions</u> is regrettably too superficial
to discover any new insights into behavioural aspects of accounting.
Chapter 2 ('Phantasmagoric Accounting') highlights such weaknesses
in traditional accounting systems but remains largely anecdotal.

Gambling raises many very interesting aspects of human behaviour
which have apparent implications for accounting policy but then
turns his attention to, again, discussing methodological techniques
- the empiricist trap: what Blaug [2] refers to as 'measurement
without theory'. He discusses aspects such as equal opportunity
employment, morale, moves to distinguishing between integrative and
abstract thinking processes in decision analysis, then proceeds
to discuss phantasmagoric accounting. To be fair all these are
discussed in relation to constructing information systems models.
By the same token it is this digressing into purely methodological
aspects which is a persistent shortcoming of the book. It
would have been more interesting to have had one, or two, of these
subjects more fully developed analytically. For example, morale is
a fairly vague concept yet one which is all important to management
policy decisions. In what way can accounting information be
utilized to lead to improvements? Gambling is very good in detailing
the shortfalls of present business oriented accounting but not so
good at detailing specifically how they would be overcome in his
system.

The question concerning his awareness of dominant or strongly held views
in the behavioural disciplines cannot yet be answered. Gambling

has not perceptibly made use of any.

Systems Methodologies

It is difficult for someone not well versed in modern systems analysis
to critically examine the work of someone seemingly well qualified. A
cynic may be moved to point out that this is why the unqualified person
found Gambling's discussion in the third chapter illuminating.
Traditional accounting has failed to provide the answers required of
it. This, Gambling argues has resulted in a collapse of confidence
in the profession: it is the 'necrosis of the central information
system' of which accounting is a major part.

> ...accounts prepared under the old rules may have as little
> relevance to present-day citizens as the nit-picking
> detail of sixteenth-century religious controvesy (p.46).

One result has been the growth of informal systems, counter information
systems, processes described as the 'Apotheosis of Uncle Fred'(pp 53-58).
Although not specifically mentioned in the book, this appears to be
what was meant by accountants researching the once fashionable topic
of the efficient market.

However, while it is acknowledged that Gambling is well qualified in
systematic analysis (as in MA) his analysis in Conventions in this
field, like that of the previously discussed behavioural aspects is
more concerned with anecdote and methodology. What seems to be
lacking is the construction of a tight theory.

Human Resource Accounting

The Preface to Conventions states that the book is directed to the
subject of HRA and it appears that a prior research study into HRA
was the immediate motivation for the book itself. A great deal has
been written on HRA with few positive conclusions emerging. Is it
a topic that illustrates Sterling's [14] point that accountants
do not resolve issues they just move to fresher fields? Or is it
a topic to which, researchers have realised, no satisfactory answer
can ever be produced? Gambling, himself, acknowledges that the
subject is 'démodé'; or, more colloquially, a 'dead horse'.

There are two immediate, major obstacles to implementing HRA -
definition and measurement. A large section of the literature
has been devoted to reporting attempts to determine measurement
within the broad definition of the traditional accounting model
Gambling, on the other hand has previously argued for the advantages
of drawing on techniques devised in other disciplines: the provision
of new ideas and techniques (Gambling [7]). This involved his
constructing a complex systems dynamics model. He demonstrated
that employees generate a complex series of resources and conventional
approaches to HRA were merely considering cash required physical
flows. Some have praised his suggestions (e.g. Cannon [3]p.17)
though generally they have been academically overlooked.

There are two basic problems in this approach to HRA. First, most
proponents of HRA have argued that amounts for human resources should
be included in accounting reports because they are no different
from other assets in that they represent investments in potential
future benefits; they are necessarily included in the economists'
purported emphasis on wealth as the source of all income. This line
of argument of course presumes a definition of assets and the function
of accounting which in turn open a Pandora's Box of problems. In
strict historical cost terms the asset is most likely to be reported
at current expenditure in acquiring it, which is then spread over its
useful life. In this respect assets are unexpired costs and accounting
reports the result of the allocation of costs and revenues to periods.
Not only is it not really possible to identify costs which imply value
to the resource (human) but also if traditional accounting allocations
are arbitrary, attempts to incorporate HRA is adding fuel to the
bonfire. Gambling is arguing for new techniques and thus separating
HRA from other assets accounting. Such combination of techniques
for assets would consequently be internally inconsistent.

The second problem concerns the methodology of those new techniques.
They are presumably derived from other fields of study. In his
case, he is suggesting a systems dynamics HRA model (see Gambling
[7]). An attractive title with the imagery of precision and order
but it is not too reassuring to read statements such as:

258

> I do believe that events like the October
> Revolution and the formation of British
> Leyland were brought about by the interaction
> of groups of auto-programming biocomputers ([10],p.107)

Does this mean that accounting is to be subsumed by a race of 'cyber-
countants'?   The first word in the title of HRA suggests that it will
be necessary to draw on work in the field of (at least) social
psychology, a subject which is itself in theoretical disarrray
and uncertainty (see Stenhouse and Gaffikin [13]). Gambling is
not unaware of these problems and admits,

> ...measurement techniques proposed for this item (HR)
> may or may not be less satisfactory than those in use
> for, say, fixed assets... ([10], p.135);

and,

> The tools we use (from econometrics and social psychology)
> moreover seem particularly unsuited to the problems we
> face. (p.140)

These, then, are the two problems in his new approach; recognized
by the author himself!

There is, in Gambling's suggestion for HRA, a nagging, apparent
logical, or at least ethical, inconsistency. The theme of **Conventions**,
continued from SA, is, as indicated earlier, the need for more
socially responsible reporting by accountants: the extension of
accounting theory to the cultural environment of a particular society.
The ledger of Francesco Dantini, in the 14th Century contained an
entry for an asset, 'Martha - our slave', (Myers and Flowers [11]p.5).
Such a description is not likely to be used today. It is certainly
true that human resources have characteristics common to other assets
owned by the firm. If handled carefully they can generate income
flows. It is, therefore, important that management are aware of
this resource in making decisions. It is equally true that they
(HR) have characteristics **not** found in most other assets - they talk,
often think and are usually capable of freedom of movement, to
mention just a few. These resources in fact make up what Gambling
refers to as 'society'. HRA requires people to report to people
the cost or value (some monetary measure) of people.

259

Accountants are often the butt of comedians because they think
in terms of monetary units. The conceptual presumption in HRA
suggestions is that accounting is the most important (if not the
only) management information system. In some instances this may
well be true. There is nevertheless, a personnel function within
organisations, however primitively adapted to the size and nature of
the business. It is the prerogative of that function to 'report'
on human resources. While researchers in that speciality have also
attempted some form of HRA their results have been and will continue
to be, equally fruitless. The so called 'monetary convention'
in accounting is the cause of a great number of ills, so it would
be better not to add to them. HRA is philosophically, methodologically
and ethically barren.

Conclusion

Conventions is, Gambling admits, 'the antithesis of what sensible
chaps who become accountants' (p.91) are accustomed to. It is
concerned with the need to reappraise the traditional accounting
function: it should generate more information for decision makers.
This sort of argument overlooks the fact that accounting is only
one of the many information systems used by managers. This is
especially so of HRA. Those associated with the personnel
function (such as, manpower, planners, personnel managers, staff
officers, industrial relations specialists) have toyed with HRA.
This should not be taken to imply that accountants should take it
on their shoulders to provide the methodology. Gambling is
right in highlighting the problems with which extant accounting is
fraught. Should we not, therefore, 'take the beam out of
our own eyes first'?

Despite confessing the methodological inadequacy of his 'tribe'
(accountants) Gambling has displayed a particular predilection for
methodological considerations. These, it is true, are important
in a work breaking new ground. However, if overemphasised they
replace the conceptual and theoretical aspects. It is maybe for
this reason that no rigorous theory is presented - there is
argument, however. Nevertheless Gambling's discussions of the

symptoms of the malaise in present accounting - its inadequacy to
meet informational requirements of all users - is interesting
and illuminating. His anecdotes are equally interesting and at
times highly amusing. Conventions achieves its aim of presenting
a refreshingly unconventional perspective of some persistent
problems in accounting and for this reason is recommended reading
for all 'sensible chaps'.

M J R Gaffikin
October 1979

References

(1) Achinstein, P. Concepts of Science Johns Hopkins Press, 1968

(20 Blaug, M. 'Kuhn versus Lakatos, or Paradigms versus Research
       Programmes in the History of Economics' History of
       Political Economy, 8, January 1976

(3) Cannon, J.A. 'Human Resource Accounting - A Critical Comment',
       Personnel Review, 3, Summer 1974

(4) Feyerabend, P. Against Method. Outline of an Anarchistic Theory
       of Knowledge, NLB 1975

(5) Gambling, T. The Accountant, the Computer and the Abacus, University
       of Birmingham: Inaugural Lecture, 1969

(6) _____ Societal Accounting, Allen & Unwin, 1974

(7) _____ 'A Systems Dynamics Approach to Human Resource
       Accounting', The Accounting Review, 49, 1974

(8) _____ Modern Accounting: Accounting as the Information
       System of Technological Change, The Macmillan Press

(9) _____ '"Societal Accounting" meets the Sandilands Report',
       The Singapore Accountant, 11, 1976

(10) _____ Beyond the Conventions of Accounting, The Macmillan
       Press, 1978

(11) Myers, M.S. & Flowers, U.S., 'A Framework for Measuring Human Assets',
       California Management Review, 16, Summer 1974

(12) Peasnell, K.V. 'Statement of Accounting Theory and Theory Acceptance',
       Accounting & Business Research, 31 1978.

(13) Stenhouse, D & Gaffikin, M.J.R. Behavioural Accounting and Ethology,
       Massey University School of Business Occasional
       Paper No.8, 1976

(14) Sterling, R.R. 'Toward a Science of Accounting', Financial Analysts
       Journal, September-October 1975

(15) Watts, R.L. & Zimmerman, J.L., 'The Demand and Supply of Accounting
       Theories: The Market for Excuses', The Accounting
       Review, 54, April 1979

QUESTIONS

(1)   To what extent is Gambling successful in developing a "gener-
        alised theory of accounting" in Societal Accounting ?

(2)   "The theme of this book is that accounting is not so much closely
        connected with the societies which it serves, but rather an
        integral part of the fabric of every society". (p.15)
        This is how Gambling opens his Societal Accounting.
                How important is this theme to Societal Accounting?
                Is the theme consistently applied?

(3)   Gambling argues that traditional accounting has been exclusively
        discussed in terms of the enterprise (firm). Has this inhibited
        the development of a broader accounting theory? Does Gambling
        successfully argue the case for a "broader" accounting?

(4)   If Gambling's suggestion for a wider application of accounting
        is acceptable, how does this affect traditional definitions of
        assets, income and expenses?

(5)   What are externalities? Can they be accounted for (in the trad-
        itional sense)?

(6)   What is the view of theories adopted by Gambling in Beyond the
        Conventions? Does he attempt to provide any sort of theory?

(7)   Who is "Uncle Fred" (p.53 etc)? Why is "he" important to Gambling's
        argument in Beyond the Conventions?

(8)   Are Gambling's ideas on accounting theory relevant to the problems
        of current accounting theory or merely an unaffordable luxury?

Theories as Problem Solutions

The main arguments presented in Thomas Kuhn's book, The Structure of
Scientific Revolutions, have been so often quoted that in many fashion-
conscious, intellectual circles they are now passé. However, for those
concerned with epistemological considerations, Kuhn's work is significant
in that it drew attention to some important questions. These include,
the intellectual maturity of a discipline, the manner in which new
ideas are accepted by those working in a discipline and the value of the
study of the history of the discipline. Kuhn was not the first to
attend to many of the questions raised by his analysis but it is probably
because of the widespread attention his book claimed that his solutions
are now either accepted or being hotly debated. Other analyses have
appeared in the philosophy of science literature but none has been so
widely applied to so many disciplines. In accounting, Wells [1976] has
uncovered possible Kuhnian schools of thought in the inflation accounting
literature. The Committee on Concepts and Standards for External
Financial Reports of the American Accounting Association (SATTA) has
attempted a more general application of Kuhnian analysis: to the entire
accounting literature [1977].

Whether or not Kuhn's analysis can be applied to accounting theory is
not at issue here. What is significant is his insistence of the value
of historical study. Such value is far greater than mere curiousity.
It is more than that which Popper claims: simply that we "can learn
from our mistakes" [1972, p.vii].

Theories provide the basis for action in solving problems. A theory can
be regarded as more successful, more useful, if it enables the solution
of more problems than its alternatives. To solve more problems is to
progress. Progress is temporal. Consequently any theory appraisal
requires an understanding of the historical context of the theory. Any
current theory of accounting which is generally acceptable indicates
that most accountants consider that it solves accounting problems
better than any previously acceptable theory. It enables more purposeful
action.

Throughout this century there have been many suggested 'theories of accounting'. Such a statement presumes some generally understood notion of theory. However, Henderson & Peirson state that the,

> ... word 'theory' like many others in the
> English language has multiple popular meanings ...
> [1977, p.1]

Hendriksen merely accepts a dictionary definition. It is:

> ... the coherent set of hypothetical, conceptual,
> and pragmatic principles forming the general frame
> of reference for a field of inquiry [1977, p.1]

Most is a little more original in claiming a theory as:

> a systematic statement of the rules or principles
> which underlie or govern a set of phenomena
> [1977, p.11]

Two more 'fashionable' scholars (seemingly oft-quoted) are even more general. Although they apparently prefer more specific use of the term, to facilitate their analysis they use the word 'theory' as a "generic term for the existing accounting literature" [1979, p.273]. Despite this they conclude that,

> *not only is there no generally accepted accounting
> theory to justify accounting standards, there will
> never be one* (p.301).

An extreme interpretation of their conclusion would seem to not only deny the rationale for this book but also any other textbook on or course of study in accounting theory. If Paton's Accounting Theory [1922] did not prove acceptable to all accountants, then it should be forgotten. Fortunately there are people around who are not so rash. Paton's Accounting Theory, for a long time out of print, is now reprinted and more readily available. It is worth studying; and not for purely emotional reasons.

The study of the works of major accounting writers is part of the study of the history of ideas. Such study facilitates an appreciation of the problems for which an acceptable theory must provide solutions. It is problems and their solution which are fundamental in evaluating a theory. All the accounting writers studied in this book were attempting to provide solutions to problems they saw existing in their professional environment. Insofar as those problems constitute the work of the accounting researcher, theories provide the answers. As Laudan says,

The function of a theory is to resolve ambiguity,
to reduce irregularity to uniformity, to show
that what happens is somehow intelligible and
predictable. [1977, p.13]

A qualification is needed. Any theory must be able to provide, in
Laudan's words, "acceptable answers to interesting questions", to
provide "satisfactory solutions to important problems" (p.13).

Problems with Problems

The use of such relative terms as, 'interesting' and 'important' may
seem to some to merely fuzz the meaning of theory. This is probably
due to an ingrained belief in theories being designed only to explain
facts. If this were so then it would not be possible to "explain most
of the theoretical activity that has taken place in science" [Laudan,
p.16]. That is, taking facts to mean true statements about the world.
Consequently solving problems is not the same as making true statements
about the world. It is only necessary that the problem be thought to be
part of the true statements of the world. Many theories have existed
which solve many empirical problems yet have later been shown to be not
in accordance with 'the facts'. For example, some of Newton's physical
laws or even blood-letting as a cure of disease.

Problems will become 'interesting' when someone (a would-be theorist)
considered it sufficiently important to warrant a solution. That is why
Sweeney wrote his Stabilized Accounting; that is why Chambers wrote his
Accounting, Evaluation and Economic Behavior; and so too many others their
works.

Unfortunately the problem-solving approach to theory appraisal is not as
simple as it first sounds. It is also important to know what a problem
is. Some would even suggest that that is part of genius: the recognition
of a problem. However, more fundamental issues are at stake. Problems
are often theory-dependent. What may seem to be a problem may exist
because of a particular theory only. For example, the rescheduling of
depreciation charges (back-log depreciation) arises out of replacement
cost (such as current cost accounting) accounting.

Problems may be artificially generated to facilitate the provision of
solutions. Maybe there is very little connection between capital asset
pricing models and the provision of accounting information There may be

problems for which it is unreasonable to expect solutions to be provided: income smoothing?

Nevertheless, if these issues can be resolved, then (following Laudan) problems can be divided into empirical problems and conceptual problems. The recent accounting literature would suggest considerable efforts are being devoted to the former but it is important to realize that there are non-empirical problems of great importance that any successful theory must solve.

Empirical problems may be sub-divided into,

- (a) unsolved problems,
- (b) solved problems, and
- (c) anomalous problems.

Unsolved problems are those which have not adequately been solved by any theory. Here the current debate over accounting for the extractive industries springs to mind. In this case the problems are exacerbated by the artificiality of the accounting period assumption.

Solved problems are the converse of unsolved problems and an appealing illustration is tax allocation accounting. Although the subject of much debate at one stage there now appear to be acceptable solutions (theories). Note, however, that what may be an acceptable solution to a problem today may not be acceptable sometime later. Although the notion of historical cost solved problems existing in the early 1930s, it does not do so today.

A problem for which a particular theory cannot, as yet, provide a solution is termed an anomalous problem. Philosophers such as Popper and Kuhn (op cit) have suggested this should entail the rejection of the theory. However, while the anomaly certainly raises doubts about that theory it need not necessitate the rejection of it. It is first necessary to examine the testing process. In addition the non compatibility of a theory with the data presupposes an infallible knowledge of that data. Research in capital market efficiency (eg Joy & Jones, 1979) has uncovered certain such anomalies.

Some problems go beyond only those the empiricist sees. Such problems are classed as conceptual. There can be internal or external conceptual problems. Where there is logical inconsistency the problem is internal. Where there is direct confrontation between competing theories the problem is external. Chambers (1965) would claim the former of Edwards & Bell (1961). Chambers & Edwards & Bell both rely on market values.

266

However, one argues for <u>exit</u> market prices, the other for <u>entry</u> market prices. Here is an example of material conceptual problem - the valuation of assets (as viewed by the two theories).

The above is an overview of the problem solving approach to theory appraisal. It is, of course, philosophically far more complicated than that described. However, it does provide a basis for appraising the theories of accounting studied in this book. A higher level question would involve the interconnection between theories. Does any exist? Depending on the line of analysis followed theories could be classified into groups. They could provide a Kuhnian paradigm (see, Wells, 1975) or a Lakatosian research programme (see SATTA, p.42, fn.2) or a research tradition described by Laudan (1977, Ch.3). It is likely that such higher level analysis would contribute significantly to the fuller understanding of accounting problems.

However, at this stage, it is only important to recognize that theory appraisal can be accommodated by determining the problem-solving effectiveness of the theory. This entails both the empirical and conceptual problems. In addition, recognition of problem-solving efficacy requires, in turn, recognition of the temporal nature of theories: one theory is only better if it solves more problems than a prior theory.

The Intellectual History of Accounting

To try to understand the theories of past writers is to try to determine what these past writers saw as problems. It is to participate in what is generally referred to as the history of ideas or intellectual history. Not only is it interesting to try to determine why a particular writer wrote as he (as in accounting) or she did, it is useful. As the great economist, Keynes said,

> Practical men, who believe themselves to be quite
> exempt from any intellectual influences are usually
> the slaves of some defunct economist.
> (quoted in Samuelson, 1962, p.17)

True intellectual history is interdisciplinary. It is this because its aim is to find "maximally adequate solutions to a divergent range of compelling intellectual problems, problems which, moreover, occur in several diverse disciplines" (Laudan, 1977, p.174). However, despite being exhibited in the same year, it is unlikely that anyone would attempt to establish the intellectual interconnections between Sweeney's

267

Stabilized Accounting and Pablo Picasso's Guernica. An extreme example
which no doubt detracts from the significance of inter-disciplinary
study. However, it is probably equally safe to claim that, in the
overall history of ideas very little attention will be paid by "outsiders"
to the intellectual development of accounting. (But do note the
Sombart proposition - see, Most, 1977, pp.25-6.) Consequently, a more
insular appreciation of accounting ideas is understandable. It is
important to accountants to be aware of the intellectual development of
their discipline. Have there been different schools of thought, as
Wells (1976) and SATTA have suggested? Or, is the literature of this
century merely, as Peasnell implies, the ingénueism of an immature field
of study?

Examining the literature in terms of problem-solving effectiveness, as
suggested above, is likely to greatly assist answering such questions.
However, there are, in the practice of uncovering the history of ideas,
certain guidelines well worth bearing in mind. First, not only does
the historiography of ideas seek to provide a description (an exegesis,
or the "what") but it seeks to explain (the "why"). It is not sufficient
to determine what new ideas were presented in Vatter's fund theory (1947).
It is also important to try to understand why he presented them. Many
accounting theory texts do not do this. They are too often summaries
(or at best syntheses) of past theories often chronologically presented.

To endeavour to provide an explanatory history of ideas is no easy
task. Skinner, in a lengthy paper (1969) has said that there have been
two main orthodoxies. The first insists that "it is the context 'of
religious, political, and economic factors' which determines the meaning
of any given text, and so must provide 'the ultimate framework' for
any attempt to understand it" (p.1). The other insists on "the autonomy
of the text itself" (p.1).

Whereas the former would seek to explain Gilman's physical and cultural
environment as the basis of appreciation of his ideas, the second would
look for explanations within his Accounting Concepts of Profit only.
The former tends to a probable solution in that it can always be argued
that insufficient attention has been devoted to a particular detail.
The latter approach tends to be achronic and, as such, seems to deny the
nomenclature history of ideas. This is, necessarily, a simplistic
interpretation, yet Skinner (1969) comes to no less a conclusion than

that both orthodoxies are inappropriate.

His suggested alternative is Collingwoodian. Whereas Collingwood (1946)
argues that the study of history requires 'getting into the minds' of
the subjects of study, Skinner, says:

> ... to understand a text must be to understand
> both the intention to be understood, and the
> intention that this intention should be understood,
> which the text itself as an intended act of
> communication must at least have embodied.
> (Skinner, 1969, p.48)

It seems, that in order to understand Canning's The Economics of
Accountancy, it is necessary to determine why Canning wrote the book.
What was he attempting to convey and what led him to want to convey his
ideas? Although this may seem complicated, for most of the earlier
texts in this study the intentions seem clear (!). It seems safe to
suggest that Sprague was intending to provide a theoretical analysis of
accounting procedures. Hatfield does appear to have wanted to provide a
rationalization of practice. Canning did want to explain the differences
in accounting and economic approaches to income determination. Sweeney
and MacNeal did see a need for improving accounting measurement-valuation
bases. And so on.

The 'ideas' contained in the Skinner quotation above provide the
rationale for the course of study this book hopes to promote. Although
Skinner has argued that the proper form of historiography of ideas does
not lie in an amalgam of the two orthodoxies it is difficult to comprehend
any process of determining the intentions of a particular theorist that
did not involve just that. Consequently eighteen different books have
been selected for study. These books contain the 'ideas' in a form the
authors consider to be best at the time of writing. However, ideas do
not appear from 'thin air'. Some appreciation of the authors' environment
can provide some clues as to why the author wrote the book. Therefore
a short biographical chronology has been provided. Other writings also
provide clues, so selected bibliographies have also been included in
this book. It is most important (for some sort of theory appraisal) to
determine how a particular theory is received at the time of its
appearance. To this end contemporary reviews have (where possible) been
provided. (A variety of reasons have prevented this in some instances.)
Again, it should be stressed that these reviews are the opinions of the

reviewers. The reviewer may very well have misinterpreted the book (maybe every reader does!). The author is rarely provided with a platform for rebuttal of a review. Fortunately, there are usually more than one review. References are, where possible, provided and should be used for comparison.

Conclusion: the Indispensability of Intellectual History for Contemporary Theory Appraisal

Many of the widely adopted accounting theory textbooks appear, at first, to acknowledge the value of past theories for contemporary theory development. For example, the first three Chapters of Hendriksen (1977), Chapters 2 and 3 in Most (1977) and Chapter 2 (and Appendices) in Henderson & Peirson (1977). Unfortunately, closer examination often (not always) indicates that the Chapters on past theories are merely 'scene-setting' for the 'real-stuff'.

Intellectual history is more than that. It defines contemporary rationality. A theory, it has been argued, should be judged in terms of its problem-solving effectiveness. Progressiveness is determined by choosing a more effective problem-solving theory. Until it is known how a particular theory has fared temporally it is not possible to choose an alternative. Consequently rationality (choosing the most progressive theory) is defined by progressiveness which in turn derives meaning only from temporal evaluation. Truth, verisimilitude and corroboration are not really possible. They are abstract concepts and are open to such criticisms as to make them unworkable.

A particular theory cannot be _proved_ to be a greater representation of the truth than another. All theory testing is also highly questionable. Therefore it is on a theory's problem-solving effectiveness that theory appraisal must depend.

It is important that accounting theorists turn their attentions to examining past theories. How effective have these theories been in solving accounting problems? Some of those used as a basis for study in this book will no doubt be seen to be quite inadequate. Others may turn out to be remarkably useful and effective. It is this sort of analysis for which this book aspires to be the motivation. As the teacher in Collingwood says:

... here our author, being neither illiterate
nor idiotic (which is why I am asking you to study
his works), has expressed in such a way that we
can understand it a thought that was worth expressing.
At first sight you cannot tell what he is trying to
say. But if you will think carefully about the
passage you will see that he is answering a question
which he has taken the trouble to formulate in his
mind with great precision. What you are reading
is his answer. Now tell me what the question was.
(Collingwood, 1939, p.71).

Michael Gaffikin
University of Sydney

REFERENCES

American Accounting Association, Committee on Concepts and Standards
      for External Financial Reports, Statement on Accounting Theory
      and Theory Acceptance (SATTA), AAA, 1977.

Chambers, R J,"Edwards & Bell on Business Income", Accounting Review,
      v.40, 1965, pp.731-41 (reproduced in this volume).

Collingwood, R G, An Autobiography (1939) Oxford University Press
      edition, 1970.

_____ , The Idea of History, Oxford University Press, 1946.

Edwards, E & Bell, S, The Theory and Measurement of Business Income,
      University of California Press, 1961.

Henderson, S & Peirson, G, An Introduction to Financial Accounting Theory,
      Longman Cheshire Pty, 1977.

Hendriksen, E S, Accounting Theory, 3 ed., Richard D Irwin, 1977.

Joy, O M & Jones, C P, "Earnings Reports & Market Efficiencies: An
      Analysis of the Contrary Evidence", Journal of Financial
      Research, 1979, pp.51-63.

Laudan, L, Progress & its Problems: Towards a Theory of Scientific
      Growth, University of California Press, 1977.

Most, K S, Accounting Theory, Grid, 1977.

Paton, W A, Accounting Theory (reprint), Scholars Book Co, 1973.

Peasnell, K V, "Statement of Accounting Theory & Theory Acceptance: A
      Review Article", Accounting & Business Research, v.8, 1978,
      pp.217-25.

Popper, K R, Conjectures & Refutations, The Growth of Scientific
      Knowledge, Routledge & Kegan Paul, 4 Ed, 1972.

Samuelson, P A, "Economists and the History of Ideas", American Economic Review, v.52, 1962, pp.1-18.

Skinner, Q, "Meaning and Understanding in the History of Ideas", History of Theory, v.8, 1969, pp.1-53.

Vatter, W J, The Fund Theory of Accounting and its Implications for Financial Reports, University of California Press, 1947.

Watts, R L & Zimmerman, J L, "The Demand for and Supply of Accounting Theories: The Market for Excuses", Accounting Review, v.54, 1979, pp.273-305.

Wells, M C, "A Revolution in Accounting Thought?", Accounting Review, v.41, 1976, pp.471-82.